Software Testing

Concepts and Operations

Ali Mili
NJIT, USA

Fairouz Tchier
KSU, KSA

WILEY

Published by John Wiley & Sons, Inc., Hoboken, New Jersey
Published simultaneously in Canada

For general information on our other products and services or for technical support, please contact our Customer Care Department within the United States at (800) 762-2974, outside the United States at (317) 572-3993 or fax (317) 572-4002.

Wiley also publishes its books in a variety of electronic formats. Some content that appears in print may not be available in electronic formats. For more information about Wiley products, visit our web site at www.wiley.com.

Library of Congress Cataloging-in-Publication Data

Mili, Ali.
Software testing : concepts and operations / Ali Mili.
     pages   cm
   Includes bibliographical references and index.
   ISBN 978-1-118-66287-8 (cloth)
1. Computer software–Testing.   I. Title.
   QA76.76.T48M56 2015
   005.1'4–dc23
                                           2015001931

Printed in the United States of America

10 9 8 7 6 5 4 3 2 1

Dedicated to my parents
in honor of their 68 years of mutual devotion
and to Amel, Noor, Farah Aisha, and Serena Aida.
May they realize their hopes and dreams.
A.M.

Dedicated to my loving parents,
my husband Jamel, and my children Sarah, Bellal, and Amine.
May their lives be filled with happiness and success.
F.T.

Contents

Preface

Software engineering is the only engineering discipline where product testing is a major technical and organizational concern, as well as an important cost factor. Several factors contribute to this state of affairs:

- The first factor that makes software testing such a big concern is, of course, the size and complexity of software products, which make the design of software products a high-risk, error-prone proposition.
- The second factor is the lack of a standardized development process for software products, which means that product quality cannot be ensured by process controls, and has to be ensured by product controls instead.
- The third factor is the scarcity of practical, scalable methods that can ensure product quality through static product analysis, shifting the burden to dynamic methods.
- Other factors include the absence of a general reuse discipline, the lack of scalability of correctness-preserving development methods, and the pervasiveness of specification changes through the development, maintenance, and evolution process, etc.

The subject of this book is the study of software testing; amongst the many books that are currently available on the same subject, this book can be characterized by the following premises:

- *Software testing as an integral part of software quality assurance*. We view software testing as part of a comprehensive strategy for software quality assurance, alongside many other techniques. The law of diminishing returns advocates the use of a variety of diverse techniques, which complement each other, in such a way that each is used wherever it delivers the greatest return on investment. Hence software testing is better studied in a broader context that also encompasses other methods rather than to be studied as an isolated set of techniques.

- *Software testing as a complementary technique to static analysis.* Since the early days of software engineering, we have witnessed a colorful debate on the respective merits of software testing versus static program analysis in terms of effectiveness, scalability, ease of use, etc. We take the position that each of these techniques is effective against some type of specifications and less effective against other types; also, very often, when we find that one technique or another is difficult to use, it is not the result of any intrinsic shortcoming of the technique, rather it is because the technique is used against the wrong kind of specification. Of course, we do not always get to choose the specification against which we must ensure product correctness; but we can, in fact, decompose a complex specification into components and map each component to the technique that is most adapted to it. This is illustrated in Chapter 6.

- *Software testing as a systematic stepwise process.* Early on, software testing earned the reputation of being a means to prove the presence of faults in programs, but never their absence; this is an undeserved reputation, in fact, because testing can be used for all sorts of goals, as we discuss in Chapter 7. Nevertheless, whether deserved or not, this reputation has had two consequences: first, the assumption that the only possible goal of testing is fault exposure, diagnosis, and removal. Second, the (consequent) belief that testing amounts merely to test data generation, specifically the generation of test data that has the greatest potential to expose faults. By contrast, we argue that testing follows a multiphase process that includes goal identification and analysis, test data generation, oracle design, test driver design, test deployment, and test outcome analysis. We devote different chapters to each one of these phases.

- *Software testing as a formal/formalizable process.* Because it requires relatively little analysis of the software product under test or its specification, testing is often perceived as an activity that can be carried out casually, and informally. By contrast, we argue that testing ought to be carried out with the same level of rigor as static program verification, and that to perform testing effectively, one must be knowledgeable in software specifications, in program correctness, in relative correctness, in the meaning of a fault, in fault removal, etc.. This is discussed in more detail in Chapter 6.

- *Software testing as a goal-oriented activity.* We argue that far from being solely dedicated to finding and removing faults, testing may have a wide range of goals, including such goals as estimating fault density, estimating reliability, certifying reliability, etc. This is discussed in detail in Chapter 7.

This book stems from lecture notes of a course on software testing and quality assurance and hence is primarily intended for classroom use; though it may also be of interest to practicing software engineers, as well as to researchers in software engineering. The book is divided into five broad parts, including 3 or 4 chapters per part, to a total of 16 chapters.

- Part I introduces software testing in the broader context of software engineering and explores the qualities that testing aims to achieve or ascertain, as well as the lifecycle of software testing.
- Part II introduces mathematical foundations of software testing, which include software specification, program correctness and verification, concepts of software dependability, and a software testing taxonomy. It is uncommon for a software testing book to discuss specifications, verification, and dependability to the extent that we do in this book. We do it in this book for many reasons:
    - First, we believe that it is not possible to study software testing without a sound understanding of software specifications, since these capture the functional attributes that are testing candidate programs against and are the basis for oracle design.
    - Second, when we test a program in the context of product certification or in the context of acceptance testing, what is at stake is whether the candidate program is correct; surely, we need to understand what correctness means, for this purpose.
    - Third, if dynamic program testing and static program analysis are to be used in concert, to reach a more complete conclusion than any one method alone, they need to be cast in the same mathematical model.
    - Fourth, the act of removing a fault from a program, which is so central to testing, can only be modeled by defining the property of *relative correctness*, which provides that the program is *more-correct* once the fault is removed than it was prior to fault removal; relative correctness, in turn, can only be defined and understood if we understand the property of (absolute) correctness.

    The taxonomy of software testing techniques classify these techniques according to a number of criteria, including in particular the criterion of goals: It is important to recognize the different goals that one may pursue in conducting software testing, and how each goal affects all the phases of the testing lifecycle, from test data generation to oracle design to test deployment to test outcome analysis.
- Part III explores a phase of software testing that has so dominated the attention of researchers and practitioners that it is often viewed as the only worthwhile issue in software testing: test data generation. In this part, we briefly discuss some general concepts of test data generation and then we explore the two broad criteria of test data generation, namely: functional criteria (Chapter 9) and structural criteria (Chapter 10). We discuss test data generation for simple programs that map initial states onto final states, as well as for state-bearing programs, whose output depends on their input history.
- Part IV discusses the remaining phases of the software testing lifecycle that arise after test data generation and include test oracle design, test driver design, and

test outcome analysis. Test oracles (Chapter 11) are derived from target specifications according to the definition of correctness and depend on whether we are talking about simple state-free programs or about programs that have an internal state. Test driver design (Chapter 12) depends on whether test data has been generated offline and is merely deployed from an existing medium, or whether it is generated at random according to some probability law. As for the analysis of test outcomes (Chapter 13), it depends of course on the goal of the test and ranges from reliability estimation to reliability certification to fault density estimation to product acceptance, etc.

• Part V concludes the book by surveying some managerial aspects of software testing, including software metrics (Chapter 14), software testing tools (Chapter 15), and software product line testing (Chapter 16).

In compiling the material of this book, we focused our attention on analyzing and modeling important aspects of software testing, rather than on surveying and synthesizing the latest research on the topic; several premises determined this decision:

• This book is primarily intended to be an educational tool rather than a research monograph.
• In an area of active research such as software testing, students are better served by focusing on fundamental concepts that will serve them in the long run regardless of what problem they may encounter rather than to focus on the *latest techniques*, which by definition will not remain *latest* for too long.

In the perennial academic debate of whether we serve our students best by making them operational in the short term or by presenting them with fundamentals and enabling them to adapt in the long run, we have decided to err on the side of the latter option.

ACKNOWLEDGMENT

Special thanks are due to the late Professor Lawrence Bernstein for inviting us to write this book for inclusion in his distinguished series.

We thank our successive cohorts of students, who tolerated our caprices as we fine-tuned and refined the contents of our lecture notes term after term. We also thank Slim Frikha, a summer intern from ParisTech, France, who reviewed and evaluated software testing tools to help us with Chapter 15. This publication was made possible in part by a grant from the Qatar National Research Fund NPRP 04-1109-1-174. Its contents are solely the responsibility of the authors and do not necessarily represent the official views of the QNRF.

F. Tchier
A. Mili

Part I

Introduction to Software Testing

In this part we introduce software testing by discussing what makes software engineering so special that testing should occupy such an important part of its lifecycle. Then we survey software qualities that testing techniques may be used to assess. Finally we review the various lifecycle models of software testing that may be followed depending on the context and goal of testing.

Software Testing: Concepts and Operations, First Edition. Ali Mili and Fairouz Tchier.
© 2015 John Wiley & Sons, Inc. Published 2015 by John Wiley & Sons, Inc.

1

Software Engineering: A Discipline Like No Other

On the face of it, software engineering sounds like an engineering discipline among others, such as chemical engineering, mechanical engineering, civil engineering, and electrical engineering. We will explore, in this chapter, in what way and to what extent software engineering differs from other engineering disciplines.

1.1 A YOUNG, RESTLESS DISCIPLINE

Civil engineering and mechanical engineering date back to antiquity or before, as one can see from various sites (buildings, road networks, utility infrastructures, etc.) around the Mediterranean basin. Chemical engineering (Lavoisier and others) and electrical engineering (Franklin and others) can be traced back to the eighteenth century. Nuclear engineering (Pierre and Marie Curie) emerged at the turn of the twentieth century and industrial engineering emerged around the time of the Second World War, with issues of logistics. By contrast, software engineering is a comparatively young discipline, emerging as it did in the second half of the twentieth century. The brief history of this discipline can be divided into five broad eras, lasting approximately one decade each, which are as follows:

- *The Sixties: The Era of Pioneers.* This era marks the first time that practitioners and researchers came face to face with the complexities, paradoxes, and anomalies of software engineering. Software projects of this era were ventures into unchartered territory, characterized by high levels of risk, unpredictable outcomes, and massive cost and schedule overruns. The programming languages that were dominant in this era are assembler, Fortran, Cobol, and (in academia) Algol.

Software Testing: Concepts and Operations, First Edition. Ali Mili and Fairouz Tchier.
© 2015 John Wiley & Sons, Inc. Published 2015 by John Wiley & Sons, Inc.

- *The Seventies: Structured Software Engineering.* This era is characterized by the general belief that software engineering problems are of a technical nature and that if we evolved techniques for software specification, design, and verification to control complexity, all software engineering problems would be resolved. Given that structure is our main intellectual tool for dealing with complexity, this era has seen the emergence of a wide range of structured techniques, including structured programming, structured design, structured analysis, structured specifications, etc. The programming languages that were dominant in this era are C and (in academia) Pascal.

- *The Eighties: Knowledge-Based Software Engineering.* This era is characterized by the realization that software engineering problems are of a managerial and organizational nature more than a technical nature. This realization was concurrent with the emergence of the Fifth Generation Computing initiative, which started in Japan and spread across the globe (the United States, Europe, Canada), and was focused on thinking machines designed with extensive use of artificial intelligence techniques. This general approach permeated the discipline of software engineering with the emergence of knowledge-based software engineering techniques. The programming languages that were dominant in this era are Prolog, Scheme/Lisp, and Ada.

- *The Nineties: Reuse-Based Software Engineering.* As it became increasingly clear that fifth-generation computing was not delivering on its promise, and worldwide fifth-generation initiatives were fading, software researchers and practitioners turned their attention to reuse as a possible savior of the discipline. Software engineering is, after all, the only discipline where reuse is not an integral part of the routine engineering process. It was felt that if only software engineers had large databases of reusable software components readily available, the industry would achieve great gains in productivity, quality, time to market, and reduced process risk. This evolution was concurrent with the emergence of object-oriented programming, which supports a bottom–up design discipline that facilitates product reuse. The programming languages that were dominant in this era are C, C++, Eiffel, and Smalltalk.

- *The First Decade of the Millennium: Lightweight Software Engineering.* While software reuse is not practical as a general paradigm in software engineering, it is feasible in limited application domains, giving rise to *product line engineering*. Other attributes of this era include Java programming, with its focus on web applications; agile programming, with its focus on rapid and flexible response to change; and component-based software engineering, with its focus on software architecture and software composition. The programming languages that were dominant in this era are Java, C++, and (in academia) Python.

Perhaps as result of this young and eventful history, the discipline of software engineering is characterized by a number of paradoxes and counter-intuitive properties, which we explore in this chapter.

1.2 AN INDUSTRY UNDER STRESS

Nowadays, software runs all aspects of modern life and accounts for a large and increasing share of the world economy. This trend started slowly with the advent of computing in the middle of the twentieth century and was further precipitated by the emergence of the World Wide Web at the end of the twentieth and the beginning of the twenty-first century. This phenomenon has spawned a great demand for software products and services and generated a market pressure that the software industry takes great pains to cater to.

Many fields of science and engineering (such as bioinformatics, medical informatics, weather forecasting, and modeling and simulation) are so dependent on software that they can almost be considered as mere applications of software engineering. Also, it is possible to observe that many computer science curricula are slowly inching toward more software engineering contents at the expense of traditional theoretical material, which may be perceived as less and less relevant to today's job market. Some engineering colleges are preempting the trend by starting software engineering degrees in computer science departments or by starting complete software engineering departments alongside traditional computer science departments.

Concurrent with a widening demand for software to serve ever-broader needs, we are also witnessing higher and higher expectations in terms of product quality. As software takes on ever more vital functions in life-critical and mission-critical applications and in applications that carry massive financial stakes, it becomes increasingly important to ensure that software products fulfill their function with a high degree of dependability. This requires that we deploy a wide range of techniques, including the following:

- *Process controls*, ensuring that software products are developed and evolved according to certified, mature processes.
- *Product controls*, ensuring that software products meet quality standards commensurate with their application domain requirements; this is achieved by a combination of techniques, including static analysis, dynamic testing, reliability estimation, fault tolerance, etc.

In summary, it is fair to argue that the software industry is under massive stress to deliver both quantity and quality; as we discuss in subsequent sections, this is both difficult and expensive.

1.3 LARGE, COMPLEX PRODUCTS

> *The demand for complex hardware/software systems has increased more rapidly than the ability to design, implement, test and maintain them.*
> **Michael Lyu, *Handbook of Software Reliability Engineering*, 1996**

Not only is it critical for us to build software products that are of high quality, it is also very difficult, due to their size and complexity. When it was built in the mid-60s, the IBM operating system OS360 (©IBM Corporation), with a million lines of code and a price tag of 500 million dollars, was considered as the most complex human artifact ever produced up to then. This size was subsequently dwarfed by Microsoft's Windows operating systems (©Microsoft): The 1993 version (Windows NT 3.1) is estimated to be 5 millions lines of code, whereas the 2003 version (Windows Server 2003) is estimated to be 50 million lines of code. Completing projects of this kind of size is not only a major engineering undertaking but also a major organizational challenge; it is estimated that the production of the Windows Server 2003 involved 2000 software personnel (programmers, analysts, engineers) for development and 2400 software personnel for software testing.

Another example of software size growth is given by NASA's flight software. A study published in 2009 by NASA's Jet Propulsion laboratory under the title *NASA Study on Flight Software Complexity* (Jet Propulsion Laboratory, 2009) plots the evolution of flight software size of the various human and robotic space programs from 1968 to 2005. Both series (flight software for human missions and flight software for robotic mission) show a near-perfect linear evolution through the years, except that they are plotted on a logarithmic scale for size, meaning in effect that flight software size grows exponentially from year to year. Hence for human missions, flight software grows from 8.5 kilo lines of code (KLOC) for the Apollo program in 1968 to 470 KLOC for the space shuttle program in 1980 to 1.5 million lines of code (MLOC) for the international space station in 1989. For robotic missions, software size grows from 30 line of code (LOC) for the Mariner-6 mission in 1968 to 3 KLOC for Voyager in 1977 to 8 KLOC for Galileo in 1989 to 349 KLOC for DS1 (Deep Space 1) in 1999 to 545 KLOC for MRO (Mars Reconnaissance Orbiter) in 2005. The same Jet Propulsion Laboratory (JPL) report describes the recent evolution of military avionics software in the following terms: between 1960 and 2000, the percentage of flight control functionality that is delegated to software jumped from 8 to 80%, leading to an increase in size from one generation of aircrafts to another; hence it went from 1000 lines of code for the F-4A to 1.7 million lines of code for the F-22 to 5.7 million lines of code for the F-35 Joint Strike Fighter. The authors of the report argue that the increase in the size and complexity of flight software stems from software serving as a '*complexity sponge*,' whereby complexity migrates from other parts of the system to software, on account of its flexibility and its adaptability.

A panel convened by the Software Engineering Institute (www.sei.cmu.edu) in 2005–2006 to analyze software systems of the future and draw a research agenda to manage such systems estimates that future software systems are expected to have sizes up to a billion lines of code. Along with this dry measure of size, such systems will be large in terms of other dimensions, such as (www.sei.cmu.edu/uls/) the amount of data stored, accessed, manipulated, and refined; the number of connections and interdependencies; the number of hardware elements; the number of computational elements; the number of system purposes and user perception of these purposes; the number of routine processes, interactions, and emergent behaviors; the number of overlapping policy domains and enforceable mechanisms; and the number of parties involved in the operation of the system (developers, maintainers, end users, stakeholders, etc.).

Size changes everything: such systems (referred to as ultra-large–Scale (ULS) systems) challenge all our knowledge and assumptions about software and are estimated to have a number of distinguishing features, such as the following:

- Decentralization in fundamental dimensions, such as decentralized development, decentralized evolution, and decentralized operation.
- Conflicting, unknown, and diverse requirements: Whereas the traditional view in software engineering is that requirements must be analyzed, compiled, and specified prior to software design and development, the view taken by the ULS approach is that at no time can we claim that all relevant requirements have been collected and specified.
- Continuous evolution and deployment: Whereas the traditional view of software engineering is that a software product proceeds sequentially through successive phases of development, then maintenance, then phase out, ULS systems are developed, evolved, and deployed concurrently (made up of parts that are at different stages in their evolutionary process).
- Heterogeneous, inconsistent, changing elements: Whereas a traditional software product is developed as a cohesive monolithic system by a development team, ULS systems emerge as the aggregate of many components, which may have evolved independently, using different paradigms and different technologies, by different teams, and from different stakeholder classes. Also, different components of the system are expected to evolve relatively independently.
- Deep erosion of the people-system boundary: Whereas traditional systems are defined in terms of a distinct boundary that separates them from the outside world, ULS systems are envisioned to include human users as an integral part so that when a user interacts with a ULS system, she/he may be engaging human actors along with system behavior.
- Failure is normal and frequent: Whereas in traditional software systems we think of failures as exceptional events and consider that failure avoidance is contingent upon fault removal, in ULS systems, we take a broader view of successful (failure-free) operation, which does not exclude the presence of faults but makes provisions for system redundancy and requirements nondeterminacy to make up for the presence of faults.

1.4 EXPENSIVE PRODUCTS

Not only are software products very large and complex, they are also very expensive to produce. Of course, if a product is large, one expects it to be costly, but what is surprising is that the *unitary* cost of software, that is, the cost per LOC, does, itself, increase with size. Whereas any programmer one asks may say that they can produce a hundred lines of code in a day or more, a more realistic figure, across all areas of software development, is closer to about 10 lines of code per day, or about 200 lines of code per person-month. This figure includes all costs that are spent producing software, including the cost of all phases of the software lifecycle, from requirements analysis and specification to software testing. If we assume the cost of a person-month to be 20,000 dollars (in salary, fringe benefits, and related expenses), this amounts to about $100 per LOC. If, for the sake of argument, we apply Boehm's COnstructive COst MOdel (COCOMO) cost estimation model to a bespoke (custom-tailored) software project of size 500,000 source lines of code developed in embedded mode (the hardest/most costly development mode), we find 80 source lines of code per person-month.

In most other engineering disciplines, one way to mitigate costs is to use economies of scale, that is, to produce in such a large volume as to lower the unitary cost. Economies of scale are possible because in most engineering disciplines, the production process requires an initial up-front cost that is all the better amortized as the volume of production increases. The same process applies in software engineering: If we invest resources to acquire software tools, to train software professionals, or to set up a programming environment, then the more software we produce the better our investment is amortized. But in software we are also dealing with a phenomenon of diseconomy of scale: the more software we produce within a single product, the more interdependencies we create between the components of the product so that the unitary cost (per LOC) of large software products is larger than that of smaller products. This phenomenon of diseconomy of scale overrides the traditional economy of scale (that comes from amortizing up-front investments); the net result is a diseconomy of scale, which is all the more acute that the software product is larger or more complex; see Figure 1.1.

Many of these costs are mitigated nowadays by the use of a variety of coarse-grained software development methods, which proceed to build software by composing existing components, rather than by painstakingly writing code from scratch line

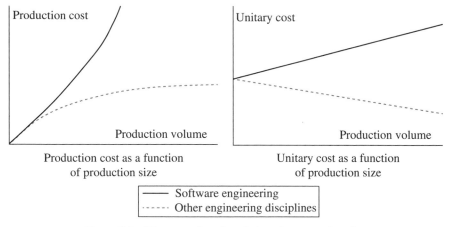

Figure 1.1 *Diseconomies of scale in software engineering.*

by line. Another trend that is emerging recently to address software cost and quality is the use of so-called Agile methodologies. These methodologies control the costs and risks of traditional lifecycles by following an iterative, incremental, flexible lifecycle, where the user participates actively in the specification and development of successive versions of the targeted software product.

1.5 ABSENCE OF REUSE PRACTICE

In the absence of economies of scale, one would hope to control costs by a routine discipline of reuse; in the case of software, it turns out that reuse is also very difficult to achieve on a routine basis. In any engineering discipline, reuse is made possible by the existence of a standard product architecture that is shared between the producer and the consumer of reusable assets: for example, automobiles have had a basic architecture that has not changed for over a century; all cars have a chassis, four wheels, an engine, a battery, a transmission, a cab, a steering column, a braking system, a horn, an exhaust system, shock absorbers, etc. Thanks to this architecture, the design of a new car is relatively straightforward and is driven primarily by design and marketing considerations; the designer of a new model does not have to reinvent a car from scratch and can depend on a broad market of companies that provide standard components, such as batteries, tires, and spare parts. The standard architecture of a car dictates market structure and creates great efficiencies in the production and maintenance of a car.

Unfortunately, no standard architecture exists in software products; this explains, to a large extent, why the expectations that software engineering researchers and practitioners pinned on a discipline of software reuse never fully materialized. Several software reuse initiatives were launched in the last decade of the last century, making available a wide range of software products and sophisticated search and assessment algorithms; but they were unsuccessful because software reuse requires not only functional matching between the available components and the requirements of the user but also architectural matching, which was often lacking. The absence of a standard architecture of software products also explains why software product lines have achieved some degree of success: product line engineering is a form of software reuse that is practiced in the context of a narrow application domain, in which it is possible to define and enforce a reference architecture. As an example, if we define a product line of e-commerce systems, we may want to define the reference architecture as being composed of the following components: a web front-end; a shopping cart component; an order-processing component; a banking component; a marketing and recommendations component; a network interface; and a database interface.

1.6 FAULT-PRONE DESIGNS

In other engineering disciplines, the presence of a standard product architecture, the availability of usable product components, the availability of compiled engineering knowledge, and the application of mandated safety requirements all contribute to reducing the design space of a product so as to make it manageable. The design of an engineering product (e.g., a bridge, a road, or a car) within this limited design space is a fairly straightforward operation that proceeds from requirements to finished product in a systematic, predictable manner.

In software engineering, the situation is significantly more complex, for several reasons, which are as follows:

- There is no standard software architecture, except perhaps for some vague architectures of broad families of software products, such as data-processing applications, transaction-processing applications, event-processing applications, and language-processing applications.
- There is little or no availability of software reusable assets, in the traditional sense of engineering assets that can be used to compose software products; the only assets that may be used widely across the industry are small assets (such as abstract data types (ADTs)) that deliver limited gains in terms of reduced lifecycle costs or reduced process risk.
- There is little software engineering knowledge that may be used across applications in the same way that engineering knowledge is reused in complied form across products in other engineering disciplines.
- Software specifications are very complex artifacts that typically involve vast amounts of detailed functional information; the breadth of the specification space precludes the ability to organize the design space in a systematic manner.

Because the design space of software products is so vast, software design is significantly more error prone than design in other engineering disciplines.

1.7 PARADOXICAL ECONOMICS

While technology can change quickly, getting your people to change takes a great deal longer. That is why the people-intensive job of developing software has had essentially the same problems for over 40 years.
Watts Humphrey, *Winning with Software: An Executive Strategy*, 2001

1.7.1 A Labor-Intensive Industry

If we consider the cost of an automobile, for example, and ponder the question of what percentage of this cost is due to the design process and what percentage is due to manufacturing, we find that most of the cost (more than 99%, perhaps) is due to manufacturing. Typically, by the time one buys a car, the effort that went into designing the new model has long since been amortized by the number of cars sold; what one is paying for is all the raw materials and the processing that went into manufacturing the car. By contrast, when one is buying a software product, one is paying

TABLE 1.1 Lifecycle cost distribution: design versus manufacturing

	Software engineering, %	Other engineering, %
Design	>99	<1
Manufacturing	<1	>99

essentially for the design effort, as there are no manufacturing costs to speak of (loading compact disks or downloading program files). Table 1.1 shows, summarily, how the cost of a software product differs from the cost of another engineering product in terms of distribution between design and manufacturing.

1.7.2 Absence of Automation

The labor-intensive nature of software engineering has an immediate impact on the potential to automate software engineering processes. In all engineering processes, one can achieve savings in manufacturing by automating the manufacturing process or at least streamlining it, as in assembly lines. This is possible because manufacturing follows a simple, systematic process that requires little or no creativity. By contrast, design cannot be automated because it requires creativity, artistic appreciation, aesthetic sense, and so on. Automating the manufacturing process has an impact in traditional engineering disciplines because it helps reduce a cost factor that accounts for more than 99% of production costs; but it has no impact in software engineering because it affects less than 1% of production costs. Hence the automated development of software products is virtually impossible in general.

The only exception to this general rule is the development of applications within a limited application domain, where many of the design decisions may be taken a priori when the automated tool is developed and hardwired into the operation of the tool. One of the most successful areas of automated software development is compiler construction, where it is possible (thanks to several decades of intensive research) to produce compilers automatically, from a syntactic definition of the source language and relevant semantic definitions of its statements. Not surprisingly, this is a very narrow application domain.

1.7.3 Limited Quality Control

The lack of automation and hence the absence of process control make it difficult to control product quality. Whereas in traditional engineering disciplines, the production process is a systematic, repeatable process, one can control quality analytically by certifying the process or empirically by statistical observation. Because the production of software proceeds through a creative process, neither approach is feasible, since the process is neither systematic nor repeatable. This shifts the control of product quality to product controls, such as static analysis, or dynamic program testing.

TABLE 1.2   Lifecycle cost distribution: development versus testing

	Software engineering, %	Other engineering, %
Development	≈50	>99
Testing	≈50	<1

1.7.4   Unbalanced Lifecycle Costs

In most other engineering disciplines, products are produced in large volume and are generally assumed to behave as expected; in software engineering, due to the foregoing discussion, such an assumption is unfounded, and the only way to ensure the quality of a software product is to subject that product to extensive analysis. This turns out to be an expensive proposition, in practice, and the source of another massive paradox in software engineering economics. Whereas testing (and more generally, verification and quality assurance) takes up a small percentage of the production cost of any engineering artifact, it accounts for a large percentage of the lifecycle cost of a software product. As a practical example, consider that the development of Windows Server 2003 (©Microsoft Corp.) was carried out by a team of 4400 software engineers, of whom 2000 formed the development team and a staggering 2400 formed the test team. More generally, testing accounts for around 50% of lifecycle costs, which is much higher than traditional manufacturing industries (where the likelihood of a defective product is so low as to make any significant amount of testing wasteful) (Table 1.2).

Good software engineering practice dictates that more effort ought to be spent on up-front specification and design activities and that such up-front investment enhances product quality and lessens the need for massive investment in *a posteriori* testing. While these practices appear to be promising, they have not been used sufficiently widely to make a tangible impact; so that software testing remains a major cost factor in software lifecycles.

1.7.5   Unbalanced Maintenance Costs

It is common to distinguish in software maintenance between several types of maintenance activity; the two most important types (in terms of cost) are as follows:

- Corrective maintenance, which aims to remove software faults
- Adaptive maintenance, which aims to adapt the software product to evolving requirements

Empirical studies show that adaptive maintenance accounts for the vast majority of maintenance costs. This contrasts with other engineering disciplines, where there is virtually no adaptive maintenance to speak of: it is not possible for a car buyer to return to the dealership to make her/his car more powerful, add seats to it, or make it more fuel-efficient. Hence, it is possible to distinguish between software products

TABLE 1.3 Maintenance cost distribution: corrective versus adaptive

	Software engineering, %	Other engineering, %
Corrective	≈20	>99
Adaptive	≈80	<1

TABLE 1.4 Corrective maintenance cost distribution: design versus wear and tear

	Software engineering, %	Other engineering, %
Design	≈100	1
Wear and tear	≈0	99

and other engineering products by the distribution of maintenance, as shown in Table 1.3.

While it is not realistic to expect a car dealership to change a car to meet different specifications, it is certainly their responsibility to repair if it no longer meets its original specifications. Another distinguishing feature arises when one considers corrective maintenance: Whereas in software products corrective maintenance consists in changing the design or implementation of the product, in other engineering disciplines products need (corrective) maintenance due to wear and tear (Table 1.4).

The only cases where a maintenance action on a brick-and-mortar product (e.g., a car) is of type *design* are cases where a manufacturer makes a product recall; these are sufficiently rare that they are usually newsworthy and are broadly advertised in public forums.

1.8 CHAPTER SUMMARY

This chapter introduces the discipline of software engineering with all its specific characteristics and paradoxes, contrasts it with more traditional engineering disciplines, and elucidates the role that software testing plays within this discipline.

1.9 BIBLIOGRAPHIC NOTES

For more information on the COCOMO cost model, consult (Boehm, 1981) or (Boehm et al., 2000); for more information on the JPL report on the evolution of avionics and space flight software, consult (Jet Propulsion Laboratory, 2009); for more information on the classification of software products into broad families of applications, consult (Somerville, 2004).

2

Software Quality Attributes

When one buys a car, one may be interested in any number of quality attributes, including purchase price, maintenance cost, reliability, safety, fuel efficiency (mpg), engine size/power, acceleration (0–60 mph), comfort, roominess, looks, noise level, trunk size, environmental impact, and so on. Likewise, a software product may feature many quality attributes, which we review briefly in this chapter, focusing in particular on those that may be of interest with respect to software testing. We distinguish between five categories of software quality attributes which are as follows:

- *Functional attributes,* which characterize the input/output behavior of the software product
- *Operational attributes,* which characterize the operational conditions of the software product
- *Usability attributes,* which characterize the extent to which the software product can be used and adapted to user needs
- *Business attributes,* which characterize the cost of developing, using, and evolving the software product
- *Structural attributes,* which characterize the internal structure of the software product

We consider these families of attributes in turn, in this chapter. For each attribute, we will present a definition and, possibly, a quantification (i.e., a way to measure the attribute quantitatively). This classification is not perfectly orthogonal, and many attributes may be listed in more than one category; but it helps us to define some structure in the set of attributes.

Software Testing: Concepts and Operations, First Edition. Ali Mili and Fairouz Tchier.
© 2015 John Wiley & Sons, Inc. Published 2015 by John Wiley & Sons, Inc.

2.1 FUNCTIONAL ATTRIBUTES

Functional attributes characterize the input/output behavior of software products. We distinguish between two broad categories of functional attributes: those that are of a Boolean nature (a software product has them or does not have them) and those that are of a statistical nature (a software product has them to a smaller or larger extent). The functional attributes of a software product depend on the existence of a specification, which describes a set of situations the product is intended to face, along with a prescription of correct program behaviors for each situation. We refer to the set of relevant situations as the *domain* of the specification.

2.1.1 Boolean Attributes

We recognize two attributes of a Boolean nature in a software product, which are as follows:

- *Correctness,* which is the property that the software product behaves according to its specification for all possible situations in the domain of the specification.
- *Robustness,* which is the property that the software product behaves according to its specification for all possible situations in the domain of the specification and behaves *reasonably* for situations outside the domain of the specification. Of course, reasonable behavior is not a well-defined condition, hence robustness is only partially defined; but it generally refers to behavior that alerts the user to the anomaly of the situation and acts prudently and conservatively (avoiding irreversible operations, avoiding irretrievable losses of information, etc.).

As defined, robustness logically implies correctness: whereas correctness refers solely to the behavior of the software product within the domain of the specification, robustness also refers to the behavior of the product outside the domain of the specification. Conversely, we can argue that robustness is not distinguishable from correctness since it is merely correctness with respect to a stronger specification (one that specifies the behavior of candidate programs inside the original specification's domain, as well as outside it); nevertheless, for a given specification, these are distinct properties.

2.1.2 Statistical Attributes

Correctness and a fortiori robustness are notoriously difficult to establish for software products of any realistic size; hence we introduce statistical attributes, which measure (over a continuum) how close a software product is to being correct or robust. We distinguish between two broad families of statistical attributes, depending on whether the obstacles to correctness and robustness are inadvertent (product complexity, programmer incompetence, etc.) or voluntary (malicious attempts to cause product failure).

- *Dependability*: Dependability is the probability that the system behaves according to its specifications for a period of operation time. We recognize two attributes within dependability, namely, *reliability* and *safety,* that differ by the stakes attached to satisfying the specification.
  - *Reliability* reflects the probability that the software product operates for a given amount of time without violating its specification.
  - *Safety* reflects the probability that the software product operates for a given amount of time without causing a catastrophic failure.

  Both reliability and safety are related to the product's ability to operate according to its specification; but whereas reliability reflects the product's ability to adhere to all the clauses of its specification, safety focuses particularly on high-stakes clauses, whose violation causes a catastrophic loss, in terms of human lives, mission success, high financial stakes, etc. Safe systems are sometimes referred as fail-safe, in the sense that it may fail to satisfy its specification but still satisfy the high-stakes requirements of its specification. A system may be reliable but unsafe (fails seldom but causes a catastrophic loss whenever it fails); and a system may be safe but unreliable (fails often, but causes low-stakes losses, and never causes catastrophic losses).

  The most commonly used metric to quantify reliability is the mean time to failure, which is the mean of the random variable that represents the operation time until the next system failure; the same metric can be used to quantify safety, if we just replace *failure* by *catastrophic failure*. Older metrics include the mean time between failures, which is the mean of the random variable that represents the time between two successive failures. More recent metrics include the mean failure cost, which measures the mean of the random variable that measures the loss of a stakeholder as a result of possible system failures.

- *Security*: Whereas dependability refers to failures that result from system design flaws, security refers primarily to voluntary actions by malicious perpetrators, although one can argue that these actions are rendered possible by system vulnerabilities, which also stem from system design flaws. We find four attributes that can be considered as aspects of security, which are as follows:
  - Confidentiality: Confidentiality refers to a system's ability to prevent unauthorized access to confidential data entrusted to its custody.
  - Integrity: Integrity refers to a system's ability to prevent loss or damage to critical data entrusted to its custody.
  - Authentication: Authentication refers to a system's ability to properly identify each user that gains access to its resources and to grant users access privileges according to their rightful status.
  - Availability: Availability refers to a system's ability to continue delivering service to its user community; it can be measured as a percentage. This attribute is usually the casualty of denial of service attacks: when the system is under attack, its ability to deliver services to its legitimate users suffers.

There is no widely accepted measure of system security. To the extent that security attacks result from system vulnerabilities, it is possible to quantify all dimensions of security (including availability) by mean time to detection (MTTD), which is the mean of the random variable that measures the time it takes perpetrators to uncover system vulnerabilities, and by mean time to exploitation (MTTE), which is the mean of the random variable that represents the time it takes perpetrators to find a way to exploit discovered system vulnerabilities.

2.2 OPERATIONAL ATTRIBUTES

Whereas functional attributes characterize the functions/services that a software product delivers to its users, operational attributes characterize the conditions under which these services are delivered. We find four attributes that can be considered as operational attributes, which are as follows:

- *Latency*: Latency (or response time) is the time that elapses between the submission of a query to the system and the response to the query; this attribute is relevant for interactive systems and can be measured in seconds. Because the time between a query and its response varies, of course, from query to query, and varies according to the system workload at the time the query is submitted, this attribute is understood to be an average over many queries, for an average workload.
- *Throughput*: Throughput is the volume of processing that the system can deliver per unit of operation time; this attribute is relevant for batch systems, such as the program that a bank runs in the middle of the night to update all the transactions of the day, and can be measured in transactions per second. Though latency and throughput appear to be related, as they both reflect the speed with which the system can process transactions, they are fairly orthogonal, in the sense that a system can have short (good) latency and small (bad) throughput (if it spends much of its time switching between queries), and long (bad) latency and large (good) throughput if its scheduler favors keeping the processor busy over the concern of fairness.
- *Efficiency*: The efficiency of a software product is its ability to deliver its functions and services with minimal computing resources, such as CPU cycles, memory space, disk space, and network bandwidth. It is difficult to quantify this attribute for a given software product in a way that prorates resource consumption to the services rendered by the product, but very easy to use this attribute to compare candidate software products for a given application.
- *Capacity*: The capacity of a system is the number of simultaneous users that a system can sustain while preserving a degree of quality of service (in terms of response time, timeliness, precision, size of data, etc.). This definition is ambiguous in a number of ways (what does it means to be simultaneous? At what level of granularity are we defining simultaneity? What degree of quality are we considering? etc.), but is a useful metric nevertheless.

- *Scalability*: The scalability of a system reflects its ability to continue delivering adequate service when its workload exceeds its original capacity. This attribute is sometimes referred to as graceful degradation: of course, as the workload increases beyond the system's preplanned capacity, one expects some degradation of the quality of service; scalability consists in ensuring that this degradation remains graceful (i.e., a progressive, continuous function of the workload).

2.3 USABILITY ATTRIBUTES

Whereas functional attributes measure the services rendered by the software product to the end user, and operational attributes reflect the operational conditions under which these services are rendered, usability attributes reflect the extent to which the software product is easy to use, and to customize to the end user's needs and circumstances. We identify five such attributes, which are as follows:

- *Ease of Use*: Ease of use is important especially in systems whose user community is broad, diverse, heterogeneous and possibly unskilled; this includes, for example, an online system in a public space. Qualities that support ease of use include simplicity of system interactions, uniformity of interaction patterns, availability of help menus, use of simple vocabulary, tolerance to misuse, and so on.
- *Ease of Learning*: Ease of learning is important especially in systems whose user community is homogeneous in terms of skill level (e.g., all the clerical staff of an organization) and who envisions to use the software product on a long-term basis (e.g., an accounting application). Qualities that support ease of learning include intuitiveness of system interactions, consistency of interaction protocols, uniformity of system outputs, and so on.
- *Customizability*: The customizability of a software product is its ability to be tuned to specific functional requirements of the end user, by the end user. The more control the end user has over the functionality of the software product, the better the customizability.
- *Calibrability*: The calibrability of a software product is its ability to be tuned to specific operational requirements of the end user, by the end user. The more control the end user has over the operational attributes of the software product, the better the calibrability.
- *Interoperability*: The interoperability of a software product is its ability to work in conjunction with other applications; it is difficult to give a general quantitative metric for this attribute, but it can be qualitatively characterized by the range of applications with which it can collaborate (for example, the breadth of file formats it can analyze and process, or by the range of file formats in which it can produce its output); it can also be qualitatively characterized by the range of technologies with which it is compatible.

The functional attributes, the operational attributes, and the usability attributes of a software product constitute all the attributes of the product that are of interest to the end user; in the remainder of this chapter, we consider other stakeholders of a software product, and review attributes that are of interest to them.

2.4 BUSINESS ATTRIBUTES

Broadly speaking, business attributes reflect the stakes of a software manager in the development, operation and evolution of a software product. They include the following attributes:

- *Development Cost*: Development cost is clearly an important attribute, and a business attribute at that. We usually quantify it in person-months invested in the development of the software product, from its requirements analysis to its acceptance testing.
- *Maintainability*: The maintainability of a software product is the amount of effort invested in the maintenance of the product during its operation phase (post delivery). We can quantify it in absolute terms, by means of person-months of maintenance effort per year, or in relative terms, by means of person-months of maintenance effort par year per line of code. Since most maintenance costs are typically spent on adaptive maintenance, which is driven by user demands rather than by any intrinsic attribute of the software product, we may want to normalize the measure of maintainability to the volume of adaptive maintenance, or exclude adaptive maintenance altogether from the person-month calculation of maintenance effort.
- *Portability*: The portability of a software product is the average cost of porting the product from one hardware/software platform to another. Portability is enhanced by reducing the platform-dependent functionality as much as possible, or by confining it to a single component of the product (hence confining changes to this component in the event of a migration of the product from one platform to another). Though it is usually thought of as a qualitative attribute, portability can be quantified by the average cost (in person-months) of a migration.
- *Reusability*: Whereas the three previous attributes reflect product cost, this attribute reflects potential benefits. The reusability of a software product is its ability to be reused, in whole or in part, in the design and development of other software products within the product's application domain. Reusability is the aggregate of two orthogonal properties, which are as follows:
  - *Usefulness,* which is the extent to which the product (or component) is widely needed in the product's application domain
  - *Usability,* which is the ease (lower cost) with which it is possible to adapt the product (or component) to the requirements of an application within the domain

Whereas usefulness is a property of the product's (or component's) specification, usability is a property of its design: well-designed components can be adapted to related requirements at low cost, by such devices as genericity and parameterization.

2.5   STRUCTURAL ATTRIBUTES

Like business attributes, structural attributes are of interest to system custodians/developers/maintainers/operators; but whereas business attributes deal with economic aspects of system management, structural attributes deal with their technical aspects. In other words, whereas business attributes are relevant to software managers, structural attributes are of interest to engineers, designers and other technical personnel. We identify four structural attributes, which are as follows:

- *Design Integrity*: The quality of a design is easier to recognize than to define, which is in turn much easier than to quantify. Qualities of a good design include simplicity, orthogonality (the quality of a design that results from a set of independent decisions), economy of concept, cohesiveness of the design rationale, consistency of design rules, adherence to a simple design discipline, and so on.
- *Modularity*: Modularity can be defined in terms of a single design principle: information hiding. The main characteristic of a modular design is that each component of the system hides a design decision that other components need not know about (i.e., be influenced by). Hence one of the main features of a modular design is the separation between the specification of a module and its implementation. Modularity can be quantified by two attributes, which are as follows:
  - o Cohesion: The cohesion of a component represents the volume of information flow within the component, and can be quantified using information theory.
  - o Coupling: The coupling between two components represents the bandwidth of information interchange that takes place between the components, and can be quantified by the entropy of the random variable that represents the flow of information interchange.
- *Testability*: The testability of a software product reflects the extent to which one can test the system or components thereof to an arbitrary level of thoroughness. Testability can be quantified by means of two attributes, which are as follows:
  - o Controllability: The controllability of a component in a system is the bandwidth (breadth) of input values we can submit (as test data) to the component by controlling system inputs. This can be quantified by the conditional entropy of the system's input given an input value of the component.
  - o Observability: The observability of a component is the extent to which we can infer the output produced by the component by observing the system output. This can be quantified by the conditional entropy of the component's output, given the system's output.

- *Adaptability*: The adaptability of a system is the ease with which it can be modified to satisfy changing requirements. This attribute sounds similar to customizability, in that they both deal with adjusting the software product to meet different sets of requirements. In fact they are different in two crucial ways, which are as follows:
  - Whereas customizability refers to changes carried out by the end user (hence accessible to her/him, by design), adaptability refers to changes carried out by the software engineer.
  - Whereas customizability refers to changes that are planned for within the design of the system, adaptability refers to changes in the system requirements.

In many instances, we find that structural attributes support business attributes; for example, modularity supports maintainability. But we consider them as distinct, on the grounds that one is a business attribute while the other is a structural/technical attribute. Also, there is no one-to-one correspondence between them: modularity supports not only maintainability but also development cost (which it reduces); also, maintainability is supported not only by modularity but also by testability.

2.6 CHAPTER SUMMARY

This chapter provides us a vocabulary for discussing software properties and enables us to explore the effects of software testing on achieving or measuring these properties, as we will do in subsequent chapters. We have presented five classes of software quality attributes, which we divide broadly into three categories, which are as follows:

- *Attributes that are relevant to software users*: These include functional attributes, operational attributes, and usability attributes and reflect the overall quality of service delivered by the software product.
- *Attributes that are relevant to software operators*: These include business attributes and reflect the cost of developing, maintaining, and evolving the software product.
- *Attributes that are relevant to software engineers*: These include structural attributes and reflect the engineering qualities of the product and their impact on analyzing and working with the software product for the duration of its lifecycle.

2.7 EXERCISES

2.1. Your colleague Joe argues that since reliability is the probability that the product operates free of failure for some unit of time and safety is the probability that the product operates free of catastrophic failures, and since catastrophic failures are failures, then a reliable system is necessarily safe. Do you agree with Joe? Why or why not?

2.2. Can a system be reliable but not secure? Can a system be secure but not reliable?

2.3. Can a system have high reliability but low availability? Can a system have high availability but low reliability?

2.4. Consider a queue simulation module M that uses an implementation of an first in/first out (FIFO) queue Q. Using information theory, propose a formula for the cohesion of M and the coupling of M and Q. What information do you need about the implementation of M and Q to compute the cohesion of M and the coupling of M and Q.

2.8 BIBLIOGRAPHIC NOTES

Some of the terminology introduced in Section 2.1, pertaining to functional attributes, is inspired by Avizienis et al. (2004); because the definitions of Avizienis et al. are too detailed for our purposes, we have not adopted them wholesale but have simplified them a little. The quantification of security by means of MTTD and MTTE is due to Nicol et al. (2004). For more information on information theory, consult Csiszar and Koerner (2011).

3

A Software Testing Lifecycle

Testing is the process of executing a software product on sample input data and analyzing its output. Unlike other engineering products, which are usually fault-free, software products are prone to be faulty, due to an accumulation of faults in all the phases of their lifecycle (faulty specifications, faulty design, faulty implementation, etc.). Also, unlike other engineering products, where faults arise as a result of product wear and/or decay, the faults that arise in software products are design faults, which are delivered with the new product.

3.1 A SOFTWARE ENGINEERING LIFECYCLE

The simplest model of a software product lifecycle views the process of developing and evolving the product as a set of phases proceeding sequentially from a requirements analysis phase to a product operation and maintenance phase. While this process model is widely believed to be simplistic, and not to reflect the true nature of software development and evolution, we adopt it nevertheless as a convenient abstraction. If nothing else, this process model enables us to situate software testing activities in their proper context within the software engineering lifecycle. For the sake of argument, we adopt the following sequence of phases:

- *Feasibility Analysis*: Feasibility analysis is the phase when the economic and technical feasibility of the development project is assessed, and a determination is made of whether to proceed with the development project, within a given budget, schedule, and technological means.
- *Requirements Analysis*: The phase of requirements analysis is the most difficult of the software lifecycle, at the same time as it is the most fateful phase, in terms of determining the fate of the project (its success or failure, its scope, its cost, its value to users, etc.). Whereas a naïve view may understand this phase as

Software Testing: Concepts and Operations, First Edition. Ali Mili and Fairouz Tchier.
© 2015 John Wiley & Sons, Inc. Published 2015 by John Wiley & Sons, Inc.

consisting of a user dictating user requirements and a software engineer who is carefully taking notes, the reality of this phase is typically much more complex: The *requirements engineer* (a software engineering specializing in analyzing requirements) must conduct a vast data gathering operation that consists in the following steps: identifying system stakeholders; gathering relevant domain knowledge (pertaining to the application domain of the system); identifying relevant outside requirements (relevant laws of nature, applicable regulations, relevant standards, etc.); collecting requirements from all relevant stakeholders (system end users, system operators, system custodians, system managers, etc.); documenting the requirements; identifying possible ambiguities, gaps, inconsistencies; resolving/negotiating inconsistencies; specifying the functional and nonfunctional requirements of the system; and finally validating the requirements specification for completeness (all relevant requirements are captured) and minimality (all captured requirements are relevant). As we shall see in Chapter 5, validating a specification has much in common with testing a program.

- *Product Architecture*: The phase of product architecture consists in determining the broad structure of the product, including a specification of the main components of the architecture, along with a specification of the coordination and communication mechanisms between the components, as well as decisions pertaining to how the system will be deployed, how it will be distributed, how data will be shared, and so on. The architecture is usually evaluated by the extent to which it supports relevant operational attributes (see Chapter 2).

- *Product Design*: In the product design phase, system designers make system-wide design decisions pertaining to data structures, data representation, and algorithms, and decompose the software product into small units to be developed independently by programmers. This phase is verified by ensuring that if all the units perform as specified, then the overall system performs as specified.

- *Programming*: The phase of programming can be carried out by a large number of programmers working independently (ideally, at least), and developing program units from unit specifications. This phase is verified by means of *Unit Testing*, where each unit is tested against the specification that it was developed to satisfy.

- *System Integration*: Once all the units have been developed, the system is put together according to its design and tested to ensure that it meets its system wide specification. This is referred to as *Integration Testing*, as it tests the integration of the units into the overall system. This phase takes usually a significant portion of the project's budget and schedule. This phase can also be used to carry out another form of testing: *Reliability Testing*, where fault removal is accompanied by an evolving estimate of reliability growth, until a target reliability is reached; this differs from integration testing in that its focus is not on finding faults, but on improving reliability (hence targeting those faults that have the greatest negative impact on reliability).

- *Delivery*: Once the system has gone through integration testing and has been deemed to be ready for delivery, it is delivered to the customer, in an operation that includes *Acceptance Testing*. Like integration testing, acceptance testing is a system-wide test. But whereas integration testing is focused on finding faults, acceptance testing is focused on showing their absence, or at least highlighting their sparsity. This phase can also be used to carry out another form of testing: *Certification Testing*, whose goal is to certify (or not) that the product meets some quality standard; this differs from acceptance testing in that the goal is not to make a particular customer happy, but rather to satisfy a generic quality standard.

• *Operations and Maintenance*: If during the operation phase, the software product fails, or the software requirements change, then a maintenance operation is initiated to alter the software product accordingly. Upon the completion of the maintenance operation, the software system must be tested; but given that the maintenance operation may involve only a limited portion of the source code, or only limited aspects of system functionality, it may be advantageous to focus the testing effort to those portions of the code that have been modified, or those functional aspects that are part of the altered requirements; this is called *Regression Testing*.

Figure 3.1 illustrates this lifecycle, and highlights the testing activities that take place therein. Each phase of this lifecycle concludes with a verification and validation step, intended to ensure that the deliverable that is produced in the phase is sufficiently trustworthy to serve as a launchpad for the next phase. Strictly speaking, validation ensures that the specification is valid (in the sense that it record *all* the valid requirements, and *nothing but* the valid requirements), whereas verification ensures that the product is correct with respect to the specification; hence, in theory, validation is used at the end of the requirements specification phase, and verification is used in all subsequent phases (see Fig. 3.2 for a summary illustration). But in practice, it is a good idea to maintain a healthy suspicion of the specification throughout the lifecycle, to test it at every opportunity (we will explore means to this end in subsequent chapters), and be prepared to adjust it as necessary.

As Figure 3.2 shows, it is much harder to ascertain specification validation than it is to ascertain program verification, for the following reasons:

• Assuming the requirements specification is written in a formal notation, the verification step consists in checking a relationship between two formal documents (the specification and the program); as hard as this may be, it is a well-defined property between two formal artifacts. By contrast, validation involves a formal artifact (the specification) and a heterogeneous collection of requirements and facts from diverse sources.

• Because verification involves a well-defined property between two well defined artifacts, it is a systematic, repeatable, possibly automatable operation.

• Because validation involves interaction with multiple stakeholders, it is an informal process that is neither repeatable nor automatable. Its success depends on the competence, cooperation and dependability of several human actors.

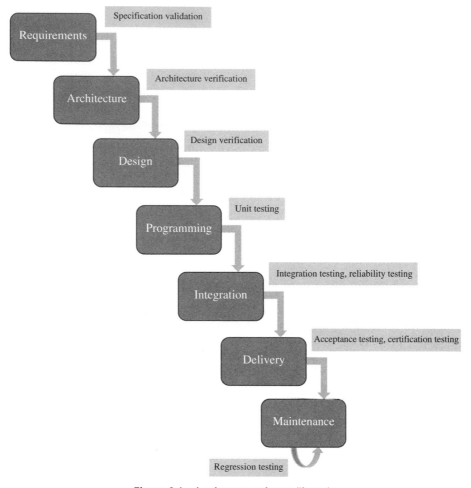

Figure 3.1   *A reference software lifecycle.*

In addition to this chronological decomposition of the lifecycle into phases, we can also consider an organizational decomposition the lifecycle into activities, where each activity represents a particular aspect of the software project carried out by a specialized team. A typical set of activities includes the following:

- Requirements Analysis
- Software Design
- Programming
- Test Planning
- Configuration Management and Quality Assurance

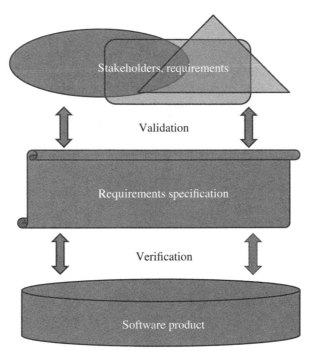

Figure 3.2   *Verification and validation.*

- Verification and Validation
- Manuals
- Project Management

So that a complete view of the lifecycle is given by a two-dimensional table that shows phases and activities; in principle, all activities are active at all phases, though to different degrees.

3.2   A SOFTWARE TESTING LIFECYCLE

So far, we have seen many testing processes, including unit testing, integration testing, reliability testing, acceptance testing, certification testing, and regression testing. We will review other forms of testing in the next chapter. While they may differ in many ways, these forms of testing all follow a generic process, which includes the following phases:

- *Preparing a Test Environment*: With the possible exception of regression testing, which takes place during the operations and maintenance, most testing happens in a development environment rather than its actual operating environment. Hence, it is incumbent on the test engineer to create a test environment that mimics the operational environment as faithfully as possible. This may be a non-trivial task, involving such steps as simulating the operational environment; creating stubs for missing parts of the operational environment; and simulating workload conditions by creating fictitious demands on the system.

- *Generating Test Data*: Ideally, to test a program, we would like to execute it on all possible inputs or combinations of inputs or combinations of inputs and internal states (if the program carries an internal state), and observe its behavior under these circumstances. Unfortunately, that is totally unrealistic for all but the most trivial programs. Hence, the challenge for the program tester is to find a set of test data that is small enough to be feasible, yet large enough to be representative. What do we mean by representative: we mean that if the program executes successfully on the test data, then we can be fairly confident that it would execute successfully on any input data (or more generally any configuration of input data and internal state). Quantitatively, if we let S be the set of all possible configurations of inputs and internal states, and D the subset of S that includes all the configurations on which the program was tested successfully; and if we let σ and δ be, respectively, the events "the program runs successfully on all elements of S" and "the program runs successfully on all elements of D," then we want the conditional probability $\Pi(\sigma \mid \delta)$ to be as close to 1.0 as possible. This, in general, is a very difficult problem; hence Dijkstra's often-cited quote that "testing can be used to prove the presence of faults, never their absence." While one can hardly argue with this premise, we will see in later chapters that while testing cannot be used to prove a program correct, it can be used to establish lesser goals, that are useful nevertheless, such as: to estimate the reliability of a program; to estimate the fault density of the program; to certify that the reliability of a program exceeds a required threshold; or, if used in conjunction with fault diagnosis and removal, to enhance the reliability of a program.

  In practice, test data is generated by means of what is called a *test selection criterion*. This is a condition that characterizes elements of S that are in D. It is not difficult to generate a test selection criterion that produces a small set D; what is very difficult is to generate a test selection criterion that is representative of S (a much harder case to make). The generation of a test selection criterion is one of the most important attributes of software testing; it is also a very difficult decision to make, as we discuss in Part III of the book, and the aspect of software testing that has mobilized the greatest share of researcher attention. Selecting what data to run the product on determines the fate of the test process, in the sense that it affects the extent to which the test achieves its goal. We can identify three broad categories of test selection criteria, which are as follows:

  o Functional criteria of test data selection: These criteria consist in generating test data by inspecting the specification of the software product; the goal of these criteria is to exercise all the functionalities and services that the product is supposed to deliver.

○ Structural criteria of test data selection: These criteria consist in generating test data by inspecting the source code of the product; the goal of these criteria is to exercise all the components of the product.

○ Random test data selection: These criteria consist in generating test data randomly over all of S (the combination of the input space and the internal state space); but this is usually done according to a specific *usage pattern*. In practice, the combined configurations of inputs and internal states are not equally likely to occur; some may be more likely to occur than others; in order for this type of selection criterion to be effective, we need to have a probability distribution function over S that quantifies the likelihood of occurrence of any element of S in normal usage. By adhering to the same probability distribution during the testing phase, we ensure that whatever behavior is observed during the testing phase is likely to arise during field usage; another advantage of this approach is that test data can be generated automatically (using random data generators), so that a software product can be tested on much more inputs than if test data were generated by hand.

• *Generating an Oracle*: Whenever we test a software product, we need an *oracle*, that is, an agent that tells us, for each execution, whether the software product behaved correctly or not. The most obvious candidate for an oracle is the specification that the software product is meant to satisfy; and the safest way to implement an oracle is to write a certified Boolean function that takes as input the test data and the output of the program and rules on whether the observed input/output behavior satisfies the specification. But there are several situations where this ideal solution is impractical, or unnecessary, which are as follows:

○ First, the specification may be so complex that writing a Boolean function to test it is difficult and/or error-prone; if the Boolean function that represents the oracle is more complex than the program under test, then this solution defeats the purpose of the test, and may in fact mislead us into the wrong conclusions and actions.

○ Second, it may be unnecessary to test the program against all the clauses of the specification: we may be interested in testing safety properties of the software product, in which case the oracle will only reflect safety critical requirements; or we may verify the correctness of the program against some aspects of the specification using alternative means (e.g., static analysis).

○ Third, the process of storing the test data prior to each test and executing the oracle after each test may be prohibitively expensive in terms of computer resources, compelling us to consider more cost-effective options.

○ Fourth, there are cases where we want to use an oracle that is in fact stronger (more demanding) than the specification: when the goal of the test is to find faults, it is not sufficient to know that the program satisfies the specification; rather it is necessary to check that the program computes the exact function that the designers intended it to compute; any deviation from this function may be an indication of a fault in the program.

• *Generating a Termination Condition*: Any test process aims to achieve a goal: For example, unit testing aims to diagnose faults in the program unit before integrating it into the project's configuration; integration testing aims to diagnose faults in the design of the system or the specifications in the system's unit; reliability testing aims to estimate the reliability of the software product, or to remove enough faults from the system to raise its reliability beyond a required threshold; acceptance testing aims to establish the dependability of the software product to the satisfaction of the customer (or to the terms of the development contract); and so on. The *Termination Condition* of a test is the condition that characterizes the achievement of the goal, that is, the condition that we test to know that we have achieved the goal of the test, hence we can terminate the test.

- *Producing a Test Driver*: The test driver is the process whereby the program is executed on the selected test data, its output is tested against the selected test oracle, and a course of action is defined for the case of a successful test and the case of an unsuccessful test, until the condition of termination is realized. If test data is generated automatically (e.g., using random test data generation, or by reading from a predefined test data repository), and if the termination condition can be checked on the fly (e.g., generating a predefined number of test data samples, or exhausting a file of test data), and if the analysis of the test outcome can be done off-line, then the test driver can be automated. A generic pattern for such a test driver may be as follows:

```
void function testdriver()
    {statetype state, initstate;
     while (! testTermination())
         {generateTest(state); initstate=state;
          Program(state); // candidate program
                          // modifies state
          if (oracle(initstate, state))
              {successfultest(initstate);}
          else
              {unsuccessfultest(initstate);}}
cout << "test report";}
```

At each iteration, the driver generates a new test data sample, stores it into variable `initstate`, then lets the program under test run, modifying the current state but keeping the initial state intact. Then, the test oracle is called to check the execution of the program on the current test data sample, and depending on the outcome of the test, takes some action; if the test is successful, it may record the initial state on which the test was successful, or simply increment a counter recording the number of successful tests; if the test is unsuccessful it may write a failure report on some file intended for the analysis of the test outcome.

- *Executing the Test*: This phase consists merely of executing, whether by hand or automatically, the test driver that is defined in the previous phase.
- *Analyzing Test Outcome:* The whole test would be in vain if we did not have a phase in which we analyze the outcome of the test and draw the conclusion that is called for, depending on the goal of the test. If the goal of the test is to find faults, then this phase consists in analyzing the outcome of the test to identify faults and remove them; if the goal of the test is to judge acceptance, then this phase

consists in determining whether the product can be deemed acceptable; if the goal of the test is to estimate reliability, then this phase consists in computing the estimated reliability on the basis of the observed successes and failures of the program under test; and so on.

The process of executing the test varies according to the type of test, but broadly follows the process depicted in Figure 3.3. There are instances where the test loop exits

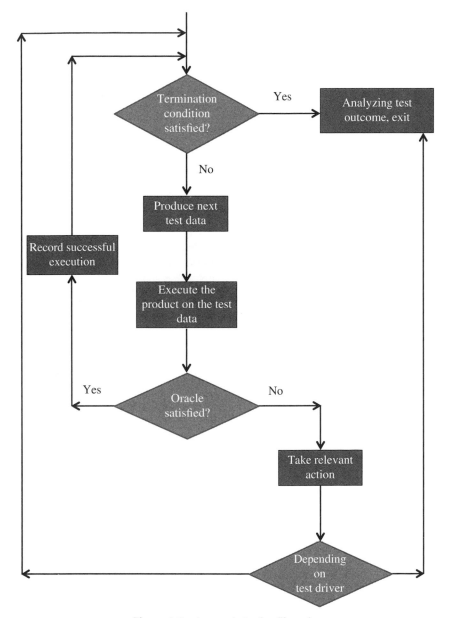

Figure 3.3 *A generic testing lifecycle.*

whenever an unsuccessful execution is encountered; in such cases, the fault that may have caused the failure of the program is diagnosed, then removed, and the test resumes by reentering the loop. In other instances, an unsuccessful test does not disrupt the loop, but does cause a record to be stored to document the circumstances of the failure. These cases will be explored in Chapter 7, when we discuss a taxonomy of testing methods.

3.3   THE V-MODEL OF SOFTWARE TESTING

Even though testing is usually thought of as a single phase, the last phase, of the software lifecycle, it is actually best viewed as an activity that proceeds concurrently through all the phases of the lifecycle, from start to finish. The following model, called the V-model, illustrates the nature of testing as an ongoing activity through the software lifecycle, and shows how testing can be planned step by step as the lifecycle proceeds; it superimposes, in effect, the software lifecycle with the testing lifecycle. We discuss later how each pair of phases connected by a horizontal arrow in the Figure 3.4 are related to each other: generally, the phase on the left branch of the V prepares the corresponding phase on the right branch; and the latter tests the validity of the former.

- It is possible to start planning for acceptance testing as soon as the phase of requirements analysis and software specification is complete. Indeed, the software specifications that emerge from this phase can be used to prepare the test oracle, and can also be used to derive, if not actual test data, at least the criteria for selecting test data, and the standards of thoroughness that acceptance testing must meet. On the other hand, acceptance testing checks the final software product against the specifications that were derived in the phase of requirements analysis and software specification.

- Whereas acceptance testing is a service to the end user, system testing is a service to the development team. Whereas the goal of acceptance testing is to show that the software behaves according to its specifications within the parameters of the agreement between the developer and the user, the goal of system testing is to find as many faults as possible prior to acceptance testing (if there are any faults, we want them to show up at system testing rather than acceptance testing). Planning for system testing can start as soon as the software architecture is drawn, when we have some idea about what function the software system fulfills, and how it operates; this information affects test data generation and oracle design.

- Whereas system testing tests the software system as a monolith, by considering its external behavior and its global specification, integration testing tests a specific attribute of the software product, namely, the ability of the system components to interact according to the design of the system. Accordingly, test data has to be targeted to exercise component interactions, and the test

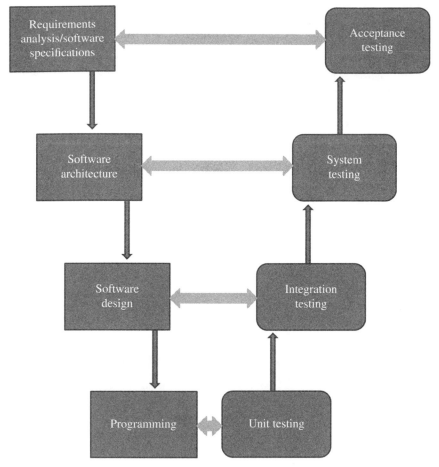

Figure 3.4 *The V-model of software testing.*

oracle focuses on whether the exercised interactions are consistent with the intent of the designer.

• Unit testing focuses on testing individual modules against module specifications generated as part of the system design. Test data may be generated in such a way as to cover all aspects of the specification, or all structural features of the unit.

3.4 CHAPTER SUMMARY

In this chapter, we have reviewed two broad lifecycles, which are as follows:

• The lifecycle of software development and maintenance, focusing in particular on the various forms of testing that take place along this lifecycle, including unit testing, integration testing, system testing, reliability testing, acceptance testing, certification testing, and regression testing.

- The lifecycle of software testing, as a sequence of phases that include preparing a test environment, generating test data, generating a test oracle, generating a termination criterion, generating a test driver, executing the test, and analyzing the outcome of the test.

3.5 BIBLIOGRAPHIC NOTES

Though there are several sources that discuss software lifecycles, the ideas presented in this chapter are most influenced by Boehm (1981), most notably his view of the software lifecycle as a two-dimensional structure that decomposes the software development process into a chronological dimension (phases) and an organizational dimension (activities). The V-model is inspired from Culbertson et al. (2002). Other examples of lifecycle models can be found in Black (2007), Kaner et al. (1999), and Kit (1995).

Part II

Foundations of Software Testing

Whereas in the previous part, we looked at software, software qualities, software engineering, and the role that testing plays in the software engineering process, in this part, we focus our attention on software testing and survey its foundations. This part includes four chapters:

- In Chapter 4, we discuss a relation-based specification model that we use throughout the book; specifications play a central role in software testing, as we always test a program against a specification that captures the properties we are interested in.
- In Chapter 5, we define the concept of program correctness, and we briefly present an inductive method to prove program correctness by static analysis.
- In Chapter 6, we introduce the fundamental concepts of fault, error, failure, and relative correctness and discuss how these concepts can be used to elucidate the goals and means of software testing.
- Finally, in Chapter 7, we present a software testing taxonomy, which characterizes each testing effort by a number of (nearly) orthogonal attributes.

Software Testing: Concepts and Operations, First Edition. Ali Mili and Fairouz Tchier.
© 2015 John Wiley & Sons, Inc. Published 2015 by John Wiley & Sons, Inc.

4

Software Specifications

The specification of a software product is a description of the functional requirements that the product must satisfy. It is not common to study software specifications in the context of software testing; we do so in this book for a variety of reasons, which are as follows:

- *Specifications are the Basis for Test Oracles*: As we discuss in Chapter 3, the design of a test oracle is a critical step in software testing; this step consists primarily in selecting a specification against which we test the program and in implementing it. This step plays an important role in determining the effectiveness of the test.

- *Testing and Relative Correctness*: We cannot talk about testing without talking about faults (testing means exposing, identifying, and/or removing faults); and we cannot talk about faults without talking about relative correctness (a program from which we have removed a fault is more correct, in some sense, than the original faulty program); and we cannot talk about relative correctness without talking about correctness (as correctness is the ultimate form of relative correctness); and we cannot talk about correctness without talking about specifications (correctness is relative to a specification).

- *A Bridge Between Testing and Verification*: It is customary to argue that dynamic testing and static verification are complementary techniques to ensure the correctness or reliability of software products. But complementarity is meaningful only if the results of these two techniques can be expressed in the same broad framework; specifications make this possible.

- *A Basis for Hybrid Verification*: In the perennial debate about the comparative merits of static analysis and dynamic testing, an important detail often gets overlooked: the observation that what makes a method ineffective is not any intrinsic shortcoming of the method but rather the fact that it is used against the wrong specification. A cost-effective approach to software quality may be

Software Testing: Concepts and Operations, First Edition. Ali Mili and Fairouz Tchier.
© 2015 John Wiley & Sons, Inc. Published 2015 by John Wiley & Sons, Inc.

to use testing for some parts of the specification and use static analysis for other parts; this is discussed in Chapter 6. This approach is possible only when the two methods are designed to deal with the same specification framework.

• *Testing in the Context of Verification and Validation*: Testing is best viewed as part of a broader policy of verification and validation. The study of software specifications will give us an opportunity to practice the activities of software verification and validation and the role that testing may play in carrying out these activities.

With these premises in mind, we discuss the topic of software specifications as an important aspect of the study of software testing. While there is a wide range of specification languages that are used in research circles, some of which are relatively widely used in industry, we choose not to commit to any language, but rather to use mathematical notation, and focus on models rather than languages.

4.1   PRINCIPLES OF SOUND SPECIFICATION

4.1.1   A Discipline of Specification

The *specification* of a software product is a description of the properties that the product must have to fulfill its purpose. The specification is usually derived by identifying all the relevant stakeholders of the (existing or planned) software product, eliciting the requirements that they expect the product to meet, formulating and combining these requirements, and compiling them into a cohesive document. While specifications typically pertain to functional and operational requirements, we focus primarily on functional requirements in this book, that is, requirements that pertain to the input/ output behavior of the software product.

As a product, a specification must meet two conditions, which are as follows:

1. *Formality*: The specification must be represented in such a way as to describe precisely what functional behavior is required.
2. *Abstraction*: The specification must describe what requirements the software product must satisfy, not how to satisfy them. In other words, it must focus on *what* candidate programs must do rather than *how* they must do it, the latter being the prerogative of the designer.

As a process (the process of identifying stakeholders, eliciting requirements, compiling them, etc.), a specification must meet two conditions, which are as follows:

1. *Completeness*: The specification must capture *all* the relevant requirements of the product.
2. *Minimality*: The specification must capture *nothing but* the relevant requirements of the product.

A specification that is deemed to be complete and minimal is said to be *valid*. In Sections 4.2 and 4.3, we will have an opportunity to discuss how to ensure the validity of specifications; in the remainder of this section, we introduce elements of relational mathematics, which we use throughout the book, starting in this chapter.

4.2 RELATIONAL MATHEMATICS

4.2.1 Sets and Relations

We represent sets using a programming-like notation, by introducing variable names and associated data type (sets of values). For example, if we represent set S by the variable declarations

x: X; y: Y; z: Z,

then S is the Cartesian product $X \times Y \times Z$. Elements of S are denoted in lower case s and are triplets of elements of X, Y, and Z. Given an element s of S, we represent its X component by $x(s)$, its Y component by $y(s)$, and its Z component by $z(s)$. A *relation* on S is a subset of the Cartesian product $S \times S$; given a pair (s,s') in R, we say that s' is an *image* of s by R. Special relations on S include the *universal relation* $L = S \times S$, the *identity relation* $I = \{(s,s') \mid s' = s\}$, and the *empty relation* $\phi = \{\}$. To represent relations graphically, we use the Cartesian plane in which set S is represented on the abscissas (for s) and the ordinates (for s'). Using this device, we represent an arbitrary relation on S, as well as L, I, and ϕ in Figure 4.1.

4.2.2 Operations on Relations

Because a relation is a set, we can apply to relations all the operations that are applicable to sets, such as union ($\cup$), intersection ($\cap$), difference ($/$), and complement ($\overline{}$). In addition, we define the following operations:

- The *converse* of relation R is the relation denoted by $\hat{R}$ and defined by $\hat{R} = \{(s,s') \mid (s,s') \in R\}$.

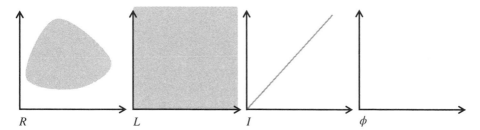

Figure 4.1 *Special relations.*

- The *domain* of relation R is the subset of S denoted by *dom(R)* and defined by $dom(R) = \{s | \exists s' : (s,s') \in R\}$.
- The *range* of relation R is the subset of S denoted by *rng(R)* and defined as the domain of $\hat{R}$.
- The *(pre)restriction* of R to (sub)set A is the relation denoted by $_A \backslash R$ and defined by $_A \backslash R = \{(s,s') | s \in A \land (s,s') \in R\}$.
- The *postrestriction* of R to (sub)set A is the relation denoted by $R_{/A}$ and defined by $R_{/A} = \{(s,s') | (s,s') \in R \land s' \in A\}$.

Figure 4.2 depicts a graphic illustration of a relation, its complement, and its converse.

Given a set A (subset of S), we define three relations of interest, which are as follows:

- The *vector* defined by A is the relation A × S.
- The *inverse* vector defined by A is the relation S × A.
- The *monotype* defined by A is the relation denoted by I(A) and defined by $I(A) = \{(s,s') | s \in A \land s' = s\}$.

Figure 4.3 represents, for set A (a subset of S), the vector, inverse vector, and monotype defined by A.

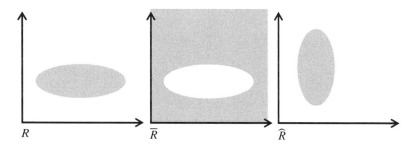

Figure 4.2 Complement and inverse.

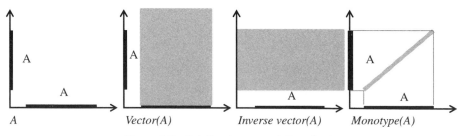

Figure 4.3 Relational representation of sets.

Given two relations R and R′, we let the product of R by R′ be denoted by R•R′ (or RR′, if no ambiguity arises) and defined by $R{\bullet}R' = \{(s,s')|\exists s'' : (s,s'')\in R \land (s'',s')\in R'\}$. The Figure 4.4 illustrates the definition of relational product.

If we denote the vector and the inverse vector defined by A by, respectively, $\omega(A)$ and $\mu(A)$, then the following identities hold, by virtue of the relevant definition:

- $\omega(A) = I(A){\bullet}L$,
- $\mu(A) = L{\bullet}I(A)$,
- $\widehat{\omega(A)} = \mu(A)$,
- $I(A) = \omega(A) \cap I = \mu(A) \cap I$.

Vectors are a convenient (relational) way to represent sets, when we want everything to be a relation. Hence, for example, the domain of relation R can be represented by the vector RL, and the range of relation R can be represented by the inverse vector LR (Fig. 4.5).

Note that we can represent the prerestriction and the postrestriction of a relation to a set, say A, using the vector and inverse vector defined by A, as shown in the Figure 4.6.

4.2.3 Properties of Relations

Among the properties of relations, we cite the following:

- A relation R is said to be *total* if and only if $RL=L$.
- A relation R is said to be *surjective* if and only if $LR=L$.

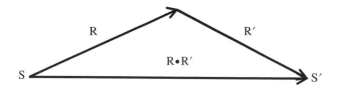

Figure 4.4 *Relational product.*

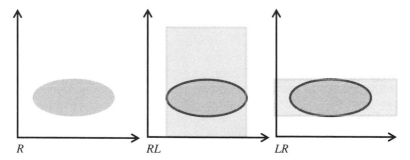

Figure 4.5 *Multiplying with universal relation.*

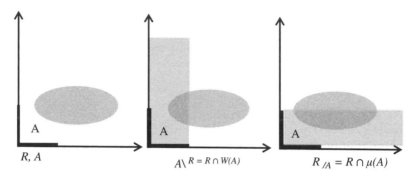

Figure 4.6 *Pre and post restriction.*

- A relation R is said to be *deterministic* if and only if $\hat{R}R \subseteq I$.
- A relation R is said to be *reflexive* if and only if $I \subseteq R$.
- A relation R is said to be *symmetric* if and only if $R \subseteq \hat{R}$.
- A relation R is said to be *transitive* if and only if $RR \subseteq R$.
- A relation R is said to be *antisymmetric* if and only if $R \cap \hat{R} \subseteq I$.
- A relation R is said to be *asymmetric* if and only if $R \cap \hat{R} \subseteq \phi$.
- A relation R is said to be *connected* if and only if $R \cup \hat{R} = L$.
- A relation R is said to be an *equivalence relation* if and only if it is reflexive, symmetric, and transitive.
- A relation R is said to be a *partial ordering* if and only if it is reflexive, antisymmetric, and transitive.
- A relation R is said to be a *total ordering* if and only if it is a partial ordering and is connected.

The Figure 4.7 illustrates some of these properties.

4.3 SIMPLE INPUT OUTPUT PROGRAMS

While the study of relations may sound alien to software testing, relations can be used to model specifications, which are an important part of software testing. They are the basis for the design and implementation of oracles, and more generally, they serve to define what is program correctness, what is a fault, what is fault removal, and what is relative correctness, all of which are essential aspects of software testing.

4.3.1 Representing Specifications

If one asks junior computer science (CS) students in a programming course to write a C++ function that reads a real number and compute its square root, they would

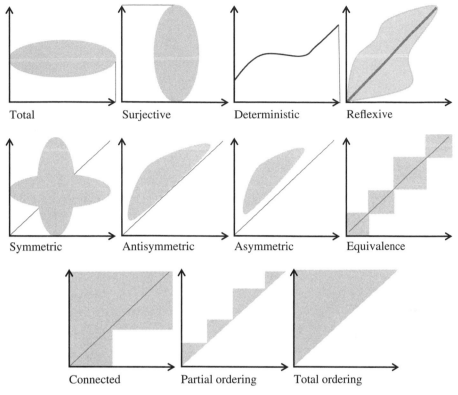

Figure 4.7 *Properties of relations.*

rush immediately to their computers to write code and run it; and yet this problem statement, despite being simple and short, leaves many questions unanswered. Consider that this statement may be interpreted in a wide range of manners, leading to a wide range of possible specifications, where space S is defined to be the set of real numbers:

1. Only nonnegative arguments will be submitted; the output is a (positive or non-positive) square root of the input value:

$$R_1 = \left\{ (s,s') | s \geq 0 \wedge s'^2 = s \right\}.$$

2. Only non-negative arguments will be submitted; the output is the nonnegative square root of the input value:

$$R_2 = \left\{ (s,s') | s \geq 0 \wedge s'^2 = s \wedge s' \geq 0 \right\}.$$

3. Only nonnegative arguments will be submitted; the output is an approximation (within a precision ε) of a (positive or non-positive) square root of the input value:

$$R_3 = \left\{ (s,s') | s \geq 0 \wedge |s'^2 = s| < \varepsilon \right\}.$$

4. Only nonnegative arguments will be submitted; the output is an approximation (within a precision ε) of the non-negative square root of the input value:

$$R_4 = \left\{ (s,s') | s \geq 0 \wedge \left| s'^2 = s \right| < \varepsilon \wedge s' \geq 0 \right\}.$$

5. Negative arguments may also be submitted; for negative arguments, the output is −1; for nonnegative arguments, the output is a (positive or nonpositive) square root of the input value:

$$R_5 = \left\{ (s,s') | s \geq 0 \wedge s'^2 = s \right\} \cup \{ (s,s') | s < 0 \wedge s' = -1 \}.$$

6. Negative arguments may also be submitted; for negative arguments, the output is −1; for nonnegative arguments, the output is the nonnegative square root of the input value:

$$R_6 = \left\{ (s,s') | s \geq 0 \wedge s'^2 = s \wedge s' \geq 0 \right\} \cup \{ (s,s') | s < 0 \wedge s' = -1 \}.$$

7. Negative arguments may also be submitted; for negative arguments, the output is arbitrary; for nonnegative arguments, the output is an approximation (within a precision ε) of a (positive or nonpositive) square root of the input value:

$$R_7 = \left\{ (s,s') | s \geq 0 \wedge \left| s'^2 = s \right| < \varepsilon \right\} \cup \{ (s,s') | s < 0 \}.$$

8. Negative arguments may also be submitted; for negative arguments, the output is arbitrary; for nonnegative arguments, the output is an approximation (within a precision ε) of the non-negative square root of the input value:

$$R_8 = \left\{ (s,s') | s \geq 0 \wedge \left| s'^2 = s \right| < \varepsilon \wedge s' \geq 0 \right\} \cup \{ (s,s') | s < 0 \}.$$

9. Only nonnegative arguments will be submitted; the output must be within ε of the exact square root of the input (comparison with specification R_4: Precision ε applies to the square root scale rather than the square scale):

$$R_9 = \{ (s,s') | s \geq 0 \wedge |s' - \sqrt{s}| < \varepsilon \}.$$

We could go on and on. This simple example highlights two lessons: First, the importance of precision in specifying program requirements and second, the premise that relations enable us to achieve the required precision.

As a second illustrative example, consider the following requirement pertaining to space S defined by an array $a[1..N]$ of some type, where N is greater than or equal to 1, a variable x of the same type, and an index variable k, which we use to address array a: Search x in a and place its index in k. Again, this simple requirement lends itself to a wide range of interpretations, some of which we write as follows, along with their relational representation:

1. Variable x is known to be in a; place in k an index where x occurs in a.

$$F_1 = \{(s,s') | (\exists h : 1 \le h \le N : a[h] = x) \wedge a[k'] = x\}.$$

2. Variable x is known to be in a; place in k the first (smallest) index where x occurs in a.

$$F_2 = \{(s,s') | (\exists h : 1 \le h \le N : a[h] = x) \wedge a[k'] = x \wedge (\forall h : 1 \le h < k' : a[h] \ne x)\}$$
$$= F_1 \cap \{(s,s') | (\forall h : 1 \le h < k' : a[h] \ne x)\}.$$

3. Variable x is known to be in a; place in k an index where x occurs in a, while preserving a and x.

$$F_3 = F_1 \cap \{(s,s') | a' = a \wedge x' = x\}.$$

4. Variable x is known to be in a; place in k the first (smallest) index where x occurs in a, while preserving a and x.

$$F_4 = F_2 \cap \{(s,s') | a' = a \wedge x' = x\}.$$

5. Variable x is not known to be in a; if it is not, place 0 in k; else place in k an index where x occurs in a.

$$F_5 = F_1 \cup \{(s,s') | (\forall h : 1 \le h \le N : a[h] \ne x) \wedge k' = 0\}.$$

6. Variable x is not known to be in a; if it is not, place 0 in k; else place in k the first (smallest) index where x occurs in a.

$$F_6 = F_2 \cup \{(s,s') | (\forall h : 1 \le h \le N : a[h] \ne x) \wedge k' = 0\}.$$

7. Variable x is not known to be in a; if it is not, place 0 in k; else place in k an index where x occurs in a, while preserving a and x.

$$F_7 = F_3 \cup \{(s,s') | (\forall h : 1 \le h \le N : a[h] \ne x) \wedge k' = 0\}.$$

8. Variable x is not known to be in a; if it is not, place 0 in k; else place in k the first (smallest) index where x occurs in a, while preserving a and x.

$$F_8 = F_4 \cup \{(s,s') \mid (\forall h: \ 1 \le h \le N : a[h] \ne x) \wedge k' = 0\}.$$

Note that F_1 can be written simply as $F_1 = \{(s,s') \mid a[k'] = x\}$ since the clause $(\exists h: \ 1 \le h \le N : a[h] = x)$ is a logical consequence of $a[k'] = x$. We draw the reader's attention to the importance of carefully watching which variables are primed and which are unprimed in a specification. By writing F_1 as we did, we mean that the final value of k points to a location in the original array a where the original value of x is located. As written, this relation specifies a search program. If, instead of F_1, we had written the specification as follows:

$$F_1' = \{(s,s') \mid a[k'] = x'\},$$

then it would be possible to satisfy this specification by the following simple program:

```
{k=1; x=a[1];}
```

If, instead of F_1, we had written the specification as follows:

$$F_1'' = \{(s,s') \mid a'[k'] = x\},$$

then it would be possible to satisfy this specification by the following simple program:

```
{k=1; a[1]=x;}
```

If, instead of F_1, we had written the specification as follows:

$$F_1''' = \{(s,s') \mid a'[k'] = x'\},$$

then it would be possible to satisfy this specification by the following simple program:

```
{k=1; x=0; a[1]=0;}
```

Neither of these three programs is performing a search of variable x in array a.

4.3.2 Ordering Specifications

When we consider specifications on a given space S, we find it natural to order them according to the strength of their requirement, that is, some of them impose more requirements than others. Let us, for the sake of illustration, consider the specifications of the search program written in the previous section:

1. $F_1 = \{(s,s') | (\exists h : 1 \leq h \leq N : a[h] = x) \wedge a[k'] = x\}$.
2. $F_2 = F_1 \cap \{(s,s') | (\forall h : 1 \leq h < k' : a[h] \neq x)\}$.
3. $F_3 = F_1 \cap \{(s,s') | a' = a \wedge x' = x\}$.
4. $F_4 = F_2 \cap \{(s,s') | a' = a \wedge x' = x\}$.
5. $F_5 = F_1 \cup \{(s,s') | (\forall h : 1 \leq h \leq N : a[h] \neq x) \wedge k' = 0\}$.
6. $F_6 = F_2 \cup \{(s,s') | (\forall h : 1 \leq h \leq N : a[h] \neq x) \wedge k' = 0\}$.
7. $F_7 = F_3 \cup \{(s,s') | (\forall h : 1 \leq h \leq N : a[h] \neq x) \wedge k' = 0\}$.
8. $F_8 = F_4 \cup \{(s,s') | (\forall h : 1 \leq h \leq N : a[h] \neq x) \wedge k' = 0\}$.

It is natural/ intuitive to consider that F_2 is stronger than F_1 since the latter would be satisfied with k' pointing to any occurrence of x in a, while the former requires that k' points to the smallest such occurrence. Also, it is natural to consider that F_3 is stronger than F_1 since the latter requires that a and x be preserved whereas the former does not; for the same reason, F_4 is stronger than F_2. On the other hand, F_5 can be considered stronger than F_1 since the latter makes provisions for the case when x is not in a, whereas the former does not; for the same reason, we can consider that F_6 is stronger than F_2, that F_7 is stronger than F_3, and that F_8 is stronger than F_4. These ordering relations are depicted in Figure 4.8.

We notice that F_2 and F_5 are both considered stronger than F_1, but while the former is a subset of F_1, the latter is a superset thereof. There appears to be two (nonexclusive) ways for a specification R to be considered stronger than a specification R': by having a larger domain, and by having fewer images for elements in the common domain. Whence the following definition.

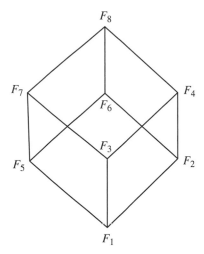

Figure 4.8 *A lattice of refinement.*

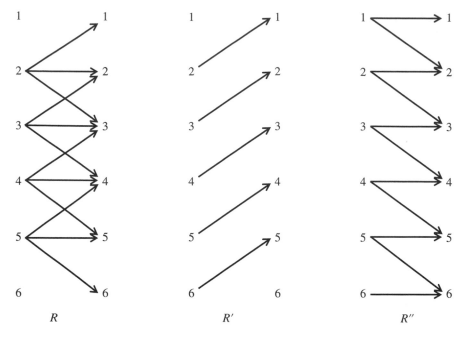

Figure 4.9 *R' and R" refine R.*

Definition: Refinement *Given a set S and two relations R and R' on S. We say that R* <u>*refines*</u> *R' if and only if R has a larger domain than R' and has fewer images for elements in the domain of R'. Formally, $RL \supseteq R'L$ and $R'L \cap R \subseteq R'$.*

Henceforth, we use the term <u>refines</u> to refer to the property of being a "stronger'" specification. We admit without proof that the relation <u>refines</u> is a partial ordering between specifications, that is, that it is reflexive, antisymmetric, and transitive. We refer to this relation as the <u>refinement</u> ordering. The graph in Figure 4.9 shows two relations, R' and R", that refine relation R.

4.3.3 Specification Generation

Let space S be defined by a real array $a[1..N]$ and a real variable x and an index variable k. We are interested to write a relation to reflect the following requirement:

Place in x the largest value of a and in k the smallest index where the largest value occurs.

For example, if array a has the following values,

1	2	3	4	5	6	7	8	9	10	11	12
8.9	9.1	5.2	9.4	9.4	0.12	4.3	8.2	9.4	3.1	2.6	9.4

then we want x' to be equal to 9.4 and k' to be equal to 4. Because it is too difficult to specify all the requirements at once, we consider them one by one:

1. Place in x a value larger than all the values in the array:

$$M_1 = \{(s,s') | \forall h : \ 1 \leq h \leq N : \ x' \geq a[h]\}.$$

2. Place in x an element of the array (note that M_1 alone ensures that x' is greater than all the elements of the array but does not ensure that it is the maximum: 500.0 could be a possible value, for the array aforementioned):

$$M_2 = \{(s,s') | \exists h : \ 1 \leq h \leq N : \ x' = a[h]\}.$$

3. Place in k' an index of a where the maximum of the array occurs:

$$M_3 = \{(s,s') | \ x' = a[k']\}.$$

4. Ensure that no index smaller than k' carries the maximum of the array (hence ensuring that k' is the smallest index):

$$M_4 = \{(s,s') | \forall h : \ 1 \leq h < k' : \ x' \neq a[h]\}.$$

Then we compute the overall specification as the intersection of M_1, M_2, M_3, and M_4, that is,

$$M = M_1 \cap M_2 \cap M_3 \cap M_4.$$

As a second example, we consider space S made up of three nonnegative real variables x, y, z, and a variable t that represents the enumerated type: {notri, scalene, isosceles, equilateral, right, rightisoceles}. We consider the following requirement:

Given that x, y, and z represent the sides of a triangle, place in t the class of the triangle represented by x, y, and z from the set {notri, scalene, isosceles, equilateral, rightisoceles, right}. We assume that the label "isosceles" is reserved for triangles that are isosceles but not equilateral and that the label 'right' is reserved for triangles that are right but not isosceles.

To write this specification, we write one relation for each type of triangle, then form their union. To this effect, we define the following predicates in triplets of real numbers:

- $Tri(x,y,z) \equiv (x \leq y+z) \wedge (y \leq x+z) \wedge (z \leq x+y).$
- $Equi(x,y,z) \equiv (x = y \wedge y = z).$

- $Iso(x,y,z) \equiv (x=y \lor y=z \lor x=z)$.
- $Right(x,y,z) \equiv (x^2=y^2+z^2 \lor y^2=x^2+z^2 \lor z^2=x^2+y^2)$.

Using these predicates, we define the following relations:

1. $T_1 = \{(s,s') | \, Tri(x,y,z) \land Equi(x,y,z) \land t' = equilateral\}$.
2. $T_2 = \{(s,s') | \, Tri(x,y,z) \land Iso(x,y,z) \land \neg Equi(x,y,z) \land \neg Right(x,y,z) \land t' = isoceles\}$.
3. $T_3 = \{(s,s') | \, Tri(x,y,z) \land Iso(x,y,z) \land Right(x,y,z) \land t' = rightisoceles\}$.
4. $T_4 = \{(s,s') | \, Tri(x,y,z) \land Right(x,y,z) \land \neg Iso(x,y,z) \land t' = right\}$.
5. $T_5 = \{(s,s') | \, Tri(x,y,z) \land \neg Iso(x,y,z) \land \neg Equi(x,y,z) \land \neg Right(x,y,z) \land t' = scalene\}$.
6. $T_6 = \{(s,s') | \, \neg Tri(x,y,z) \land t' = notri\}$.

Using these relations, we form the relational specification of the triangle classification problem:

$$T = T_1 \cup T_2 \cup T_3 \cup T_4 \cup T_5 \cup T_6.$$

From these two examples, we want to discuss the question of how do we generate a complex specification from simple/ elementary specifications?

1. In the case of the specification that finds the maximum of the array, we compute the overall specification as the intersection of elementary specifications; in the case of the specification of triangle classification, we compute the overall specification as the union of elementary specifications.
2. It appears that we use the intersection when the domains of the elementary specifications are identical and we use the union when the domains of the elementary specifications are disjoint. In the former case we generate the compound specification as the conjunction of elementary properties; whereas in the latter case, we generate the compound specification by case analysis.

The question that we wish to address then is as follows: Given two relations *R1* and *R2* on space *S*, how do we compose them into a specification that captures all the requirements of *R1* and all the requirements of *R2* (for the sake of completeness) and nothing more (for the sake of minimality), assuming that the domains of *R1* and *R2* are neither (necessarily) identical nor (necessarily) disjoint? Consider the following graph depicting the configuration of *dom(R1)* and *dom(R2)* (Fig. 4.10).

If we want R to capture all the specification information of R1 and all the specification information of R2, then R has to be identical to R1 outside the domain of R2 and identical to R2 outside the domain of R1, and for each element of the

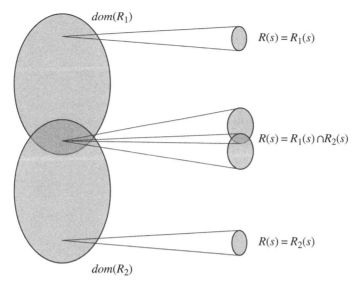

Figure 4.10 *Least upper bound of relations R_1 and R_2.*

intersection of the domains of R1 and R2, it has to be identical to the intersection of R1 and R2. This justifies the following definition.

Definition: Join of Specifications *The join of two relations R_1 and R_2 on set S is denoted by $R_1 \oplus R_2$ and defined by $R_1 \oplus R_2 = \overline{R_2 L} \cap R_1 \cup \overline{R_1 L} \cap R_2 \cup (R_1 \cap R_2)$.*

This formula is a mere relational representation of the Figure 4.10, depicting how $R = R_1 \oplus R_2$ can be derived from R_1 and R_2 The following proposition, which we present without proof, gives an important property of the *join* operator.

Proposition: Compatibility Condition *Let R_1 and R_2 be two relations on set S. If R_1 and R_2 satisfy the following condition,*

$$R_1 L \cap R_2 L = (R_1 \cap R_2) L,$$

which we call the compatibility condition, *then $R_1 \oplus R_2$ is the least refined relation that refines R_1 and R_2 simultaneously. If R_1 and R_2 do not satisfy the compatibility condition, then there exists no relation that refines them both.*

The Figure 4.11 shows an example of two relations R_1 and R_2 that satisfy the compatibility condition and shows their join.

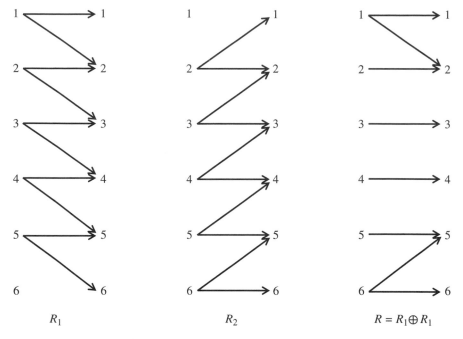

Figure 4.11   The Join of compatible relations.

To check whether R_1 and R_2 verify the compatibility condition, we compute the following:

- $R_1 L = \{1,2,3,4,5\} \times S.$
- $R_2 L = \{2,3,4,5,6\} \times S.$
  - ○ $R_1 L \cap R_2 L = \{2,3,4,5\} \times S.$
- $(R_1 \cap R_2) = \{(2,2),(3,3),(4,4),(5,5)\}.$
  - ○ $(R_1 \cap R_2)L = \{2,3,4,5\} \times S.$

Hence the condition is verified. Since R_1 and R_2 verify the compatibility condition, their join $(R = R_1 \oplus R_2)$ represents the least refined relation that refines them both. On input 1 (outside the domain of R_2), R behaves as R_1; on input 6 (outside the domain of R_1), R behaves like R_2; and on inputs $\{2,3,4,5\}$ (the intersection of the domains of R_1 and R_2), R behaves like the intersection of R_1 and R_2 (which includes $\{(2,2),(3,3),(4,4),(5,5)\}$).

As a second example, consider the following relations R_1 and R_2 (Fig. 4.12).

In this case, R_1 and R_2 do not satisfy the compatibility condition since 4 belongs to the domain of each one of them but does not belong to the domain of their intersection. Indeed, it is not possible to find a relation that refines them simultaneously since R_1

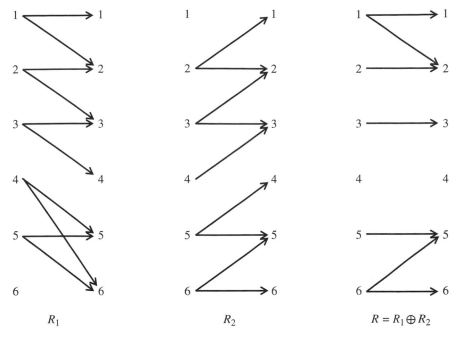

Figure 4.12 *Incompatible relations.*

assigns images 5 and 6 to 4, where R_2 assigns images 2 and 3; there is no value that R may assign to 4 to satisfy both R_1 and R_2.

4.3.4 Specification Validation

The software engineering literature is replete with examples of software projects that fail, not because programmers do not know how to write code or how to test it, but rather because analysts and engineers fail to write valid specifications, that is, specifications that capture all the relevant requirements (for the sake of completeness) and nothing but relevant requirements (for the sake of minimality). Consequently, it is important to validate specifications for completeness and minimality and to invest the necessary resources to this effect before proceeding with subsequent phases of the software lifecycle. In this section, we briefly and cursorily discuss the process of specification validation, in the narrow context of the relational specifications that we introduce in this chapter, with the modest goal of giving the reader some sense of what it may mean to validate a specification.

Let us start with a very simple illustrative example: We consider space S defined by natural variables x and y, and we consider the following requirement:

Increase x while preserving the sum of x and y.

We submit the following relations as possible specifications for this requirement:

1. $N_1 = \{(s,s') | \ x \leq x' \wedge x + y = x' + y'\}$.
2. $N_2 = \{(s,s') | \ x + y = x' + y' \wedge y \geq y'\}$.
3. $N_3 = \{(s,s') | \ x' = x + 3 \wedge y' = y - 3\}$.
4. $N_4 = \{(s,s') | \ x < x' \wedge y > y'\}$.
5. $N_5 = \{(s,s') | \ x - x' = y' - y \wedge y > y'\}$.
6. $N_6 = \{(s,s') | \ x < x' \wedge x - x' = y' - y\}$.
7. $N_7 = \{(s,s') | \ x' = x + 1 \wedge x + y = x' + y'\}$.
8. $N_8 = \{(s,s') | \ x + y = x' + y' \wedge y' = y - 2\}$.

We invite the reader to ponder the following questions: which of these specifications is complete; and for those that are complete, which are minimal. The following table shows our answers to these questions (if a specification is not complete, it makes no sense to check its minimality):

Specification	Complete?	Minimal?	Valid?
$N_1 = \{(s,s') | \ x \leq x' \wedge x + y = x' + y'\}$	No	N/A	No
$N_2 = \{(s,s') | \ x + y = x' + y' \wedge y \geq y'\}$	No	N/A	No
$N_3 = \{(s,s') | \ x' = x + 3 \wedge y' = y - 3\}$	Yes	No	No
$N_4 = \{(s,s') | \ x < x' \wedge y > y'\}$	No	N/A	No
$N_5 = \{(s,s') | \ x - x' = y' - y \wedge y > y'\}$	Yes	Yes	Yes
$N_6 = \{(s,s') | \ x < x' \wedge x - x' = y' - y\}$	Yes	Yes	Yes
$N_7 = \{(s,s') | \ x' = x + 1 \wedge x + y = x' + y'\}$	Yes	No	No
$N_8 = \{(s,s') | \ x + y = x' + y' \wedge y' = y - 2\}$	Yes	No	No

Specifications N_5 and N_6 are complete and minimal (and are identical, in fact); they specify that x must be increased while preserving the sum of x and y. Specifications N_1 and N_2 are not complete because they do not stipulate that x must increase (they allow it to stay constant); and specification N_4 is not complete because it fails to specify that the sum of x and y must be preserved. Specifications N_3, N_7, and N_8 are complete but not minimal because they specify by how much x must be increased, which is not stipulated in the requirement.

In the example aforementioned, we wrote the specifications on the basis of the proposed requirement (to *Increase x while preserving the sum of x and y*) and we judged the completeness and minimality of candidate specifications by considering the same source, that is, the proposed requirement. If the same person or group is tasked with generating the candidate specifications and judging their validity (completeness and minimality), then the same biases that cause the person to write invalid specifications may cause him/ her to overlook the invalidity of their specification. The only way to ensure a measure of confidence in the validation of the specification is to separate the team that generates the specification from the team that validates it. To this effect, we propose the following two-team, two-phase approach:

Activity Phase	Specification Generation	Specification Validation
Specification Generation	Generating the specification from sources of requirements	Generating validation data from the same sources of requirements
Specification Validation	Updating the specification according to feedback from the validation team	Testing the specification against the validation data generated earlier

- *The Specification Generation Phase*: In the specification generation phase, the specification team generates the specification by referring to all the sources of requirements (requirements documents). Using the exact same sources, the validation team generates validation data that it intends to test the specification against. We distinguish between two types of validation data, which are as follows:
  - Completeness properties: These are properties that the specification must have but the validation team suspects the specification team may fail to record.
  - Minimality properties: These are properties that the specification must not have but the validation team suspects the specification team may record inadvertently. For the sake of redundancy, the specification team and the validation team must work independently of each other.
- *The Specification Validation Phase*: In the specification validation phase, the validation team tests the specification against completeness and minimality data generated in the previous phase, while the specification team updates the specification if it turns out that it was not complete or not minimal.

It remains to discuss the following: what form does the validation data take, and how does one test a specification against the generated validation data. The answers to these questions are given in the following definitions.

Definition: Completeness *Given a requirements document, a* <u>completeness</u> <u>property</u> *V is a relation that represents requirements information that candidate specifications must capture. A specification R is said to be* <u>complete</u> *with respect to V if and only if R refines V.*

Implicit in this definition is that a good completeness property is one that has the potential to detect an incomplete specification; in other words, a good completeness property is one that the validation team believes the specifier team may have overlooked.

Definition: Minimality *Given a requirements document, a* <u>Minimality Property</u> *W is a relation that represents requirements information that candidate specifications must not capture. A specification R is said to be* <u>minimal</u> *with respect to W if and only if R does not refine W.*

Implicit in this definition is that a good minimality property is one that has the potential to detect a nonminimal specification; in other words, a good minimality property is one that the validation team believes the specifier team may have inadvertently recorded in the specification.

Completeness and minimality are not absolute attributes but rather relative with respect to selected completeness and minimality properties, as provided in the following definition.

Definition: Validity *A specification R is said to be* <u>valid</u> *with respect to completeness properties* $V = \{V_1, V_2, ..., V_n\}$, *and minimality properties* $W = \{W_1, W_2, ..., W_m\}$ *if and only if R is complete with respect to every element of V and minimal with respect to every element of W.*

We admit without proof that if R refines all of V_1, V_2, ..., V_n, then it refines their join. Hence, the range of valid specifications with respect to completeness properties $V = \{V_1, V_2, ..., V_n\}$ and minimality properties $W = \{W_1, W_2, ..., W_m\}$ is represented in the Figure 4.13.

As a illustrative example of specification validation, consider the following requirement pertaining to space S defined by an array $a[1..N]$ of some type, a variable x of the same type, and an index variable k, which we use to address array a: <u>Given that</u> <u>x is known to be in</u> a, <u>place in k the smallest index where x occurs</u>. This is a variation of the example discussed in Section 4.2.1.

4.3.4.1 *Specification Generation Phase* Examples of completeness properties include the following:

1. If each cell of array a contains the index of that cell and if x=1, then k′ should be 1.

$$V_1 = \{(s,s') | \; (\forall h: \; 1 \leq h \leq N : a[h] = h) \wedge x = 1 \wedge k' = 1\}.$$

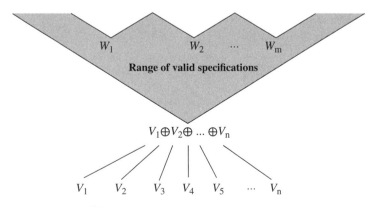

Figure 4.13 *Range of valid specifications.*

2. If array a contains 1 everywhere and $x=1$, then k' should be 1.

$$V_2 = \{(s,s')| \ (\forall h: \ 1 \le h \le N : a[h] = 1) \wedge x = 1 \wedge k' = 1\}.$$

3. If array a contains the sequence $1..N$ in increasing order and $x=N$, then k' should be N.

$$V_3 = \{(s,s')| \ (\forall h: \ 1 \le h \le N : a[h] = h) \wedge x = N \wedge k' = N\}.$$

Examples of minimality properties include the following:

1. There is no requirement to preserve x.

$$W_1 = \{(s,s')| \ (\exists h: \ 1 \le h \le N : a[h] = x) \wedge x' = x\}.$$

2. There is no requirement to preserve a.

$$W_2 = \{(s,s')| \ (\exists h: \ 1 \le h \le N : a[h] = x) \wedge a' = a\}.$$

4.3.4.2 Specification Validation Phase So far, we have looked at the requirements documentation, but we have not looked at candidate specifications; generating validation data independently of specification generation is important, for the sake of redundancy. Now, let us consider a candidate specification and check whether it is complete with respect to the completeness properties and minimal with respect to the minimality properties. We consider specification F_2, introduced in Section 4.2.1 as

$$F_2 = \{(s,s')| \ (\exists h: \ 1 \le h \le N : a[h] = x) \wedge a[k'] = x \wedge (\forall h: \ 1 \le h < k' : a[h] \ne x)\}$$

To prove that F_2 refines V_1, we must prove that F_2 has a larger domain than V_1 and that the restriction of F_2 to the domain of V_1 is a subset of V_1. We find the following:

$$F_2L = \{(s,s')| \ (\exists h: \ 1 \le h \le N : a[h] = x)\}.$$

$$V_1L = \{(s,s')| \ (\forall h: \ 1 \le h \le N : a[h] = h) \wedge x = 1 \}.$$

Clearly, V_1L is a subset of F_2L. We compute the restriction of F_2 to V_1L, and we find the following:

$$F_2 \cap V_1L$$

= {substitution}

$\{(s,s')|(\forall h: \ 1 \leq h \leq N: a[h] = h) \wedge x = 1 \wedge$

$\qquad (\exists h: \ 1 \leq h \leq N: a[h] = x) \wedge a[k'] = x \wedge (\forall h: \ 1 \leq h < k': a[h] \neq x)\}$

= {simplification}

$\{(s,s')|(\forall h: \ 1 \leq h \leq N: a[h] = h) \wedge x = 1 \wedge a[k'] = x \wedge (\forall h: \ 1 \leq h < k': a[h] \neq x)\}$

= {logic simplification}

$\{(s,s')|(\forall h: \ 1 \leq h \leq N: a[h] = h) \wedge x = 1 \wedge k' = 1 \wedge (\forall h: \ 1 \leq h < k': a[h] \neq x)\}$

= {logic simplification}

$\{(s,s')|(\forall h: \ 1 \leq h \leq N: a[h] = h) \wedge x = 1 \wedge k' = 1\}$

= {substitution}

V_1.

We now consider the completeness property V_2. To prove that F_2 refines V_2, we must prove that F_2 has a larger domain than V_2 and that the restriction of F_2 to the domain of V_2 is a subset of V_2. We find the following:

$$F_2 L = \{(s,s')| \ (\exists h: \ 1 \leq h \leq N: a[h] = x)\}.$$
$$V_2 L = \{(s,s')| \ (\forall h: \ 1 \leq h \leq N: a[h] = 1) \wedge x = 1\}.$$

Clearly, $V_2 L$ is a subset of $F_2 L$. We compute the restriction of F_2 to $V_2 L$, and we find the following:

$F_2 \cap V_2 L$

= {substitution}

$\{(s,s')|(\forall h: \ 1 \leq h \leq N: a[h] = 1) \wedge x = 1 \wedge$

$\qquad (\exists h: \ 1 \leq h \leq N: a[h] = x) \wedge a[k'] = x \wedge (\forall h: \ 1 \leq h < k': a[h] \neq x)\}$

= {simplification, redundancy}

$\{(s,s')|(\forall h: \ 1 \leq h \leq N: a[h] = 1) \wedge 1 \leq k' \leq N \wedge x = 1 \wedge (\forall h: \ 1 \leq h < k': a[h] \neq 1)\}$

$= \{\text{logic}\}$

$\{(s,s')|(\forall h: 1 \le h \le N: a[h]=1) \wedge x=1 \wedge k'=1\}$

$= \{\text{substitution}\}$

$V_2.$

We now consider the completeness property V_3. To prove that F_2 refines V_3, we must prove that F_2 has a larger domain than V_3 and that the restriction of F_2 to the domain of V_3 is a subset of V_3. We find the following:

$$F_2 L = \{(s,s')| (\exists h: 1 \le h \le N: a[h]=x)\}.$$
$$V_3 L = \{(s,s')| (\forall h: 1 \le h \le N: a[h]=h) \wedge x=N\}.$$

Clearly, $V_3 L$ is a subset of $F_2 L$. We compute the restriction of F_2 to $V_3 L$, and we find the following:

$F_2 \cap V_3 L$

$= \{\text{substitution}\}$

$\{(s,s')|(\forall h: 1 \le h \le N: a[h]=h) \wedge x=N \wedge$

$\qquad (\exists h: 1 \le h \le N: a[h]=x) \wedge a[k']=x \wedge (\forall h: 1 \le h < k': a[h] \ne x)\}$

$= \{\text{simplification}\}$

$\{(s,s')|(\forall h: 1 \le h \le N: a[h]=h) \wedge x=N \wedge a[k']=N \wedge (\forall h: 1 \le h < k': a[h] \ne x)\}$

$= \{\text{logic}\}$

$\{(s,s')|(\forall h: 1 \le h \le N: a[h]=h) \wedge x=N \wedge k'=N \wedge (\forall h: 1 \le h < k': a[h] \ne x)\}$

$= \{\text{simplification, redundancy}\}$

$\{(s,s')| (\forall h: 1 \le h \le N: a[h]=h) \wedge x=N \wedge k'=N\}$

$= \{\text{substitution}\}$

$V_3.$

We turn our attention to checking the minimality of F_2 with respect to W_1 and W_2.

$$F_2 = \{(s,s') | \; (\exists h : \; 1 \leq h \leq N : a[h] = x) \; \wedge \; a[k'] = x \; \wedge \; (\forall h : \; 1 \leq h < k' : a[h] \neq x)\}$$

$$W_1 = \{(s,s') | \; (\exists h : \; 1 \leq h \leq N : a[h] = x) \; \wedge \; x' = x\}.$$

Because F_2 and W_1 have the same domain, the only way to prove that F_2 does not refine W_1 is to prove that $F_2 \cap W_1 L$ is not a subset of W_1. To this effect, we compute the following:

$$F_2 \cap W_1 L$$

$$= \{ \; F_2 \text{ and } W_1 \text{ have the same domain}\}$$

$$F_2.$$

which is not a subset of W_1. Hence F_2 is minimal with respect to W_1. We can prove, likewise, that it is minimal with respect to W_2. Indeed, F_2 does not preserve x, nor a.

4.4 RELIABILITY VERSUS SAFETY

The introduction of the refinement ordering introduced in this chapter enables us to revisit a concept we had discussed in Chapter 2, namely, the contrast between reliability and safety. As we remember, the reliability of a system is its ability/likelihood of avoiding failure whereas the safety of a system is its ability/likelihood of avoiding catastrophic failure; because catastrophic failures are failures, one may be tempted to argue that a reliable system is necessarily safe but that is not the case. Indeed, reliability and safety are not logical/Boolean properties but stochastic properties, hence the argument that catastrophic failures are failures does not enable us to infer that reliable systems are necessarily safe. Rather, because the stakes attached to meeting the safety requirements are much higher than those attached to meeting the reliability requirement, the threshold of probability that must be reached for a system to be considered safe is much higher than the threshold of probability that must be reached for a system to be considered reliable.

This idea can be elucidated by means of the refinement ordering: Let R be the specification that represents the reliability requirements of a system, and let F be the specification that represents its safety requirements. For the sake of illustration, we consider a simple example of a system that controls the operation of traffic lights at an intersection.

- Specification R captures the requirements that the traffic light must satisfy in terms of how it schedules the green, orange, and red light of each incoming street, along with the _walk_ and _do not walk_ signs for pedestrians crossing the streets. Such requirements must dictate the sequence of light configurations (which streets have green, which streets have orange, which streets have red, which walkways have a _walk_ signal, which walkways have a flashing _walk_ signal, which walkways

have a *do not walk* signal, etc.), as well as how much each configuration lasts in order to optimize traffic flow, fairness, pedestrian safety, and so on.
* Specification F focuses on two safety critical requirements: First that no orthogonal streets have a green light at the same time; and second no street has a green light for cars and pedestrians at the same time.

The following observations are typical of a reliability–safety relationship:

* The stakes attached to violating a safety requirement are much heavier than the stakes attached to a reliability requirement. Violating a reliability requirement may cause a relatively minor inconvenience, such as a traffic jam or a low throughput of vehicles and pedestrians across the intersection; by contrast, violating a safety requirement may cause an accident that involves injuries or loss of life.
  ○ As a consequence of this difference in stakes, we impose different probability thresholds to the different properties. To consider that a system is reliable, it suffices that it meets the reliability requirements with a probability of 0.99 over a unit of operation time (e.g., an hour): having a traffic jam 1% of the time is acceptable. But to consider that a system is safe, we need a higher probability of meeting the safety requirements: having a fatal accident 1% of the time is not acceptable; a probability threshold of 0.999999 is more palatable.
* The reliability requirements specification (*R*) refines the safety requirements specification (*F*). If we consider the sample example of traffic lights and we assume that the requirements specification is valid, then the reliability requirement clearly subsumes the safety requirement since any behavior that abides by the reliability requirement excludes that two orthogonal streets have a green light simultaneously or that a street has a green light while at the same time a walkway that crosses it has a *walk* signal.
* It is much easier to prove that a candidate program satisfies a safety requirement (*F*) than it is to prove that it satisfies the reliability requirement (*R*), for the simple reason that a reliability requirement is typically significantly more complicated. Fortunately, because the safety requirement is simpler, we can verify candidate programs against it with greater thoroughness, hence achieve greater confidence (reflected in higher probability) that a candidate program meets this requirement.

The Figure 4.14 shows specifications R and F, ordered by refinement, and illustrates the relationship between the various possible behaviors of candidate programs, with corresponding probabilities of the behaviors in question: reliable behavior, (possibly unreliable but) fail-safe behavior, and unsafe behavior.

4.5 STATE-BASED SYSTEMS

Whereas specifications we have studied so far are adequate for specifying programs that take an input (or initial state) and map it onto an output (or final state), they are

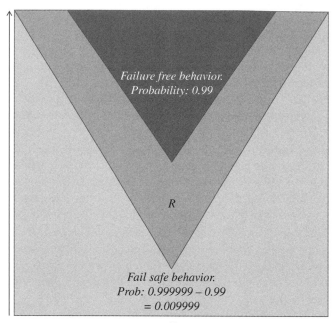

Failure free behavior.
Probability: 0.99

R

Fail safe behavior.
Prob: 0.999999 − 0.99
= 0.009999

F
Unsafe behavior. Probability: 0.000001

Figure 4.14 *Safety vs. reliability.*

inadequate to represent programs whose response depends not only on their input but also on their internal state; the subject of this section is to explore ways to specify such systems.

4.5.1 A Relational Model

As we recall from our discussion in Section 4.1, specifications have to have two key attributes, which are formality and abstraction. We can achieve formality by using a mathematical notation, which associates precise semantics to each statement. As for abstraction, we can achieve it by ensuring that the specifications describe the externally observable attributes of candidate software products, but do not specify, dictate, or otherwise favor any specific design or implementation.

We consider the following description of a stack data type: A stack is a data type that is used to store items (through operation *push*()) and to remove them in reverse order (through operation *pop*()); operation *top*() returns the most recently stored item that has not been removed, operation *size*() returns the number of items stored and not removed, and operation *empty*() tells whether the stack has any items stored; operation *init*() reinitializes the stack to an initial situation, where it contains no elements. Imagine that we want to specify a stack without saying anything about how to implement it. How would we do it? Most data structure courses introduce stacks by showing a data structure made up of an array and an index into the array and by explaining how *push* and *pop* operations affect the array and its index; but such an approach violates the principle of abstraction since it specifies the stack by describing a possible implementation thereof. An alternative could be to specify the stack by means of an abstract list, along with list operations, without specifying how the list is implemented. We argue that this too violates the principle of abstraction as it dictates a preferred implementation; in fact, a stack does not necessarily require a list of elements, regardless of how the list is represented, as we show here.

- Consider that a stack that stores identical elements can be implemented by a simple natural number, say n:

  - `init():` `{n=0;}`
  - `push(a):` `{n=n+1;}` // a is the only value that can be
    //stacked
  - `pop():` `{if (n>0) {n=n-1;}}`
  - `top():` `{if (n>0) {return a;} else {return error;}}`
  - `size():` `{return n;}`
  - `empty():` `{return (n==0);}`

- Consider that a stack that stores two possible symbols (e.g., '{' and '}') can also be implemented without any form of list, using a simple natural number, say n:

  - `init():` `{n=1;}`
  - `push(a):` `{n=2*n+code(a);}` // where code(a) maps the two
    //symbols onto 0 and 1.
  - `pop():` `{if (n>1) {n=n div 2;}}`
  - `top():` `{if (n==1) {return error;} else {return decode`
    `(n mod 2);}}` // decode() is the inverse of code().
  - `size():` `{return floor(log2(n));}`
  - `empty():` `{return (n==1);}`

- We can likewise implement a stack that stores any number (k) of symbols by using base-k numeration rather than base 2 (used earlier).

Hence, for the sake of abstraction, we resolve to specify the stack by describing its externally observable behavior, without making any assumption, regardless of how vague, about its internal structure. To this effect, we specify a stack by means of three parameters, which are as follows:

- An *input space*, say X, which includes all the operations that may be invoked on the stack. Hence,
  $X = \{init, pop, top, size, empty\} \cup \{push\} \times itemtype,$
  where *itemtype* is the data type of the items we envision to store in the stack.

We distinguish, in set X, between inputs that affect the state of the stack (namely, $AX = \{init, push, pop\}$) and inputs that merely report on it (namely, $VX = \{top, size, empty\}$).

From the set of inputs X, we build the set of input histories, H, where an input history is a sequence of inputs; this is needed because the behavior of the stack is not determined solely by the current input but involves past inputs as well.

○ Hence, we introduce the set of input histories, $H = X^*$.

- An *output space*, say Y, which includes all the values returned by all the elements of VX. In the case of the stack, the output space is as follows:
$Y = (itemtype \cup \{error\}) \cup integer \cup boolean$,
which correspond, respectively, to inputs *top*, *size*, and *empty*.

- A *relation* from H to Y, which represents the pairs of the form (h, y), where h is an input history and y is an output that the specifier considers correct for h. We denote this relation by <u>stack</u> and we use the notation *stack* (h) to refer to the image of h by stack (if that image is unique) or to the set of images of h by stack (if h has more than one image). We present here some pairs of the form (h, y) for relation <u>stack</u>:

○ *stack* $(pop.init.push\,(a).init.push\,(a).top) = a$.
○ *stack* $(pop.init.pop.push(a).push(b).top.top) = b$.
○ *stack* $(init.pop.push(a).pop.push(a).pop.push(a).size) = 1$.
○ *stack* $(pop.push\,(a).pop.init.pop.push(a).top.push(a).top.push(a).$
pop.empty$) = false$.
○ *stack*$(init.pop.pop.pop.push\,(a).push\,(b).push\,(c).top.push\,(c).push\,(b).$
empty.top$) = b$.

We can go on describing possible input histories and corresponding outputs. In doing so, we are specifying how operations interact with each other but we are not prescribing how each operation behaves; this leaves maximum latitude to the designer, as mandated by the principle of abstraction.

It is clearly impractical to specify data types by listing elements of their relations; in the next section, we explore a closed-form representation for such relations.

4.5.2   Axiomatic Representation

We propose to represent the relation of a specification by means of an inductive notation, where we do induction on the structure of the input history; this notation includes two parts, which are as follows:

- *Axioms*, which represent the behavior of the system for trivial input histories.
- *Rules*, which represent the behavior of the system for complex input histories as a function of its behavior for simpler input histories.

4.5.2.1 Specification of a Stack   As an illustration, we represent the specification of the stack using axioms and rules. Throughout this presentation, we let *a* be an arbitrary element of itemtype and *y* an arbitrary element of *Y*; also, we let *h*, *h'*, *h''* be arbitrary elements of *H* and *h*+ an arbitrary non-null element of *H*.

Axioms. We use axioms to represent the output of input histories that end with an operation in set *VX* (that reports on the state), namely in this case *top*, *size*, and *empty*. It is understood that input histories that end with an operation in set *AX* (that affects the state) produce no meaningful output; hence we assume that for such input histories, the output is any element of *Y*.

- Top Axioms
  - stack(init.top) = error.
    Seeking the top of an empty stack returns an error.
  - stack(init.h.push(a).top) = a.
    Operation top returns the most recently stacked item.
- Size Axiom
  - stack(init.size) = 0.
    The size of an empty stack is zero.
- Empty Axioms
  - stack(init.empty) = true.
    An initial stack is empty.
  - stack(init.push(a).empty) = false.
    A stack that contains element *a* is not empty.

Rules: Whereas axioms characterize the behavior of the stack for simple input sequences, rules establish relations between the behavior of the stack for complex input histories and their behavior for simpler input histories.

- Init Rule
  - stack(h'.init.h) = stack(init.h).
    Operation init reinitializes the stack; whether sequence *h'* intervened prior to init or did not makes no difference for the future behavior (*h*) of the stack.
- Init Pop Rule
  - stack(init.pop.h) = stack(init.h).
    A pop operation on an empty stack has no effect: whether it occurred or did not occur makes no difference for the future behavior (*h*) of the stack.
- Push Pop Rule
  - stack(init.h.push(a).pop.h+) = stack(init.h.h+).
    A pop operation cancels the most recent push: whether the sequence push(a). pop occurred or did not makes no difference to the future behavior of the stack, though not to the present (if h ends with an operation in VX, we could not say that stack(init.h)=stack(init.h.push(a).pop) as the left-hand side returns a specific value but the right-hand side returns an arbitrary value).

- Size Rule
  - ○ stack(init.h.push(a).size) = 1+stack(init.h.size).
    We assume that the stack is unbounded; hence any push operation increases the size by 1.
- Empty Rules
  - ○ stack(init.h.push(a).h'.empty) ⇒ stack(init.h.h'.empty).
  - ○ stack(init.h.h'.empty) ⇒ stack(init.h.pop.h'.empty).
    Removing a push or adding a pop to the input history of a stack makes it more empty (i.e., if it was empty prior to removing push or adding pop, it is a fortiori empty afterward).
- VX Rules
  - ○ stack(init.h.top.h+) = stack(init.h.h+).
  - ○ stack(init.h.size.h+) = stack(init.h.h+).
  - ○ stack(init.h.empty.h+) = stack(init.h.h+).
    VX operations leave no trace of their passage; once they are serviced and another operation follows them, they are forgotten: whether they occurred or did not occur has no impact on the future behavior of the stack.

We have written a closed-form specification of the stack in such a way that we describe solely the externally observable properties of the stack, without any reference to how a stack ought to be implemented; a programmer who reviews this specification has all the latitude he/she needs to implement this stack as he/she sees fit.

4.5.2.2 *Specification of a Queue*

We discuss how to represent the specification of a queue, in the same way that we wrote the specification of a stack earlier. We represent in turn the input space (from which we infer the set of input histories), then the output space, then the relation, which we denote by queue.

Input Space. We let X be defined as $X = \{$init, dequeue, front, size, empty$\} \cup \{$enqueue$\} \times$ itemtype. We partition this set into $AX = \{$init, enqueue, dequeue$\}$ and $VX = \{$front, size, empty$\}$. We let H be the set of sequences of elements of X.

Output Space. We let the output space be defined as $Y =$ itemtype $\cup$ integer $\cup$ Boolean $\cup \{$error$\}$.

Axioms. We propose the following axioms:

- Front Axioms
  - ○ queue(init.front) = error.
    Invoking front on an empty queue returns an error.
  - ○ queue(init.enqueue(a).enqueue*().front) = a,
    where enqueue(_)* designates an arbitrary number (including zero) of

enqueue operations, involving arbitrary items as parameters. Interpretation: Invoking *front* on a non-empty queue returns the first element enqueued.

- Size Axioms
  - ○ queue(init.size) = 0.
    The size of an empty queue is zero.
- Empty Axioms
  - ○ queue(init.empty) = true.
  - ○ queue(init.enqueue(a).empty) = false.
    An initial queue is empty. A queue in which an element has been enqueued is not empty.

Rules: We propose the following rules.

- Init Rule
  - ○ queue(h'.init.h) = queue(init.h).
    The init operation reinitializes the stack, that is, renders all past input history immaterial.
- Init Dequeue Rule
  - ○ queue(init.dequeue.h) = queue(init.h)
    A dequeue operation executed on an empty queue has no effect.
- Enqueue Dequeue Rule
  - ○ queue(init.enqueue(a).enqueue*(_).dequeue.h) = queue(init.enqueue*(_).h)
    A dequeue operation cancels the first enqueue, by virtue of the first in, first out (FIFO) policy of queues.
- Size Rule
  - ○ queue(init.h.enqueue(a).size) = 1+queue(init.h.size).
    Assuming queues of unbounded size, any enqueue operation increases the size of the queue by 1.
- Empty Rules
  - ○ queue(init.h.enqueue(a).h'.empty) $\Rightarrow$ queue(init.h.h'.empty).
  - ○ stack(init.h.h'.empty) $\Rightarrow$ stack(init.h.dequeue.h'.empty).
    Removing an enqueue or adding a dequeue to the input history of a queue makes it more empty (i.e., if it was empty prior to removing enqueue or adding dequeue, it is a fortiori empty afterward).
- VX Rules
  - ○ queue(init.h.front.h+) = queue(init.h.h+).
  - ○ queue(init.h.size.h+) = queue(init.h.h+).
  - ○ queue(init.h.empty.h+) = queue(init.h.h+).
    VX operations leave no trace of their passage; once they are serviced and another operation follows them, they are forgotten: whether they occurred or did not occur has no impact on the future behavior of the queue.

4.5.2.3 *Specification of a Set*   As a third illustrative example, we discuss how to represent the specification of a set, in the same way that we wrote the specifications of a stack and a queue earlier. We represent in turn the input space (from which we infer the set of input histories), then the output space, then the relation, which we denote by *set*.

Input Space: Before we introduce the input space, let us review quickly what we want this set abstract data type (ADT) to do: we want the ability to reinitialize the set, pick a random element of the set, enumerate all its elements, and return its smallest element and its largest element (assuming its elements are ordered). Also, we want to be able to insert, delete, and search designated elements of the set. Hence, we let X be defined as

$$X = \{\text{init, pick, min, max, enumerate, size}\} \cup \{\text{insert, delete, search}\} \times \text{itemtype}.$$

We partition this set into $AX = \{\text{init, insert, delete}\}$ and $VX = \{\text{pick, min, max, size, enumerate, search}\}$. We let H be the set of sequences of elements of X.

Output Space: We let the output space be defined as

$$Y = \text{itemtype} \cup \mathbf{P}(\text{itemtype}) \cup \{\text{error}\} \cup \text{integer} \cup \text{boolean},$$

where $\mathbf{P}(\text{itemtype})$ is the power set of itemtype.

Axioms: We propose the following axioms:

- Pick Axioms
  - set(init.pick) = error.One cannot pick an element from an empty set.
  - Set(init.h.insert(a).pick) = a.If *a* is an element of the set, then it is a possible pick; we will add a commutativity rule later to make it possible to pick other elements than the most recently inserted element.
- Size Axiom
  - set(init.size) = 0.
    The size of an empty set is zero.
- Enumerate Axiom
  - set(init.enumerate) = ∅.
    The enumeration of an empty set returns empty.
- Search Axiom
  - set(init.search(a)) = false.
    The search of *a* in an empty set returns false.
- Min Axiom
  - set(init.min) = +∞.
    Plus infinity is the neutral element of operation *min*.

- Max Axiom
  - set(init.max) = −∞.
    Minus infinity is the neutral element of operation *max*.

Rules: We propose the followng rules:

- Init Rule
  - set(h'.init.h) = set(init.h).
    Operation *init* makes the previous history irrelevant.
- Null Delete Rule
  - set(init.delete(a).h) = set(init.h).
    A *delete* operation has no effect on an empty set.
- Insert Delete Rule
  - set(init.insert(a).delete(a).h) = set(init.h).
    Operation *delete* cancels the effect of operation insert.
- Idempotence Rule
  - Insert Insert Rule
    set(init.h'.insert(a).insert(a).h) = set(init.h'.insert(a).h) if is already in the set, inserting it makes no difference.
- Commutativity Rule
  - set(init.h'.op1(a).op2(b).h) = set(init.h'.op2(b).op1(a).h).
    where op1 and op2 are any of *insert* and *delete* and *a* and *b* are distinct. Interpretation: The order of operations of *insert* and *delete* of distinct elements is immaterial.
- Size Rules
  - If set(init.h.search(a)) = true then set(init.h.insert(a).size) = set(init.h.size).
  - If set(init.h.search(a)) = false then set(init.h.insert(a).size) = 1+set(init.h.size).
    Operation *insert(a)* increases the size of the set only if element *a* is not in the set prior to insertion.
- Inductive Rules
  - set(init.h.insert(a).search(b)) = (a=b) ∨ set(init.h.search(b)).
    If (a=b) then return true (since *b* is found in the set), else check prior to the insertion of *a*.
  - set(init.h.insert(a).enumerate) = {a} ∪ set(init.h.enumerate).
    If *a* has been inserted, it should be enumerated.
  - set(init.h.insert(a).min) = MIN (a, set(init.h.min)).
    Inductive argument on the min.
  - set(init.h.insert(a).max) = MAX (a, sct(init.h.max)).
    Inductive argument on the max.
- VX Rules
  - set(init.h.search(a).h+) = set(init.h.h+).
  - set(init.h.pick.h+) = set(init.h.h+).

○ set(init.h.enumerate.h+) = set(init.h.h+).

○ set(init.h.size.h+) = set(init.h.h+).

○ set(init.h.min.h+) = set(init.h.h+).

○ set(init.h.max.h+) = set(init.h.h+).

VX operations leave no trace of their passage once they have been passed.

4.5.3   SPECIFICATION VALIDATION

In the previous section, we have written specifications of a number of ADTs, namely, a stack, a queue, and a set. How do we know that our specifications are valid, that is, that they capture all the properties we want them to capture (completeness) and nothing else (minimality)? To bring a measure of confidence in the validity of these specifications, we envision a validation process, similar to the process we advocated in Section 4.2.3, though this time (for the sake of simplicity) we focus solely on completeness. We imagine that while we are writing these specifications, an independent verification and validation team is generating formulas of the form

$$stack(h) = y$$

for different values of h and y, on the grounds that whatever we write in our specification should logically imply these statements. Then the validation step consists in checking that the proposed formulas can be inferred from the axioms and rules of our specification. If they do, then we can conclude that our specification is complete with respect to the proposed formulas; if not, then we need to check with the verification and validation team to see whether our specification is incomplete or perhaps the validation data is erroneous.

For the sake of illustration, we check whether our specification is valid with respect to the formulas written in Section 4.3 as sample input/output pairs of our stack specification:

- $V_1 : stack(pop.init.push(a).init.push(a).top) = a.$
- $V_2 : stack(pop.init.pop.push(a).push(b).top.top) = b.$
- $V_3 : stack(init.pop.push(a).pop.push(a).pop.push(a).size) = 1.$
- $V_4 : stack(pop.push(a).pop.init.pop.push(a).top.push(a).top.push(a).pop.empty) = false.$
- $V_5 : stack(init.pop.pop.pop.push(a).push(b).push(c).top.push(c).push(b).empty.top) = b.$

For V_1, we find the following:
stack(pop.init.push(a).init.push(a).top)
= {by the init Rule}
stack(init.push(a).top)
= {by the second top axiom}
$a.$ **QED**

For V_2, we find the following:
stack(pop.init.pop.push(a).push(b).top.top)
= {by the init Rule}
stack(init.pop.push(a).push(b).top.top)
= {by the VX Rule pertaining to top}
stack(init.pop.push(a).push(b).top)
= {by the second top axiom}
b.   **QED**

For V_3, we find the following:
stack(init.pop.push(a).pop.push(a).pop.push(a).size)
= {by the init pop Rule}
stack(init.push(a).pop.push(a).pop.push(a).size)
= {by the push pop Rule, applied twice}
stack(init.push(a).size)
= {by the size Rule}
1+stack(init.size)
= {by the size axiom}
1.   **QED**

For V_4, we find the following:
stack(pop.push(a).pop.init.pop.push(a).top.push(a).top.push(a).pop.empty)
= {by the init rule}
stack(init.pop.push(a).top.push(a).top.push(a).pop.empty)
= {by the init pop rule}
stack(init.push(a).top.push(a).top.push(a).pop.empty)
= {by the VX rule, as it pertains to top}
stack(init.push(a).push(a).push(a).pop.empty)
= {by the push pop rule}
stack(init.push(a).push(a).empty)
⇒ {by the empty rule}
stack(init.push(a).empty)
= {by the empty axiom}
false.
If the left-hand side logically implies false, then it is false.   **QED**

For V_5, we find the following:
stack(init.pop.pop.pop.push(a).push(b).push(c).top.push(c).push(b).empty.top)
= {by virtue of the VX rules, applied to empty}
stack(init.pop.pop.pop.push(a).push(b).push(c).top.push(c).push(b).top)
= {by virtue of the second top axiom}
b.   **QED**

Because our specification has survived five tests unscathed, we gain a bit more confidence in its validity.

4.6 CHAPTER SUMMARY

The main ideas/concepts that you need to keep from this chapter are the following:

- The algebra of relations, including operations, and properties.
- Principles of sound specification, and how relations support these.
- The concept of join of relations, its significance, and its role in specification generation.
- The concept of refinement, its significance, and its role in specification validation.
- The relational specification of systems that maintain an internal state.
- The axiomatic representation of the relational specification of systems that maintain a state.
- The generation and validation of axiomatic specifications.

4.7 EXERCISES

4.1. Given relations R and Q on set S, write a relational expression that represents the following: the prerestriction of R to the domain of Q; the prerestriction of R to the range of Q; the postrestriction of R to the domain of Q; the postrestriction of R to the range of Q.

4.2. Consider the following relations on the set S of natural numbers:
$R = \{(s,s')| \; s'= 7s\}$
$R' = \{(s,s')| \; s' = s+5\}$
Compute the following:
  a. $dom(R), \; rng(R)$.
  b. $dom(R'), \; rng(R')$.
  c. $R \bullet R'. \; dom(R.R')$.
  d. $R' \bullet R. \; dom(R'.R)$.
  e. Prerestriction of R to $A = \{s| \; s \; mod \; 5=0\}$.
  f. Postrestriction of R' to $B = \{s| \; s<4\}$.

4.3. Consider the following relations on the set S of natural numbers (starting at zero).
$R = \{(s,s')| \; s' = s-7\}$
$R' = \{(s,s')| \; s' = 5s - 32\}$
Compute the following expressions:
  a. $dom(R), \; rng(R)$.
  b. $dom(R'), \; rng(R')$.
  c. $R \cdot \hat{R}$, and $\hat{R} \cdot R$.

d. $R' \cdot \hat{R}'$, and $\hat{R}' \cdot R'$.

e. $R \cdot R'$, and $dom (R \cdot R')$.

f. $R' \cdot R$, and $dom (R' \cdot R)$.

4.4. For each relation R given here on space S defined by natural variables x and y, tell whether R has the properties defined in Section 4.2.3.

    a. $R = \{(s,s')| \; x+y = x'+y'\}$

    b. $R = \{(s,s')| \; x' = x+1 \; \wedge \; y' = y-1\}$

    c. $R = \{(s,s')| \; x \geq x' \; \wedge \; y' = y\}$

    d. $R = \{(s,s')| \; x-y \geq x'- y'\}$

    e. $R = \{(s,s')| \; x \geq 1 \; \wedge \; y \geq x\}$

4.5. Let S be the set of persons and let P and M be the following relations on S:

    • $P = \{(s,s')| \; s' \text{ is a parent of } s\}$.

    • $M = \{(s,s')| \; s \text{ is male}\}$.

    From these three relations, compose the following relations: female (the complement of male), mother, father, daughter, son, half-sibling, sibling, half brother, half sister, brother, sister, maternal grandfather, paternal grandfather, maternal grandmother, paternal grandmother, grandson, granddaughter, uncle, aunt, niece, nephew, and cousin. All of these relations can be built from P and M.

4.6. Consider the square root specification given in Section 4.3.1; give five more possible interpretations of the square root requirement, and present a relation for each.

4.7. Consider the specification of the search programs, given in Section 4.3.2. Write five new interpretations, along with corresponding relations. Hint: Consider, for example, the situation where a and x are preserved whether x is or is not in a; or the case where no output requirement is imposed when x is not in a.

4.8. Consider the following specifications on space S defined by an array $a[1..N]$ of real numbers and a variable x of type real and say whether or not they represent the specification of a program to compute the sum of a into x; if not, give an example of a program that satisfies the specification but is not computing the sum of a into x.

    a. $M_1 = \left\{ (s,s') | x' = \sum_{i=1}^{N} a[i] \right\}$

    b. $M_2 = \left\{ (s,s') | x' = \sum_{i=1}^{N} a'[i] \right\}$

    c. $M_3 = \left\{ (s,s') | x = \sum_{i=1}^{N} a'[i] \right\}$

    d. $M_4 = \left\{ (s,s') | x' = \sum_{i=1}^{N} a'[i] \wedge a' = a \right\}$

4.9. Consider the square root specifications $R_1 \ldots R_9$ given in Section 4.3.1. Rank them by the refinement ordering and draw a graph showing their refinement relations, similar to that given for the search specifications $F_1 \ldots F_8$.

4.10. Consider a space S defined by an array a[1..N] of type T, an index variable k and a variable x of type T. Write the following specifications and rank them by strength:

a. Place in x the largest element of a.

b. Place in x the largest element of a and in k an index where the largest element of a occurs.

c. Place in x the largest element of a and in k the largest index where the largest element of a occurs.

d. Place in x the largest element of a and in k an index where the largest element of a occurs, while preserving a.

4.11. Consider a space S defined by an array a[1..N] of type T, an index variable k and a variable x of type T. Write the following specifications and rank them by strength:

a. Place in x a value less than or equal to all the elements of the array.

b. Place in x an arbitrary value of the array.

c. Place in x an arbitrary value of the array and in k an index where x occurs.

d. Place in x the smallest element of the array and in k an index where x occurs.

e. Place in x the smallest element of the array and in k the smallest index where x occurs.

4.12. Prove that the refines relation between relational specifications is a partial ordering relation; that it is reflexive, antisymmetric and transitive.

4.13. Let space S be defined by three variables a, b, c of type natural, and consider the requirement that these three variables be rearranged in increasing order, that is, we want to permute their values in such a way that $a' \le b' \le c'$. Write the relational specification of this requirement, by proceeding: first by case analysis (consider all the possible orderings of the three values of a, b, c) and second, by conjunction of properties (consider all the relations that must hold between a, b, c and a', b', c').

4.14. Consider the following specifications on space S defined by an array a[1..N] of some type, a variable x of the same type, and an index variable k, which we use to address array a.

a. $F_1 = \{(s,s') | (\exists h : 1 \le h \le N : a[h] = x) \wedge a[k'] = x\}$

b. $F_5 = F_1 \cup \{(s,s') | (\forall h : 1 \le h \le N : a[h] \ne x) \wedge k' = 0\}$

Do these specifications satisfy the compatibility condition? If so, compute their join. If not, explain why.

4.15. Consider the following specifications on space S defined by an array $a[1..N]$ of some type, a variable x of the same type, and an index variable k, which we use to address array a.

  a. $F_1 = \{(s,s') \mid (\exists h: 1 \le h \le N: a[h] = x) \wedge a[k'] = x\}$
  b. $F_5 = F_1 \cup \{(s,s') \mid (\forall h: 1 \le h \le N: a[h] \ne x) \wedge k' = 0\}$
  c. $F_9 = F_1 \cup \{(s,s') \mid (\forall h: 1 \le h \le N: a[h] \ne x)\}$

Do specifications F_5 and F_9 satisfy the compatibility condition? If so, compute their join. If not, explain why.

4.16. Consider the following specifications on space S defined by an array $a[1..N]$ of some type, a variable x of the same type, and an index variable k, which we use to address array a.

  a. $F_1 = \{(s,s') \mid (\exists h: 1 \le h \le N: a[h] = x)\, a[k'] = x\}$
  b. $F_5 = F_1 \cup \{(s,s') \mid (\forall h: 1 \le h \le N: a[h] \ne x) \wedge k' = 0\}$
  c. $F_{10} = F_1 \cup \{(s,s') \mid (\forall h: 1 \le h \le N: a[h] \ne x) \wedge k' = -1\}$

Do specifications F_5 and F_{10} satisfy the compatibility condition? If so, compute their join. If not, explain why.

4.17. Check whether Specification F_1 (given in Section 4.3.2) is complete with respect to completeness properties V_1, V_2, V_3 and whether it is minimal with respect to minimality properties W_1, W_2.

4.18. Check whether Specification F_3 (given in Section 4.3.2) is complete with respect to completeness properties V_1, V_2, V_3 and whether it is minimal with respect to minimality properties W_1, W_2.

4.19. Check whether Specification F_4 (given in Section 4.3.2) is complete with respect to completeness properties V_1, V_2, V_3 and whether it is minimal with respect to minimality properties W_1, W_2.

4.20. Check whether Specification F_5 (given in Section 4.3.2) is complete with respect to completeness properties V_1, V_2, V_3 and whether it is minimal with respect to minimality properties W_1, W_2.

4.21. Check whether Specification F_6 (given in Section 4.3.2) is complete with respect to completeness properties V_1, V_2, V_3 and whether it is minimal with respect to minimality properties W_1, W_2.

4.22. Check whether Specification F_7 (given in Section 4.3.2) is complete with respect to completeness properties V_1, V_2, V_3 and whether it is minimal with respect to minimality properties W_1, W_2.

4.23. Check whether Specification F_8 (given in Section 4.3.2) is complete with respect to completeness properties V_1, V_2, V_3 and whether it is minimal with respect to minimality properties W_1, W_2.

4.24. Generate validation data for the stack specification given in Section 4.5.2.1, and check its validity against your data.

4.25. Generate validation data for the queue specification given in Section 4.5.2.2, and check its validity against your data.

4.26. Generate validation data for the set specification given in Section 4.5.2.3, and check its validity against your data.

4.27. Follow the example discussed in Section 4.5.1 to derive a stack that stores four symbols, e.g. the arithmetic operators +, −, ∗, and /.

4.8 PROBLEMS

4.1. This ADT stores and retrieves elements in a linearly ordered structure. We let the list be defined by the following operations:

AX-operations: These are operations that alter the state of the ADT but produce no visible output.

- **init**: This operation initializes or re-initializes the list to empty.
- **insertlast (itemtype x)**: This operation inserts x at the end of the list.
- **insertfirst (itemtype x)**: This operation inserts x at the beginning of the list.
- **insertat (itemtype x, integer n)**: If the size of the list allows, this operation inserts x at position n; else it does not change the list.
- **deletelast ()**: This operation deletes the element at the end of the list.
- **deletefirst ()**: This operation deletes the element at the beginning of the list.
- **deletetat (integer n)**: If the size of the list allows, this operation deletes the element at position n; else it does not change the list.

VX-operations: These are operations that return values but do not change the state.

- **boolean: empty ()**: It returns T if and only if the list is empty.
- **integer: size ()**: It returns the number of elements in the list.
- **boolean: search (itemtype x)**: It tells whether x is in the list.
- **integer: multisearch (itemtype x)**: It gives the multiplicity of x in the list.
- **itemtype: choose ()**: It returns an arbitrary element of the list.
- **itemtype: first ()**: It returns the first element in the list.
- **itemtype: last ()**: It returns the last element in the list.
- **itemtype: smallest ()**: It returns the smallest element.
- **itemtype: largest ()**: It returns the largest element.

Write this specification and validate it. If this work is done in a team, divide the team in two, for specification and specification validation. Hint: Convert all insert operations into insertlast operations, and all delete operations into deletelast operations; then specify insertlast and deletelast.

4.2. In discrete mathematics, a multiset is a collection of objects where duplication is permitted. We let *multiset* be defined by the following operations:

- **AX**-operations: These are operations that alter the state of the ADT but produce no visible output.
  - **init**: This operation initializes or re-initializes the multiset to empty.
  - **insert (itemtype x)**: If x is not in the multiset, this operation adds it; if not, it increments its multiplicity.
  - **insert (itemtype x, integer n)**: Inserts n copies of x, where n is non-negative.
  - **remove (itemtype x)**: If x is not in the set, then this operation is null; if x does belong in a single copy, it no longer exists in the set; if x belongs in multiple copies, its multiplicity is reduced by 1.
  - **remove (itemtype x, integer n)**: It performs remove(x) n times.
  - **removeall (itemtype x)**: If x does not belong to the multiset, then this operation is null; else all instances of x are removed.
  - **removeany()**: It removes an arbitrary element of the set, reducing its multiplicity by 1; if the set is empty, this operation is null.
  - **eraseany()**: It removes all the instances of an arbitrary element; if the multiset is empty, this operation is null.

- **VX**-operations: These are operations that return values but do not change the state.
  - **boolean: empty ()**: It returns T if and only if the set is empty.
  - **integer: size ()**: It returns the number of distinct elements.
  - **integer: multisize ()**: It returns the multisize of the multiset.
  - **boolean: search (itemtype x)**: It tells whether x is in the multiset.
  - **integer: multisearch (itemtype x)**: It gives the multiplicity of x.
  - **itemtype: choose ()**: It returns an arbitrary element of the multiset.
  - **itemtype∗ list ()**: It lists the elements of the multiset.
  - **itemtype∗ list (integer n)**: It lists the elements of the multiset with a multiplicity greater than or equal to n.
  - **itemtype: least ()**: It returns an element with minimal multiplicity.
  - **itemtype: most ()**: It returns an element with maximal multiplicity.
  - **itemtype: smallest ()**: It returns the smallest element.
  - **itemtype: largest ()**: It returns the largest element.

Write this specification and validate it. If this work is done in a team, divide the team in two, for specification and specification validation.

4.9 BIBLIOGRAPHIC NOTES

Software specification has been the subject of active research since the early days of software engineering, highlighting both the criticality and the difficulty of this phase and its products; it is impossible to do justice to all the work that was published in this area or to any significant portion thereof. We will merely cite a few of the specification languages that have emerged: Z, a relational notation that has been widely used in industry and academia (Spivey, 1998); B, a relational notation that has an object-oriented flavor, and supports refinement, in addition to specification (Abrial, 1996); Alloy, a language inspired by Z and B and used to represent structures by means of sets of constraints (Jackson, 2011). For a general overview of specification languages and issues, consult (Habrias and Frappier, 2013).

5

Program Correctness and Verification

This being a book on software testing, one may wonder why we need to talk about program correctness. There are several reasons and some of them are as follows:

- The focus of software testing is to run the candidate program on selected input data and check whether the program behaves correctly with respect to its specification. The behavior of the program can be analyzed only if we know what is a correct behavior; hence the study of correctness is an integral part of software testing.
- The study of program correctness leads to analyze candidate programs at arbitrary levels of granularity; in particular, it leads to make assumptions on the behavior of the program at specific stages in its execution and to verify (or disprove) these assumptions; the same assumptions can be checked at run-time during testing, giving us valuable information as we try to diagnose the program or establish its correctness. Hence the skills that we develop as we try to prove program correctness enable us to be better/more effective testers.
- It is common for program testers and program provers to make polite statements about testing and proving being complementary and then to assiduously ignore each other (each other's methods). But there is more to complementarity than meets the eye. Very often, what makes a testing method or a proving method ineffective is not an intrinsic attribute of the method, but rather the fact that the method is used against the wrong type of specification. Hence it is advantageous, given a complex/compound specification, to decompose it into two broad components— one that lends itself to testing and the other that lends itself to proving—and apply each method against the appropriate specification component. Consider a simple

Software Testing: Concepts and Operations, First Edition. Ali Mili and Fairouz Tchier.
© 2015 John Wiley & Sons, Inc. Published 2015 by John Wiley & Sons, Inc.

example: imagine that we want to verify a sorting routine, whose specification is $Sort(s,s') = Ord(s') \land Prm(s,s')$, where s designates an array of elements with some ordering key, $Ord(s')$ means that s' is ordered (according to selected key), and $Prm(s,s')$ means that s' is a permutation of s. Testing the sorting routine against specification $Prm(s,s')$ is at the same time inefficient, complex, and error prone: it is inefficient because it requires that we save the initial array s to check the property $Prm(s,s')$ at the end; it is complex because checking that two sequences are permutations of each other is difficult, especially if we allow multiple identical elements; it is error-prone because it is complex. But proving that a sorting routine satisfies the condition $Prm(s,s')$ is very easy: it suffices to ensure that whenever the array is modified, it is modified in the context of a swap of two of its cells, thereby ensuring the preservation of $Prm(s,s')$ at each step. By contrast, proving that the sort routine achieves the property $Ord(s')$ may be tedious and error-prone, as it involves a painstaking inductive argument, and may depend on the stepwise update of index variables and on maintaining complex program invariants; however, checking $Ord(s')$ at run-time can be done efficiently and reliably; it is efficient because it does not require saving a prior state and can be carried out in $O(n)$ steps (n: the size of the array), and it is reliable because its formula is very simple (ensuring that each element of s' is not greater than the next element). Hence by testing the program against specification Ord(s') and proving it against Prm(s,s'), we achieve great gains in efficiency, quality, and reliability.

- It is best to view software testing, not as an isolated effort, but rather as an integral part of a broad, multi-pronged policy of quality assurance that deploys each method where it is most effective by virtue of the *Law of Diminishing Returns*.
- The study of program verification, which we conduct in this chapter, prepares the ground for the next chapter, where we discuss faults and fault removal.

5.1 CORRECTNESS: A DEFINITION

We let space S be the set of natural numbers and let R be the following specification on S:

$$R = \{(0,0),(0,1),(0,2),(1,1),(1,2),(1,3),(2,2),(2,3),(2,4),(3,3),(3,4),(3,5)\}.$$

We consider the following candidate programs (represented by their functions on S), and we ask the question: which of these programs is correct with respect to R?

$$P_1 = \{(0,1),(1,2),(2,3),(3,4)\},$$
$$P_2 = \{(0,1),(1,2),(2,3),(3,4),(4,5),(5,6),(6,7)\},$$
$$P_3 = \{(0,0),(1,2),(2,4)\},$$
$$P_4 = \{(0,0),(1,2),(2,4),(4,8),(5,10),(6,12)\},$$

$$P_5 = \{(0,0),(1,2),(2,4),(3,6)\},$$

$$P_6 = \{(0,0),(1,2),(2,4),(3,6),(4,8),(5,10),(6,12)\},$$

We submit:

- Only programs P1 and P2 are <u>correct</u> with respect to specification R since they return correct values for all the inputs of interest for R (which are inputs 0, 1, 2, 3).
- We say that programs P3 and P4 are <u>partially correct</u> with respect to R: they are not defined for all relevant inputs (which are 0, 1, 2, 3) since they are not defined for 3; but whenever they are defined for a relevant input (which is the case for 0, 1, 2), they return a correct value.
- We say that programs P5 and P6 are <u>defined</u> with respect to R (or that they <u>terminate normally</u> with respect to R): they produce an output for all relevant inputs (which are 0, 1, 2, 3), though for 3 they produce an incorrect output (6, rather than 3, 4, or 5).

As a second example, we let space S be defined by two integer variables x and y, and we let R be the following relation (specification) on S:

$$R = \{(s,s') | x(s') = x(s) + y(s)\}.$$

We consider the following candidate programs (written in C-like notation), and we ask the question: which of these programs is correct with respect to R?

```
p1: {while (y<>0) {x=x+1; y=y-1;}}.
p2: {while (y>0) {x=x+1; y=y-1;}}
p3: {if (y>0) {while (y>0) {x=x+1; y=y-1;}
         else {while (y<0) {x=x-1; y=y+1;}}
```

Before we make judgments on the correctness of these programs, we compute their respective functions:

$$P_1 = \{(s,s') | y \geq 0 \wedge x' = x+y \wedge y' = 0\},$$

$$P_2 = \{(s,s') | y \geq 0 \wedge x' = x+y \wedge y' = 0\} \cup \{(s,s') | y < 0 \wedge x' = x \wedge y' = y\},$$

$$P_3 = \{(s,s') | x' = x+y \wedge y' = 0\}.$$

We submit:

- That P1 is <u>partially correct</u> with respect to R; it is not (totally) correct because it is not defined for negative values of y; but it is partially correct with respect to R because whenever it is defined (for nonnegative values of y), it satisfies specification R (computing the sum of x and y into x).

- That P2 is defined with respect to R; it is not totally correct because for negative y it fails to compute the sum of x and y into x; but it is defined because it produces a final state for all relevant initial states (which, in the case of R, are all states in S).
- That P3 is totally correct with respect to R because it is defined for all relevant initial states and satisfies specification R for all relevant states, by computing the sum of x and y into x.

As a third example, we consider the following program on space S defined by integer variables x and y:

```
p: {while (y<>0) {x=x+1; y=y-1;};}
```

and we consider the following specifications:

$$R_1 = \{(s,s')|x' = x+y\},$$
$$R_2 = \{(s,s')|y \geq 0 \land x' = x+y\},$$
$$R_3 = \{(s,s')|y > 0 \land x' = x+y\},$$
$$R_4 = \{(s,s')|y > 10 \land x' = x+y\},$$
$$R_5 = \{(s,s')|y \geq 0 \land x' = x+1 \land y' = y-1\},$$
$$R_6 = \{(s,s')|y = 1 \land x' = x+1 \land y' = y-1\},$$
$$R_7 = \{(s,s')|x' = x+1 \land y' = y-1\}.$$

As a reminder, consider that the function of program p is:

$$P = \{(s,s')|y \geq 0 \land x' = x+y \land y' = 0\}.$$

Whence we submit:

- Program p is not correct with respect to R_1 because it does not terminate for all relevant initial states (which, according to specification R_1 are all initial states).
- Program p is correct with respect to specifications R_2, R_3, R_4, and R_6. For all these specifications, the program terminates normally for all relevant initial states and delivers a correct final state.
- Program p is defined with respect to specification R_5; it is defined for all relevant inputs (which are states such that $y \geq 0$), but it is not partially correct, since it delivers a different output from what specification R_5 demands.
- Finally, program p is neither correct, nor partially correct, nor defined with respect to specification R_7.

We are now ready to cast the intuition gained through these examples into formal definitions.

Definition: Correctness *Let R be a specification (relation) on space S and let p be a program on space S whose function we denote by P. We say that program p is correct (or totally correct) with respect to R if and only if:*

$$\forall s: \ s \in dom(R) \Rightarrow s \in dom(P) \wedge (s, P(s)) \in R.$$

Definition: Partial Correctness *Let R be a specification (relation) on space S and let p be a program on space S whose function we denote by P. We say that program p is partially correct with respect to R if and only if:*

$$\forall s: \ s \in dom(R) \wedge s \in dom(P) \Rightarrow (s, P(s)) \in R.$$

Note that partial correctness provides for the correct behavior of the program *only* whenever the program terminates; so that a program that never terminates is, by default, partially correct with respect to any specification. Despite this gaping weakness, partial correctness is a useful property that is often considered valuable in practice.

Definition: Termination *Let R be a specification (relation) on space S and let p be a program on space S whose function we denote by P. We say that program p is defined (or terminates) with respect to R if and only if:*

$$\forall s: s \in dom(R) \Rightarrow s \in dom(P).$$

We conclude this section with a simple proposition, which stems readily from the definitions.

Proposition: Correctness Properties *Let R be a specification (relation) on space S and let p be a program on space S whose function we denote by P. Program p is totally correct with respect to specification R if and only if it is partially correct and defined with respect to R.*

5.2 CORRECTNESS: PROPOSITIONS

In this section, we introduce a number of propositions pertaining to correctness, partial correctness, and termination; for the sake of readability, we do not prove them, but comment on their intuitive significance.

5.2.1 Correctness and Refinement

As we remember, the refinement ordering was introduced in Chapter 4 to rank specifications in terms of strength, reflecting how demanding a specification is or how hard a specification is to satisfy. As we recall, this ordering plays a role in determining whether a given specification is complete with respect to a completeness property and whether a given specification is minimal with respect to a minimality property. Surprisingly, or on second thought not surprisingly, the same refinement ordering plays an important role in defining program correctness, as the following propositions provide. For the sake of simplicity, we restrict our attention to deterministic programs (i.e., programs that produce a uniquely determined final state for any given initial state).

Proposition: Correctness, Refinement-based Formula *Let R be a specification (relation) on space S and let p be a program on space S whose function we denote by P. Program p is correct with respect to specification R if and only if P refines R.*

Function P refines relation R if and only if it has a larger domain that R and for all elements s in the domain of R, the pair $(s,P(s))$ is an element of R; this is exactly how we defined (total) correctness in Section 5.1.

Proposition: Partial Correctness, Refinement-based Formula *Let R be a specification (relation) on space S and let p be a program on space S whose function we denote by P. Program p is partially correct with respect to specification R if and only if P refines $(R \cap PL)$.*

Unlike with total correctness, in partial correctness P does not have to satisfy R for all initial states in the domain of R; rather it suffices that it satisfies R for elements of the domain of R for which p terminates normally (whence the term PL). Note that if we take $P=\emptyset$ (i.e., program p fails to terminate for all initial states), then this condition is satisfied.

Proposition: Termination, Refinement-based Formula *Let R be a specification (relation) on space S and let p be a program on space S whose function we denote by P. Program p is defined with respect to R if and only if P refines RL.*

Relation RL has the same domain as relation R, but because it assigns all the elements of S to any element of the domain of R, it imposes no condition on the final state; this is exactly what termination is about.

We conclude this section by revisiting the definition of refinement: so far we have interpreted the refinement to mean that a specification is stronger than another, more demanding than another, and so on. There is a simple way to characterize refinement, now that we have defined correctness; it is given in the following proposition.

Proposition: Characterizing Refinement by Correctness *Given two specifications R and R' on space S, R refines R' if and only if any program p that is correct with respect to R is correct with respect to R'.*

Isn't the essence of being a stronger specification to admit fewer correct programs? Any program that is correct with respect to the stronger/more demanding/more refined specification is necessarily correct with respect to the weaker/less demanding/less refined specification. The necessary condition of this Proposition is a mere consequence of the transitivity of the refinement ordering: if a program p is correct with respect to R, then its function P refines R; since R refines R', then a fortiori P refines R', hence p is correct with respect to R'.

5.2.2 Set Theoretic Characterizations

Whereas in Section 5.1 we introduced definitions of correctness and in Section 5.2.1 we introduced propositions that formulate correctness in terms of refinement, in this section we introduce propositions that formulate correctness in terms of set theoretic formulae. In practice, these are more tractable than either the definitions or the refinement-based characterizations.

Proposition: Correctness, Set Theoretic Formula *Let R be a specification (relation) on space S and let p be a program on space S whose function we denote by P. Program p is correct with respect to specification R if and only if*

$$dom(R \cap P) = dom(R).$$

Interpretation of this formula: The set $dom(R)$ is the set of initial states for which program p must behave as R mandates. The set $dom(R \cap P)$ is the set of initial states for which program p does behave as R mandates (see Fig. 5.1 for an illustration). Program p is correct with respect to specification R if and only if these two sets are identical.

Proposition: Partial Correctness, Set Theoretic Formula *Let R be a specification (relation) on space S and let p be a program on space S whose function we denote by P. Program p is partially correct with respect to specification R if and only if*

$$dom(R \cap P) = dom(R) \cap dom(P).$$

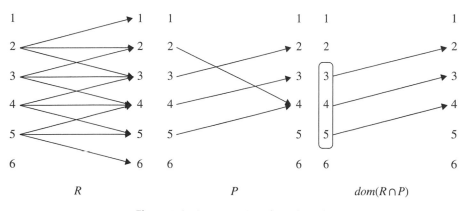

Figure 5.1 *Interpretation of $dom(R \cap P)$.*

Interpretation of this formula: The set $dom(R \cap P)$ is the set of initial states for which program p behaves as R mandates (see Fig. 5.1 for an illustration). The set $dom(R) \cap dom(P)$ is the set of states for which program p terminates and specification R has a requirement. Program p is partially correct with respect to specification R if and only if it behaves according to R whenever it terminates.

Proposition: Termination, Set Theoretic Formula *Let R be a specification (relation) on space S and let p be a program on space S whose function we denote by P. Program p is defined with respect to R if and only if $dom(R) \cap dom(P) = dom(R)$.*

This condition simply means that *dom(R)* is a subset of *dom(P)*.

5.2.3 Illustrations

As an illustration of the propositions given in the previous section, we revisit the examples of Section 5.1 and check the formulas of these propositions to ensure that we reach the same conclusions. We consider the specification and the candidate programs of the first example:

$$R = \{(0,0),(0,1),(0,2),(1,1),(1,2),(1,3),(2,2),(2,3),(2,4),(3,3),(3,4),(3,5)\}.$$
$$P_1 = \{(0,1),(1,2),(2,3),(3,4)\},$$
$$P_2 = \{(0,1),(1,2),(2,3),(3,4),(4,5),(5,6),(6,7)\},$$
$$P_3 = \{(0,0),(1,2),(2,4)\},$$
$$P_4 = \{(0,0),(1,2),(2,4),(4,8),(5,10),(6,12)\},$$
$$P_5 = \{(0,0),(1,2),(2,4),(3,6)\},$$
$$P_6 = \{(0,0),(1,2),(2,4),(3,6),(4,8),(5,10),(6,12)\},$$

The following table shows, for each candidate program P, the values of $dom(R \cap P)$, $dom(R)$, $dom(P)$, and the correctness property of P: total correctness (TC), partial correctness (PC), termination (T), or none (N).

Candidate	dom(R∩P)	dom(R)	dom(P)	TC	PC	T	N
P_1	{0,1,2,3}	{0,1,2,3}	{0,1,2,3}				
P_2	{0,1,2,3}	{0,1,2,3}	{0,1,2,3,4,5,6}				
P_3	{0,1,2}	{0,1,2,3}	{0,1,2}				
P_4	{0,1,2}	{0,1,2,3}	{0,1,2,4,5,6}				
P_5	{0,1,2}	{0,1,2,3}	{0,1,2,3}				
P_6	{0,1,2}	{0,1,2,3}	{0,1,2,3,4,5,6}				

These are indeed the conclusions we had reached earlier for the first example. For the second example, we list the specification and programs, then we draw the same table.

$$R = \{(s,s')\,|\,x(s') = x(s) + y(s)\}.$$

$$P_1 = \{(s,s')\,|\,y \geq 0 \wedge x' = x+y \wedge y' = 0\},$$

$$P_2 = \{(s,s')\,|\,y \geq 0 \wedge x' = x+y \wedge y' = 0\} \cup \{(s,s')\,|\,y < 0 \wedge x' = x \wedge y' = y\},$$

$$P_3 = \{(s,s')\,|\,x' = x+y \wedge y' = 0\}.$$

Candidate	dom(R∩P)	dom(R)	dom(P),	TC	PC	T	N
P_1	$\{(s,s')\,|\,y\geq 0\}$	S	$\{(s,s')\,|\,y\geq 0\}$				
P_2	$\{(s,s')\,|\,y\geq 0\}$	S	S				
P_3	S	S	S				

These are indeed the conclusions we had reached earlier for the second example. For the third example, we had a single program and many specifications, which we present below:

```
p: {while (y<>0) {x=x+1; y=y-1;};}
```

$$R_1 = \{(s,s')\,|\,x' = x+y\},$$

$$R_2 = \{(s,s')\,|\,y \geq 0 \wedge x' = x+y\},$$

$$R_3 = \{(s,s')\,|\,y > 0 \wedge x' = x+y\},$$

$$R_4 = \{(s,s')\,|\,y > 10 \wedge x' = x+y\},$$

$$R_5 = \{(s,s')\,|\,y \geq 0 \wedge x' = x+1 \wedge y' = y-1\},$$

$$R_6 = \{(s,s')\,|\,y = 1 \wedge x' = x+1 \wedge y' = y-1\},$$

$$R_7 = \{(s,s)\,|\,x' = x+1 \wedge y' = y-1\}.$$

We remember that the function of program p is $P = \{(s,s')\,|\,y \geq 0 \wedge x' = x+y \wedge y' = 0\}$, whence the domain of P is $\{s\,|\,y \geq 0\}$; for each specification R we write, in the table below, the values of $dom(R \cap P)$, $dom(R)$, and $dom(P)$, then make a judgment about the correctness properties of P with respect to the specification in question.

Specification	$dom(R\cap P)$	$dom(R)$	$dom(P)$,	TC	PC	T	N
R_1	$\{(s,s')\|y\geq 0\}$	S	$\{(s,s')\|y\geq 0\}$				
R_2	$\{(s,s')\|y\geq 0\}$	$\{(s,s')\|y\geq 0\}$	$\{(s,s')\|y\geq 0\}$				
R_3	$\{(s,s')\|y> 0\}$	$\{(s,s')\|y> 0\}$	$\{(s,s')\|y\geq 0\}$				
R_4	$\{(s,s')\|y> 10\}$	$\{(s,s')\|y> 10\}$	$\{(s,s')\|y\geq 0\}$				
R_5	$\{(s,s')\|y= 1\}$	$\{(s,s')\|y\geq 0\}$	$\{(s,s')\|y\geq 0\}$				
R_6	$\{(s,s')\|y= 1\}$	$\{(s,s')\|y= 1\}$	$\{(s,s')\|y\geq 0\}$				
R_7	$\{(s,s')\|y= 1\}$	S	$\{(s,s')\|y\geq 0\}$				

5.3 VERIFICATION

All the formulas of correctness we have seen so far have an important attribute in common: They define correctness by an equation that involves the function of the candidate program as well as the specification that the program is judged against. In order to use any of these formulas, we need to begin by computing the function of the program. This approach raises two problems: First, computing the function of a program is very complex and error-prone and does not lend itself to automation because it depends (to capture the function of iterative loops) on inductive arguments that are virtually impossible to codify; second, computing the function of a program in all its detail may be wasteful if the specification refers to only partial functional attributes of the program.

For the sake of illustration, consider the following program p on natural variables n, f, k:

```
{natural n, f, k;
f=1; k=1;  while (k!=n+1) {f=f*k; k=k+1;}}
```

and consider the following specifications

$$R_1 = \{(s,s')|n = n'\}.$$

$$R_2 = \{(s,s')|k' = n' + 1\}.$$

$$R_3 = \{(s,s)|k \leq k'\}.$$

$$R_4 = \{(s,s')|f \leq f'\}.$$

According to the foregoing definitions and propositions, in order to prove that program p is correct with respect to any of the proposed specifications, we must first compute the function of p. Given that the specifications refer to very partial aspects of the function of the program, it seems very wasteful to have to compute the function of the program in all its minute detail before we can prove correctness.

In this section, we present an alternative verification method that is commensurate with the complexity of the specification, and proceeds by recursive descent on the control structure of the program at hand. The core formula of this method takes the form of a triplet:

$$\{\phi\} \; p \; \{\psi\}$$

Where p is a program or program part and ϕ and ψ are assertions on (variables of) the space of the program. This formula is interpreted as follows: If ϕ holds prior to execution of program p and p executes and terminates, then ψ holds after the execution of p. Such formulas are called *Hoare formulas*; ϕ is called a *precondition* and ψ is called a *postcondition* to program p.

5.3.1 Sample Formulas

As a way to nurture the reader's understanding of this notation, we give below a number of formulas, which we want to consider as valid (in reference to the definition above); we let x and y be integer variables and we classify the sample formulas by the control structure of the program p.

Assignment statement:
- $\{x=1\}$ x=x+1; $\{x=2\}$
- $\{x\geq 1\}$ x=x+1; $\{x\geq 2\}$
- $\{x\geq 1\}$ x=x+1; $\{x\geq 1\}$
- $\{x=1 \;\wedge\; y=4\}$ x=x+1; $\{x=2 \;\wedge\; y=4\}$
- $\{x=x0\}$ x=x+1 $\{x=x0+1\}$, for some constant x0.
- $\{x=x0 \;\wedge\; y=y0\}$ x=x+1 $\{x=x0+1 \;\wedge\; y=y0\}$, for some constants x0 and y0.
- $\{x=x0 \;\wedge\; y=y0\}$ x=x+1 $\{x\geq x0+1 \;\wedge\; y\geq y0\}$, for some constants x0 and y0.

Sequence statement:
- $\{x=3\}$ x=x+3; y=x*x; $\{x=6 \;\wedge\; y-36\}$
- $\{x=3\}$ x=x*x; y=x+9 $\{x=9 \;\wedge\; y=18\}$
- $\{x=x0 \;\wedge\; y=y0\}$ x=x+3; y=x*x; $\{x=x0+3 \;\wedge\; y=(x0+3)^2\}$, for some constants x0 and y0.
- $\{x=x0 \;\wedge\; y=y0\}$ x=x*x; y=x+9; $\{x=x0^2 \;\wedge\; y=x0^2+9\}$, for some constants x0 and y0.
- $\{x=x0 \;\wedge\; y=y0\}$ x=x+y; y=x–y; x=x–y; $\{x=y0 \;\wedge\; y=x0\}$, for some constants x0 and y0.
- $\{x=x0 \;\wedge\; y=y0\}$ x=x+1; y=y–1; $\{x=x0+1 \;\wedge\; y=y0–1\}$, for some constants x0 and y0.

- $\{x=x0 \ \wedge \ y=y0\}$ x=x+1; y=y-1; $\{x+y=x0+y0\}$, for some constants x0 and y0.
- $\{x+y=A\}$ x=x+1; y=y-1; $\{x+y=A\}$, for some constant A.

Conditional statement:
- $\{$true$\}$ if (x<0) $\{x=-x;\}$ $\{x\geq 0\}$.
- $\{x=x0\}$ if (x<0) $\{x=-x;\}$ $\{x=|x0|\}$.
- $\{$true$\}$ if (x<y) $\{x=x+y; y=x-y; x=x-y;\}$ $\{x\geq y\}$.
- $\{x=x0 \ \wedge \ y=y0\}$ if (x<y) $\{x=x+y; y=x-y; x=x-y;\}$ $\{x=\max(x0,y0) \ \wedge \ y=\min (x0,y0)\}$, for some constants x0 and y0.

Alternation statement:
- $\{x=x0 \ \wedge \ y=y0 \ \wedge \ x>0 \ \wedge \ y>0 \ \wedge \ x\neq y\}$ if (x>y) $\{x=x-y;\}$ else $\{y=y-x;\}$ $\{\gcd(x,y)=\gcd(x0,y0)\}$, for some constants x0 and y0.
- $\{\gcd(x,y)=A \ \wedge \ x>0 \ \wedge \ y>0 \ \wedge \ x\neq y\}$ if (x>y) $\{x=x-y;\}$ else $\{y=y-x;\}$ $\{\gcd(x,y)=A\}$, for some constant A.

Iteration:
- $\{$true$\}$ while (y$\neq$0) $\{x=x+1; y=y-1;\}$ $\{y=0\}$
- $\{y\geq 0\}$ while (y$\neq$0) $\{x=x+1; y=y-1;\}$ $\{y=0\}$
- $\{y<0\}$ while (y$\neq$0) $\{x=x+1; y=y-1;\}$ $\{y=0\}$
- $\{x=x0 \ \wedge \ y=y0\}$ while (y$\neq$0) $\{x=x+1; y=y-1;\}$ $\{x=x0+y0 \ \wedge \ y=0\}$, for some constants x0 and y0.
- $\{y\geq 0\}$ while (y>0) $\{x=x+1; y=y-1;\}$ $\{y=0\}$
- $\{x=x0 \ \wedge \ y\geq 0\}$ while (y>0) $\{x=x+1; y=y-1;\}$ $\{x\geq x0\}$
- $\{y<0\}$ while (y>0) $\{x=x+1; y=y-1;\}$ $\{y<0\}$
- $\{x=x0 \ \wedge \ y=y0 \ \wedge \ y\geq 0\}$ while (y>0) $\{x=x+1; y=y-1;\}$ $\{x=x0+y0 \ \wedge \ y=0\}$, for some constants x0 and y0.
- $\{x=x0 \ \wedge \ y=y0 \ \wedge \ y<0\}$ while (y>0) $\{x=x+1; y=y-1;\}$ $\{x=x0 \ \wedge \ y= y0 \ \wedge \ y<0\}$, for some constants x0 and y0.
- $\{y<0\}$ while (y$\neq$0) $\{x=x+1; y=y-1;\}$ $\{y=-1\}$
- $\{y<0\}$ while (y$\neq$0) $\{x=x+1; y=y-1;\}$ $\{y=1\}$
- $\{y<0\}$ while (y$\neq$0) $\{x=x+1; y=y-1;\}$ $\{y=2\}$

We leave it to the reader to ponder, by reference to the definition of this notation, why each one of the formulas above is valid. So far we have established the validity of these formulas by inspection, in reference to the definition. For larger and more complex programs, this may not be practical; in the next section, we introduce a deductive process that aims to establish the validity of complex formulas by induction on the complexity of the program structure.

5.3.2 An Inference System

An inference system is a system for inferring conclusions from hypotheses in a systematic manner. Such a system can be defined by means of the following artifacts:

- A set *F* of (syntactically defined) <u>formulas</u>.

- A subset *A* of *F*, called the <u>set of axioms</u>, which includes formulas that we assume to be valid by hypothesis.

- A set of <u>inference rules</u>, which we denote by *R*, where each rule is made up of a set of formulas called the <u>premises of the rule</u>, and a formula called the <u>conclusion of the rule</u>. We interpret a rule to mean that whenever the premises of a rule are valid, so is its conclusion; we usually represent a rule by listing its premises above a line and its conclusion below the line.

An <u>inference</u> in an inference system is an ordered sequence of formulas, say $v_1, v_2, \ldots, v_n$, such each formula in the sequence, say v_i, is either an axiom or the conclusion of a rule whose premises appear prior to v_i, that is, amongst $v_1, v_2, \ldots, v_{i-1}$. A <u>theorem</u> of a deductive system is any formula that appears in an inference.

In this section, we propose an inference system that enables us to establish the validity of Hoare formulas by induction on the complexity of the program component of the formulas. To this effect, we present in turn, the formulas, then the axioms, and finally the rules.

- *Formulas.* Formulas of our inference system include all the formulas of logic, as well as Hoare formulas.

- *Axioms.* Axioms of this inference system include all the tautologies of logic, as well as the following formulas:
  - {false} p {ψ}, for any program p and any postcondition ψ.
  - {φ} p {true}, for any program p and any precondition φ.

- *Rules.* We present below a rule for each statement of a simple C-like programming language.

Assignment Statement Rule: We consider an assignment statement that affects a program variable (and implicitly preserving all other variables), and we interpret it as an assignment to the whole program state (changing the selected variable and preserving the other variables), which we denote by *s=E(s)*, where *s* is the state of the program. We submit the following rule,

$$\frac{\phi \Rightarrow \psi(E(s))}{\{\phi\}\, s = E(s)\, \{\psi\}}.$$

Interpretation: If we want ψ to hold after execution of the assignment statement, when s is replaced by $E(s)$, then $\psi(E(s))$ must hold before execution of the assignment; hence the precondition ϕ must imply $\psi(E(s))$.

Sequence Rule: Let p be a sequence of two subprograms, say $p1$ and $p2$. We have the following rule,

$$\exists int:$$

$$\{\phi\}p1\{int\}$$

$$\frac{\{int\}p2\{\psi\}}{\{\phi\}p1;p2\{\psi\}}$$

Interpretation: if we can find an intermediate predicate *int* that serves as a postcondition to p1 and a precondition to p2, then the conclusion is established.

Conditional Rule: Let p be a conditional statement of the form: **if (condition) {statement;}**. We have the following rule,

$$\{\phi \wedge t\}B\{\psi\}$$
$$\frac{(\phi \wedge -t) \Rightarrow \psi}{\{\phi\}if(t)\{B\}\{\psi\}}.$$

Interpretation: The two premises of this rule correspond to the two execution paths through the flowchart of the conditional statement (Fig. 5.2).

Alternation Rule: Let p be an alternation statement of the form: **if (condition) {statement;} else {statement;}**. We have the following rule,

$$\{\phi \wedge t\}B1\{\psi\}$$
$$\frac{\{\phi \wedge \neg t\}B2\{\psi\}}{\{\phi\}if(t)\{B1\}else\{B2\}\{\psi\}}.$$

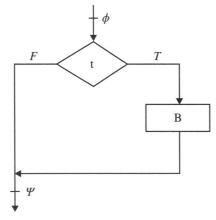

Figure 5.2   *Flowchart of if-statement.*

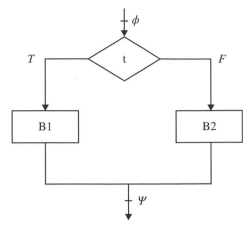

Figure 5.3 *Flowchart of if-else statement.*

Interpretation: The two premises of this rule correspond to the two execution paths through the flowchart of the conditional statement (Fig. 5.3).

Iteration Rule: Let p be an iterative statement of the form: `while (condition) {statement;}`. We have the following rule,

$$
\begin{array}{c}
E\,inv: \\
\phi \Rightarrow inv \\
\{inv \wedge t\}B\{inv\} \\
\underline{inv \wedge \neg t \Rightarrow \psi} \\
\{\phi\}\,while\,(t)\,\{B\}\{\psi\}
\end{array}.
$$

Interpretation: The first and second premises establish an inductive proof to the effect that predicate *inv* holds after any number of iterations. The third premise provides that upon termination of the loop, the combination of predicate *inv* and the negation of the loop condition must logically imply the postcondition. Predicate *inv* is called an *invariant assertion*. It must be chosen so as to be sufficiently weak to satisfy the first premise, yet sufficient strong to satisfy the third premise (and the second). See the flowchart below, which highlight the points at which each of the relevant assertions is supposed to hold. Note that *inv* is placed upstream of the loop condition; hence the loop condition is never part of *inv* (since upstream of the loop condition we do not know whether t is true or not) (Fig. 5.4).

Consequence Rule: Given a Hoare formula, we can always strengthen the precondition and/or weaken the postcondition. We have the following rule:

$$
\begin{array}{c}
\phi \Rightarrow \phi' \\
\psi' \Rightarrow \psi \\
\underline{\{\phi'\}p\{\psi'\}} \\
\{\phi\}p\{\psi\}
\end{array}
$$

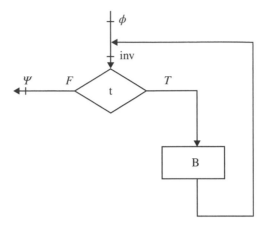

Figure 5.4 *Flowchart of while statement.*

Interpretation: This rule stems readily from the definition of these formulas.

Using the proposed axioms and rules, we can now generate theorems of the form *{ϕ} p {ψ}*. The question that arises then is: what good does it do us to generate such theorems? What does that tell us about *p*? The following Proposition provides the answer.

Proposition: Proving Partial Correctness *If the formula*

$$\{\phi\}\ p\ \{\psi\}$$

is a theorem of the deductive system, then p is partially correct with respect to the specification $R = \{(s,s') | \phi(s) \wedge \psi(s')\}$.

In the following section, we present sample illustrative examples of the inference system presented herein.

5.3.3 Illustrative Examples

We consider the following program on space S defined by variables x and y of type real, and we form a triplet by embedding it between a precondition and a postcondition:

- Program: while (y≠0) {x=x+1; y=y−1;}.
- Precondition: $x = x0 \wedge y = y0$, for some constants $x0$ and $y0$.
- Postcondition: $x = x0 + y0$.

We form the following formula and we attempt to prove that this formula is a theorem of the proposed inference system:

$$v: \{x = x0 \wedge y = y0\}\ \texttt{While (y≠0)\{x=x+1;y=y-1;\}}\ \{x = x0 + y0\}$$

We apply the iteration rule to *v*, using the invariant assertion $inv \equiv (x + y = x0 + y0)$. This yields the following three formulas:

$v_0 : x = x0 \wedge y = y0 \Rightarrow (x + y = x0 + y0)$.

$v_1 : \{(x + y = x0 + y0) \wedge (y \neq 0)\}$ `x=x+1;y=y-1` $\{(x + y = x0 + y0)\}$.

$v_2 : (x + y = x0 + y0) \wedge (y = 0) \Rightarrow x = x0 + y0$.

We find that v_0 and v_2 are both tautologies and hence they are axioms of the inference system. We consider v_1, to which we apply the sequence rule, with the intermediate assertion $int \equiv (x + y = x0 + y0 + 1)$. This yields two formulas:

$v_{10} : \{(x + y = x0 + y0) \wedge (y \neq 0)\}$ `x=x+1` $\{(x + y = x0 + y0 + 1)\}$.

$v_{11} : \{(x + y = x0 + y0 + 1)\}$ `y=y-1` $\{(x + y = x0 + y0)\}$.

We apply the assignment statement rule to v_{10} and v_{11}, which yields the following formulas:

$v_{100} : (x + y = x0 + y0) \wedge (y \neq 0) \Rightarrow ((x + 1) + y = x0 + y0 + 1)$.

$v_{110} : \{(x + y = x0 + y0 + 1) \Rightarrow (x + (y-1)) = x0 + y0\}$.

We find that v_{100} and v_{110} are both tautologies and hence they are axioms of the inference system. This concludes our proof to the effect that v is a theorem, since the sequence

$$v_{100}, v_{110}, v_{10}, v_{11}, v_0, v_1, v_2, v$$

is an inference, as the reader may check: each formula in this sequence is either an axiom or the conclusion of a rule whose premises are to the left of the formula. By virtue of the proposition labeled *Proving Partial Correctness,* we conclude that program p is partially correct with respect to the following specification:

$$R = \{(s, s') \mid \exists x0, y0 : (x = x0 \wedge y = y0) \wedge (x' = x0 + y0)\} = \{(s, s') \mid x' = x + y\}.$$

It may be more expressive to view this inference as a tree structure, where leaves are the axioms and internal nodes represent the rules that were invoked in the inference; the root of the tree represents the theorem that is established in the inference (Fig. 5.5).

As a second illustrative example, we let space S be defined by three integer variables n, f, k, such that n is nonnegative, and we let program p be defined as:
`{f=1; k=1; while (k≠n+1) {f=f*k; k=k+1;};}.`

We choose the following precondition and postcondition:

- $\phi(s) \equiv (n = n0)$.
- $\psi(s) \equiv (f = n0!)$.

This produces the following formula:

$v : \{(n = n0)\}$ `f=1; k=1; while (k≠n+1) {f=f*k; k=k+1;}` $\{f = n0!\}$.

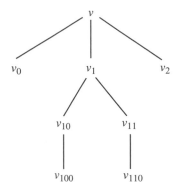

Figure 5.5 Structure of an Inference.

We apply the sequence rule to v, using the intermediate predicate $int \equiv (n = n0 \wedge f = 1 \wedge k = 1)$. This yields

$v_0 : \{(n = n0)\}$ **f=1; k=1** $\{n = n0 \wedge f = 1 \wedge k = 1\}$.

$v_1 : \{n = n0 \wedge f = 1 \wedge k = 1\}$ **while (k≠n+1) {f=f*k; k=k+1;}** $\{f = n0!\}$.

We apply the sequence rule to v_0, using the intermediate assertion $int \equiv (n = n0 \wedge f = 1)$. This yields

$v_{00} : \{(n = n0)\}$ **f=1** $\{n = n0 \wedge f = 1\}$.

$v_{01} : \{(n = n0 \wedge f = 1)\}$ **k=1** $\{n = n0 \wedge f = 1 \wedge k = 1\}$.

We apply the assignment statement rule to v_{00} and v_{01}. This yields respectively:

$v_{000} : n = n0 \Rightarrow n = n0 \wedge 1 = 1$.

$v_{010} : n = n0 \wedge f = 1 \Rightarrow n = n0 \wedge f = 1 \wedge 1 = 1$.

We find that v_{000} and v_{010} are both tautologies and hence axioms of the inference system. We now focus on v_1, to which we apply the iteration rule, with the invariant assertion $inv \equiv (n = n0 \wedge f = (k-1)!)$. This yields:

$v_{10} : n = n0 \wedge f = 1 \wedge k = 1 \Rightarrow (n = n0 \wedge f = (k-1)!)$.

$v_{11} : \{(n = n0 \wedge f = (k-1)!) \wedge k \neq n+1\}$ **f=f*k; k=k+1** $\{(n = n0 \wedge f = (k-1)!)\}$.

$v_{12} : (n = n0 \wedge f = (k-1)!) \wedge (k = n+1) \Rightarrow f = n0!$.

We find that formula v_{10} is a tautology, since the factorial of 0 is 1, and we find that formula v_{12} is a tautology, by simple substitution. Hence we now focus on v_{11}, to which we apply the sequence rule, with the intermediate assertion $int \equiv (n = n0 \wedge f = (k)!)$. This yields:

v_{110} : $\{(n = n0 \wedge f = (k-1)!) \wedge k \neq n+1\}$ `f=f*k` $\{(n = n0 \wedge f = (k)!)\}$.
v_{111} : $\{(n = n0 \wedge f = (k)!)\}$ `k=k+1` $\{(n = n0 \wedge f = (k-1)!)\}$.

Application of the assignment statement rule to v_{110} and v_{111} yields:

v_{1100} : $(n = n0 \wedge f = (k-1)!) \wedge (k \neq n+1) \Rightarrow (n = n0 \wedge f \times k = (k)!)$.
v_{1110} : $(n = n0 \wedge f = (k)!) \Rightarrow (n = n0 \wedge f = (k+1-1)!)$.

We find that v_{1100} and v_{1110} are both tautologies and hence axioms of the inference system. This concludes our proof; we leave it to the reader to verify that the following sequence is an inference in the proposed inference system:

$$v_{1100}, v_{1110}, v_{110}, v_{111}, v_{11}, v_{10}, v_{12}, v_{000}, v_{010}, v_{00}, v_{01}, v_{0}, v_{1}, v.$$

Because v is a theorem, we conclude that program p is partially correct with respect to the following specification (formed from the precondition and postcondition of v):

$$R = \{(s,s') | \exists n0 : n = n0 \wedge f' = n0!\} = \{(s,s') | f' = n!\}.$$

As a third example, we consider the following GCD program on positive integer variables x and y:

`{while (x≠y) {if (x>y) {x=x-y;} else {y=y-x;};},`

and we consider the following precondition/postcondition pair:

- $\phi(s) \equiv (x = x0 \wedge y = y0)$,
- $\psi(s) \equiv (x = \gcd(x0, y0))$.

We form the following formula:

v: $\{x = x0 \wedge y = y0\}$
$\qquad$ `while (x≠y) {if (x>y) {x=x-y;}else {y=y-x;}}`
$$\{x = \gcd(x0, y0)\}.$$

We apply the iteration rule to v with the following invariant assertion: $inv \equiv (\gcd(x,y) = \gcd(x0, y0))$. This yields:

v_0 : $(x = x0 \wedge y = y0) \Rightarrow (\gcd(x,y) = \gcd(x0, y0))$,

v_1 : $\{(\gcd(x,y) = \gcd(x0, y0)) \wedge (x \neq y)\}$
$\qquad$ `if (x>y) {x=x-y;} else {y=y-x;}`
$$\{(\gcd(x,y) = \gcd(x0, y0))\}$$

v_2 : $(\gcd(x,y) = \gcd(x0, y0)) \wedge (x = y) \Rightarrow (x = \gcd(x0, y0))$.

We find that v_0 and v_2 are tautologies and hence axioms of the inference system. We focus on v_1, to which we apply the alternation rule, which yields:

$$v_{10} : \{(\gcd(x,y) = \gcd(x0,y0)) \wedge (x \neq y) \wedge (x > y)\}$$

$$\mathbf{x = x - y}$$

$$\{(\gcd(x,y) = \gcd(x0,y0))\}$$

$$v_{11} : \{(\gcd(x,y) = \gcd(x0,y0)) \wedge (x \neq y) \wedge (x \leq y)\}$$

$$\mathbf{y = y - x}$$

$$\{(\gcd(x,y) = \gcd(x0,y0))\}$$

We apply the assignment statement rule to v_{10} and v_{11}, which yields:

$$v_{100} : (\gcd(x,y) = \gcd(x0,y0)) \wedge (x \neq y) \wedge (x > y) \Rightarrow (\gcd(x-y,y) = \gcd(x0,y0)).$$

$$v_{110} : (\gcd(x,y) = \gcd(x0,y0)) \wedge (x \neq y) \wedge (x \leq y) \Rightarrow (\gcd(x,y-x) = \gcd(x0,y0)).$$

We find that both of these formulas are tautologies and hence axioms of the inference system. This concludes the proof that v is a theorem; hence program p is partially correct with respect to

$$R = \{(s,s') \mid \exists x0, y0 : x = x0 \wedge y = y0 \, x' = \gcd(x0,y0)\} = \{(s,s') \mid x' = \gcd(x,y)\}.$$

5.4 CHAPTER SUMMARY

Among the most important lessons to retain from this chapter, we cite:

- Understanding that the study of program testing requires that we understand the meaning of program correctness.
- Understanding that a program under test is considered to fail with respect to a specification if it fails to terminate for an initial state in the domain of the specification, or if it does terminate but fails to deliver a state that the specification considers correct.
- Understanding the hierarchy of correctness levels, including total correctness, partial correctness and termination.
- Understanding that all three levels of program correctness can be captured by means of the refinement ordering; in particular, total correctness means precisely that the function of the program refines the specification.
- Understanding the construct of an inference system and how it mechanizes the process of inferring theorems from hypotheses.

- Knowing how to use the proposed inference system to prove that a program is partially correct with respect to a specification that takes the form of a precondition/postcondition.
- Understanding the mapping between a relational specification and a specification that takes the form of a precondition/postcondition.
- Understanding how constants are introduced (and eliminated) from specifications that take the form of a precondition and a postcondition.

5.5 EXERCISES

5.1. Prove that the following formula is a theorem of the inference system presented in Section 5.3. Draw a conclusion about the partial correctness of the program.

$$v: \{x=x0 \wedge y=y0 \wedge y \geq 0\} \ \texttt{while (y>0) \{x=x+1; y=y-1;\}} \ \{x=x0+y0\}.$$

5.2. Consider the following program on space S defined by variables x, y, z of type integer.

$$\{\texttt{z=0; while (y}\neq\texttt{0) \{y=y-1; z=z+x;\};\}}$$

This program computes the product of x and y into z. Write an appropriate precondition and postcondition for this program and prove the resulting formula; compute the binary relation that stems from the precondition/postcondition pair and infer a partial correctness property of the program.

5.3. Consider the following program on space S defined by variables n and f of type integer.

$$\{\texttt{f=1; while (n}\neq\texttt{0) \{f=f*n; n=n-1;\};\}}$$

Write an appropriate precondition and postcondition that capture the function of this program, and prove the resulting formula; compute the binary relation that stems from the precondition/postcondition pair and infer a partial correctness property of the program.

5.4. Same as Exercise 3, for the following program on integer variables x, y, z.

$$\{\texttt{z=0; while (y}\neq\texttt{0) \{if (y\%2==0) \{x=2*x; y=y/2;\} else \{z=z+x; y=y-1;\};\};\}}.$$

5.5. Same as Exercise 3, for the following program on real array a of size N (≥ 1), variable x of type real, and index variable k:

$$\{\texttt{x=0; k=0; while (k<N) \{x=x+a[k]; k=k+1;\};\}}.$$

5.6. Same as Exercise 3, for the following program on real array a of size N (≥ 1), variable x of type real, variable f of type Boolean, and index variable k:

```
{k=N-1; a[0]=x; while (a[k]≠x) {k=k-1;}; f=(k>0);}
```

5.7. Draw the inference tree of the proof of the second example (the factorial program) in Section 5.3.3.

5.8. Draw the inference tree of the proof of the third example (the gcd program) in Section 5.3.3.

5.6 PROBLEMS

5.1. Imagine that we have a program p on space S and a specification R on S, and we wish to prove that p is partially correct with respect to R using the inference system of Section 5.3. How we do convert specification R into a precondition and a postcondition? Is this conversion unique? Give illustrative examples.

5.2. When we are given a precondition ϕ and a postcondition ψ of a program p, we can use them to form a relational specification R by the formula $R = \{(s,s') | \phi(s) \wedge \psi(s')\}$. When constants (such as $x0$ and $y0$) are involved in the precondition or postcondition, we must quantify them existentially in the formula of R; justify this step. Give an example of a precondition/postcondition pair that adequately describes the function of a program but can be defined without reference to constants.

5.7 BIBLIOGRAPHIC NOTES

The definitions and propositions pertaining to program correctness are due to Linger et al. (1979) and Mills et al. (1986) or inspired from Mili et al. (1994). The proof method that is presented in Section 5.3.2 is due to C.A.R. Hoare (1969).

6

Failures, Errors, and Faults

To the extent that software testing is the task of finding and removing faults in programs, the study of software testing requires that we study the nature and properties of faults; these are usually viewed as part of a hierarchy that also includes errors and failures; hence the subject of this chapter.

6.1 FAILURE, ERROR, AND FAULT

Now that we know what a correct program is, we can easily define what a program failure is: it is any behavior of the program that belies, or is in contradiction with, its claim of correctness with respect to a given specification. Defining errors or faults is more complicated, because it relies on detailed design knowledge that has no officially sanctioned existence (in the way that a specification is an officially sanctioned document, which is part of the lifecycle deliverables), except possibly in the mind of the designer.

We use a simple example to introduce these concepts and then we present tentative definitions thereof. Let S be the space defined by a variable of type integer, and let R be the following specification:

$$R = \left\{ (s, s') \mid s' = (s+1)^2 \bmod 3 + 12 \right\}$$

and let p be the following program on space S:

```
{s=s+1;        // line 1
  s=2*s;       // line 2
  s = s % 3;   // line 3
  s=s+12;}     // line 4
```

Software Testing: Concepts and Operations, First Edition. Ali Mili and Fairouz Tchier.
© 2015 John Wiley & Sons, Inc. Published 2015 by John Wiley & Sons, Inc.

Given the expression that the specification mandates to compute, we would expect the candidate program to add 1 to s, then compute the square of the result, then compute the remainder by 3, then add 12; yet on line 2, the program multiplies s by 2 rather than raise it to the power 2. Hence it may be natural to consider that line 2 is a *fault*, and that it should be s=s*s rather than s=2*s. Notice that in order to determine that line 2 is a fault, we have to refer to a hypothetical design, which we assume the programmer had intended to follow; this matter will be discussed in subsequent sections.

We consider possible initial values of s and investigate how the program behaves on each:

- For initial state s=1, line 1 produces state s=2, which line 2 maps into 4. Because for s=2, 2*s and s*s are the same, the fault has no impact on this execution. We say that the *fault is not sensitized*, that is, it is not causing the state to be different from the correct state.
- For initial state s=2, line 1 produces state s=3, which line 2 maps onto 6. Because the correct state at this step of the computation is 3*3=9 rather than 2*3=6, we say that we are observing an *error*. In this case, we say that the *fault has been sensitized*: unlike in the previous case, it has produced a state that is distinct from the expected state at this step. Notice that in the same way that the identification of a fault refers to a hypothetical program design against which individual statements of program parts are judged, the identification of an error refers to a sequence of expected/correct states against which actual states are compared. Even though the fault is sensitized and generates an error, it causes no long-term impact, since by line 3 the program generates a correct state: indeed (6 mod 3) is the same as (9 mod 3). So that at the end of the program (after line 4), the state of the program is s=12. We say that the *error has been masked*.
- For initial state s=3, line 1 produces state s=4, which line 2 maps onto state s=8. Because the correct state at this step of the computation ought to be s=16 instead of s=8, we observe again that the fault has been sensitized and has caused an error. By line 3, the state becomes (8 mod 3)=2 rather than (16 mod 3)=1, hence the *error is propagated* to the next state. By line 4, the state becomes s=2+12=4 rather than s=1+12=13. The error is again propagated causing a *failure* of the program.

Hence in this example,

- The *fault* is the statement in line 2, which should be (s=s*s) rather than (s=2*s);
- An *error* is the impact of the fault on program states; not all executions of the program give rise to an error; those that do are said to sensitize the fault. Executions on initial states s=2 and s=3 lead to errors.
- A *failure* is the event whereby an execution of the program on some initial state violates the specification; not all errors give rise to a failure; those that do are said to be propagated; those that do not are said to be masked.

In this example, the specification is total and deterministic and the program is expected (if it weren't for its fault) to compute the function defined by the specification.

6.2 FAULTS AND RELATIVE CORRECTNESS

6.2.1 Fault, an Evasive Concept

The discussions in Section 6.1 make it sound like faults are a simple concept, they are easy to characterize and locate, and easy to remove; reality is more complicated than that.

Let us consider again the program of Section 6.1:

```
{s=s+1;          // line 1
  s=2*s;         // line 2
  s = s % 3;     // line 3
  s=s+12;}       // line 4
```

We assume that the fault is in line 2 and that correcting the fault consists in replacing the statement (s=2*s) by the statement (s=s*s). Alternatively, we could also argue that a way to correct this program is to change line 3 from (s=s%3) to (s=((s/2)**2)%3). Alternatively, we could also argue that a way to correct the program is to insert a statement between lines 2 and 3 that reads (s=(s/2)**2). Alternatively, we could also argue that a way to correct the program is to change line 1 from (s=s+1) to (s=(s+1)**2–2) and line 2 from (s=2*s) to (s=s+2). Alternatively, we could argue that a way to correct the program is to change line 1 from (s=s+1) to (s=(s+1)**2) and to remove line 2. Of course, all these alternatives sound convoluted and far-fetched, but any definition of fault ought to make equal provisions for all these possibilities.

Furthermore, if we consider a non-deterministic specification, then we now have two degrees of failure: the program may fail because it violates its (non deterministic) specification or because it fails to compute the function it was designed to compute. This distinction is important in practice: if we are conducting unit testing, for example, then we want to judge the program against its intended function, but if we are conducting acceptance testing, then we want to judge it against its (possibly non-deterministic, much less-refined) specification.

We let space S be the set of natural variables and let R be the following specification on S:

$$R = \left\{ (s,s') \mid s' mod 3 = (s+1)^2 mod 3 \right\}.$$

Imagine that upon inspecting R, the programmer decides to write a program that computes the following function:

$$\pi = \left\{ (s,s') \mid s' = (s+1)^2 mod 3 \right\}.$$

We consider the following candidate programs on S:

- p1: {s=s+1; s=s*s; s=s%3; s=s+12}
- p2: {s=s+1; s=s*s; s=s%6; s=s+12}
- p3: {s=s+4; s=s*s; s=s%3; s=s+12}

These programs are not correct with respect to π but they are correct with respect to R. Hence whether these programs have faults or not depends on whether we are judging them against R or against π.

From these discussions, we draw the following conclusions about faults in programs:

- A fault is not a characteristic of a program but rather depends on a program and a specification.
- Neither the existence, nor the number, nor the location, nor the nature of faults is uniquely determined: the same faulty program behavior can be remedied in a number of different ways, involving a number of locations and involving different types of corrective actions (changing an existing statement, adding a statement, removing a statement, changing the location of a statement, etc.). This observation should give us an opportunity to ponder what it means to measure fault density in a program, or fault proneness, or other fault-related metrics.
- Designating a particular statement as a fault is often a tentative decision that is contingent on assumptions made about other parts of the program; as such, the designation of a statement as faulty is as valid as the assumptions made about other parts of the program.
- Very often, when we designate a program part (a statement or a set of statements that may or may not be contiguous) as faulty, we do so on the basis of an assumption we have about the specification of the program part; hence we are in effect second-guessing the designer by presuming to know what his intent is with respect to the designated program part. Clearly, our diagnosis of the fault is only as good as our assumption.

In this chapter, we give a definition of a fault that has the following attributes: It involves the program, the (possibly) faulty program part, and the specification; it makes no assumption on the correctness of incorrectness of any other part except the faulty program part; and it makes no assumption about the intent of the program designer.

6.2.2 Relative Correctness

Implicit in the definition of a fault is the idea that the program would be better off without it. If we are talking about the last remaining fault of a program (how do we ever know that?), then we can characterize it by the fact that with the fault, the program is incorrect, and without the fault, the program is correct. But in general, programs have (many) more than one fault, and removing one fault does not make the program correct, but it ought to make it *more-correct*. Whence the following definition.

Definition: Relative Correctness *Let R be a specification on space S and let p and p' be two programs on space S, whose functions are P and P'. We say that p' is* <u>*more-correct*</u> *than p with respect to R if and only if*

$$dom(R \cap P') \supseteq dom(R \cap P).$$

We say that P is *strictly-more-correct* than P' with respect to R if and only if:

$$dom(R \cap P') \supset dom(R \cap P).$$

Interpretation: $dom(R \cap P)$ represents the set of initial states on which program p delivers an output that specification R considers correct; we refer to this set as the *competence domain* of program p with respect to specification R. Clearly, the larger the competence domain, the better: when p' is more-correct than p with respect to R, then whenever p behaves correctly on an initial state, so does p'. The following proposition links the novel concept of relative correctness to a well-known property: reliability.

Proposition: Relative Correctness and Reliability *Let R be a specification on space S and let p and p' be two programs such that p' is more-correct than p with respect to R. Then program p' is more reliable with respect to R than p.*

The proof of this proposition is straightforward: We equate reliability with probability of a successful execution of a program on an arbitrary element of the domain of R; reliability is usually quantified in terms of MTTF, which is clearly monotonic with respect to the said probability. If we consider a probability distribution over the domain of R, which reflects the likelihood of inputs submitted to the programs, then it is clear that the probability of a successful execution of p' is larger than the probability of a successful execution of p, since each probability of successful execution is computed as the integral of the probability distribution over the competence domain. See the Figure 6.1; the gain in probability is indicated by the integral (or the sum, for discrete probability distributions) of the probability distribution over the range of inputs in $dom(R \cap P)/dom(R \cap P')$.

Given that $dom(R \cap P)$ is, by construction, a subset of $dom(R)$, the best that a program p can do is to achieve the equality $dom(R \cap P) = dom(R)$. But we have seen in Chapter 5 that this is the condition under which p is correct with respect to specification R. Whence the following proposition.

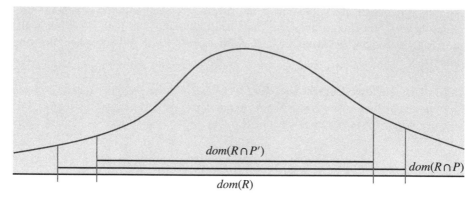

Figure 6.1   *Relative correctness and relative reliability.*

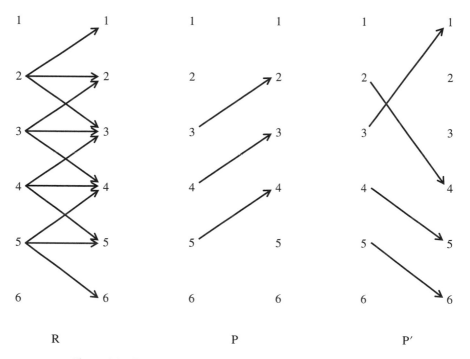

Figure 6.2   *To be more-correct without duplicating correct behavior.*

Proposition: Maximum Relative Correctness *Let R be a specification on space S and let p be a program on space S. If and only if p′ is correct with respect to R, p′ is more-correct with respect to R than any program p on space S.*

The interest of this proposition is that it presents program correctness as an extreme form of relative correctness: a faulty program can become fault-free by shedding its faults and augmenting its competence domain $dom(R \cap P)$ until it reaches its maximum value, that is, $dom(R)$, when the program become totally fault-free.

Note that for program p' to be more-correct than program p with respect to specification R, p' has to behave correctly with respect to R for all initial states for which p behaves correctly. Note that this does not mean that program p and program p' behave identically on $dom(R \cap P)$. Because R may be non-deterministic, programs p and p' may both satisfy specification R on $dom(R \cap P)$ while being distinct. In particular, several programs may be correct with respect to specification R and still be distinct from each other, even within $dom(R)$. See the Figure 6.2. In this example, program p' is more-correct than program p; yet program p does not coincide with program p' on $dom(R \cap P) = \{4,5\}$.

6.3 CONTINGENT FAULTS AND DEFINITE FAULTS

6.3.1 Contingent Faults

Now that we have defined the concept of relative correctness, whereby a program can be considered more-correct than another (in a way: getting closer to a correct program), we are ready to define a fault. A fault may be localized at an arbitrary level of granularity: at the level of a line of code, or at the level of a simple statement (e.g., assignment statement and condition), or the level of a compound statement (sequence, if-then, if-then-else, while-loop), or the level of a block (unnamed block, with variable declarations and executable statements, or named block, such as a function body), and so on. We want to define faults in such a way that the definition applies equally to any scale of granularity. Hence in general, we view a program as an aggregate of components linked by programming constructs; the size of these components determines, for our purposes, the level of granularity at which we want to localize faults in a program. As an example, we consider the following program:

```
#include <iostream> ... ... ...                          // line 1
void count (charq[]) {int let, dig, other, I, l; char c; //     2
   i=o; let=0; dig=0; other=0; l=strlen(q); /* init */   //     3
   while (i<l) {                            /* t     */  //     4
      c=q[i];                               /* b0     */ //     5
      if ('A'≤c && 'Z'>c) let=+2;           /* c1, b1 */ //     6
      else                                              //     7
      if ('a'≤c && 'z'≥c) let=+1;           /* c2, b2 */ //     8
      else                                              //     9
      if ('0'≤c && '9'≥c) dig=+1;           /* c3, b3 */ //    10
      else                                              //    11
         other+=1;                          /* b4     */ //    12
      i++;}                                 /* inc    */ //    13
   printf("%d %d %d\n", let, dig, other);} /* print */  //    14
```

Using the abbreviations given in the comments (between /* and */), we can rewrite this program as follows:

```
{init;
While(t) {b0; if (c1) {b1} else if (c2) {b2} else if (c3) {b3}
else b4; inc};
Print;}
```

We can rewrite this program at a finer grain (by decomposing conditions into their conjuncts, for example) or at a coarser grain (by coalescing statements into larger blocks), depending on the precision with which we wish to identify/localize faults. The definition of a fault, which we give below, is based on two assumptions:

1. First, we are not questioning the structure of the program; rather we are only questioning the correctness of each part thereof. If we feel that the structure may be at fault, then we need to rewrite the program at a coarser level of granularity.
2. Second, the designation of a particular program part as faulty is somewhat discretionary: we are assuming for a moment that other components are not in question and pondering whether modifying the selected component will make the program more-correct. This explains why we refer to these faults as *contingent* faults: They are faulty if we assume for the time being that other parts are not; also once the designated fault is corrected, the existence, number, location, and nature of other faults may change.

Whence the following definition.

Definition: Contingent Fault *We let R be a specification on space S and we let p be a program on space S, which is written at some level of granularity as* $p = C(p_1, p_2, p_3, \ldots, p_i, \ldots, p_n)$. *We say that p_i is a* contingent fault *(or simply a* fault*) in program p with respect to specification R if and only if there exists a program component p'_i such that the program p' defined by* $p' = C(p_1, p_2, p_3, \ldots, p'_i, \ldots, p_n)$ *is strictly-more-correct with respect to R than p.*

Note that we require that p' be strictly-more-correct than p; it is not sufficient that it be merely more-correct. The reason for this requirement is that if we accepted that p' be more-correct than p, then any statement of p will be considered a fault—of course we do not want that; we want to consider as faults statements whose modification leads to an effective increase in the competence domain of the program.

As an illustration, we consider the program above and investigate its faults with respect to the following specification:

$$R = \{(s, s') \mid q \in list(char) \wedge os' = os \oplus \#_A(q) \oplus \#_0(q) \oplus \#_\#(q)\},$$

where:

- *os* designates the output stream of the program (declared by the **#include<iostream>** statement),
- $\oplus$ represents concatenation,
- $\#_A(q)$, $\#_0(q)$, $\#_\#(q)$ designate, respectively, the number of alphabetic characters, numeric characters, and special symbols in array q.

We argue *b1* is a fault in p with respect to R; to this effect, we must offer an alternative statements *b1'* that makes the set $dom(R \cap P)$ larger. We propose $b1' =$ (let+=1;) and we show that this yields a more-correct program. We find,

$$dom(R \cap P) = \{s \mid q \in list(char/CHAR)\},$$

where CHAR represents the set of upper case alphabetical characters. Indeed, this program works correctly with respect to R as long as the input sequence does not include any upper case letters: all upper case letters from "A" to "Y" are counted twice in *let*, and "Z" is counted as a special character (variable other) rather an alphabetical character (let). As for program p', which is obtained by changing b1 into b1', we find

$$dom(R \cap P') = \{s \mid q \in list(char/'Z')\}.$$

Indeed, now the program counts the number of all upper case letters properly, except for "Z"; as it is written, the program counts occurrences of "Z" as special characters (variable *others*), rather than alphabetical characters (variable *let*). Clearly, we do have

$$dom(R \cap P') \supset dom(R \cap P),$$

hence p' is strictly-more-correct than p and hence *b1* is a contingent fault.

6.3.2 Monotonic Fault Removal

All programmers have war stories about a program that was running fine until they made a slight alteration to its code thinking they were improving it, when all of a sudden it started behaving erratically. Yet, fixing programs is supposed to make them behave better, nor worse. Whence the following definition.

Definition: Monotonic Fault Removal *We let R be a specification on space S and we let p be a program on space S, which is written at some level of granularity as:* $p = (p_1, p_2, p_3, \ldots, p_i, \ldots, p_n)$. *We assume that p_i is a fault in program p with respect to specification R and we let component p_i' be a program component on S. We say that the replacement of p_i by p_i' constitutes a* <u>monotonic fault removal</u> *if and only if* *the program p' defined by* $p' = C(p_1, p_2, p_3, \ldots, p'_i, \ldots, p_n)$ *is strictly-more-correct with respect to R than program p.*

Note the distinction between being a *fault*, which is a unary property that characterizes a component of program p, and being a monotonic fault removal, which is a binary property, that characterizes a faulty program part and its candidate substitution. Just because p_i is a fault does not mean that any p'_i we substitute it with will be a monotonic fault removal. In other words, the fact that p_i is a fault means that there exists (at least one) p'_i that will make p' more-correct than p. To obtain a monotonic fault removal we need to find such a p'_i, whereas to prove that p_i is a fault, it suffices to prove that such a p'_i exists.

As an illustration of the concept of monotonic fault removals, we consider again the program introduced in Section 6.3.1, and we let p″ be the program obtained from p′ by substituting condition c1 by c1′ defined as:

$$('A' \le c) \,\&\&\, ('Z' \ge c).$$

Because this program is correct with respect to R, we know that $dom(R \cap P'') = dom(R)$, which we write as:

$$dom(R \cap P'') = \{s \mid q \in list(char)\}.$$

For the sake of comparison, we also write the domains of correctness of programs p and p':

$$dom(R \cap P) = \{s \mid q \in list(char/CHAR)\},$$
$$dom(R \cap P') = \{s \mid q \in list(char/'Z')\}.$$

Clearly, we have

$$dom(R \cap P) \subset dom(R \cap P') \subset dom(R \cap P'') = dom(R).$$

Hence the transition from program p to program p″ via program p′ is uniformly monotonic: with each fault removal, we obtain a more-correct program, until all faults are removed and we get a correct program.

Let us consider for a moment the case when we remove faults in reverse order: let $p°$ be the program obtained from p by changing condition $c1$ into condition $c1'$ defined as above:

$$('A' \le c) \,\&\&\, ('Z' \ge c).$$

We write below the domain of correctness of this program:

$$dom(R \cap P°) = \{s \mid q \in list(char/CHAR)\}.$$

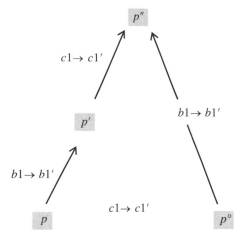

Figure 6.3 *Ordering candidate programs by relative correctness.*

Because this is not a strict superset of the domain of correctness of p with respect to R, the transition from p to p° does not represent a monotonic fault removal. However, if we take program p° and change statement $b1$ therein into $b1' =$ (let+=1), we find program p″, which is strictly-more-correct than p°. Whereas the transition from p to p″ via p' is uniformly monotonic, the transition from p to p″ via p° is not, because p° is not strictly-more-correct than p. These relations are illustrated in Figure 6.3.

As another illustrative example, consider the following specification on space S = natural:

$$R = \left\{ (s, s') \mid s' \bmod 7 = \left(s^2 \bmod 3 + 8\right) \bmod 7 \right\}.$$

And we consider the following three programs:

```
p  = {s= 2*s; s= s mod 6; s= s+8;}
p' = {s= 2*s; s= s mod 3; s= s+8;}
p" = {s= s^2; s= s mod 3; s= s+8;}
```

We find that p is not correct with respect to R. Indeed,

$$dom(R \cap P) = \left\{ s \mid 2s \bmod 6 = s^2 \bmod 3 \right\},$$

while $dom(R)=S$. We conjecture that the statement $\{$ s= s mod 6 ; $\}$ is a contingent fault; to prove our claim, we consider program p', where this statement is replaced by $\{$ s= s mod 3 ; $\}$ and we prove that p' is strictly-more-correct than p with respect to R. To this effect, we compare the competence domains of programs p and p′. We find:

$$dom(R \cap P') = \left\{ s \mid 2s \bmod 3 = s^2 \bmod 3 \right\}.$$

We argue that $dom(R \cap P) \subset dom(R \cap P')$, since if $2s \, mod6 = s^2 mod3$, then $2s \, mod6$ is necessarily between 0 and 2, in which case $2s \, mod6$ is identical to $2s \, mod3$. Hence p' is strictly-more-correct than p: indeed, p' stems from p by replacing the statement $\{s= s \, mod \, 6 ; \}$ by the statement $\{s= s \, mod \, 3 ; \}$. But we are not out of the woods yet: Program p' is not correct with respect to R since the expression of the domain of competence of p', which is evaluated above, is not equal to the domain of R, which is S. We consider statement $\{s= 2*s ; \}$ in program g', and we resolve to replace it with statement $\{s= s*s ; \}$, yielding program p''. We find that p'' is correct with respect to R, since we have:

$$dom(R \cap P'') = dom(R).$$

The following table shows, for some values of the initial state s, the final states delivered by programs p, p', and p''; we also show, by a shaded box, whether each program behaves correctly with respect to specification R. Note that while p behaves correctly once out of three times (whenever s is a multiple of 3), and while program p' behaves correctly twice out of three times (whenever s is a multiple of 3, or 2 plus a multiple of 3), program p'' behaves correctly with respect to R every time (for all initial states).

s	P		P'		P''	
	Value	Correct?	Value	Correct?	Value	Correct?
0	8		8		8	
1	10		10		9	
2	12		9		9	
3	8		8		8	
4	10		10		9	
5	12		9		9	
6	8		8		8	
7	10		10		9	
8	12		9		9	
9	8		8		8	
10	10		10		9	
11	12		9		9	
12	8		8		8	
13	10		10		9	

We have moved from program p to program p'' via program p' by successive transitions that yielded more and more correct programs; but things are not always so smooth. If instead of changing the second statement of program p (from $\{s= s \bmod 6;\}$ to $\{s= s \bmod 3;\}$) before the first (from $\{s= 2*x;\}$ to $\{s= s*s;\}$), we changed the first statement first, we would have obtained the following program, which we denote by p^o:

```
{s= s*s; s= s mod 6; s= s+8;}.
```

We are unable to prove that p^o is more-correct than p, and for good reason: the table below shows that it is not, since the column that corresponds to p^o does not subsume the column that corresponds to P.

s	P		p^o		P''	
	Value	Correct?	Value	Correct?	Value	Correct?
0	8		8		8	
1	10		9		9	
2	12		12		9	
3	8		11		8	
4	10		12		9	
5	12		9		9	
6	8		8		8	
7	10		9		9	
8	12		12		9	
9	8		11		8	
10	10		12		9	
11	12		9		9	
12	8		8		8	
13	10		9		9	

We conclude this section by asking a simple question: do all fault removals have to be monotonic in practice? As we can see from the transitions from p to p^o in the two examples above, a substitution may be perfectly reasonable in the sense that it is bringing the program (syntactically) closer to being correct, and yet not produce a monotonic fault removal. While ideally it would be desirable if every substitution produced a monotonic fault removal, those that do not ought to be part of a sequence of substitutions that, together, yield a strictly-more-correct program. This is the case for the transition from p to p'' via p^o in the two examples above.

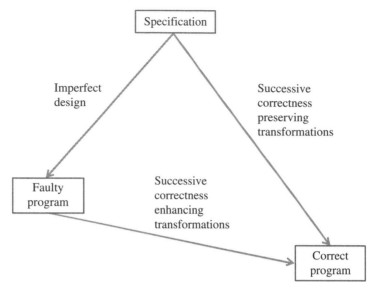

Figure 6.4 *A framework for monotonic fault removal.*

6.3.3 A Framework for Monotonic Fault Removal

The discussion of monotonic fault removal leads us to consider a logical framework for software testing that mimics/parallels the well-known frameworks of program derivation:

- In the same way that refinement calculi provide us with a mathematical framework for program derivation by successive *correctness-preserving* transformations starting from specifications and culminating in a correct program,
- we argue that relative correctness provides us with a mathematical framework for fault removal by means of successive *correctness-enhancing* transformations starting in an incorrect program and culminating in a correct program.

This framework is illustrated in Figure 6.4.

6.3.4 Definite Faults

Let us consider the following program, which is obtained from the program discussed in Section 6.3.1 by changing c1 into c1′, as discussed above:

```
#include <iostream> ... ... ...                          //  line 1
void count (charq[]) {int let, dig, other, I, 1;
   char c;                                               //  2
  i=o; let=0; dig=0; other=0;
   l=strlen(q);                         /* init  */  //  3
  While (i<1) {                         /* t     */  //  4
```

```
c=q[i];                              /* b0       */  // 5
if ('A'≤c && 'Z'≥c) let=+2;          /* c1', b1*/   // 6
else                                                 // 7
if ('a'≤c && 'z'≥c) let=+1;          /* c2, b2  */   // 8
else                                                 // 9
if ('0'≤c && '9'≥c) dig=+1;          /* c3, b3  */   // 10
else                                                 // 11
   other+=1;                         /* b4      */    // 12
i++;}                                /* inc     */    // 13
printf("%d %d %d\n", let, dig, other);} /* print */  // 14
```

If we are interested to make this program correct with respect to specification R, defined by

$$R = (s,s') \mid q \in list(char) \wedge os' = os \oplus \#_A(q) \oplus \#_0(q) \oplus \#_\#(q)\},$$

we can do so by changing $b1$ into $b1'$ defined as (let+=1;). But we can also correct it by changing $b2$ into $b2'$ defined as (let+=2), and changing *print* into *print'* defined as (printf("%d %d %d\n", let/2, dig, other);). Alternatively, we can correct it by changing $b2$ into $b2'$ and adding a statement between lines 13 and 14 that divides *let* be 2. Our point is that there is some degree of discretion in designating faults: often, a statement can be considered faulty only if we resolve, arbitrarily, to assume that other parts of the program are not; this is why we refer to this type of faults as *contingent* faults. Yet there are cases where we do not get the luxury to decide which parts of the program to question and which parts to absolve; whence the following definition.

Definition: Definite Fault *We let R be a specification on space S and we let p be a program on space S, which is written at some level of granularity as $p = C(p_1, p_2, p_3, \ldots, p_i, \ldots, p_n)$. We say that p_i is a definite fault in program p with respect to specification R if and only if for all $p'_1, p'_2, ..p'_{i-1}, p'_{i+1}, \ldots p'_n$, the program p' defined as $C(p'_1, p'_2, p'_3, \ldots, p_i, \ldots, p'_n)$ is not correct with respect to R.*

In other words, component p_i is single-handedly precluding program p from being correct: assuming that the program structure (defined by C) is not in question (only the components of the structure are), no change to the program that preserves p_i can make the program correct with respect to R. We consider two simple situations where definite faults are easy to characterize; we briefly review them in turn, below. In both cases, we do not present any theory but rather content ourselves with offering a simple illustrative example; also in both cases we take a simple sequential structure for program p.

6.3.4.1 *Loss of Injectivity*

Let S be the set of natural numbers and let R be the specification defined on space S by:

$$R = \{(s,s') \mid s' = 5 + s \, mod \, 6\}.$$

We let p be a program of the form $p = \{p_1; p_2\}$ and we consider a number of possibilities for p_1:

- $p_1 = \{s = s \% 6;\}$. Then p_2 may be $\{s=s+5;\}$.
- $p_1 = \{s = s+6;\}$. Then p_2 may be $\{s = 5 + s \% 6;\}$.
- $p_1 = \{s = s+5;\}$. Then p_2 may be $\{s = 5 + (s-5) \% 6;\}$
- $p_1 = \{s = s \% 12;\}$. Then p_2 may be $\{s = 5 + s \% 6;\}$.

But if we choose $p_1 = \{s = s \% 3\}$, then no function p_2 can salvage the state of the program and produce a correct outcome; knowing the value of (s mod 3) does not inform us on the value of (s mod 6), yet we need this information to ensure a successful execution. Hence component $p1$ is definitely faulty because program p cannot be correct with respect to R unless p_1 is changed.

6.3.4.2 Loss of Surjectivity

We consider space S defined as the set of naturals and we let R be the following relation on S:

$$R = \left\{ (s,s') \mid s' = s^2 mod 6 \right\}.$$

We let p be a program of the form $p = \{p_1; p_2\}$ and we consider a number of possibilities for p_2:

- $p_2 = \{s = s \% 6;\}$. Then p_1 may be $\{s=s*s;\}$.
- $p_2 = \{s = (s+5) \% 6;\}$. Then p_1 may be $\{s = s*s-5;\}$.

But if we choose $p_2 = \{s = s \% 3\}$, then there is nothing that function p_1 can do to make up for the loss of surjectivity inflicted by p_2. Unlike the first two examples, the third example of p_2 has caused a loss of surjectivity beyond what R can tolerate (the range of R is the interval $[0..5]$ whereas the range of P_2 is $[0..2]$). We say that p_2 is a definite fault because there is nothing that p_1 can do to ensure that $p = \{p_1; p_2\}$ is correct with respect to R.

6.4 FAULT MANAGEMENT

6.4.1 Lines of Defense

Programs fail to be correct or reliable because they have faults. Hence any effort to improve reliability and/or to enhance the probability of correctness ought to focus on faults. Ways to deal with faults are traditionally divided into three broad categories:

1. *Fault Avoidance*. Methods that fall under the header of fault avoidance focus on developing software products that are free of faults by construction. These methods use the type of techniques that we discuss in Chapter 5 to verify that

programs are correct as they are constructed. More sophisticated methods turn the verification techniques around to generate methods for developing programs from specifications, by stepwise manipulation of the specification, in a way that ensures the correctness of the final program by construction, rather than by inspection; some models of program construction cast the task of program derivation as a calculation involving the target specification and a design that is taking shape as design decisions are taken. The main difficulty with fault avoidance methods is that they do not scale up easily or reliably to large scale development.

2. *Fault Removal*. If we cannot avoid faults at program construction, perhaps we can try to remove them once the program is developed; this is the philosophy of fault removal methods and the focus of software testing. Fault removal methods face two obstacles in practice:

   - First, we can never be sure that we have removed all the faults in a program; the methods discussed in Chapter 5 are intended to ensure the absence of faults, to the extent that they scale up to programs of realistic size.

   - Second, we can never be sure that while removing one fault we are not inadvertently introducing others. The framework of monotonic fault removal introduced in this chapter is intended to ensure that the programs become increasingly more-correct with each fault removal, to the extent that it can scale up to programs of significant size and complexity.

     One way to increase the effectiveness of fault removal is to ensure that we target the most egregious faults first, that is, those that have the greatest (negative) effect on reliability, to maximize the return on investment on the fault removal effort; also it is generally agreed that a software may be reliable despite having faults, provided the residual faults have a low impact on reliability.

3. *Fault Tolerance*. If we can neither avoid faults as we develop software products, nor remove them from the product after development, we ought to tolerate them and learn to live with them. Fault tolerance consists in admitting the presence of faults in operating software products but taking steps to ensure that faults do not cause failures. This is possible if we monitor program states for any sign that a fault has caused an error and we intervene upon detecting an error to ensure that we avoid failure. Fault tolerance includes run-time steps, namely error detection, damage assessment, and error recovery; it also includes off-line steps, which are to analyze error reports to diagnose the fault that may have caused the error.

Each of these three families of methods has its strengths and weaknesses. The *Law of Diminishing Returns* advocates using them in concert, deploying each one where it is most effective. The focus of this book is on fault removal, but we may overstep the boundaries of fault removal to the extent that program testing includes any technique that involves observing and analyzing the behavior of candidate programs in execution.

6.4.2   Hybrid Validation

According to the foregoing discussion, it is advantageous to deploy more than one method of verification, by virtue of the law of diminishing returns; according to this law, each method offers high returns on some aspects of verification and lower returns on others. If we deploy different methods that offer high returns on complementary aspects, then we can afford the luxury of applying each method where its returns are high. As a simple illustration of this philosophy, we consider the following algorithm for selection sort. While this algorithm is fairly straightforward, one may be forgiven for having some doubt that it is correct; some examples are as follows: Are all the indices initialized properly? Are they incremented properly? Are they tested properly, against the right boundaries? Are the inequalities correct (strict or large)? Does this algorithm work for N=1?

```
void somesort (itemtype a[MaxSize], indextype N)      // line 1
{                                                      // 2
   indextype i; i=0;                                   // 3
      while (i<=N-2)                                    // 4
      {indextype j; indextype mindx; itemtype minval;  // 5
       j=i; mindx=j; minval=a[j];                      // 6
      while (j<=N-1)                                    // 7
         {if (a[j]<minval) {mindx=j; minval=a[j];}     // 8
          j++;}                                         // 9
      itemtype temp;                                   // 10
      temp=a[i]; a[i]=a[mindx]; a[mindx]=temp;         // 11
      i++;}                                             // 12
}                                                      // 13
```

To lift these doubts, one may want to use the technique discussed in Chapter 5; to this effect, we would have to derive a precondition and a postcondition for this routine. To check that the function sorts array *a*, we would write the following precondition/postcondition pair:

- Precondition: $\phi(s) \equiv (s=s0)$.
- Postcondition: $\psi(s) \equiv prm(s,s0) \wedge sorted(s)$,

where *prm(s,s0)* means that array *a* is a permutation of array *a0*, and *sorted(s)* means that array *a* is sorted.

Applying the proof technique presented in Chapter 5 involves a few pages of proof, and requires the invention of several intermediate assertions, and two invariant assertions, one for each loop. Any wrong choice of an intermediate assertion or an invariant assertion will leave us in limbo, unsure whether the program is incorrect or our choice of assertion is inappropriate. On the other hand, if we wanted to test this program using the same specification as an oracle, then we would have to write a Boolean function that checks whether the final array is a permutation of the initial array; such a Boolean function is difficult to write and is perhaps more complex and more error prone than writing the sort algorithm itself.

As an alternative, we choose to prove the correctness of the program with respect to $prm(s,s0)$ and to test the program using the oracle $sorted(s)$. As far as proving the correctness of the program with respect to $prm(s,s0)$, it suffices to consider that the only location in the program where array a is changed at all, is line 11, where cells a[i] and a [mindx] are swapped. Swapping two cells of an array preserves the property $prm(s,s0)$, hence this specification is satisfied. Specifically, we would define the following precondition/postcondition pair:

- Precondition: $\phi(s) \equiv (s=s0)$,
- Postcondition: $\psi(s) \equiv prm(s,s0)$,

which would yield the following verification condition:

v: $\{s=s0\}$
```
indextype i; i=0;
  while (i<=N-2)
  {indextype j; indextype mindx; itemtype minval;
   j=i; mindx=j; minval=a[j];
  while (j<=N-1)
    {if (a[j]<minval) {mindx=j; minval=a[j];}
     j++;}
  itemtype temp;
  temp=a[i]; a[i]=a[mindx]; a[mindx]=temp;
  i++;}
```

$\{prm(s,s0)\}$

By virtue of the consequence rule, we derive the following verification condition:

v0: $\{prm(s,s0)\}$
```
indextype i; i=0;
  while (i<=N-2)
  {indextype j; indextype mindx; itemtype minval;
   j=i; mindx=j; minval=a[j];
  while (j<=N-1)
    {if (a[j]<minval) {mindx=j; minval=a[j];}
     j++;}
  itemtype temp;
  temp=a[i]; a[i]=a[mindx]; a[mindx]=temp;
  i++;}
```

$\{prm(s,s0)\}$

We can easily verify this formula, using *prm(s,s0)* as an intermediate assertion and an invariant assertion throughout the program (it is preserved vacuously since most statements do not affect array *a*), until we generate the verification condition: w: {*prm(s,s0)*} **temp=a[i]; a[i]=a[mindx]; a[mindx]=temp;** {*prm(s,s0)*} which we assume to hold since all it does is to permute two cells of array *a*.

Now, to test this routine for specification *sorted(s)*, we write the following test driver:

```cpp
#include <iostream>
#include <fstream>
#include <string>
#include <iomanip>
#include "rand.cpp"
using namespace std;

// types
typedef int itemtype;
typedef int indextype;

// constants
const indextype MaxSize = 60;
const itemtype ValueRange = 200;
const int TestLength = 10000;

// variables, current state
indextype N;
itemtype a [MaxSize];

// working variables
int testnumber=0;   // counting tests
int nbfail = 0;     // counting failures
string tf="testfile.dat";

// function headers
int drawint (int ValueRange);
void generatetestdata (itemtype a [MaxSize], indextype& N);
bool moretests ();
void testreport ();

// program and specification/ oracle
void somesort (itemtype a[MaxSize], int N);  // any sorting
                                             algorithm
bool Oracle(itemtype a [MaxSize], indextype N);
```

```
fstream teststream (tf.data(), ios::out);

int main ()
{SetSeed(684);   // random value
Iwhile (moretests())
  {generatetestdata (a,N);
  somesort (a,N);
  if (!Oracle(a,N)){nbfail=nbfail+1;}};
testreport();}

int drawint (int ValueRange)
  {int val; val = 1+ int(NextRand()*ValueRange);
  return val;}

void generatetestdata (itemtype a [MaxSize], indextype& N)
  {N = drawint(MaxSize);
  for (int k=0; k<N; k++) {a[k]=drawint(ValueRange);}}

bool Oracle(itemtype a[MaxSize], indextype N)
  {bool sorted; sorted=true;
  for (int k=0; k<N-1; k++) {sorted = sorted && (a[k]<=
    a[k+1]);};
  return sorted;}
```

The oracle of this test is very simple, since it merely checks that the current array is sorted. Also because this test driver is written on the basis of the specification of a sorting algorithm, it can be applied to any sorting function; it is not specific to the selection sort.

Execution of the test driver on the selection sort function, generating ten thousand random arrays of random size between 1 and 60, of random values between 1 and 200, yields no failure. While we have not proven that the program has no faults, we have shown that if it does have faults, they do not appear to be causing frequent failures; this does not prove that the program never fails but makes it unlikely that failure is frequent. We have reached this conclusion with relatively little effort.

6.5 CHAPTER SUMMARY

The most important ideas to remember from this chapter are the following:

- The hierarchy of fault, error, and failure, and the cause–effect relationships between them; also the concepts of fault sensitization, error masking, error propagation.
- The difference between failure with respect to the intended function versus failure with respect to the relevant specification. To the extent that the intended

function is just an example of (highly refined) specification, it is important to remember that failure, error, and fault are all defined with respect to a specification.

- The concept of relative correctness and its intuitive significance.
- The concept of contingent fault and what the attribute of contingent refers to; the concept of definite fault and their intuitive significance.
- The classification of software improvement methods according to how they deal with the presence and possible sensitization of faults.
- The law of diminishing returns and its application in dealing with faults.

6.6 EXERCISES

6.1. Consider the second sample example presented in Section 6.1, with space S defined as the set of natural variables, the specification R, and the intended function π, defined by:

$$R = \left\{ (s,s') \mid s' mod\, 3 = (s+1)^2 mod3 \right\}.$$

$$\pi = \left\{ (s,s') \mid s' = (s+1)^2 mod\, 3 \right\}.$$

a. Show that π refines R.
b. Show that p1: {s=s+1; s=s*s; s=s%3; s=s+12} is correct with respect to R.
c. Show that p2: {s=s+1; s=s*s; s=s%6; s=s+12} is correct with respect to R.
d. Show that p1: {s=s+4; s=s*s; s=s%3; s=s+12} is correct with respect to R.

6.2. Consider the sample program given in Section 6.3.1 and the following specification; tell if the program has any faults; if you believe it does, show that they are faults, using relevant definitions.

$$R = \{(s,s') \mid q \in list(char/CHAR) \wedge os' = os \oplus \#_A(q) \oplus \#_0(q) \oplus \#_\#(q)\},$$

6.3. Consider the sample program given in Section 6.3.1 and the following specification; tell if the program has any faults; if you believe it does, show that they are faults, using relevant definitions.

$$R = \{(s,s') \mid q \in list(char') \wedge os' = os \oplus \#_A(q) \oplus \#_0(q) \oplus \#_\#(q)\},$$

where *char'* is the set of all ascii characters excluding lower case alphabetic characters. Consider that in this case the print statement (line 14) may be considered a fault (if only we printed *let/2* rather than *let*).

6.4. Consider the sample program given in Section 6.3.1 and the following specification; tell if the program has any faults; if you believe it does, show that they are faults, using relevant definitions.

$$R = \{(s, s') \mid q \in list(char' / 'Z') \wedge os' = os \oplus \#_A(q) \oplus \#_0(q) \oplus \#_\#(q)\},$$

where $char'$ is the set of all ascii characters excluding lower case alphabetic characters.

6.5. Consider the sample program given in Section 6.3.1 and the following specification; tell if the program has any faults; if you believe it does, show that they are faults, using relevant definitions.

$$R = \{(s, s') \mid q \in list(char') \wedge tail^2(os') = \#_0(q) \wedge tail(os') = \#_\#(q)\},$$

where $char'$ is the set of all ascii characters excluding lower case alphabetic characters and operation $tail^n(os)$ represents the nth most recently written element of stream os.

6.6. Consider the sample program given in Section 6.3.1 and the following specification; tell if the program has any faults; if you believe it does, show that they are faults, using the relevant definitions.

$$R = \{(s, s') \mid q \in list(char) \wedge tail^2(os') = \#_0(q)\},$$

where $char$ is the set of all ascii characters and operation $tail^n(os)$ represents the nth most recently written element of stream os.

6.7. Apply the method discussed in Section 6.4.2 to an insertion sort function.

6.8. Apply the method discussed in Section 6.4.2 to a quick sort function.

6.7 PROBLEMS

6.1. In the definition of contingent fault, we have assumed that faults involve a single component. Show on the sample program of Section 6.3.1 that there are cases when more than one component must be considered as the locus of a fault. What impact does this new definition have on the concept of monotonic fault removal? Can all fault removals be monotonic?

6.2. Let $p1$ and $p2$ be two programs on space S and let $P1$ and $P2$ be their respective functions. Show that if $P1$ refines $P2$, then $p1$ is more-correct than $p2$ with respect to any specification R. Show that if $p1$ is more-correct than $p2$ with respect to any specification R, then $P1$ refines $P2$.

6.8 BIBLIOGRAPHIC NOTES

The hierarchy of faults, errors, and failures is due to Laprie et al. (Laprie, 1992, 1995; Avizienis et al., 2004). The concepts of relative correctness, contingent fault, and definite fault are due to Mili et al. (2014); an earlier analysis of the concept of fault is due to Offutt and Hayes (1996).

7

A Software Testing Taxonomy

7.1 THE TROUBLE WITH HYPHENATED TESTING

When reading about software testing, we often encounter types of testing that include such samples as black box testing, white box testing, unit testing, system testing, regression testing, mutation testing, stress testing, and so on. The trouble with this list is that the qualifiers that we put before testing refer to different attributes of the testing activity: depending on the case, they may refer to a test data selection criterion, or to the scale of the asset under test, or to the assumptions of the test activity, or to the product attribute being tested, and so on. The purpose of this chapter is to classify software testing activities in a systematic manner, using orthogonal dimensions; like all classifications schemes, ours aims to capture in a simple abstraction a potentially complex set of related attributes. A software testing activity can be characterized by a number of interdependent attributes; in order to build an orthogonal classification scheme, we must select a set of independent attributes that is sufficiently small so that its elements are indeed independent, yet sufficiently large to cover all classes of interest. In Section 7.2, we introduce this classification scheme, by identifying the set of attributes that we use for the purpose of classification, along with the secondary attributes that depend on these. In Section 7.3, we consider a number of important testing activities, analyze how they can be projected on our classification scheme, and discuss what inferred attributes they have by virtue of their classification.

Software Testing: Concepts and Operations, First Edition. Ali Mili and Fairouz Tchier.
© 2015 John Wiley & Sons, Inc. Published 2015 by John Wiley & Sons, Inc.

7.2 A CLASSIFICATION SCHEME

While all testing activities consist in executing a software product on selected input data, observing its outputs and analyzing the outcome of the experiment, there is a wide variance in how testing is conducted, depending, broadly, on the goal of the test, the asset under test, the circumstances of the test, and the assumptions being made about the product and its environment. We identify four independent attributes of a software testing activity, and seven dependent attributes. We refer to the first set as primary attributes and refer to the second set as secondary attributes.

- The primary attributes of a software testing activity are as follows:
  - *Scale*: This refers to the scale of the product under test, and can be a module, a subsystem, a system, and so on.
  - *Goal*: There is a wide range of reasons why one may want to test a program, including finding faults, estimating the number of faults, estimating the reliability of the product, improving the reliability of the product, certifying that the product exceeds some reliability threshold, and so on.
  - *Property*: While testing is most often used to check functional properties of software assets and systems, it may also be used to assess their average performance, their performance under stress, their robustness, and so on.
  - *Method*: This attribute refers to the method that is used to generate test data and can, broadly, take three possible values; one may choose test data by considering the specifications (to cover all services, all functions, all circumstances) or by considering the software product (to exercise all components, all interfaces, all data flows, all control flows, etc.) or by random data generation, possibly adhering to a usage pattern (defined by a probability distribution).
- Once these primary attributes are selected, a number of secondary attributes fall in place in a nearly deterministic manner. We identify the following secondary attributes:
  - *Oracle*: The oracle of a test is the agent that determines, for each execution, whether the outcome of the execution is consistent with the correctness of the product under test. The oracle of a test depends first and foremost on the property that we want to prove: while most typically we want to test the functional properties of a program, we may also want to test some operational attribute; clearly, the oracle depends on this choice. Also, for a given property, the oracle depends on the goal that we want to achieve through the test; the more ambitious the goal, the stronger the oracle.
  - *Test life cycle*: The life cycle of a test is the set of phases that the test has to proceed through. As such, the life cycle depends, of course, on goal of the test; it also depends on the property being tested and on the method being deployed to generate test data.
  - *Test assumptions*: Each test makes assumptions about the product, what may or may not be at fault, and to what extent the test environment mimics the operating environment of the software product.

○ *Test completion*: Test completion is the condition under which the test activity is deemed to have achieved its goal. Of course, this attribute depends heavily on what the goal is, and consequently on what product property is being tested.

○ *Required artifacts*: To plan and conduct a test, one may need any combination of the source code, the executable code, the specification of the product, the intended function of the product, the intended properties of the product, the design documentation of the product, the test data, and so on. This is heavily dependent on the goal of the test, the property being tested, and the test data generation method.

○ *Stakeholders*: Different testing activities throughout the software life cycle involve different stakeholders/ participants, such as developers, designers, specifiers, users, verification and validation teams, quality assurance teams, and so on. This attribute depends on the goal of the test as well as the scale of the software product, and the phase of the software life cycle where the test takes place.

○ *Test environment*: The environment of a test is the set of interfaces that the product under test interacts with as it executes. A software product may be tested in a variety of environments, depending on the scale of the product and the phase of the life cycle: the development environment, the operating environment, or a simulation of the operating environment.

○ *Position in the life cycle*: Each phase of the software life cycle lends itself to a verification step, which can be carried out through testing. The position in the life cycle affects the scale of the asset to be tested, and thereby affects all the other primary attributes (goal, property, and method).

In Sections 7.2.1 and 7.2.2, we review in turn the primary then the secondary attributes, by discussing what values each attribute may take, and any dependencies that each value entails.

7.2.1 Primary Attributes

We consider four primary attributes: the scale, the goal, the property, and the method. We review these in turn in the following:

The Scale: We consider three possible values for this attribute:

- *A unit*: This represents a programming unit that implements a data abstraction or a functional abstraction. As such, it can be a class in an object-oriented language, the implementation of an abstract data type, or a routine.

- *A subsystem*: This represents a component in an integrated software system. To test such a component in a credible manner, we may have to run the whole system and observe the behavior of this particular component within the system. This situation arises in the context of maintenance, for example, where we may change a component and then test the whole system to check whether the changes are satisfactory, and whether the new subsystem works smoothly within the overall system.

- *A system*: This represents a complete autonomous software system.

The Goal: This is perhaps the most important attribute of a test. The values it may take include the following:

- *Finding and removing faults*: The most common goal of software testing is to observe the behavior of the program on test data, and to diagnose and remove faults whenever the program fails to satisfy its specification.
- *Proving the absence of faults/certifying compliance with quality standards*: While in practice it is virtually impossible to test a program on all possible combinations of inputs and configurations, this possibility cannot be excluded in theory. Also, we can imagine cases where the set of possible input data is small, or cases where we can design a test data D such that if the program runs successfully on D, then it runs successfully on all the input space S.
- *Estimating fault density*: Software testing can be used to estimate the fault density of a product, as will be discussed in Chapter 13. This is done by seeding faults, then running a test to compute how many seeded faults have been recovered and how many unseeded faults have been uncovered; fault density can then be estimated by interpolation.
- *Estimating the frequency of failures*: While the previous goals are concerned with faults, this and the next goal are concerned with failures instead; there is a sound rationale for focusing on failures rather than faults, because it is better to reason about observable/relevant effects than about hypothetical causes. To pursue this goal, we run the software product under conditions that simulate its operational environment, and estimate its failure rate; the estimate is reliable only to the extent that the test environment is a faithful reflection of the operating environment, and that the test data reflects, in its distribution, the usage pattern of the software product. It is only under such conditions that the failure rate observed during testing can be borne out during field usage. We identify three possible instances of this goal, depending on whether we want to estimate the reliability, the safety, or the security of the product:
  - ○ *Estimating reliability*
  - ○ *Estimating safety*
  - ○ *Estimating security*

  We get one instance or another, depending on the oracle that we use for the test: To estimate reliability, we use the functional specifications of the software product; to estimate safety, we use the safety-critical requirements of the product; to estimate security, we use the security requirements of the product.
- *Ensuring the infrequency of failures*: As an alternative to proving the absence of faults, we may want to prove that faults are not causing frequent failures; after all, a program may have faults and still be reliable, or more generally experience infrequent failure. Also, as an alternative to estimating the frequency of failures, we may simply establish that the frequency of failure is lower than a required

threshold. Whereas estimating the frequency of failure is a mere analytical process, that analyzes the product as it is, ensuring the infrequency of failures may involve diagnosing and removing faults until the frequency of failures of the software product is deemed to be lower than the mandated threshold. As we argued in the last item, in order for the estimate of the failure rate to be reliable, the software product must be tested in an environment that mimics its operating environment, and the test data must be distributed according to the usage pattern of the product in the field. Also, this goal admits three instances, depending on what oracle is used in the test:

- *Certifying reliability*
- *Certifying security*
- *Certifying safety*

We get one instance or another, depending on the oracle that we use for the test.

Method: Given a limited amount of resources (time, manpower, and budget), we cannot run the software product on the set S of all possible input data; as a substitute, we want to run the software product on a set of test data, say D (a subset of S), that is large enough to help us achieve our goal, yet small enough to minimize costs. The test data generation method is the process that enables us to derive set D according to our goal; the criterion that we use to derive D from S depends on the goal of the test, as follows:

- If the goal of the test is to diagnose and remove faults, then D should cause the maximum number of failures, that is, uncover/sensitize the maximum number of faults.
- If the goal of the test is to prove correctness, then D should be chosen in such a way that if the program runs successfully on D, we can be reasonably confident (or assured) that it runs successfully on all of S.
- If the goal of the test is to estimate the product's failure rate or to ensure that the product's failure rate exceeds a mandated threshold, then D must be a representative sample of the usage pattern of the product.

Test data generation methods are usually divided into three broad families:

- *Structural methods*, which generate test data by analyzing the structure of the software product and targeting the data in such a way as to exercise relevant components of the product.
- *Functional methods*, which generate test data by analyzing the specification of the software product or its intended function, and targeting the data in such a way as to exercise all the services or functionalities that are part of the specification or intended function.
- *Random, with respect to a usage pattern*. This method generates test data in such a way as to simulate the conditions of usage of the software product in its operating environment.

It is possible to map the goal of the test to the test data generation method in a nearly deterministic manner, as shown in the following table:

Method Goal	Structural	Functional	Random
Finding and removing faults	√		
Proving the absence of faults		√	
Estimating the frequency of failure			√
Ensuring the infrequency of failure			√
Estimating fault density			√

Target Attribute: Most typically, one tests a software product to affect or estimate some functional quality of the product, such as correctness, reliability, safety, security, and so on; but as the following list indicates, one may also be interested in testing the product for a broad range of attributes.

- *Functionality*: Testing a software product for functional properties such as correctness, reliability, safety, security, and so on is the most common form of testing, and is the default option is all our discussions.
- *Robustness*: Whereas correctness mandates that the software product behaves according to the specification for all inputs in the specified domain, robustness further mandates that the program behaves reasonably (whatever that means: we can all recognize unreasonable program behavior when we see it) outside of the specification domain, that is, on inputs or situations for which the specification made no provisions.
- *Design and structure*: In integration testing, the focus of the test is on ensuring that the parts of the software system interact with each other as provided by the design; here the attribute we want to test or ensure is the proper realization of the design.
- *Performance*: We may want to test a software product for the purpose of empirically analyzing its performance under normal usage conditions (e.g., normal workload).
- *Graceful degradation*: In the same way that we distinguish between *correctness* (functional behavior for normal inputs) and *robustness* (functional behavior for exceptional or unplanned inputs), we distinguish between *performance* (operational behavior under normal workloads) and *graceful degradation* (operational behavior under excessive workloads). To test a software product for graceful degradation, we operate it under excessive workloads and observe whether its performance decreases in a continuous, acceptable manner.

In Section 7.2.2, we review the secondary attributes and discuss how they are affected by the choices made for the primary attributes reviewed in this section.

7.2.2 Secondary Attributes

We consider the secondary attributes listed earlier and review the set of values that are available for each attribute, as well as how these values are impacted by the primary attributes.

The Oracle: If the target attribute of the test is an operational attribute, such as the response time of the product under normal workloads, or under exceptional workloads, then the oracle takes the form of an operational condition (a response time, or a function plotting the response time as a function of the workload). If the target attribute of the test is functional, then the oracle depends on whether the goal of the test is to find faults or to certify failure freedom. The following table highlights these dependencies.

<table>
<tr><td colspan="2" rowspan="2">Oracle</td><td colspan="5">Target attribute</td></tr>
<tr><td>Functionality</td><td>Robustness</td><td>Design</td><td>Performance</td><td>Graceful degradation</td></tr>
<tr><td rowspan="4" style="writing-mode: vertical-rl;">Goal of testing</td><td>Fault removal</td><td rowspan="2" colspan="2">Use the strongest (most refined) possible oracle, e.g., the intended program function</td><td rowspan="2">Oracle checks relevant interactions</td><td rowspan="2" colspan="2">Performance requirements under normal/exceptional conditions</td></tr>
<tr><td>Proving absence of faults</td></tr>
<tr><td>Estimating frequency of failures</td><td rowspan="2" colspan="2">Use the weakest (least refined) possible oracle that the end user considers acceptable.</td><td rowspan="2">Oracle checks overall system function</td><td>N/A</td><td></td></tr>
<tr><td>Ensuring infrequency of failures</td><td></td><td></td></tr>
</table>

The Oracle as a Function of the Goal of Testing and the Target Attribute Being Tested

The Test Life Cycle: Whereas in Chapter 3 we have presented a generic test lifecycle, we can imagine three variations thereof, which we present in the following text:

- *A sequential life cycle*, which proceeds sequentially through three successive phases of test data generation, test execution, and test outcome analysis. An algorithmic representation of this cycle may look like this

```
{testDataGeneration(D);    // D: test data set;
  T=empty;                 // T: report
while (not empty(D))
   {d=removeFrom(D);
   d'=P(d);
   if (not(oracle(d,d'))) {add(d,T;}}
analyze(T);}
```

In this cycle, the phases of test data generation, test execution, and test analysis take place sequentially.

- *A semisequential life cycle*, where the execution of tests pauses whenever a failure is observed; this life cycle may be adopted if we want to remove faults as the test progresses. An algorithmic representation of this cycle may look like this:

```
{testDataGeneration(D); // D: test data set;
  while (not empty(D))
   {repeat {d=removeFrom(D); d'=P(d);}
   until not(oracle(d,d'));
     offLineAnalysis(d); // fault diagnosis and removal
   }
}
```

- An iterative life cycle, which integrates the test data generation into the iteration. An algorithmic representation of this cycle may look like this:

```
{while (not completeTest())
   {d=generateTestData();
    d'=P(d);
    if (oracle(d,d')) {successfulTest(d);}
    else {unsuccessfulTest(d);}
    }
}
```

The following table shows how the value of this attribute may depend on the primary attributes of goal and method.

Life cycle			Goal of testing			
			Fault removal	Proving absence of faults	Estimating frequency of failures	Ensuring infrequency of failures
Test data generation method		Structural	Semi sequential	Sequential		Semi sequential
		Functional				
		Random	Iterative			Iterative

Test Assumptions: A test can be characterized by the assumptions it makes about the product under test and/or about the environment in which it runs. As such, this attribute can take three values, depending on the scale of the product being tested, as shown in the following table.

Assumptions	Scale		
	Unit	Subsystem	System
Test assumption	The oracle/specification of the unit is not in question. Only the unit's correctness is.	Only the targeted subsystem is in question, not the remainder of the system.	The test environment mimics the product's operating environment.

Test Completion: Test completion is the condition under which the test activity is deemed to achieve its goal. Such conditions are as follows:

- The software product has passed the certification standard.
- The software product has performed to the satisfaction of the user.
- It is felt that all relevant faults have been diagnosed and removed.
- The reliability of the software product has been estimated.
- The reliability of the software product has grown beyond the required threshold.
- The test data generated for the test have been exhausted, and so on.

The following table illustrates how this attribute depends on the goal of the test and the test data generation method.

Completion criterion		Goals of testing			
		Fault removal	Proving absence of faults	Estimating frequency of failures	Ensuring Infrequency of Failures
Test data generation method	Structural	Test data exhausted	Desired conclusion reached	N/A	N/A
	Functional			Estimation completed	
	Random	Desired level of coverage achieved			Target threshold reached or exceeded

Required Artifacts: Many artifacts may be needed to conduct a test, including any combination of the following artifacts:

- The source code
- The executable code
- The product specification
- The product's intended function
- The product's design
- The signature of the software product (i.e., a specification of its input space)
- The usage pattern of the software product (i.e., a probability distribution over its input space)
- The test data generated for the test

This attribute depends on virtually all four primary attributes; for the sake of parsimony, we only show its dependence on the goal of testing and on the test data generation method.

Artifacts		Goals of testing			
		Fault removal	Proving absence of faults	Estimating frequency of failures	Ensuring infrequency of failures
Test data generation method	**Structural**	Source + Executable + Function			
	Functional	Executable + Specification + Function		Executable + Specification	Source + Function + Specification + Signature + Usage pattern
	Random	Executable + Function + Signature + Usage pattern		Executable + Signature + Usage pattern	Source + Specification + Signature + Usage pattern

Stakeholders: A stakeholder in a test is a party that has a role in the execution of the test, or has a role in the production of the software asset being tested, or has a stake in the outcome of the test. Possible stakeholders include the product developer, the product specifier, the product user, the quality assurance team, the verification and validation team, the configuration management team, and so on. The following table shows how this attribute depends on the goal of the test and the scale of the asset.

Stakeholders		Goals of testing			
		Fault removal	Proving absence of faults	Estimating frequency of failures	Ensuring infrequency of failures
Scale	Unit	Unit developer	Unit developer, CM/QA team		
	Subsystem (maintenance)	Subsystem developer, maintenance engineer	Subsystem developer, maintenance engineer, CM/QA team		
	System			Verification and validation team Design team	Specifier team, design team, and end users

Test Environment: The environment of a test is the set of interfaces that the product under test interacts with as it executes. The following table shows the different values that this attribute may take, depending on the goal of the test and the scale of the software product under test.

Test Environment		Goals of testing			
		Fault removal	Proving absence of faults	Estimating frequency of failures	Ensuring infrequency of failures
Scale	Unit	Development environment	Project configuration		
	Subsystem (maintenance)	Software system			
	System	Development environment	Operating environment	Simulated operating environment	

Position in the Life Cycle: As we have seen in Chapter 3, several phases of the software life cycle include a testing activity. The software activity at each phase can be characterized by primary attributes; the following table shows how the goal of testing and the scale of the product under test determine the phase at which each test activity takes place.

Position in the Lifecycle		Goals of testing			
		Fault removal	Proving absence of faults	Estimating frequency of failures	Ensuring infrequency of failures
Scale	Unit	Unit testing	Adding the asset into the project configuration		
	Subsystem (maintenance)	Maintenance	Regression testing		
	System	Integration testing	Acceptance testing	Reliability estimation	Reliability growth

7.3   TESTING TAXONOMY

In this section, we consider a number of different test activities, analyze them, and discuss to what extent the classification scheme presented in this chapter enables us to characterize them in a meaningful manner.

7.3.1   Unit-Level Testing

We distinguish between two types of unit-level testing:

- *Unit-Level Fault Removal*: This test is carried out by the unit's developer as part of the coding and unit testing phase of the software life cycle; its purpose is to detect, isolate, and remove faults as part of the development life cycle.
- *Unit-Level Certification*: This test is carried out by the configuration management/quality assurance team for the purpose of ensuring that the unit under test meets the quality standards mandated for the project.

The following table illustrates how these two tests differ from each other, by comparing and contrasting their attributes.

Attributes		Unit-level fault removal	Unit-level certification
Primary attributes	**Scale**	Unit (module, routine, function)	Unit (module, routine, function)
	Goal	Finding and removing faults	Certifying compliance with project-wide quality standards
	Property	Functionality	Functionality
	Method	Structural (attempting to sensitize and expose as many faults as possible)	Functional (attempting to exercise as many functional aspects as possible)
Secondary attributes	**Oracle**	The function that the unit is designed to compute	The specification that the unit is designed to satisfy
	Test life cycle	Semisequential	Sequential (generate test data, run the unit on the test data, and record outcomes, rule on certification)
	Test assumptions	The intended function is not in question (the correctness of the unit is)	The unit specification is not in question (the correctness of the unit is)
	Completion criterion	Confidence that most egregious faults have been removed	Confidence that the unit has passed/ or has failed the certification standard
	Required artifacts	Executable code + Source code + test environment + Intended function	Executable code + test environment + Unit specification
	Test stakeholders	Unit developer	Unit developer + Configuration management/quality Assurance team
	Test environment	Simulated environment	Existing (evolving) system + Simulated environment
	Position in the SW life cycle	During the programming phase	Concludes the programming phase for each individual unit

7.3.2 System-Level Testing

We consider three system-level tests:

1. *Integration test*, which arises at the end of the programming phase, when programming units that have been developed, tested, and filed into the product configuration are combined according to the product design to produce an integrated product.
2. *Reliability test*, which arises as the end of the software development project, prior to product delivery, to evaluate the reliability of the product (and eventually, ascertain that the product reliability exceeds the product's required reliability).
3. *Acceptance test*, which is conducted jointly by the development team and the user team to check that the software product meets its requirements.

Even though these tests are all at the same scale (system-wide), they differ from each other in significant ways, as we see in the table below.

Attributes		Integration test	Reliability test	Acceptance test
Primary attributes	Scale	System	System	System
	Goal	Find and remove design faults (dealing with inter-component coordination)	Assess the reliability of the product	Check whether the system meets its requirements to the satisfaction of the user
	Property	Design	Functionality	Functionality
	Method	Structural	Functional (compatible with usage pattern)	Functional (as per user requirements)
Secondary attributes	Oracle	System function	System Specification (or subspecification with respect to which we want to estimate reliability)	System specification
	Test life cycle	Semisequential	Iterative	Sequential
	Test assumptions	Units are not in question; only system design is	Test environment mimics operating environment	Test environment mimics operating environment
	Completion criterion	All relevant interactions exercised, all possible faults removed	Reliability adequately estimated/ or reliability requirement met	Contractual obligation met

(continued)

(*continued*)

Required artifacts	Executable code + source code + design documentation + expected function	Executable code + usage pattern + Relevant specification	Executable code + contractual requirements
Test stakeholders	Product designers	Product designers + verification and validation	Requirements engineers + user representative + managers
Test environment	Development environment	Operating environment (or simulation thereof)	Operating environment (or simulation thereof)
Position in the SW life cycle	Integration	Prior to delivery	At delivery

7.4 EXERCISES

7.1. Consider the software product that operates an automatic teller machine at a bank, and let S be the input space of the product:

- Define set S, assuming that each query to the automatic teller takes the form of an identification sequence (including a card ID followed by a PIN), followed by a query to the card database to authenticate the customer, followed (in case of successful identification) by a customer query (account balance, cash withdrawal, cash deposit, check deposit), followed by a query to the account database (to perform the requested operation), followed by an actuation of the cash dispenser (if the customer requests a withdrawal and it is approved), or followed by an actuation of the deposit unit (that accepts cash or checks) and updates the accounts database accordingly.
- Using empirical knowledge of how automated teller machines are usually used, define the usage pattern of the software product as a probability distribution over S.
- Write a program that generates random test data according to the probability distribution you have computed in Question (b).

7.2. Regression testing takes place at the end of any maintenance operation. You are asked to characterize the activity of regression testing in the context of corrective maintenance, that is, maintenance that aims to correct a fault in a software product.

7.3. Regression testing takes place at the end of any maintenance operation. You are asked to characterize the activity of regression testing in the context of adaptive maintenance, that is, maintenance that aims to accommodate a change in the requirements of a software product.

7.4. Naik and Tripathy (2008) discuss the following types of tests:

- Functionality
- Robustness
- Interoperability
- Performance
- Scalability
- Stress
- Load and stability
- Regression
- Documentation
- Regulatory

Characterize these types of test using the classification scheme proposed in this chapter.

7.5 BIBLIOGRAPHIC NOTES

Alternative classification schemes for software testing can be found in the following references: Culbertson et al. (2002); Mathur (2008); Naik and Tripathy (2008); Perry (2002).

Part III
_____

Test Data Generation

Test data generation is one of the most critical phases of software testing in the sense that it has the greatest impact on the success or failure of the test to achieve its purpose. The problem of test data selection can be formulated simply as follows: Given an input space S (which is assumed to be so large that it is impractical to test the program on all elements of S), choose a small subset T of S such that we can achieve the goal of the test by executing the candidate program on T rather than on S. Clearly, the requirement that T must satisfy depends on the goal of the test. We consider two possible requirements:

1. *A Logical Requirement.* Any program that runs successfully for all elements of T runs successfully for all elements of S. Note that this is equivalent to the following property: If a candidate program P fails on some element s of S, then there exists an element t of T such that execution of P on the element t fails.

2. *A Stochastic Requirement.* The reliability observed on the execution of a candidate program P on T is lower than, or the same as (an approximation of), the reliability observed on the execution of a candidate program P on S. So that any reliability claim made on the basis of observations made during the testing phase, when input data is limited to T, will be borne out during the operation phase, when the input ranges over all of S.

It is important to note that these two requirements are dependent on the oracle used in the test; it is conceivable that for each requirement, the stronger the oracle (corresponding to a more-refined specification), the larger is set T; this will be discussed in Chapter 11.

Software Testing: Concepts and Operations, First Edition. Ali Mili and Fairouz Tchier.
© 2015 John Wiley & Sons, Inc. Published 2015 by John Wiley & Sons, Inc.

8

Test Generation Concepts

Whereas Chapters 9 and 10 explore strategies for test data generation, this chapter introduces concepts that help us streamline the discussion of test data generation, by reviewing such questions as the following: How does the target attribute that we are trying to achieve through the test influence test data generation? What requirements does the generated test data satisfy? What criteria can we deploy to generate test data? How do we assess the quality of generated test data (i.e., the extent to which the generated test data fulfills its requirements)? How do we measure test coverage, that is, the extent to which a test achieves its goal?

8.1 TEST GENERATION AND TARGET ATTRIBUTES

In Chapter 7, we have surveyed several different goals of a test operation, and several distinct attributes that a test operation may aim to establish. If we focus exclusively on test processes that aim to establish a functional property (dealing with input/output behavior, rather than performance or resource usage, for example) then we can identify the following possible categories:

1. Testing a program to establish correctness with respect to a specification (as in acceptance testing).
2. Testing a program to ensure that it computes its intended function (as in unit testing).
3. Testing a program to ensure that it is robust (i.e., that it behaves appropriately outside the domain of its specification).
4. Testing a program to ensure its safety (i.e., that even when it fails to meet its specification, it causes no safety violations).

Software Testing: Concepts and Operations, First Edition. Ali Mili and Fairouz Tchier.
© 2015 John Wiley & Sons, Inc. Published 2015 by John Wiley & Sons, Inc.

5. Testing a program to ensure its security, that is, that it meets relevant security requirements, such as confidentiality (ability to protect confidential data from unauthorized disclosure), integrity (ability to protect critical data from unauthorized modification), authentication (ability to authenticate system users), and so on.

In this section, we make the case that all these attributes can be modeled uniformly as the property that the function of the candidate program refines a given specification. What changes from one attribute to another is merely the form of the specification at hand; so that in the sequel, when we talk about testing a candidate program against a specification, we could be talking about any one of these attributes.

We review in turn the five attributes listed earlier and model them as refinement properties with respect to various specifications.

1. *Correctness*: According to Chapter 5, a program p is correct with respect to a specification R if and only if the function P of program p refines relation R.

2. *Precision*: Whereas correctness tests the candidate program against its specification, precision tests the candidate program against the function that it is designed to compute, to which we refer as the *intended function* of the program. By definition, the intended function of the program is a deterministic relation; for all intents and purposes, being correct with respect to a deterministic specification is indistinguishable from computing the function defined by this specification. Whereas the specification is used for acceptance testing, the intended function of the program is used for unit testing or system testing (depending on scale) where the emphasis is not on proving correct behavior, but rather on finding faults. To illustrate the difference, consider the following simple example: We let space S be defined by positive natural variables x and y, and let specification R on S be defined as follows:

$$R = \{(s,s') \mid x' = \gcd(x,y)\},$$

where gcd (x, y) refers to the greatest common divisor of x and y. Assume that upon inspecting the specification, the program designer decides to implement the *gcd* using Euclid's algorithm. The intended function is then

$$F = \{(s,s') \mid x' = \gcd(x,y) \wedge y' = \gcd(x,y)\}.$$

If the candidate program fails to deliver *gcd* (x, y) in variable y during acceptance testing, that does not count as a failure since the specification does not require the condition $y' = \gcd(x,y)$. But if the candidate program fails to deliver $\gcd(x, y)$ in variable y during unit testing (when the emphasis is on finding faults), that does count as a failure, since it indicates that the program is not computing its intended function.

3. *Robustness*: By definition, a program is said to be robust with respect to a specification if and only if it behaves appropriately (even) in situations for which the specification makes no provisions; we do not have a general definition of what is appropriate behavior, but it should at least encompass normal termination in a well-defined final state, with appropriate alerts or error messages. For a relational specification R, the set of initial states for which the specification makes provisions is RL; hence, the set of states for which it makes no provisions is $\overline{RL}$. If we limit ourselves to specification $\overline{RL}$ for initial states outside the domain of R, it means we merely want candidate programs to terminate normally in such cases; if we want to impose additional appropriateness conditions, we further restrict the behavior of candidate programs outside the domain of R by taking the intersection of $\overline{RL}$ with some other term, say A. Hence, a program that is correct and robust with respect to R refines the following specification:

$$R \cup \overline{RL} \cap A.$$

As an illustration, we consider the space S defined by integer variables x and y, and we consider the following specification:

$$R = \{(s,s') \mid x > 0 \wedge y > 0 \wedge x' = \gcd(x,y)\},$$

where $gcd\ (x, y)$ refers to the greatest common divisor of x and y. If we also want candidate programs to be robust, then we can write a more refined specification under this form:

$$R' = R \cup \overline{RL} \cap A.$$

We find $\overline{RL} = \{(s,s') \mid x \le 0 \vee y \le 0\}$; if we choose to post an error message in x whenever x or y are not positive, we find the following composite specification:

$$R' = \{(s,s') \mid x > 0 \wedge y > 0 \wedge x' = \gcd(x,y)\}$$
$$\cup \{(s,s') \mid x \le 0 \vee y \le 0 \wedge x' = \text{errormsg}\}.$$

A candidate program is robust if and only if it refines specification R'.

4. *Safety*: By definition, safety means correctness with respect to safety-critical requirements. Most typically, the product specification refines the safety critical requirements; but because safety-critical requirements carry much heavier stakes and their violation costs a great deal more than other requirements, they are the subject of special scrutiny, and are the subject of more thorough testing and verification. From a logical standpoint, safety can be modeled by the property that the function of the program refines the safety-critical requirements.

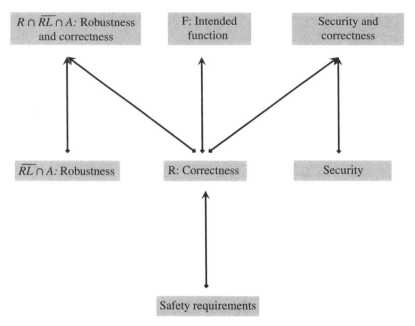

Figure 8.1 *A hierarchy of attributes.*

5. *Security*: By definition, security means correctness with respect to security requirements, such as confidentiality, integrity, authentication, availability, and so on.

Hence, while correctness (with respect to a possibly nondeterministic specification), precision (the property of computing the exact intended function), robustness (the property of behaving appropriately for unexpected situations), safety (the property of avoiding safety violations), and security (the property of evading or mitigating security threats) all sound different, they can all be modeled as the property that the function of the candidate program refines a specification; what varies from one attribute to the next is the specification in question. These specifications are ranked by the refinement ordering as shown in Figure 8.1.

Henceforth, we will talk about testing a program against a specification without specifying what form the specification has, hence which attribute we are testing it for.

8.2 TEST OUTCOMES

It is clear, from the foregoing discussions, that when we want to test a program against a specification R, there is no reason to consider test data outside the domain of R. Indeed, even if we are testing the behavior of candidate programs outside their normal operating conditions, as we must do for robustness, this amounts to testing the candidate program for correctness with respect to a more refined specification. We consider the following definition:

Definition 1: Successful Execution *We consider a specification R on space S, whose domain is X, and we let s be an element of X. We say that execution of a candidate program p on initial state s is successful if and only if: $s \in dom(R \cap P)$, where P is the function computed by program p.*

The set of initial states on which execution of candidate program p yields a successful outcome is $dom(R \cap P)$. This set is clearly a subset of $X = dom(R)$. We give two examples to illustrate the set of states that yield a successful outcome, for a given specification R and a given program p.

We consider a specification R on space S defined by variables x and y of type integer, which is defined as follows:

$$R = \{(s, s') | x' = x + y\}.$$

We let p be the following candidate program on the same space S:

```
p: {while (y!=0) {y=y-1; x=x+1;}}.
```

The function P that this program computes on space S is defined as follows:

$$P = \{(s, s') | y \geq 0 \wedge x' = x + y \wedge y' = 0\}.$$

From this, we find

$dom(R \cap P)$

= {since $P \subseteq R$}

$dom(P)$

= {quantifying over s', and simplifying}

$\{s | y \geq 0\}$.

Indeed, execution of p on s yields a successful outcome only if $y(s) \geq 0$.

As a second example, we consider a specification R on space S defined by variables x, y, and z of type integer, which is defined as follows:

$$R = \{(s, s') | y \geq 0 \wedge z' = xy\}.$$

We let p be the following candidate program on the same space S:

```
p: {while (y!=0) {y=y-1; z=z+x;}}.
```

The function P that this program computes on space S is defined as follows:

$$P = \{(s, s') \mid y \geq 0 \wedge x' = x \wedge y' = 0 \wedge z' = z + xy\}.$$

From this, we find

$dom(R \cap P)$

= {by substitution}

$dom(\{(s, s') \mid y \geq 0 \wedge x' = x \wedge y' = 0 \wedge z' = z + xy \wedge z' = xy\})$

= {simplification}

$dom(\{(s, s') \mid y \geq 0 \wedge z = 0 \wedge x' = x \wedge y' = 0 \wedge z' = xy\})$

= {quantifying over s', and simplifying}

$\{s \mid y \geq 0 \wedge z = 0\}.$

Indeed, execution of p on s yields a successful outcome only if $(y(s) \geq 0 \wedge z = 0)$.

8.3 TEST GENERATION REQUIREMENTS

The purpose of a test operation is to run a candidate program on sample inputs and observe its behavior in order to draw conclusions about the quality of the program. In general, we cannot make certifiable claims about the quality of the candidate program unless we have observed its execution on all possible inputs under all possible circumstances. Because this is most generally impossible, we must find substitutes; this is the focus of test data generation.

Given a candidate program p and a specification R whose domain is X, we are interested to choose a subset T of X such that we can achieve the goal of the test by executing the candidate program on T rather than on X. Clearly, the requirement that T must satisfy depends on the goal of the test. As we remember from Chapter 7, we identify several possible goals of testing, including the following:

- Finding and removing faults
- Proving the absence of faults
- Estimating the frequency of failures
- Ensuring the infrequency of failures

These goals impose different requirements on T, which we review below:

- A *Logical Requirement*: Set T must be chosen in such a way that if there exists an input x in X such that a candidate program p fails when executed on x, then there exists t in T such that program p fails when executed on t. This requirement provides, in effect, that set T is sufficiently rich to detect all possible faults in candidate programs.
- A *Stochastic Requirement*: The reliability observed on the execution of a candidate program p on T is the same as (or an approximation of) the reliability observed on the execution of the candidate program p on X. So that any reliability claim made on the basis of observations made during the testing phase, when input data are limited to T, will be borne out during the operation phase, when the input ranges over all of X.
- A *Sufficient Stochastic Requirement*: The reliability observed on the execution of a candidate program p on T is lower than, or the same as, the reliability observed on the execution of a candidate program p on X. So that any reliability claim made on the basis of observations made during the testing phase, when input data is limited to T, will be matched or exceeded during the operation phase, when the input ranges over all of X.

Given that the set of states that yield a successful execution of a candidate program p is $dom(R \cap P)$, the logical requirement can be expressed as follows:

$$\left(X \cap \overline{dom(R \cap P)} \neq \emptyset\right) \Rightarrow \left(T \cap \overline{dom(R \cap P)} \neq \emptyset\right).$$

This requirement provides, in effect, that if program p has a fault, test data set T will expose it; as such, this requirement serves the first goal, whose focus is to expose all faults of the program. In order for T to serve the second goal of testing, it needs to satisfy the following condition:

$$(T \subseteq dom(R \cap P)) \Rightarrow (X \subseteq dom(R \cap P)),$$

which provides, in effect, that if program p executes successfully on T, then it executes successfully on X (hence is correct). The following proposition provides that these two conditions are equivalent.

Proposition: Test Data Adequacy *Let R be a specification on space S, whose domain is X and let p be a program on space S, and T a subset of X. The following two conditions are equivalent:*

- $\left(X \cap \overline{dom(R \cap P)} \neq \emptyset\right) \Rightarrow \left(T \cap \overline{dom(R \cap P)} \neq \emptyset\right).$
- $(T \subseteq dom(R \cap P)) \Rightarrow (X \subseteq dom(R \cap P)).$

Proof

We proceed by equivalence:

$$\left(X \cap \overline{dom(R \cap P)} \neq \emptyset\right) \Rightarrow \left(T \cap \overline{dom(R \cap P)} \neq \emptyset\right)$$

$\Leftrightarrow$ {De Morgan's laws}

$$\left(T \cap \overline{dom(R \cap P)} = \emptyset\right) \Rightarrow \left(X \cap \overline{dom(R \cap P)} = \emptyset\right)$$

$\Leftrightarrow$ {by set theory, $\left(A \cap B = \emptyset\right.$ is equivalent to $\left.\left(A \subseteq \overline{B}\right)\right\}$

$$\left(T \subseteq \overline{\overline{dom(R \cap P)}}\right) \Rightarrow \left(X \subseteq \overline{\overline{dom(R \cap P)}}\right)$$

$\Leftrightarrow$ {by set theory, $\left(\overline{\overline{A}} = A\right)$}

$$(T \subseteq dom(R \cap P)) \Rightarrow (X \subseteq dom(R \cap P)).$$

QED

This proves that a test set T is adequate for the first goal of testing (finding and removing faults) if and only if it is adequate for the second goal of testing (proving the absence of faults). Figures 8.2, 8.3, and 8.4, respectively, show three configurations of X, $dom(R \cap P)$ and T: a case where a test data T is certainly inadequate, a case where test data T may be adequate, and a set of two cases where test data T is certainly adequate. The cases where T is provably adequate are both of limited practical interest: one arises when the program is correct, the other arises when T is all of S.

The test data T of Figure 8.2 is certainly inadequate: The left-hand side of the implications in proposition test data adequacy is valid, but the right-hand side is not.

Test data T of Figure 8.3 may be adequate.

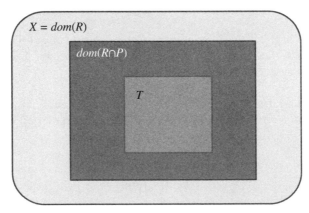

Figure 8.2 *Inadequate test data.*

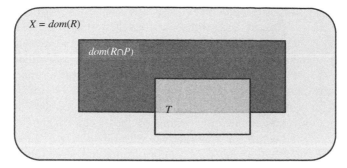

Figure 8.3 *Possibly adequate test data.*

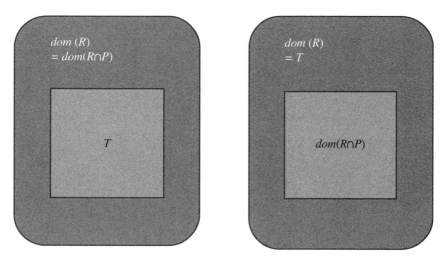

Figure 8.4 *Certainly adequate test data.*

Figure 8.4 shows cases where T is certainly adequate: (a) if p is correct or (b) if T is exhaustive test.

The testing goals can be mapped onto test data requirements as shown in the following table:

Testing goals	Test data requirements
Finding and removing faults	Logical requirement
Proving the absence of faults	Logical requirement
Estimating the frequency of failures	Stochastic requirement
Ensuring the infrequency of failures	Stochastic requirement Sufficient stochastic requirement

Note that the stochastic requirement logically implies the sufficient stochastic requirement; hence, any test data set that satisfies the former satisfies the latter; for the same reason, the former can be used whenever the latter is adequate. Note that we focus our attention on X, the domain of the specification, rather than the domain (or the state space) of the program, since candidate programs are judged for their behavior on the domain of the specification they are supposed to satisfy.

In practice, it is very difficult to generate test data that meets these requirements, especially the logical requirement; nevertheless, these requirements serve a useful function, in that they define the goal that we must attain as we generate test data, and a yardstick by which we judge the quality of our choices. In the next section, we discuss the concept of a test selection criterion, which is a criterion by which we characterize test data to satisfy some requirement among the three introduced in this section.

8.4   TEST GENERATION CRITERIA

Given a test generation requirement, among the three we have discussed earlier, it is common to generate a *test generation criterion*, that is, a condition on set T that dictates how to generate it in such a way as to satisfy the requirement.

For the logical requirement, the most compelling (and most common) criterion is to partition the domain of the specification by an equivalence relation, say EQ, and to mandate that T contain one representative element for each equivalence class of X modulo EQ. Formally, these conditions are written as follows:

- $EQ(T) = X$
- $(T \times T) \cap EQ \subseteq I$

The first condition provides that each equivalence class of X modulo EQ is represented by at least one element of T, as illustrated in Figure 8.5 (where the equivalence classes are represented by the quadrants). As for the second condition, it merely provides that T contains no unnecessary elements, that is, no two elements of the same equivalence class.

The rationale for this criterion depends on the definition of EQ: Ideally, EQ is defined in such a way that all the elements of the same equivalence class of X modulo EQ have the same fault diagnosis capability, that is, either the candidate program runs successfully on all of them or it fails on all of them; hence, there is no reason to test candidate programs on more than one element per equivalence class. Formally, this condition can be written as follows:

$$EQ \subseteq \{(s, s') \mid (s \in dom(R \cap P) \Leftrightarrow s' \in dom(R \cap P))\}.$$

We refer to this condition (on EQ) as the *condition of partition testing*, and we have the following proposition.

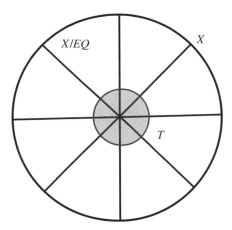

Figure 8.5 *Partitioning the domain of the specification.*

Proposition: Partition Testing *Let R be a specification whose domain is X, and let EQ be an equivalence relation on X. If relation EQ satisfies the condition of partition testing, then any set T that satisfies the condition $EQ(T) = X$ necessarily satisfies the logical requirement of test selection.*

Proof. We must prove:

$$(T \subseteq dom(R \cap P)) \Rightarrow (X \subseteq dom(R \cap P)).$$

To this effect, we assume the left-hand side and prove the right-hand side. By hypothesis, we have $X = EQ(T)$, from which we infer, by the left-hand side of the aforementioned implication:

$$X \subseteq EQ(dom(R \cap P)).$$

On the other hand, from the condition of partition testing, we infer

$$X \subseteq EQ'(dom(R \cap P)),$$

where

$$EQ' = \{(s, s') \mid (s \in dom(R \cap P) \Leftrightarrow s' \in dom(R \cap P))\}.$$

Now, we compute $EQ'(dom(R \cap P))$:

$EQ'(dom(R \cap P))$

= {definition}

$\{s' \mid \exists s : \ s \in dom(R \cap P) \land (s, s') \in EQ'\}$

= {substitution}

$\{s' \mid \exists s : \ s \in dom(R \cap P) \land (s \in dom(R \cap P) \Leftrightarrow s' \in dom(R \cap P))\}$

= {logical equivalence}

$\{s' \mid s' \in dom(R \cap P) \ \land \exists s : \ s \in dom(R \cap P) \land (s \in dom(R \cap P) \Leftrightarrow s' \in dom(R \cap P))\}$

$\subseteq$ {simplification}

$\{s' \mid s' \in dom(R \cap P)\}$

$\subseteq$ {identity }

$dom(R \cap P)$.

QED

The condition $EQ(T) = X$ provides, in effect, that each element of X is related to at least one element of T; in other words, each equivalence class of X modulo EQ has a representative in T. As for the condition $(T \times T) \cap EQ \subseteq I$, it is not needed for the proof of this proposition, because it only limits the size of T (it provides that no more than one representative per equivalence class is needed in T). In practice, the hypothesis that EQ does indeed satisfy this property is usually hard to support, and the criterion is only as good as the hypothesis.

For the stochastic requirement and the sufficient stochastic requirement, the most common generation criterion that we invoke provides that set T has the same probability distribution as the expected usage pattern of the software product. The rationale for this criterion is to imitate the operating conditions of the software product to the largest extent possible, so that whatever behavior we observe during testing is sure to be borne out during the product's operation. Given a specification R whose domain is X, we consider the following criterion on a subset T of X: We let χ be a random variable on X that reflects the usage pattern of candidate programs in operation, and we let θ be a random variable on T that reflects the distribution of test data during the testing phase. Then the probability distribution p_θ of θ over T must be identical to the probability distribution p_χ of χ over X, in the following sense:

$$\forall A, A \subseteq X : \int_{x \in A} p_\theta(x) dx = \int_{x \in A} p_\chi(\chi) d\chi.$$

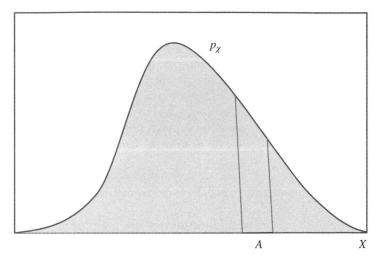

Figure 8.6 *Mimicking a probability distribution.*

The probability of occurrence of a test data point in any sub set A of X is identical to the probability of occurrence of an actual input data point in subset A during typical system operation. As an additional requirement, T must also be large enough so that observations of the candidate program on T provide a statistically significant sample of the program's behavior. In practice, depending on how large (or how dense) T is, it may be impossible to define a probability distribution p_θ that mimics exactly the probability distribution p_χ; we then let distribution p_θ approximate the probability distribution p_χ (Fig. 8.6).

In order to mimic the probability distribution p_χ, set T must have more elements where p_χ is high than where p_χ is low. This matter will be revisited in Chapter 9, when we discuss random test generation.

8.5 EMPIRICAL ADEQUACY ASSESSMENT

Whereas in the foregoing discussions, we have attempted to characterize the adequacy of a test data T with respect to test selection requirements by means of analytical arguments, in this section we consider empirical arguments. Specifically, we ponder the question: How can we assess the ability of a test set T to expose faults in candidate programs? A simple-minded way to do this is to run candidate programs on a test set T and see what proportion of faults we are able to expose; the trouble with this approach is that we do not usually know what faults a program has. Hence, if execution of program p on test set T yields no failures, or few failures, we have no way to tell whether this is because the program has no (or few) faults or because test set T is inadequate. To obviate this difficulty, we generate mutants of program p, which are programs obtained by making small changes to p, and we run all these mutants on test set T; we can then assess the adequacy of test set *T* by its ability to distinguish all the mutants from the original *p*, and to distinguish them from each other. A note of caution is in order, though: it is quite possible for mutants to be indistinguishable, in the sense that the original program p and its mutant compute the same function; in such cases, the inability of set T to distinguish the two programs does not reflect negatively on T. This means that in theory, we should run this experiment only on mutants which we know to be distinct (i.e., to compute a different function) from the original; but because it is very difficult in practice to tell whether a mutant does or does not compute the same function as the original, we may sometimes (for complex programs) run the experiment on the assumption that all mutants are distinct from the original, and from each other.

As an illustrative example, we consider the following sorting program, which we had studied in Chapter 6; we call it *p*.

```
void somesort (itemtype a[MaxSize], indextype N)    // line 1
{                                                    // 2
  indextype i; i=0;                                  // 3
  while (i<=N-2)                                      // 4
    {indextype j; indextype mindx; itemtype minval;  // 5
     j=i; mindx=j; minval=a[j];                       // 6
     while (j<=N-1)                                    // 7
       {if (a[j]<minval) {mindx=j; minval=a[j];}      // 8
        j++;}                                          // 9
     itemtype temp;                                   // 10
     temp=a[i]; a[i]=a[mindx]; a[mindx]=temp;         // 11
     i++;}                                             // 12
}                                                    // 13
```

Imagine that we have derived the following test data to test this program:

T	Index N	Array a[..]	Comment/rationale
t_1	1	[5]	Trivial size
t_2	2	[5,5]	Borderline size, identical elements
t_3	2	[5,9]	Borderline size, sorted
t_4	2	[9,5]	Borderline size, inverted
t_5	6	[5,5,5,5,5,5]	Random size, identical elements
t_6	6	[5,7,9,11,13,15]	Random size, sorted
t_7	6	[15,13,11,9,7,5]	Random size, inverted
t_8	6	[9,11,5,15,13,7]	Random size, random order

The question we ask is: How adequate is this test data? If we run our sorting routine on this data and all executions are successful, how confident can we be that our program is correct? The approach advocated by mutation testing is to generate mutants of program *p* by making small alterations to its source code and checking to what extent the test data is sensitive to these alterations. Let us, for the sake of argument, consider the following mutants of program *p*:

```
void m1 (itemtype a [MaxSize] , indextype N)        // line 1
   {                                                 // 2
     indextype i; i=0;                               // 3
     while (i<=N-1)    // changed N-2 into N-1       // 4
        {indextype j; indextype mindx; itemtype minval;  // 5
        j=i; mindx=j; minval=a[j];                   // 6
        while (j<=N-1)                               // 7
           {if (a[j]<minval) {mindx=j; minval=a[j];} // 8
           j++;}                                     // 9
        itemtype temp;                               // 10
        temp=a[i]; a[i]=a[mindx] ; a[mindx]=temp;    // 11
        i++;}                                        // 12
   }                                                 // 13
```

```
void m2 (itemtype a [MaxSize] , indextype N)        // line 1
   {                                                 // 2
     indextype i; i=0;                               // 3
     while (i<=N-2)                                  // 4
        {indextype j; indextype mindx; itemtype minval;  // 5
        j=i; mindx=j; minval=a[j];                   // 6
        while (j<N-1)    // changed <= into <        // 7
           {if (a[j]<minval) {mindx=j; minval=a[j];} // 8
           j++;}                                     // 9
        itemtype temp;                               // 10
        temp=a[i]; a[i]=a[mindx] ; a[mindx]=temp;    // 11
        i++;}                                        // 12
   }                                                 // 13
```

```
void m3 (itemtype a [MaxSize] , indextype N)        // line 1
   {                                                 // 2
     indextype i; i=0;                               // 3
     while (i<=N-2)                                  // 4
        {indextype j; indextype mindx; itemtype minval;  // 5
        j=i; mindx=j; minval=a[j];                   // 6
        while (j<=N-1)                               // 7
           {if (a[j]<=minval) {mindx=j; minval=a[j];}
                    // changed < into <=             // 8
           j++;}                                     // 9
```

```
        itemtype temp;                                      //  10
        temp=a[i]; a[i]=a[mindx]; a[mindx]=temp;            //  11
        i++;}                                               //  12
    }                                                       //  13



void m4 (itemtype a[MaxSize], indextype N)                  //  line 1
    {                                                       //  2
    indextype i; i=1;    // changed 0 into 1                //  3
    while (i<=N-2)                                           //  4
        {indextype j; indextype mindx; itemtype minval;     //  5
        j=i; mindx=j; minval=a[j];                          //  6
        while (j<=N-1)                                       //  7
            {if (a[j]<minval) {mindx=j; minval=a[j];}        //  8
            j++;}                                           //  9
        itemtype temp;                                      //  10
        temp=a[i]; a[i]=a[mindx]; a[mindx]=temp;            //  11
        i++;}                                               //  12
    }                                                       //  13



void m5 (itemtype a[MaxSize], indextype N)                  //  line 1
    {                                                       //  2
    indextype i; i=0;                                       //  3
    while (i<=N-2)                                           //  4
        {indextype j; indextype mindx; itemtype minval;     //  5
        j=i; mindx=j; minval=a[j];                          //  6
        while (j<=N-1)                                       //  7
            {if (a[j]<minval) {mindx=j; minval=a[j];}        //  8
            j++;}                                           //  9
        itemtype temp;                                      //  10
        a[i]=a[mindx]; temp=a[i]; a[mindx]=temp;
                    // inverted the first two statements     //  11
        i++;}                                               //  12
    }                                                       //  13
```

Given these mutants, we now run the following test driver, which considers the mutants in turn and checks whether test set T distinguishes them from the original program p.

```
void main ()
{for (int i=0; i<=5; i++) // does T distinguish
                          // mutant (i) from p
  {for (int j=1; j<=8; j++) // is p(tj) different from mi(tj)?
    {load tj onto N, a;
```

```
run p, store result in a';
load tj onto N, a;
run mutant i, compare outcome to a';}
if one of the tj returned a different outcome from p, announce:
  "mutant i distinguished"
  else announce: "mutant i not distinguished";}
}; // assess T according to how many mutants were distinguished
```

The actual source code for this is shown in the appendix. Execution of this program yields the following output, in which we show for each test datum t_j and for each mutant m_i whether execution of the mutant on the datum yields a different result from execution of the original program p on the same datum.

T	Mutants				
	m_1	m_2	m_3	m_4	m_5
t_1	True	True	True	True	True
t_2	True	True	True	True	True
t_3	True	True	True	True	True
t_4	True	True	True	False	False
t_5	True	True	True	True	True
t_6	True	True	True	True	True
t_7	True	True	True	False	False
t_8	True	True	True	False	False
Mutant distinguished?	No	No	No	Yes	Yes

Before we make a judgment on the adequacy of our test data set, we must first check whether the mutants that have not been distinguished from the original program are identical to it or not (i.e., compute the same function). For example, it is clear from inspection of the source code that mutant m_1 is identical to program p: indeed, since program p sorts the array by selection sort, then once it has selected the smallest $(N-1)$ elements of the array, the remaining element is necessarily the largest; hence, the array is already sorted. What mutant m_1 does is to select the Nth element of the array and permute it with itself—a futile operation, which program p skips. Mutant m_3 also appears to compute the same function as the original program p, though it selects a different value for variable **mindx** when the array contains duplicates; this difference has no impact on the overall function of the program. The question of whether mutant m_2 computes the same function as the original program is left as an exercise.

In general, once we have ruled out mutants that are deemed to be equivalent to the original program, we must consider the mutants that the test data did not distinguish from the original program even though they are distinct and raise the question: What additional test data should we generate to distinguish all these mutants? Conversely, we can view the proportion of distinct mutants that the test data has not distinguished as a measure of inadequacy of the test data, a measure that we should minimize by adding extra test data or refining existing data.

Note that the test data t_1, t_2, t_3, t_5, and t_6 does not appear to help much in testing the sorting program, as they are unable to distinguish any mutant from the original program.

In addition to its use to assess test sets, mutation is also used to automatically correct minor faults in programs, when their specification is available and readily testable: one can generate many mutants and test them against the specification using an adequate test set, until it encounters a mutant that satisfies the specification. There is no assurance that such a mutant can be found, nor that only one mutant can be found to satisfy the specification, nor that a mutant that satisfies the specification is more correct than the original program; nevertheless, this technique may find some uses in practice.

8.6 CHAPTER SUMMARY

From this chapter, it is important to remember the following ideas and concepts:

- One does not generate test data in an ad hoc manner; rather, one generates test data to fulfill specific requirements, which depend on the goal of the test. We have identified several possible requirements that a test data set must satisfy.
- It is customary to articulate a test data generation criterion, as a first step in test data generation; this criterion defines what condition a test data must satisfy to meet a selected requirement.
- Any test data selection criterion must be assessed with respect to the target requirement: To what extent does the criterion ensure that the requirement is fulfilled? This is usually very difficult to ascertain, but having well-defined requirements, even if they are not ever fulfilled, serves as a yardstick against which we can assess criteria.
- The adequacy of a criterion can be assessed analytically, by referring to the targeted requirement, or empirically, using mutants. A test data set is all the more adequate for finding program faults that it is capable of distinguishing the candidate program against mutants thereof (obtained by slight modifications).
- The only mutants that should be used to assess the adequacy of a test data set are those that are functionally distinct from the original candidate program. But determining whether a mutant is or is not functionally equivalent to the original program can take a great deal of effort, and may be error prone.

8.7 EXERCISES

8.1. Consider the following specification R on space S defined by integer variables x, y and z:

$$R = \{(s, s') \mid z' = x \times y\}$$

and consider the following program p (whose function is P) on the same space:

```
{while (y!=0) {y=y-1; z=z+x;}}.
```

Compute $dom(R \cap P)$, and interpret your results.

8.2. Same question as Exercise 8.1, for the space and specification, and the following program:

```
{z=0; while (y!=0) {y=y-1; z=z+x;}}.
```

8.3. Same question as Exercise 8.1, for the space and specification, and the following program:

```
{z=0; while (y>0) {y=y-1; z=z+x;}}.
```

8.4. Consider the following specification R on space S defined by integer variables x, y and z:

$$R = \{(s, s') \mid y \geq 0 \wedge z' = x \times y\},$$

and consider the following program p (whose function is P) on the same space:

```
{while (y!=0) {y=y-1; z=z+x;}}.
```

Compute $dom(R \cap P)$, and interpret your results.

8.5. Same question as Exercise 8.4, for the space and specification, and the following program:

```
{z=0; while (y!=0) {y=y-1; z=z+x;}}.
```

8.6. Same question as Exercise 8.4, for the space and specification, and the following program:

```
{z=0; while (y>0) {y=y-1; z=z+x;}}.
```

8.7. Consider the following specification R on space S defined by integer variables x, y and z:

$$R = \{(s, s') \mid y \geq 0 \wedge z' = z + x \times y\},$$

and consider the following program p (whose function is P) on the same space:

```
{while (y!=0) {y=y-1; z=z+x;}}.
```

Compute $dom(R \cap P)$, and interpret your results.

8.8. Same question as Exercise 8.7, for the space and specification, and the following program:

```
{z=0; while (y!=0) {y=y-1; z=z+x;}}.
```

8.9. Same question as Exercise 8.7, for the space and specification, and the following program:

```
{z=0; while (y>0) {y=y-1; z=z+x;}}.
```

8.10. Consider the mutant m_2 in the example discussed in Section 8.5. If this mutant is identical to the original program p, explain why. If not, find additional test data to distinguish it from p.

8.11. Consider the following sorting program; generate five mutants for it and perform the same analysis as we present in Section 8.5, using the same test data. If you conclude that the test data is inadequate for the mutants you generate, generate additional test data.

```
void insertSort(int a[], int length)
{
   int i, j, value;
   for(i = 1; i < length; i++)
   {
      value = a[i];
      for (j = i - 1; j >= 0 && a[j] > value; j--)
      {
         a[j + 1] = a[j];
      }
      a[j + 1] = value;
   }
}
```

8.8 BIBLIOGRAPHIC NOTES

The concept of test data selection criterion is due to Goodenough and Gerhart (1975). The concept of program mutations and mutation testing is due to Richard Lipton; an early presentation of the topic is given in DeMillo et al. (1978).

8.9 APPENDIX: MUTATION PROGRAM

```
void m1 (int a[6], int N);
void m2 (int a[6], int N);
void m3 (int a[6], int N);
void m4 (int a[6], int N);
void m5 (int a[6], int N);
void m6 (int a[6], int N);
void loaddata (int j);

// state variables
int a[6];
int N;
int aa[9][7];
int Na[9];
int ap[6];

int main ()
{
Na[1]=1; aa[1][1]=5;
Na[2]=2; aa[2][1]=5; aa[2][2]=5;
Na[3]=2; aa[3][1]=5; aa[3][2]=9;
Na[4]=4; aa[4][1]=9; aa[4][2]=5;
Na[5]=6; aa[5][1]=5; aa[5][2]=5; aa[5][3]=5; aa[5][4]=5;
aa[5][5]=5; aa[5][6]=5;
Na[6]=6; aa[6][1]=5; aa[6][2]=7; aa[6][3]=9; aa[6][4]=11;
aa[6][5]=13; aa[6][6]=15;
Na[7]=6; aa[7][1]=15; aa[7][2]=13; aa[7][3]=11; aa[7][4]=9;
aa[7][5]=7; aa[7][6]=5;
Na[8]=6; aa[8][1]=9; aa[8][2]=11; aa[8][3]=5; aa[8][4]=15;
aa[8][5]=13; aa[8][6]=7;
for (int i=1; i<=5; i++) // does T distinguish mutant (i) from p
  {bool discumul; discumul=true;
    for (int j=1; j<=8; j++) // is p(tj) different from mi(tj)?
      {// load tj onto N, a;
       bool dis; dis=true;
       loaddata(j);
       p(a,N);
       for (int k=0; k<N; k++) {ap[k]=a[k];}
       // load tj onto N, a;
       loaddata(j);
       switch(i) {case 1: m1(a,N); case 2: m2(a,N);
                  case 3: m3(a,N);
                  case 4: m4(a,N); case 5: m5(a,N);}
       for (int k=0; k<N; k++) {dis = dis && (a[k]==ap[k]);}
```

```
        if (dis) {cout << "  test t" << j << " returns True"
                 << endl;}
        else   {cout << "  test t"  << j << " returns False"
                 << endl;}
      discumul=discumul && dis;
      }
  if (discumul) {cout << "mutant " << i << " not distinguished
                   from p." << endl;}
  else {cout << "mutant " << i << " distinguished from p."
        << endl;}
  };
}


void loaddata(int j)
  {
   N=Na[j];
   for (int k=0; k<N; k++) {a[k]=aa[j][k+1];}
   }
```

9

Functional Criteria

Given a program p and a specification R whose domain is X, we are interested to generate test data T as a subset of X in such a way that when we execute the candidate program p on all the elements of set T and observe its behavior, we can make meaningful inference on the functional properties of program p. In Chapter 8, we have discussed the requirements that set T must satisfy, depending on the goal of testing, and we have analyzed possible generation criteria that yield such data sets. The generation of test data may proceed either by analyzing the specification of the program or by analyzing the source code of the program. In this chapter, we focus on the first approach.

9.1 DOMAIN PARTITIONING

The criterion of *domain partitioning* is based on the premise that the input space X of the specification can be partitioned into equivalence classes such that in each class, candidate programs either runs successfully on all the states in the class or fails on all the states in the class; this criterion may be rationalized if we define equivalence classes to include all the input data that are processed the same way. Under such a condition, we can let T be a subset of S that includes a single element of each equivalence class. The selection criterion on a test set T can be formulated as follows:

Test Data Selection Criterion: Domain Partitioning

Let EQ be an equivalence relation on set X, the domain of the specification, choose a subset T of S such that

- $EQ(T) = X$,
- $EQ \cap T \times T \subseteq I$.

Software Testing: Concepts and Operations, First Edition. Ali Mili and Fairouz Tchier.
© 2015 John Wiley & Sons, Inc. Published 2015 by John Wiley & Sons, Inc.

The first condition means that all equivalence classes are represented in T; the second condition means that each equivalence class is represented by no more than one element in T.

A special example of equivalence relation arises when the specification of the program is deterministic (in particular, when the specification used is the intended function of the program); hence the following heuristic:

> If we want to generate test data for a program p to satisfy the logical requirement with respect to a deterministic specification F, we may apply the space partitioning technique with the equivalence relation $EQ = \{(s,s') | F(s) = F(s')\}$. We refer to this relation as the *nucleus* of F.

This relation has as many equivalence classes as F has elements in its range; hence for functions F with a finite and small range, this produces a small test data set T. The rationale for this criterion may be that all the inputs that are mapped to the same output are processed using the same sequence of operations; hence if the sequence is correct, it will work correctly for all the inputs in the same class, and if it is incorrect, it will fail for all the inputs in the same class. This criterion is as good as the assumption it is based on.

As an illustration, we consider the following example: We let the input space be defined by three real positive variables x, y, and z, which we assume to represent the sides of a triangle, and we consider the following specification, which analyzes the properties of the triangle represented by the input variables: Given that x, y, and z represent the sides of a triangle, place in t the class of the triangle represented by x, y, and z from the set {scalene, isosceles, equilateral, rightisosceles, right}. We assume that the label "isosceles" is reserved for triangles that are isosceles but not equilateral and that the label "right" is reserved for triangles that are right but not isosceles.

This specification can be written by means of the following predicates:

- $Equi(x,y,z) \equiv (x = y \wedge y = z)$.
- $Iso(x,y,z) \equiv (x = y \vee y = z \vee x = z)$.
- $Right(x,y,z) \equiv (x^2 = y^2 + z^2 \vee y^2 = x^2 + z^2 \vee z^2 = x^2 + y^2)$.

Using these predicates, we define the following relations:

- $T_1 = \{(s,s') | Equi(x,y,z) \wedge t' = equilateral\}$.
- $T_2 = \{(s,s') | Iso(x,y,z) \wedge \neg Equi(x,y,z) \wedge \neg Right(x,y,z) \wedge t' = isoceles\}$.
- $T_3 = \{(s,s') | Iso(x,y,z) \wedge Right(x,y,z) \wedge t' = rightisoceles\}$.
- $T_4 = \{(s,s') | Right(x,y,z) \wedge \neg Iso(x,y,z) \wedge t' = right\}$.

- $T_5 = \{(s,s') \mid \neg Iso(x,y,z) \wedge \neg Equi(x,y,z) \wedge \neg Right(x,y,z) \wedge t' = scalene\}$.

Using these relations, we form the relational specification of the triangle classification problem:

$$T = T_1 \cup T_2 \cup T_3 \cup T_4 \cup T_5.$$

We leave it to the reader to check that T is a function; clearly, relation $EQ = \{(s,s') \mid F(s) = F(s')\}$ is an equivalence relation on the domain of T. Its equivalence classes are:

- $C_1 = \{s \mid Equi(x,y,z)\}$.
- $C_2 = \{s \mid Iso(x,y,z) \wedge \neg Equi(x,y,z) \wedge \neg Right(x,y,z)\}$.
- $C_3 = \{s \mid Iso(x,y,z) \wedge Right(x,y,z)\}$.
- $C_4 = \{s \mid Right(x,y,z) \wedge \neg Iso(x,y,z)\}$.
- $C_5 = \{s \mid \neg Iso(x,y,z) \wedge \neg Equi(x,y,z) \wedge \neg Right(x,y,z)\}$.

This partition is illustrated in Figure 9.1 (where it is superimposed on the division of space S into the set of right triangles, the set of isosceles triangles, the set of equilateral triangles, and the set of scalene triangles).

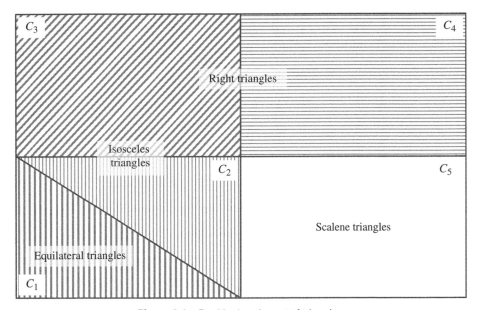

Figure 9.1 *Partitioning the set of triangles.*

From this partition of S, we derive an arbitrary set of test data:

Partition		Test data		
Name	Definition	x	y	z
C_1	$Equi(x,y,z)$	2	2	2
C_2	$Iso(x,y,z) \wedge \neg Equi(x,y,z) \wedge \neg Right(x,y,z)$	2	2	1
C_3	$Iso(x,y,z) \wedge Right(x,y,z)$	2	2	$2\sqrt{2}$
C_4	$Right(x,y,z) \wedge \neg Iso(x,y,z)$	3	4	5
C_5	$\neg Iso(x,y,z) \wedge \neg Equi(x,y,z) \wedge \neg Right(x,y,z)$	2	3	4

The rationale of space partitioning is that any program that runs successfully on these five test data triplets will run successfully on any triplet of positive reals. We have no reason to subscribe to this rationale, except for the fact that, in all likelihood, candidate programs operate by comparing the relative values of x, y, and z; hence any two states s and s' whose x-, y-, and z-components are in the same relations relative to each other are processed the same way by the program; therefore the program succeeds for both or fails for both. Notice that, because this test generation method is functional, then (by definition) we generate the test data without ever looking at the program that we are supposed to test with this data.

Now that the data has been generated, let us now look at a possible implementation of the specification presented above:

```
#include <iostream>
#include <cmath>
using namespace std;
/*   constants        */
float eps = 0.000001;
/*  state variables */
float x, y, z;
/*  functions  */
bool equal(float a, float b);
bool equi(float x, float y, float z);
bool iso(float x, float y, float z);
bool right(float x, float y, float z);
int main ()
  {cout << "enter the triangle sides on one line" << endl;
   cin >> x >> y >> z;
   if (equi(x,y,z))
     {cout << "equilateral" << endl;}
   else
```

```
    {if (iso(x,y,z))
        {if (right(x,y,z))
            {cout << "isosceles right" << endl;}
    else {cout << "isosceles" <<endl;}}
    else
        {if (right(x,y,z)) {cout << "right" << endl;}
        else {cout << "scalene" << endl;}}}}
bool equal (float a, float b)
    {return abs(a-b)<eps;}
bool equi(float x, float y, float z)
    {return (equal(x,y) && equal(y,z));}
bool iso(float x, float y, float z)
    {return (equal(x,y) || equal(y,z) || equal(x,z));}
bool right(float x, float y, float z)
    {return (equal(x*x+y*y,z*z) || equal(x*x+z*z,y*y) ||
equal(y*y+z*z,x*x));}
```

Execution of this program on the proposed test data yields the following results:

Input variables			Output
x	y	z	
2	2	2	Equilateral
2	2	1	Isosceles
2	2	$2\sqrt{2}$	Right isosceles
3	4	5	Right
2	3	4	Scalene

The behavior of the program on the selected test data is correct; according to the heuristic of space partitioning, and to the extent that it is valid, we can infer from this test that the program will behave correctly for any triplet of positive real numbers that define a triangle.

So far we have assumed that the input values x, y, and z define a triangle and have focused on the correctness of candidate programs with respect to a relation whose domain is the set of triangles; but assume that, for the sake of robustness, we wish to lift this assumption and consider cases where the input does not define a triangle (e.g., the triplet (3,3,10) does not define a triangle). We introduce the following predicate:

- $Tri(x,y,z) \equiv (x \leq y+z) \vee (y \leq x+z) \vee (z \leq x+y)$.

Using this predicate, we define a new specification T' in terms of the previous specification T, according to the following formula:

$$T' = \{(s,s') | \neg Tri(x,y,z) \wedge t' = notriangle\} \cup \{(s,s') | Tri(x,y,z)\} \cap T.$$

To make our program robust (i.e., able to handle any triplet of real numbers), we modify it to be correct with respect to specification T'. We obtain the following program:

```cpp
#include <iostream>
#include <cmath>
using namespace std;
/*   constants       */
float eps = 0.000001;
/*   state variables */
float x, y, z;
/*   functions */
Bool tri(float x, float y, float z);
bool equal(float a, float b);
bool equi(float x, float y, float z);
bool iso(float x, float y, float z);
bool right(float x, float y, float z);
int main ()
   {cout << "enter the triangle sides on one line" << endl;
    cin >> x >> y >> z;
    if (!tri(x,y,z))
       {cout << "not a triangle" << endl;}
    else
       {if (equi(x,y,z))
             {cout << "equilateral" << endl;}
       else
            if (iso(x,y,z))
                 {if (right(x,y,z))
                      {cout << "isosceles right" << endl;}
                  else {cout << "isosceles" <<endl;}
             else
                 {if (right(x,y,z)) {cout << "right" << endl;}
                  else {cout << "scalene" << endl;}}}}
bool tri (float x, float y, float z)
   {return ((x<=y+z) && (y<=x+z) && (z<=x+y));}
bool equal (float a, float b)
   {return abs(a-b)<eps;}
bool equi (float x, float y, float z)
   {return (equal(x,y) && equal(y,z));}
bool iso(float x, float y, float z)
```

```
    {return (equal(x,y) || equal(y,z) || equal(x,z));}
bool right(float x, float y, float z)
    {return (equal(x*x+y*y,z*z) || equal(x*x+z*z,y*y) ||
             equal(y*y+z*z,x*x));}
```

From the viewpoint of test data generation, this adds a new output value, hence a new equivalence class in the domain of the specification, for which we must select a representative. We choose (3,3,10), yielding the following table:

Input variables			Output
x	y	z	
2	2	2	Equilateral
2	2	1	Isosceles
2	2	$2\sqrt{2}$	Right isosceles
3	4	5	Right
2	3	4	Scalene
3	3	10	Not a triangle

Remember that for our purposes, if it weren't for the fact that it is impractical, X is the most effective test data set; selecting the test data set T = X would enable us, if it were feasible, to run the program exhaustively on all its possible inputs. Notice that the criterion of domain partitioning enables us, in effect, to run the program exhaustively on all its possible outputs, instead.

9.2 TEST DATA GENERATION FROM TABULAR EXPRESSIONS

In the previous section, we have analyzed a criterion for test data selection that applies to deterministic specifications and partitions the domain of the specification (say F) using the nucleus of F as the equivalence relation EQ ($= \{(s,s')|$ $F(s) = F(s')\}$). In this section, we see instances where the nucleus of F is either too coarse-grained or too fine-rained for our purposes, and we choose a different equivalence relation.

Tabular specifications are a form of formal specifications where complex functions that take different expressions according to many parameters can be represented in a way that highlights their dependencies and facilitates their analysis and their understanding. As an example, consider a table that specifies the tax rates of individual taxpayers in a particular jurisdiction, as a function of their income, their marital status, and their number of dependents.

Function: Tax(X, d, t)						
t: Marital status	**d:** Number of dependents	**X:** Income bracket (in $K)				
		X ≤ 20	20 < X ≤ 60	60 < X ≤ 150	150 < X ≤ 250	250 < X
Single	1	0.08 × X	1.6 + 0.10×(X − 20)	5.6 + 0.15 × (X − 60)	19.1 + 0.20 × (X − 150)	39.1 + 0.25 × (X − 250)
	2	0.07 × X	1.4 + 0.09(X − 20)	5.0 + 0.14 × (X − 60)	17.6 + 0.19 × (X − 150)	36.6 + 0.24 × (X − 250)
	3 or more	0.06 × X	1.2 + 0.08(X − 20)	4.4 + 0.13 × (X − 60)	16.1 + 0.18 × (X − 150)	34.1 + 0.23 × (X − 250)
Married/ filing singly	1	0.07 × X	1.4 + 0.09(X − 20)	5.0 + 0.14 × (X − 60)	17.6 + 0.19 × (X − 150)	36.6 + 0.24 × (X − 250)
	2	0.06 × X	1.2 + 0.08(X − 20)	4.4 + 0.13 × (X − 60)	16.1 + 0.18 × (X − 150)	34.1 + 0.23 × (X − 250)
	3	0.05 × X	1.0 + 0.07(X − 20)	3.8 + 0.12 × (X − 60)	14.6 + 0.17 × (X − 150)	31.6 + 0.22 × (X − 250)
	4 or more	0.04 × X	0.8 + 0.06(X − 20)	3.2 + 0.11 × (X − 60)	13.1 + 0.16 × (X − 150)	29.1 + 0.21 × (X − 250)

We let X, d, and t be variables that represent, respectively, the taxpayer's income, his/her number of dependents, and his/her marital status (filing status). The input space of this specification is defined by the set of values that these three variables take, where X is a real number, d is an integer, and t is a binary value (single, married). If we assume, for the sake of argument, that incomes of interest range between 0 and 1000,000, and that taxes are rounded to the nearest dollar figure, then the output of this function ranges between 0 and 186,600. If we were to apply the criterion of domain partitioning strictly, we would find that this function partitions its domain into 186,601 equivalence classes, hence T would have to have that many elements.

Yet, without knowing how candidate programs compute this function, we can assume with some level of confidence that each entry in this tabular expression corresponds to a distinct execution path; hence if we generated one test datum for each entry rather than one test datum for each tax value, we would get a much smaller test data set (35 elements rather than 186,601) without perhaps much loss of effectiveness. To this effect, we apply domain partitioning to a function Tax' derived from Tax by replacing each expression in the tabular representation of Tax by a (distinct) constant. The rationale for this substitution is the assumption that if and only if an expression in the table of Tax produces a correct value for one element within its domain of application, then it produces a correct value for all elements within its domain of application. This yields the following function.

Function: $Tax'(X, d, t)$						
t: Marital status	d: Number of dependents	X: Income bracket (in \$K)				
		$X \leq 20$	$20 < X \leq 60$	$60 < X \leq 150$	$150 < X \leq 250$	$250 < X$
t = Single	$d = 1$	$C_{1,1,1}$	$C_{1,1,2}$	$C_{1,1,3}$	$C_{1,1,4}$	$C_{1,1,5}$
	$d = 2$	$C_{1,2,1}$	$C_{1,2,2}$	$C_{1,2,3}$	$C_{1,2,4}$	$C_{1,2,5}$
	$d \geq 3$	$C_{1,3,1}$	$C_{1,3,2}$	$C_{1,3,3}$	$C_{1,3,4}$	$C_{1,3,5}$
t = Married	$d = 1$	$C_{2,1,1}$	$C_{2,1,2}$	$C_{2,1,3}$	$C_{2,1,4}$	$C_{2,1,5}$
	$d = 2$	$C_{2,2,1}$	$C_{2,2,2}$	$C_{2,2,3}$	$C_{2,2,4}$	$C_{2,2,5}$
	$d = 3$	$C_{2,3,1}$	$C_{2,3,2}$	$C_{2,3,3}$	$C_{2,3,4}$	$C_{2,3,5}$
	$d \geq 4$	$C_{2,4,1}$	$C_{2,4,2}$	$C_{2,4,3}$	$C_{2,4,4}$	$C_{2,4,5}$

Applying space partitioning to function Tax' using the nucleus of this function, we find the following test data.

Marital status/ Taxpayer status	Number of dependents	Income bracket (X, in \$K)				
		$X \leq 20$	$20 < X \leq 60$	$60 < X \leq 150$	$150 < X \leq 250$	$250 < X$
t = Single	$d = 1$	$(10, 1, S)$	$(40, 1, S)$	$(100, 1, S)$	$(200, 1, S)$	$(300, 1, S)$
	$d = 2$	$(10, 2, S)$	$(40, 2, S)$	$(100, 2, S)$	$(200, 2, S)$	$(300, 2, S)$
	$d \geq 3$	$(10, 4, S)$	$(40, 4, S)$	$(100, 4, S)$	$(200, 4, S)$	$(300, 4, S)$
t = Married	$d = 1$	$(10, 1, M)$	$(40, 1, M)$	$(100, 1, M)$	$(200, 1, M)$	$(300, 1, M)$
	$d = 2$	$(10, 2, M)$	$(40, 2, M)$	$(100, 2, M)$	$(200, 2, M)$	$(300, 2, M)$
	$d = 3$	$(10, 3, M)$	$(40, 3, M)$	$(100, 3, M)$	$(200, 3, M)$	$(300, 3, M)$
	$d \geq 4$	$(10, 5, M)$	$(40, 5, M)$	$(100, 5, M)$	$(200, 5, M)$	$(300, 5, M)$

To check that the boundaries between the various income brackets are processed properly by candidate programs, we may also want to duplicate this table for all boundary values of X, namely *X=20, 60, 150, 250,* and *1000* (assuming that 1M is the maximum income under consideration). This yields the following test data.

Marital status/ Taxpayer status	Number of dependents	Income bracket (X, in $K)				
		$X \leq 20$	$20 < X \leq 60$	$60 < X \leq 150$	$150 < X \leq 250$	$250 < X$
t = Single	$d = 1$	(10, 1, S)	(40, 1, S)	(100, 1, S)	(200, 1, S)	(300, 1, S)
		(20, 1, S)	(60, 1, S)	(150, 1, S)	(250, 1, S)	(1000, 1, S)
	$d = 2$	(10, 2, S)	(40, 2, S)	(100, 2, S)	(200, 2, S)	(300, 2, S)
		(20, 2, S)	(60, 2, S)	(150, 2, S)	(250, 2, S)	(1000, 2, S)
	$d \geq 3$	(10, 4, S)	(40, 4, S)	(100, 4, S)	(200, 4, S)	(300, 4, S)
		(20, 4, S)	(60, 4, S)	(150, 4, S)	(250, 4, S)	(1000, 4, S)
t = Married	$d = 1$	(10, 1, M)	(40, 1, M)	(100, 1, M)	(200, 1, M)	(300, 1, M)
		(20, 1, M)	(60, 1, M)	(150, 1, M)	(250, 1, M)	(1000, 1, M)
	$d = 2$	(10, 2, M)	(40, 2, M)	(100, 2, M)	(200, 2, M)	(300, 2, M)
		(20, 2, M)	(60, 2, M)	(150, 2, M)	(250, 2, M)	(1000, 2, M)
	$d = 3$	(10, 3, M)	(40, 3, M)	(100, 3, M)	(200, 3, M)	(300, 3, M)
		(20, 3, M)	(60, 3, M)	(150, 3, M)	(250, 3, M)	(1000, 3, M)
	$d \geq 4$	(10, 5, M)	(40, 5, M)	(100, 5, M)	(200, 5, M)	(300, 5, M)
		(20, 5, M)	(60, 5, M)	(150, 5, M)	(250, 5, M)	(1000, 5, M)

Assuming that the specification is valid (is not in question) and a candidate program p computes taxes as a linear function of income within each partition of the input space, it is highly unlikely that program p runs successfully on all the test data presented above, yet fail on any other valid input.

We consider a second example, where we show that the important criterion for space partitioning is not the nucleus of the function, but rather how the specification is represented in tabular form. We consider a (fictitious) tabular specification that represents the graduate admissions criteria at a university, depending on standard graduate record examination (GRE) scores for quantitative reasoning (G) and grade point average (GPA) (A); also the admissions committee lends different levels of credibility to different institutions and hence interprets the GPA with different levels of confidence, according to whether the candidate did his undergraduate degree in the same institution, in another North American institution, or elsewhere, as shown by the table below. We assume that the specification provides three distinct outcomes and they are admission (Ad), rejection (Re), and conditional acceptance (Cond), where the latter outcome places the application on hold until an admitted student declines the admission, thereby freeing up a spot for admission.

Admission criteria					
Institution, *I*	GPA, *A*	GRE score, *G*			
		G < 155	155 ≤ *G* < 160	160 ≤ *G* < 165	165 ≤ *G*
Same Institution	2.9 ≤ A	Ad	Ad	Ad	Ad
	2.3 ≤ A < 2.9	Cond	Cond	Ad	Ad
	A < 2.3	Re	Re	Cond	Cond
Another North American Institution	2.9 ≤ A	Cond	Ad	Ad	Ad
	2.3 ≤ A < 2.9	Re	Cond	Ad	Ad
	A < 2.3	Re	Re	Cond	Cond
Overseas	2.9 ≤ A	Re	Cond	Ad	Ad
	2.3 ≤ A < 2.9	Re	Re	Cond	Ad
	A < 2.3	Re	Re	Re	Cond

The input space for this function is the Cartesian product of three variables, namely *G*, *A*, and *I*. If we apply space partitioning using the nucleus of this function, we find three equivalence classes, corresponding to the three possible outputs. But in practice, any candidate program most likely proceeds by combining the conditions shown above; hence it makes more sense to partition the input space by combining these conditions, which gives 36 classes rather than 3. If for each class we select a test datum in the middle of the interval and at the boundary, we find the following test data set.

Admission criteria					
Institution, *I*	GPA, *A*	GRE score, *G*			
		G < 155	155 ≤ *G* < 160	160 ≤ *G* < 165	165 ≤ *G*
Same Institution (S)	2.9 ≤ A	(120,S,3.5) (0,S,2.9)	(158,S,3.5) (155,S,2.9)	(162,S,3.5) (160,S,2.9)	(168,S,3.5) (165,S,2.9)
	2.3 ≤ A < 2.9	(120,S,2.5) (0,S,2.3)	(158,S,2.5) (155,S,2.3)	(162,S,2.5) (160,S,2.3)	(168,S,2.5) (165,S,2.3)
	A < 2.3	(120,S,2.0) (0,S,.0)	(158,S,2.0) (155,S,.0)	(162,S,2.0) (160,S,.0)	(168,S,2.0) (165,S,.0)

Another North American Institution (N)	$2.9 \le A$	(120,N,3.5) (0,N,2.9)	(158,N,3.5) (155,N,2.9)	(162,N,3.5) (160,N,2.9)	(168,N,3.5) (165,N,2.9)
	$2.3 \le A < 2.9$	(120,N,2.5) (0,N,2.9)	(158,N,2.5) (155,N,2.9)	(162,N,2.5) (160,N,2.9)	(168,N,2.5) (165,N,2.9)
	$A < 2.3$	(120,N,2.0) (0,N,.0)	(158,N,2.0) (155,N,.0)	(162,N,2.0) (160,N,.0)	(168,N,2.0) (165,N,.0)
Overseas (O)	$2.9 \le A$	(120,O,3.5) (0,O,2.9)	(158,O,3.5) (155,O,2.9)	(162,O,3.5) (160,O,2.9)	(168,O,3.5) (165,O,2.9)
	$2.3 \le A < 2.9$	(120,O,2.5) (0,O,2.9)	(158,O,2.5) (155,O,2.9)	(162,O,2.5) (160,O,2.9)	(168,O,2.5) (165,O,2.9)
	$A < 2.3$	(120,O,2.0) (0,O,.0)	(158,O,2.0) (155,O,.0)	(162,O,2.0) (160,O,.0)	(168,O,2.0) (165,O,.0)

For completeness, we could enrich the data set by combining normal values with boundary values.

9.3 TEST GENERATION FOR STATE BASED SYSTEMS

A state-based system is a system whose output depends not only on its (current) input but also on an internal state, which is itself dependent on past inputs. As we discussed in Chapter 4, such systems can be specified in relational form by means of the following artifacts:

- An *input space X*, from which we derive a set H of sequences of X
- An *output space Y*
- A *relation* R from H to Y.

It is common to specify such systems in a way that makes their internal state explicit, by means of the following artifacts:

- An *input space X*
- An *output space Y*
- An *internal state space,* Σ
- An *output function,* ω from $X \times \Sigma$ to Y
- A *state transition function,* θ from $X \times \Sigma$ to Σ.

We argue that it is possible to map a specification of the form (X,Y,R) into a specification of the form $(X,Y,\Sigma,\omega,\theta)$, as follows:

- X and Y are preserved.

- We define the equivalence relation E on H $(=X^*)$ by:

$$E = \{(h, h') | \forall h'', \forall y : (h.h'', y) \in R \Leftrightarrow (h'.h'', y) \in R\}.$$

In other words, the pair (h, h') is in E if and only if they are equivalent histories, in the sense that they produce the same output now (for h'' empty) and in the future (for h'' not empty). Using this equivalence relation, we define the internal state space of the system as the quotient (H/E), that is, the set of equivalence classes of H modulo E. Whereas the output of the system depends on its input history, this does not mean that the system must remember its input history in all its detail; rather it must only remember the equivalence class of its input history; this is exactly the *internal state* of the system.

- The output function is defined as follows:

$$\omega = \{((x, \sigma), y) | \exists h \in \sigma : (h.x, y) \in R\}.$$

Given a current internal state σ and a current input symbol x, we let h be an arbitrary element of σ, and we let y be an image of $(h.x)$ by R. Because σ is an equivalence class of H modulo E, the choice of h within σ is immaterial, by definition.

- The state transition function is defined as follows:

$$\theta = \{((x, \sigma), \sigma') | \exists h \in \sigma : \sigma' = E(h.x)\},$$

where $E(h.x)$ designates the set of images of $(h.x)$ by relation E, which is the equivalence class of $(h.x)$ modulo E.

We have made the observation that even software systems that carry an internal state can, in theory, be modeled by a mere relation from an input set (structured as the set of lists formed from the input space) to an output space. This observation is important because it means that we can, in theory, select test data for such a system in the same way as we do for a system that has no internal state, except for considering the special structure of the input set.

As an illustration of the mapping between the (X, Y, R) model of specification and the $(X, Y, \Sigma, \omega, \theta)$ model, we consider the specification of the stack given in Chapter 4 in the (X, Y, R) format and we discuss (informally) the terms of its $(X, Y, \Sigma, \omega, \theta)$ specification.

- X: The input space of the stack is defined as

$$X = \{init, pop, top, size, empty\} \cup \{push\} \times itemtype,$$

where *itemtype* is the data type of the items we envision to store in the stack. We distinguish, in set X, between inputs that affect the state of the stack (namely: $AX = \{init, push, pop\}$) and inputs that merely report on it (namely: $VX = \{top, size, empty\}$).
  - From the set of inputs X, we build the set of input histories, H, defined as, $H = X^*$.

- *Y*: The output space includes all the values returned by all the inputs of *VX*, namely:

$$Y = (itemtype \cup \{error\}) \cup integer \cup boolean.$$

- Σ: The equivalence relation *E* includes two histories *h* and *h'* if and only if any subsequent history *h''* produces the same outcomes. Examples of histories that are equivalent modulo relation *E* include, for instance:
  - pop.top.init.pop.push(a).
  - init.push(a).
  - init.pop.top.size.push(a).empty.push(b).top.pop.
  - init.push(a).push(b).push(c).push(d).top.pop.pop.pop.

  All these histories belong to the same equivalence class modulo *E*, that is, they are part of the same state; we represent this state by its simplest element, which is
  - init.push(a).

- *ω*: The output function of the stack maps an internal state *σ* and a current input *x* into an output *y* by virtue of the equation:

$$(h.x, y) \in R,$$

  where *h* is an element of *σ*. If we consider the internal state *σ* that is the equivalence class of init.push(a), and we let *h* = init.push(a) be a representative element of state *σ*, then the output of the stack for internal state *σ* and input *x* is characterized by the following equation:

$$(init.push(a).x, y) \in stack.$$

  For $x = top$, $y = \omega(\sigma, x) = a$.
  For $x = size$, $y = \omega(\sigma, x) = 1$
  For $x = empty$, $y = \omega(\sigma, x) = false$.
  For $x = $ pop, push(_), or init, $y = \omega(\sigma, x)$ is arbitrary (an arbitrary element of *Y*), since these are elements of *AX* that change the state of the stack but generate no output.

- *θ*: The state transition function of the stack maps an internal state *σ* and a current input *x* into a new internal state *σ'* by virtue of the equation:

$$\sigma' = E(h.x),$$

  where *h* is an element of *σ*. If we consider the internal state *σ* that is the equivalence class of init.push(a), and we let *h* = init.push(a) be a representative element of state *σ*, then the next state of the stack for internal state *σ* and input *x* is characterized by the following equation:

$$\sigma' = E(init.push(a).x).$$

The following table shows the result of applying function θ to the `init.push(a)` and to the input sympols of *AX*.

x	θ (init.push(a), x)
init	*init*
push(b)	*init.push(a).push(b)*
pop	*init*

Because formally, state-based systems can be specified by binary relations, then in theory we can apply to them any criterion that we apply to simple input/output systems which are also specified by (homogeneous) binary relations. But in recognition of the special structure that implementations of state-based systems have (in terms of an input space, an internal space, and an output space), it makes sense to formulate test data selection criteria accordingly. Among the test data selection criteria that we may adopt, we mention the following:

- *Select Test Data to Visit Every State.* The question that arises with this criterion is that the specification of the product is defined in terms of input sequences and outputs and has no cognizance of internal states; also, even if we derive the states from the trace specifications as we have discussed above, the implementation does not have to adopt these very states. We obviate this dilemma by considering that, for an outside observer, a state is characterized by the values of all the *VX* operations at that state. In other words, to check that the software product is in the right state (without looking at the internal data of the product) with respect to the specification, we generate the sequence of operations that leads us to that state, and then we append to it in turn all the *VX* operations of the specification. The procedure that generates data according to this criterion proceeds as follows:
  - Partition the set of histories into equivalence classes modulo the equivalence relation *E* defined above.
  - Choose an element of each equivalence class, and add to it, in turn, all the *VX* operations of the specification.

In practice, relation *E* may have an infinity of equivalence classes, forcing us to take supersets of it by merging in the same equivalence class input sequences for which we suspect that candidate programs have the same behavior (i.e., they succeed for both or fail for both); we will see examples of this merger below. This criterion is illustrated in the Figure 9.2, where the quadrants represent equivalence classes of H^* modulo E, $h_1, h_2, \ldots, h_8$ represent the elements of the equivalence classes, and $v_1, v_2, \ldots, v_i$ represent the *VX* operations of the specification.

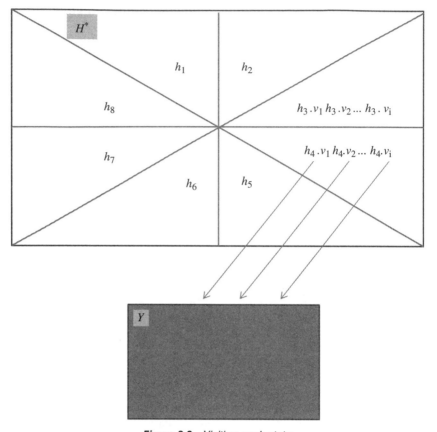

Figure 9.2 *Visiting each state.*

- *Select Test Data to Perform Every State Transition.* We perform state transitions by appending *AX* operations to existing sequences for all the *AX* operations of the specification, then appending in turn all the *VX* operations to identify the new state, and check its validity with respect to the specification. This criterion is illustrated in the Figure 9.3, where the quadrants represent equivalence classes of H^* modulo E, $h_1, h_2, ..., h_8$ represent the elements of the equivalence classes, and $v_1, v_2, ..., v_i$ represent the *VX* operations of the specification, and $a_1, a_2, ..., a_j$ represent its *AX* operations.

From this discussion we infer that the set of test data that we ought to generate to visit all the states and traverse all the state transitions is the union of two terms:

1. $(X^*/E) \times VX$ (by virtue of the criterion of visiting all the states) and
2. $(X^*/E) \times AX \times VX$ (by virtue of traversing all the state transitions).

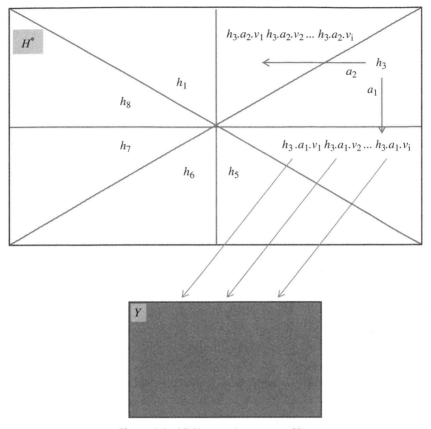

Figure 9.3 *Visiting each state transition.*

Whence the following test data generation criterion:

> If we want to generate test data for a program p to satisfy the logical requirement with respect to a state-based specification R from input space X to output space Y, we let E be the quivalence relation defined on $H = X^*$ by
>
> $$E = \{(h, h') | \forall h'' \in H, \forall y \in Y : (h''.h, y) \in R \Leftrightarrow (h''.h', y) \in R\},$$
>
> and we generate test data T as:
>
> $$T = (X^+ / E) \times VX \cup (X^* / E) \times AX \times VX.$$

Whereas the formula of T (above) provides for composing sets (X^*/E), AX, and VX by means of the Cartesian product, we in fact mean to obtain a set of sequences constructed by concatenation of elements of these sets; this is illustrated in the example below.

While *AX* and *VX* are usually small, $(X*/E)$ is usually infinite, requiring some additional assumptions to replace it by a finite/small subset. As an illustration, we consider again the stack specification, and we argue that two input sequences of this specification are equivalent if and only if they are reducible to the same sequence of the form:

$$init.push(t_1).push(t_2).push(t_3)....push(t_k).$$

This set of states is clearly infinite, given that k can be arbitrarily large, and $t_1, t_2, t_3,$ $..., t_k$, can take arbitrary values. If we assume that the success or failure of a stack implementation will not depend, perhaps, on the value that we store in the stack at any position, then we can represent states as follows, where $push(-)^n$ represents a sequence of n instances of push() for arbitrary values on the stack, then we can write the states of the stack as:

$$init.push(-)^k.$$

This set is also infinite, since k may take arbitrary natural values; hence further assumptions are needed. We may assume (with some risk) that any implementation of the stack that works for stacks of size 3 works for stacks greater than 3, provided we have assurances that overflow is not an issue (either because our stack size is bounded or because our supply of memory is unbounded). Hence $(X*/E)$ can be approximated with the following set:

$$\{init, \quad init.push(), \quad init.push().push(), \quad init.push().push().push()\}.$$

This gives the following test data, which we present in two different tables that correspond to the two terms of the union in the formula of *T*:

		(X^*/E)			
		init	*init.push(–)*	*init.push( ). push( )*	*init.push( ). push( ). push( )*
VX	*top*	*init.top*	*init.push(a). top*	*init.push(–). push(a).top*	*init.push(–).push(–). push(a).top*
	size	*init.size*	*init.push(a). size*	*init.push(–). push(a).size*	*init.push(–).push(–). push(a).size*
	empty	*init.empty*	*init.push(a). empty*	*init.push(–). push(a).empty*	*init.push(–).push(–). push(a).empty*

AX	VX	$(X^*/E) \times AX \times VX$			
		init	init.push(–)	init.push( ).push( )	init.push( ).push( ).push( )
init	top	init.init.top	init.push(a).init.top	init.push(–).push(a).init.top	init.push(–).push(–).push(a).init.top
	size	init.init.size	init.push(a).init.size	init.push(–).push(a).init.size	init.push(–).push(–).push(a).init.size
	empty	init.init.empty	init.push(a).init.empty	init.push(–).push(a).init.empty	init.push(–).push(–).push(a).init.empty
push	top	init.push(b).top	init.push(a).push(b).top	init.push(–).push(a).push(b).top	init.push(–).push(–).push(a).push(b).top
	size	init push(b).size	init.push(a).push(b).size	init.push(–).push(a).push(b).size	init.push(–).push(–).push(a).push(b).size
	empty	init.push(b).empty	init.push(a).push(b).empty	init.push(–).push(a).push(b).empty	init.push(–).push(–).push(a).push(b).empty
pop	top	init.pop.top	init.push(a).pop.top	init.push(–).push(a).pop.top	init.push(–).push(–).push(a).pop.top
	size	init.pop.size	init.push(a).pop.size	init.push(–).push(a).pop.size	init.push(–).push(–).push(a).pop.size
	empty	init.pop.empty	init.push(a).pop.empty	init.push(–).push(a).pop.empty	init.push(–).push(–).push(a).pop.empty

How do we test an implementation using this test data? Simply by declaring an instance of the class that implements the specification R and by writing sequences of method calls that represent the data shown in this table. For example,

```
#include <iostream>
#include "stack.cpp"
using namespace std;
/* state variables */
stack s;
itemtype t; int z; bool e; // to store outputs of VX operations
```

```
int main ()
  {
    s.init(); t=s.top(); cout << t; // test datum: init.top
    // ... ... ...
    s.init(); s.push(c); s.push(d); s.push(a); s.push(b);
    // test datum: init.push(_).push(_).push(a).pop.empty
  }
```

As for the question of whether these executions took place according to the specification, it will be addressed when we discuss oracle design, in Chapter 11.

9.4   RANDOM TEST DATA GENERATION

Test data generation is a difficult, labor-intensive, time-consuming and error-prone activity. Like all such activities, it raises the question of whether it can be automated. To automate the generation of specific test data that meet specific generation criteria using specifications is very difficult, especially if one considers that very often the specification is not available in the form and with the precision that is required for this purpose. What is possible, however, is to generate great volumes of random test data, according to arbitrary probability distributions; there are many cases where this approach provides an excellent return on investment, in terms of test effectiveness versus testing effort. Random number generators are widely available, in conjunction with common programming languages, or as part of mathematical packages; they can be used to generate a wide range of probability laws. Also, because they operate automatically, they can be used to generate arbitrarily large volumes of data and provide arbitrary levels of test thoroughness at relatively little cost and little risk.

- Using the package "**rand.cpp**", we can generate random numbers between 0 (inclusive) and 1 (non-inclusive) by calling the function **NextRand()** as many times as we need; prior to the first call, we must initialize the random generation process by calling the function **SetSeed()** with an arbitrary numeric parameter.
- Using function **NextRand()**, we can generate random real numbers that range uniformly 0.0 inclusive and M (non-inclusive) for an arbitrary value of real number M.

  ```
  float function randomReal(float M)
    {return M*NextRand();}
  ```

- Using function **NextRand()**, we can generate random integers that range uniformly between 1 (inclusive) and N (inclusive), for an arbitrary positive integer N.

```
int function randomInt(int N)
  {return 1+ int(N*NextRand());}
```

* Using function **NextRand()**, we can generate a Boolean function that returns true with a given probability (and false otherwise); the following function returns true with probability p.

```
bool function randomBool(float p)
  {return (NextRand() <= p);}
```

* Using function **randomBool()**, we can generate a Boolean function that returns true, on average, once every N times that it is called.

```
bool function randomEvent(int N)
  {return (randomBool(1.0/N));}
```

* Using function **randomInt()**, we can generate an integer function that ranges uniformly between two values $N1$ and $N2$, where $N1 \le N2$.

```
int function randomInterval(int N1, int N2)
  {return (N1-1+randomInt(N2-N1+1));}
```

* Using function **randomInterval()**, we can generate an integer function that ranges uniformly between $-N$ and N, for $N \ge 0$.

```
int function randomSym(int N)
  {return (randomInterval(-N,N));}
```

* Using function **NextRand()**, we can generate a function that produces a set of discrete outcomes with a specific probability distribution.

```
itemtype randomItems (itemtype items[],
                  float distribution[])
{float cumul[nbitems];
for (int i=0; i<nbitems; i++)
{cumul[i]=0;
for (int j=0; j<=i; j++) {cumul[i]=cumul[i]
                          +distribution[j];}}
float p; p=NextRand(); int i; i=0; while (p>cumul[i])
{i++;}
return (items[i]);
      }
```

This function proceeds by taking the array that represents the probability distribution and building an array of cumulative probability distributions, as follows:

index	0	1	2	3	...	nbitems-1
items	a_0	a_1	a_2	a_3	...	$a_{nbitems-1}$
distribution.	p_0	p_1	p_2	p_3	...	$p_{nbitems-1}$
cumul	p_0	p_0+p_1	$p_0+p_1+p_2$	$p_0+p_1+p_2+p_3$	...	1.0

Once the cumulative array is loaded, the function draws a random number p between 0.0 (inclusive) and 1.0 (exclusive) and returns the first item a_i for which p is less than or equal to **cumul[i]**. Such a value **i** satisfies the following condition:

$$cumul[i-1] < p \leq cumul[i].$$

The length of this interval is the difference between $cumul[i-1]$ and $cumul[i]$, which is p_i. The bigger the value of p_i, the more likely p is to fall in this interval, the more a_i is to be selected. To test this function, we invoke a large number of times and show that the distribution with which it generates the various items mimics the given probability distribution. To this effect, we execute the following program on a set of five items (which we represent by 0, 1, 2, 3, 4) with a probability distribution of (0, 0.1, 0.2, 0.3, and 0.4). The program that runs this experiment is given below:

```
#include <iostream>
#include "rand.cpp"
using namespace std;

// constants
int nbitems = 5;

// type defs
typedef int itemtype;

// functions
itemtype randomItems (itemtype items [] , float distribution []);

int main ()
  {SetSeed(684);
  int stats[5];
  itemtype items[5];  float distribution[5];
  for (int k=0; k<5; k++)
    {items[k]=k; distribution[k]=k/10.0;stats[k]=0;}
  for (int k=0; k<100000; k++)
    {stats[randomItems(items,distribution)]++;}
  for (int i=0; i<5; i++)
```

```
   {cout << stats[i] << " ";}
cout << endl;
}
```

Execution of this program yields the following outcome, which reflects a very consistent behavior with respect to our original distribution.

```
0  100749  199899  300003  399349
```

As a simple illustration of this toolbox of functions for random test data generation, we consider that we must generate test data for a small function that searches an item in an array, where:

- Arrays vary in size between 1 and 100.
- The contents of arrays are integers that vary between −20 and 80.
- The item to be searched in the array is an element of the array in 34% of the cases

To this effect, we write the following program:

```
#include <iostream>
#include "rand.cpp"
using namespace std;

// constants
int maxN = 100;          // max array size
int N1=-20; int N2=80;   // range of array values
int maxX=200000;
float prob=0.34;

// type defs
typedef int itemtype;

// functions
int randomInt (int maxval);
int randomInterval (int N1, int N2);
int randomSym (int N);
bool randomBool (float p);

int main ()
   {
   itemtype a[maxN]; itemtype X; SetSeed(684);
   int N; N=randomInt(maxN); cout << "array a: " << endl;
   for (int i=0; i<N; i++)
      {a[i]=randomInterval(N1,N2); cout << a[i] << " ";}
```

```
cout << endl << "item to search, X: " ;
if (randomBool(prob))
   {int i; i=randomInt(N); X=a[i];}  // assured to be in a
else {X=randomSym(maxX);}            // unlikely to be in a
cout << X << endl;
}
```

If we iterate the sequence of code given in the main program an arbitrary number of times, we get as many test data samples as we wish.

9.5 TOURISM AS A METAPHOR FOR TEST DATA SELECTION

In his book titled *Exploratory Software Testing*, Jim Whittaker, test engineering director at Google, discusses strategies for functional test data selection that equate testing a software product to exploring its various recesses, nooks and crannies so as to expose all its faults. Because these strategies are widely applicable, and cut across most existing techniques, we briefly present them in this section. The software product is mapped into districts (just like a city), and the tours are partitioned by district (just like city tours). Specifically, six districts are identified:

1. The *business district*, which is the code that performs the core functionality of the product.
2. The *historic district*, which is the legacy code on which the application may have been built.
3. The *tourist district*, which is the code that delivers elementary functionality for novice system users.
4. The *entertainment district*, which is the code that delivers supportive features of the product.
5. The *hotel district*, which is the code that is active when the software is at rest.
6. The *seedy district*, which is the code that few users ever activate, but that may contain product vulnerabilities.

Many tours are scheduled for each one of these districts; we cite a few, referring the interested reader to the original source.

- Tours of the Business District
  - *The guidebook tour:* This tour advocates reading the user manual in detail and exercising the product's functionalities according to the manual's guidelines. This tour tests the system's ability to deliver its advertised function, as well as the user manual's precision in describing the system's function.
  - *The skeptical customer tour:* This tour advocates running the software product through a demo used by salespeople, but constantly interrupting the sequence

of the demo to try variations that an end-user may be interested in, such as the following: What if I wanted to do this? How would I do that?

- Tours through the Historical District

  o *The bad neighborhood tour:* This tour advocates running the software product in such a way as to exercise parts of its codes that are likely to have faults; the assumption is that faults tend to congregate in a software product, and the more faults one finds in a part of the product, the more likely other faults are to be found therein.

  o *The museum tour:* This tour advocates running the software product in such a way as to exercise parts of it that stems from legacy code; the rationale of this tour is to expose any faults that may exist in the interface between legacy code and new code.

- Tours through the Entertainment District

  o *The supporting actor tour:* This tour advocates exercising features of the software product that share the screen with core features that most users typically use; they may be less visited than typical functions, but equally likely to have faults.

  o *The back alley tour:* This tour advocates exercising features that are at the low end of the feature table of the software product, on the grounds that they may also correspond to the least covered code of the product.

- Tours through the Tourist District

  o *The collector's tour:* This tour advocates running the application on a sufficiently broad set of inputs and under a sufficiently diverse set of circumstances that you can generate all the possible outcomes that the product is designed to deliver.

  o *The supermodel tour.* This tour advocates to test the application, not on the basis of its functionality, but on the basis of its appearance.

- Tours through the Hotel District

  o *The rained out tour:* This tour advocates initiating actions by the software product and then canceling them as the earliest convenience offered by the application, to check whether the product resets its state properly and diligently.

  o *The couch potato tour:* This tour advocates running the software product in such a way as to provide as little data as possible, to check the product's ability to proceed with incomplete information or by using default values.

- Tours through the Seedy District

  o *The saboteur tour:* This tour advocates initiating operations by the software product and then interfering with the proper execution of these operations (e.g., launching an I/O operation and disconnecting the relevant device); the purpose of this tour is to test the product's ability to handle exceptions.

  o *The obsessive compulsive tour:* This tour advocates initiating the same operation with the same input data over and over again and observing whether the behavior of the system (in terms of whether the successive operations are interpreted as multiple queries, whether they are properly separated from each other, whether they override each other, etc.) is consistent with its requirements.

9.6 CHAPTER SUMMARY

The focus of this chapter is generating test data by considering the specification of the software product for inspiration. We have reviewed a few criteria for test data generation, namely:

- Generating test data by recognizing, or assuming (on the basis of some rationale), that some attributes of input test data are irrelevant from the standpoint of testing: they have no effect on whether candidate programs succeed or fail on an input data. By abstracting away the irrelevant attributes, we find an equivalence relation that places in the same equivalence class all the inputs that have the same effectiveness in exposing faults in candidate programs. Once such an equivalence relation is defined, we test candidate programs by selecting a single element in each equivalence class.
- When the specification of the software requirements is structured in tabular form, it is sensible to use the tabular structure as a guideline to generate test data.
- State-based systems can be specified by relations, albeit heterogeneous relations defined on structured spaces, from which we can derive a theoretical state space, which may or may not be the state space adopted by candidate implementations; regardless, we can generate test data for such implementation using coverage criteria of (theoretical) states and state transitions.
- It is possible to automatically generate random test data for a wide range of purposes using elementary random data generators that are standard features of common programming languages.

9.7 EXERCISES

9.1. Let F be a function. Compute the relation $EQ = F\hat{F}$. Show that this is an equivalence relation and define its equivalence classes. These are called the *level sets* of function F; explain.

9.2. Show that the domains of relations T_1, T_2, T_3, T_4, and T_5 form a partition of the domain of $T = T_1 \cup T_2 \cup T_3 \cup T_4 \cup T_5$.

9.3. Consider the specification of the Tax application given in Section 9.2, and write a program that meets this specification.

   a. Consider the test data generated for this program and use the specification to record the expected output for each test datum.

    b. Check that your program meets the specification, and correct it as needed.

    c. Introduce five different faults in the program (in conditions, or assignments, or structured statements, etc.); check whether the generated test data can detect the fault.

9.4. Same exercise as above, for the admissions specification.

9.5. Consider a system that computes the tuition and fees for students at a university, as a function of the following parameters:

    a. The number of credits taken by the student for the current term, according to some sliding scale.

    b. Whether the student is graduate or undergraduate.

    c. Whether the student is resident in the state, an out-of-state national, or an international student.

Give a tabular specification of this function and generate test data accordingly.

9.6. Consider a system that checks whether a date, given by a month, day, and year is legitimate. The year is an arbitrary positive number, the month is an integer between 1 and 12, and the day is an integer between 1 and 31 whose value varies according to the month and (for February) according to the year. Write a tabular specification of this system and generate test data accordingly. Discuss the rationale of your test generation criterion.

9.7. Consider the specification of a queue ADT given in Chapter 4.

    a. List the states of this ADT according to the formula presented in this chapter.

    b. Generate test data to visit all the states and all the transitions of this ADT.

9.8. Consider the specification of a set ADT given in Chapter 4.

    a. List the states of this ADT according to the formula presented in this chapter.

    b. Generate test data to visit all the states and all the transitions of this ADT.

9.9. Consider the sample stack implementations discussed in Section 4.10.1, that use an integer rather than an array and index. Run them on the test data generated in this chapter.

9.10. In the English language, the letters of the alphabet do not appear with the same frequency. The following table shows their frequency of appearance:

a	0.082
b	0.015
c	0.028
d	0.042
e	0.126
f	0.022

g	0.020
h	0.061
i	0.070
j	0.002
k	0.008
l	0.040
m	0.024
n	0.067
o	0.075
p	0.019
q	0.001
r	0.060
s	0.063
t	0.091
u	0.028
v	0.010
w	0.024
x	0.001
y	0.020
z	0.001

Generate a function that produces characters of the alphabet with the given frequency. Run a large number of times and estimate the frequency of appearance of each letter; compare it with the table given above.

9.11. Generate a random sorted array whose values are included between a lower bound *Low* and a higher value *High*.

9.8 BIBLIOGRAPHIC NOTES

For more details on tabular specifications and their semantics, consult (Janicki et al., 1997; Janicki and Khedhri, 2001). The criterion of test data generation for state-based software product, which provides for visiting all states and exercising all state transitions, is due to Mathur (2008). Whereas in this chapter we used a simple random number generator that produces a uniform distribution over a unitary interval, specialized environments such as MATLAB (©Mathworks) offer functions for a wide range of probability laws. For a detailed discussion of James Whittaker's criteria for exploratory software testing, consult (Whittaker, 2010).

10

Structural Criteria

Whereas the functional criteria discussed in Chapter 9 generate test data by analyzing the specification of the product, the techniques we discuss in this chapter do so by analyzing the source code of the product. Structural test generation criteria may sound counter-intuitive, since they are using the program to test the program. It is like recruiting the prime suspect in a crime to help in the crime investigation; in the same way that the criminal will bias the investigation away from himself, a faulty program may focus the attention of the tester away from its shortcomings. This is not an idle comparison: Consider that if the program fails to make provisions for half of the input data that it is supposed to process (a massive gap), no amount of structural testing will expose this fault; only by referring back to the specification can we uncover such a failure. More generally, when we endeavor to verify a program, our main resource is redundancy (redundancy between a program and its specification, redundancy between two presumably equivalent programs, redundancy between a program and an executable specification, redundancy between a program and a test oracle, etc.); if we use a program to test the same program, we have no redundancy to depend on. On the other hand, consider that in order to make any claim about the functional attributes of candidate programs, a test-generation strategy must focus on the domain of the specification as a starting point; to the extent that structural test generation analyzes the program rather than its specification, such information is not available.

With these qualifications in mind, we focus our attention in this chapter on generating test data by analyzing the candidate programs; the broad rationale for this type of approach is that if we want to test a program for the purpose of exposing its possible faults, it is sensible to try to exercise all its features, such as all its statements, all its conditions, all its paths, etc. We may argue, in fact, that while functional criteria are more effective at proving the absence of faults (or at least the infrequency of failures caused by these faults), structural criteria are more effective at finding faults, since they focus on the source of the faults.

Software Testing: Concepts and Operations, First Edition. Ali Mili and Fairouz Tchier.
© 2015 John Wiley & Sons, Inc. Published 2015 by John Wiley & Sons, Inc.

10.1 PATHS AND PATH CONDITIONS

10.1.1 Execution Paths

Now that we are interested in structural test data generation, we need to look at programs rather than specifications. We assume that our programs are written in a traditional C-like programming language, which includes the following statements:

- *Variable declarations*, of the form `<data type><variable name>`.
- *Labeled statements*, of the form `<label>: <statement>`.
- *Assignment statements*, of the form `<variable name> = <expression>`.
- *Sequence statements*, of the form `<statement1> ; <statement2>`.
- *Conditional statements,* of the form `if <condition><statement>`.
- *Alternation statements*, of the form `if <condition><statement1> else <statement2>`.
- *Iteration statements*, of the form `while <condition><statement>`.
- *Statement blocks*, of the form `{<statement>}`.
- *Function calls*, of the form `<function name> ( <parameter list> )`.

Because we use structured constructs exclusively, any program is executed in sequence from the first statement to the last statement (we have no exits or return statements in the middle of a program). Hence all executions of our programs start from the first statement and proceed through the code according to the outcome of the various conditions that appear therein. Hence the following definitions.

An *elementary statement* is any one of the following

- An assignment statement
- A function call
- A condition test of the form
  - `( <condition> ? true )`
  - `( <condition> ? false )`

A *path* through a program is a sequence of elementary statements separated by semicolons such that whenever two elementary statements <es1> and <es2> follow each other in the path, then one of the following conditions holds:

- <es1> and <es2> follow each other in the program, or
- <es2> is derived from the condition of a conditional statement or an alternative statement or an iterative statement which follows <es1> in the program, or

- <es1> is the last elementary statement of a conditional statement or an alternative statement that precedes <es2> in the program, or
- <es1> is derived from the condition of an iterative statement that precedes <es2> in the program.
- <es1> has the form (c? true), where c is the condition of a conditional statement or an alternative statement, and <es2> is the first statement of the then-branch, or
- <es1> has the form (c? false), where c is the condition of an alternative statement and (es2> is the first statement of the else branch, or
- <es1> has the form (c? true), where c is the condition of an iterative statement and <es2> is the first statement of the loop body.

As an application, we consider the following program and write some of its paths. Note that the definition of paths does not stipulate that they start from the beginning of the programs nor that they end with its last statement, as we want to have the liberty to define partial paths through the code. Nevertheless the sample paths we show below start at the first statement of the program and end at its last statement.

Program g:

```
{int x; int y; read(x); read(y);       // assuming x>0, y>0

  while (x!=y) {if (x>y) {x=x-y;} else {y=y-x;}};

  write(x);}
```

Sample paths through this program include the following:

- p0: int x; int y; read(x); read(y);
     ((x!=y)? false); write(x);

- p1: int x; int y; read(x); read(y);
      ((x!=y)? true); ((x>y)? true); x=x-y;
      ((x!=y)? false); write(x);

- p2: int x; int y; read(x); read(y);
      ((x!=y)? true); ((x>y)? false); y=y-x;
      ((x!=y)? false); write(x);

- p3: int x; int y; read(x); read(y);
      ((x!=y)? true); ((x>y)? true); x=x-y;
      ((x!=y)? true); ((x>y)? true); x=x-y;
      ((x!=y)? false); write(x);

- p4: int x; int y; read(x); read(y);
    ((x!=y)? true); ((x>y)? false); y=y-x;
    ((x!=y)? true); ((x>y)? false); y=y-x;
    ((x!=y)? false); write(x);

- p5: int x; int y; read(x); read(y);
    ((x!=y)? true); ((x>y)? true); x=x-y;
    ((x!=y)? true); ((x>y)? false); y=y-x;
    ((x!=y)? false); write(x);

- p6: int x; int y; read(x); read(y);
    ((x!=y)? true); ((x>y)? false); y=y-x;
    ((x!=y)? true); ((x>y)? true); x=x-y;
    ((x!=y)? false); write(x);

- p7: int x; int y; read(x); read(y);
    ((x!=y)? true); ((x>y)? true); x=x-y;
    ((x!=y)? true); ((x>y)? false); y=y-x;
    ((x!=y)? true); ((x>y)? true); x=x-y;
    ((x!=y)? false); write(x);

- p8: int x; int y; read(x); read(y);
    ((x!=y)? true); ((x>y)? false); y=y-x;
    ((x!=y)? true); ((x>y)? true); x=x-y;
    ((x!=y)? true); ((x>y)? false); y=y-x;
    ((x!=y)? false); write(x);

and so on. Each path represents a trace of execution through the original program.

10.1.2 Path Functions

The following definition introduces the semantics of paths, in terms of the function that they define on their space.

- The effect of each variable declaration of the form "**<type> x**" is to change the state of the program from what it was prior to the declaration (say, S) to S × **<type>**.
- We assume that prior to any variable declarations, the space of the program is limited to two implicit state variables, namely the *input stream* and the *output stream*; both of these can be modeled as sequences, where **read(x)** returns the first element of the input stream and removes it therefrom, while **write (x)** appends x to the output stream.
- The semantics of an assignment statement is defined by:

$$[x = E] = \{(s, s') \mid s \in \text{def}(E) \wedge x' = E(s) \wedge \_(s) = \_(s')\},$$

where def(E) is the set of states on which E can be evaluated, and the symbol _ stands for all the other (than x) variables of the space.

- The semantics of a condition is defined by the following equations:

$$[(c?true)] = \{(s,s') \,|\, s' = s \wedge c(s)\}.$$
$$[(c?false)] = \{(s,s') \,|\, s' = s \wedge \neg c(s)\}.$$

- The semantics of sequence is defined by the following equation:

$$[es1;es2] = [es1][es2].$$

Definition: Path Function *The function of a path is the function computed inductively according to the semantic rules provided above.*

As an illustration of these rules, we compute, for example, the function of path p8 in the gcd program, which reads as follows:

```
• p8:  int x; int y;                          // line  1

       read(x); read(y);                      //        2
       ((x!=y)? true); ((x>y)? false); y=y-x; //        3
       ((x!=y)? true); ((x>y)? true); x=x-y;  //        4
       ((x!=y)? true); ((x>y)? false); y=y-x; //        5
       ((x!=y)? false);                       //        6
       write(x);                              //        7
```

We let *is* and *os* designate, respectively, the input stream and the output stream, and we let head and tail designate, respectively, the operation that returns the head of a stream and its tail (remainder once the head is removed). We interpret the first line as letting the space of the program be defined as:

$$S = is \times os \times int \times int.$$

The functions of line 2 and line 7 are then defined on space S by, respectively:

$$F_2 = \{(s,s') \,|\, length(is) \geq 2 \wedge x' = head(is) \wedge y' = head(tail(is)) \wedge is' = tail^2(is) \wedge os' = os\}.$$
$$F_7 = \{(s,s') \,|\, x' = x \wedge y' = y \wedge is' = is \wedge os' = os.x\},$$

where we use the dot to designate concatenation. Lines 3 and 5 have the same code: hence they compute the same function, which is:

$$F_3 = F_5 = \{(s,s') \,|\, x < y \wedge x' = x \wedge y' = y - x \wedge is' = is \wedge os' = os\}.$$

As for line 4, it computes the following function:

$$F_4 = \{(s,s') \,|\, x > y \wedge x' = x - y \wedge y' = y \wedge is' = is \wedge os' = os\}.$$

Finally, line 6 computes a subset of identity, as follows:

$$F_6 = \{(s,s') \mid x = y \wedge x' = x \wedge y' = y \wedge is' = is \wedge os' = os\}.$$

Computing the product $F_2 \bullet F_3 \bullet F_4 \bullet F_5 \bullet F_6 \bullet F_7$, we find:

$F_2 \bullet F_3 \bullet F_4 \bullet F_5 \bullet F_6 \bullet F_7$

$= \{$associativity, substitution$\}$

$F_2 \bullet \{(s,s') \mid x < y \wedge x' = x \wedge y' = y - x \wedge is' = is \wedge os' = os\} \bullet$
$\{(s,s') \mid x > y \wedge x' = x - y \wedge y' = y \wedge is' = is \wedge os' = os\} F_5 \bullet F_6 \bullet F_7$

$= \{$relational product$\}$

$F_2 \bullet \{(s,s') \mid x < y \wedge x > y - x \wedge x' = 2x - y \wedge y' = y - x \wedge is' = is \wedge os' = os\} F_5 \bullet F_6 \bullet F_7$

$= \{$associativity, substitution$\}$

$F_2 \bullet \{(s,s') \mid x < y \wedge x > y - x \wedge x' = 2x - y \wedge y' = y - x \wedge is' = is \wedge os' = os\} \bullet$
$\{(s,s') \mid x < y \wedge x' = x \wedge y' = y - x \wedge is' = is \wedge os' = os\} \bullet F_6 \bullet F_7$

$= \{$relational product$\}$

$$F_2 \bullet \left\{ (s,s') \,\middle|\, \begin{array}{c} x < y \wedge x > y - x \wedge 2x - y < y - x \wedge x' = 2x - y \wedge y' = 2y - 3x \wedge is' = is \\ \wedge\, os' = os \end{array} \right\} \bullet F_6 \bullet F_7$$

$= \{$associativity, substitution (post-restriction)$\}$

$$F_2 \bullet \left\{ (s,s') \,\middle|\, \begin{array}{c} x < y \wedge x > y - x \wedge 2x - y < y - x \wedge x' = 2x - y \wedge y' = 2y - 3x \wedge is' = is \\ \wedge\, os' = os \wedge x' = y' \end{array} \right\} \bullet F_7$$

$= \{$simplification, assumption that x and y are both positive$\}$

$F_2 \bullet \{(s,s') \mid 5x = 3y \wedge x' = 2x - y \wedge y' = 2y - 3x \wedge is' = is \wedge os' = os\} \bullet F_7$

$= \{$relational product, abbreviating each function by its initial$\}$

$$\left\{ (s,s') \,\middle|\, \begin{array}{c} l(is) \geq 2 \wedge 5 \times h(is) = 3 \times h(t(is)) \wedge x' = 2 \times h(is) - h(t(is)) \\ \wedge y' = 2 \times h(t(is)) - 3 \times h(is) \\ \wedge\, is' = t^2(is) \wedge os' = os \end{array} \right\} \bullet F_7$$

$= \{$relational product$\}$

$$\left\{ (s,s') \,\middle|\, \begin{array}{c} l(is) \geq 2 \wedge 5 \times h(is) = 3 \times h(t(is)) \wedge x' = 2 \times h(is) - h(t(is)) \\ \wedge y' = 2 \times h(t(is)) - 3 \times h(is) \\ \wedge\, is' = t^2(is) \wedge os' = os.(2 \times h(is) - h(t(is))) \end{array} \right\}.$$

This function reflects the impact of the path on the state variables; remember that $l(is)$, $h(is)$, and $h(t(is))$ are (respectively) the length, first element, and second element of the input stream. Note that if the first element is 18 and the second element is 30, then upon execution of this path, the input stream is truncated by two, and the output stream is augmented by a new element, whose value is: $2 \times 18 - 30 = 6$. Indeed, 6 is the greatest common divisor of 18 and 30.

Before we close this section, we give a useful rule on how to compute the product of two functions that are written in the following form (on some space S defined by two variables x and y):

$$\{(s,s')|p(x,y) \wedge x' = Ex(x,y) \wedge y' = Ey(x,y)\}.$$

Let functions F_1 and F_2 be written as:

$$F_1 = \left\{(s,s')|p_1(x,y) \wedge x' = E_x^1(x,y) \wedge y' = E_y^1(x,y)\right\},$$
$$F_2 = \left\{(s,s')|p_2(x,y) \wedge x' = E_x^2(x,y) \wedge y' = E_y^2(x,y)\right\}.$$

Then the product of functions F_1 and F_2 is given by the following formula:

$$F_1 \bullet F_2 = \left\{(s,s')|p_1(x,y) \wedge p_2\left(E_x^1(x,y), E_y^1(x,y)\right) \wedge \right.$$
$$\left. x' = E_x^2\left(E_x^1(x,y), E_y^1(x,y)\right) \wedge y' = E_y^2\left(E_x^1(x,y), E_y^1(x,y)\right)\right\}.$$

As an illustration, consider the following functions on a space S defined by integer variables x and y:

$$F_1 = \{(s,s')|x > y \wedge x' = 2x + y \wedge y' = 2y + x\},$$
$$F_2 = \{(s,s')|x > 2y \wedge x' = 3x + 2y \wedge y' = 3y + 2x\}.$$

Then the product of these two functions yields the following result:

$$F_1 \bullet F_2 = \{(s,s')|x > y \wedge 2x + y > 2(2y + x) \wedge x' = 3(2x + y) + 2(2y + x) \wedge$$
$$y' = 3(2y + x) + 2(2x + y)\}.$$

After simplification, we find:

$$F_1 \bullet F_2 = \{(s,s')|x > y \wedge y < 0 \wedge x' = 8x + 7y \wedge y' = 8y + 7x\}.$$

The product of two functions takes a special, simpler, form whenever one of the factors is a subset of the identity; specifically, we have

$$\{(s,s')|q(x,y) \wedge s' = s\} \bullet \{(s,s')|p(x,y) \wedge x' = Ex(x,y) \wedge y' = Ey(x,y)\}$$
$$= \{(s,s')|q(x,y) \wedge p(x,y) \wedge x' = Ex(x,y) \wedge y' = Ey(x,y)\}$$

and

$$\{(s,s')|p(x,y) \wedge x' = Ex(x,y) \wedge y' = Ey(x,y)\} \bullet \{(s,s')|q(x,y) \wedge s' = s\}$$
$$= \{(s,s')|p(x,y) \wedge x' = Ex(x,y) \wedge y' = Ey(x,y) \wedge q(x',y')\}.$$

In order to spare the reader the trouble of having to refer to the definition whenever he/she must compute the product of two functions, we present below a set of rules that streamline this process.

Computing the Product of Two Functions. We let space S be defined by two variables x and y of types X and Y, and we let F and G be defined as follows:

$$F = \{(s,s')|f(x,y) \wedge x' = Fx(x,y) \wedge y' = Fy(x,y)\}$$
$$G = \{(s,s')|g(x,y) \wedge x' = Gx(x,y) \wedge y' = Gy(x,y)\}$$

Where f and g are predicates and Fx, Fy, Gx, Gy are expressions that return values of the right type (X, Y, X, Y). Then, the product $F \bullet G$ can be written as:

$$\{(s,s')|f(x,y) \wedge g(Fx(x,y),Fy(x,y)) \wedge$$
$$x' = Gx(Fx(x,y),Fy(x,y)) \wedge y' = Gy(Fx(x,y),Fy(x,y))\}.$$

As an illustration of this formula, we consider the product of the following functions on space S defined by natural variables $n, f,$ and k:

- $F = \{(s,s')|k \neq n+1 \wedge n' = n \wedge f' = f \times k \wedge k' = k+1\}.$
- $G = \left\{(s,s')|k \leq n+1 \wedge n' = n \wedge f' = f \times \frac{n!}{(k-1)!} k' = n+1\right\}.$

Applying the proposed formula, we find the following relation:

$F \bullet G$

$= \{\text{proposed formula}\}$

$$\left\{(s,s')|k \neq n+1 \wedge k+1 \leq n+1 \wedge n' = n \wedge f' = f \times k \times \frac{n!}{((k+1)-1)!} k' = n+1\right\}$$

$= \{\text{merging the preconditions, simplifying}\}$

$$\left\{(s,s')|k < n+1 \wedge n' = n \wedge f' = f \times k \times \frac{n!}{k!} \wedge k' = n+1\right\}$$

$= \{\text{because } k! = k \times (k-1)!\}$

$$\left\{(s,s')|k < n+1 \wedge n' = n \wedge f' = f \times \frac{n!}{(k-1)!} \wedge k' = n+1\right\}.$$

10.1.3 Path Conditions

Definition: Path Condition *The <u>condition of a path</u> is the domain of its path function.*

The condition of a path is the condition that an initial state must satisfy in order for that path to be taken during an execution of the program. As an illustrative example, we consider path **p8**, and we find that its path condition is:

$$\{s \mid 5 \times h(is) = 3 \times h(t(is))\}.$$

We let the first and second elements of the input stream *is* be, respectively, 18 and 30; they clearly satisfy the path condition of path p8, since $5 \times 18 = 3 \times 30$. We draw a flowchart of program p and analyze what path the execution of this program follows for the selected values.

statement	is	os	x	y	(x!=y)	(x>y)
	(18, 30, ..)	(..)				
int x; int y;	(18, 30, ..)	(..)	?	?	N/A	N/A
read(x);	(30, ..)	(..)	18	?	N/A	N/A
read(y);	(..)	(..)	18	30	N/A	N/A
while (x!=0)	(..)	(..)	18	30	True	N/A
if (x>y)	(..)	(..)	18	30	N/A	False
y=y-x	(..)	(..)	18	12	N/A	N/A
while (x!=0)	(..)	(..)	18	12	True	N/A
if (x>y)	(..)	(..)	18	12	N/A	True
x=x-y	(..)	(..)	6	12	N/A	N/A
while (x!=0)	(..)	(..)	6	12	True	N/A
if (x>y)	(..)	(..)	6	12	N/A	False
y=y-x	(..)	(..)	6	6	N/A	N/A
while (x!=0)	(..)	(..)	6	6	False	N/A
Write(x);	(..)	(..).6	6	6	N/A	N/A

The reader can see that the sequence of statements in the first column of the table above does indeed correspond to path p8 (Fig. 10.1).

The ability to represent paths, compute their function, and their path condition, will all be useful in the remainder of this chapter as we explore criteria for generating test data.

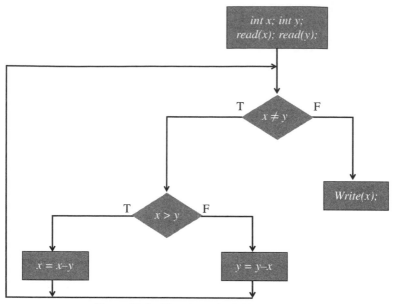

Figure 10.1   *Flowchart of a GCD program.*

10.2   CONTROL FLOW COVERAGE

Control flow coverage criteria provide for generating sufficient test data to exercise various features of the control structure of candidate programs.

10.2.1   Statement Coverage

The statement coverage criterion provides for generating sufficient test data to execute each statement of the candidate program at least once. This is a very weak criterion, since the only faults it is likely to expose are those that are so egregious that any execution of the faulty statement will cause an error, and that the error is so extensive that it will propagate and cause a failure; by statement, this criterion usually refers to elementary statements, typically assignment statements and atomic system calls. This criterion can also be applied at a higher level of abstraction than the elementary statement, and calls for exercising all the components of a composite system, with the same qualification: it can only expose faulty components that are so egregiously faulty that any execution of these components will sensitize their fault and subsequently propagate the resulting error to cause failure. Because this criterion is so weak, a single path may, conceivably, satisfy it, in some simple cases.

As an illustration, we consider the following simple program g:

```
{int x; int y; read(x); read(y);      // assuming x>0, y>0
 while (x!=y) {if (x>y) {x=x-y;} else {y=y-x;}};
 write(x);}
```

Execution of the following path through the program will exercise all the elementary statements:

```
p:  int x; int y;                                      // F0
      read(x); read(y);                                // F1
      ((x!=y)? true); ((x>y)? true); {x=x-y;}          // F2
      ((x!=y)? true); ((x>y)? false); {y=y-x;}         // F3
      ((x!=y)? false);                                 // F4
      {write(x);                                       // F5
```

The effect of F0 is to let the space of the program be defined by variables *is* and *os* of type *file stream* and variables *x* and *y* of type integer; all subsequent functions will be defined on this space. We find:

$$F_1 = \{(s,s') \,|\, length(is) \geq 2 \wedge x' = head(is) \wedge y' = head(tail(is)) \wedge is' = tail^2(is) \wedge os' = os\}.$$

$$F_2 = \{(s,s') \,|\, x > y \wedge x' = x - y \wedge y' = y \wedge is' = is \wedge os' = os\}.$$

$$F_3 = \{(s,s') \,|\, x < y \wedge x' = x \wedge y' = y - x \wedge is' = is \wedge os' = os\}.$$

$$F_4 = \{(s,s') \,|\, x = y \wedge x' = x \wedge y' = y \wedge is' = is \wedge os' = os\}.$$

$$F_5 = \{(s,s') \,|\, x' = x \wedge y' = y \wedge is' = is \wedge os' = os.x\},$$

The product of F_2 by F_3 yields:

$$F_2 \bullet F_3 = \{(s,s') \,|\, x > y \wedge x - y < y \wedge x' = x - y \wedge y' = 2y - x \wedge is' = is \wedge os' = os\}.$$

Whence, the product of $F_2 \bullet F_3$ by F_4 yields:

$$F_2 \bullet F_3 \bullet F_4 = \{(s,s') \,|\, x > y \wedge x - y < y \wedge x' = x - y \wedge y' = 2y - x \wedge is' = is \wedge os' = os \wedge x' = y'\}$$

which we simplify to become:

$$F_2 \bullet F_3 \bullet F_4 = \{(s,s') \,|\, 2x = 3y \wedge x' = x - y \wedge y' = x' \wedge is' = is \wedge os' = os\}.$$

Multiplying on the left by F_1, we find

$$F_1 \bullet F_2 \bullet F_3 \bullet F_4 = \{(s,s') \,|\, length(is) \geq 2 \wedge 2 \times head(is) = 3 \times head(tail(is)) \wedge$$
$$x' = head(is) - head(tail(is)) \wedge$$
$$y' = x' \wedge is' = tail^2(is) \wedge os' = os\}.$$

Multiplying on the right by F_5, we find

$$PF_1 \bullet F_2 \bullet F_3 \bullet F_4 \bullet F_5 = \{(s,s') \,|\, length(is) \geq 2 \wedge 2 \times head(is) = 3 \times head(tail(is)) \wedge$$
$$x' = head(is) - head(tail(is)) \wedge$$
$$y' = x' \wedge is' = tail^2(is) \wedge os' = os.x'\}.$$

The domain of this function is:

$$dom(P) = \{(s,s')|length(is) \geq 2 \wedge 2 \times head(is) = 3 \times head(tail(is))\}.$$

Any element of this domain is a possible test data that satisfies the criterion of statement coverage; we choose the initial state s defined by:

$$\left\{ \begin{array}{c} is = (21,14) \\ os = () \\ x = ? \\ y = ? \end{array} \right\}.$$

Even though a single path (and a single element in the domain of the path) enabled us to satisfy the criterion of statement coverage, it may be beneficial, in practice, to cover different statements with different paths (whenever possible) to minimize the likelihood of error masking (the longer the path, the more likely it is for an error to be masked). To this effect, we may satisfy the statement coverage with the following two paths:

```
p1:  int x; int y;                                      // F0
     read(x); read(y);                                  // F1
     ((x!=y)? true); ((x>y)? true); {x=x-y;}            // F2
     ((x!=y)? false);                                   // F3
     {write(x);                                         // F4
p2:  int x; int y;                                      // F0
     read(x); read(y);                                  // F1
     ((x!=y)? true); ((x>y)? false); {y=y-x;}           // F2
     ((x!=y)? false);                                   // F3
     {write(x);                                         // F4
```

We leave it as an exercise to the reader to generate test data from these two paths.

10.2.2 Branch Coverage

The criterion of branch coverage provides that we generate test data so that for each branch in the control structure of the candidate program (whether it arises in an if-then statement, an if-then-else statement, or a while statement), the program proceeds through each of the True branch and the False branch at least once. As an illustration of this criterion, we consider the following program:

```
#include <iostream>
#include <cmath>
using namespace std;
/* constants          */
float eps = 0.000001;
/* state variables  */
```

```
float x, y, z;
/* functions */
Bool tri(float x, float y, float z);
bool equal(float a, float b);
bool equi(float x, float y, float z);
bool iso(float x, float y, float z);
bool right(float x, float y, float z);
int main ()
    {cout << "enter the triangle sides on one line" << endl;
     cin >> x >> y >> z;
     if (!tri(x,y,z))
        {cout << "not a triangle" << endl;}
     else
     {if (equi(x,y,z))
{cout << "equilateral" << endl;}
else
if (iso(x,y,z))
{if (right(x,y,z)) {cout << "isoceles right" << endl;}
    else {cout << "isoceles" <<endl;}
else
{if (right(x,y,z)) {cout << "right" << endl;}
else {cout << "scalene" << endl;}}}}
bool tri (float x, float y, float z)
    {return ((x<=y+z) && (y<=x+z) && (z<=x+y));}
bool equal (float a, float b)
    {return abs(a-b)<eps;}
bool equi(float x, float y, float z)
    {return (equal(x,y) && equal(y,z));}
bool iso(float x, float y, float z)
    {return (equal(x,y) || equal(y,z) || equal(x,z));}
bool right(float x, float y, float z)
    {return (equal(x*x+y*y,z*z) || equal(x*x+z*z,y*y) ||
     equal(y*y+z*z,x*x));}
```

The following set of paths allows us to traverse every branch at least once:

- p1: cout << "enter the triangle sides on one line" << endl;
      cin >> x >> y >> z;
      ((!tri(x,y,z))? True) {cout << "not a triangle" << endl;}

- p2: cout << "enter the triangle sides on one line" << endl;
      cin >> x >> y >> z;
      ((!tri(x,y,z))? False); ((equi(x,y,z))? True)
          {cout << "equilateral" << endl;}

- p3: cout << "enter the triangle sides on one line" << endl;
  cin >> x >> y >> z;
  ((!tri(x,y,z))? False); ((equi(x,y,z))? False);
  ((iso(x,y,z))? True); ((right(x,y,z))? True);
  {cout << "isoceles right" << endl;}

- p4: cout << "enter the triangle sides on one line" << endl;
  cin >> x >> y >> z;
  ((!tri(x,y,z))? False); ((equi(x,y,z))? False);
  ((iso(x,y,z))? True); ((right(x,y,z))? False);
  {cout << "isoceles" << endl;}

- p5: cout << "enter the triangle sides on one line" << endl;
  cin >> x >> y >> z;
  ((!tri(x,y,z))? False); ((equi(x,y,z))? False);
  ((iso(x,y,z))? False); ((right(x,y,z))? True);
  {cout << "right" << endl;}

- p6: cout << "enter the triangle sides on one line" << endl;
  cin >> x >> y >> z;
  ((!tri(x,y,z))? False); ((equi(x,y,z))? False);
  ((iso(x,y,z))? False); ((right(x,y,z))? False);
  {cout << "scalene" << endl;}

A brief inspection of the paths presented above enables us to check that each condition appears at least once with the outcome *True* and once with the outcome *False*. In the following table, we list the paths, along with their path conditions and a test vector that satisfies the path condition.

Path	Path condition	Test vector
p1	((!tri(x,y,z))? True)	2 2 10
p2	((!tri(x,y,z))? False); ((equi(x,y,z))? True)	2 2 2
p3	((!tri(x,y,z))? False); ((equi(x,y,z))? False); ((iso(x,y,z))? True); ((right(x,y,z))? True);	$2\ 2\ 2\sqrt{2}$
p4	((!tri(x,y,z))? False); ((equi(x,y,z))? False); ((iso(x,y,z))? True); ((right(x,y,z))? False);	2 2 1
p5	((!tri(x,y,z))? False); ((equi(x,y,z))? False); ((iso(x,y,z))? False); ((right(x,y,z))? True);	3 4 5
p6	((!tri(x,y,z))? False); ((equi(x,y,z))? False); ((iso(x,y,z))? False); ((right(x,y,z))? False);	3 4 6

10.2.3 Condition Coverage

A variation of the previous criterion can be applied for programs that have compound conditions and it provides for generating test data to let each term of any condition (rather than the condition as a whole) take both truth values, true and false. So that if the condition has the form

$$a \wedge b,$$

it is not enough to let the condition be true then false, but we want to ensure that each individual term takes both truth values through the test. To generate test data according to this criterion, we proceed as follows:

> For each term, say a, of each condition of the program, say C, choose a path in the program that starts at the beginning of the program and ends at C; let P be the function of this path. Then generate:
>
> • A state in $dom(P_{/a})$ and
> • A state in $dom(P_{/\neg a})$.

As an illustration, we consider the following triangle program, which we modify specifically to create compound conditions.

```cpp
#include <iostream>
#include <cmath>
using namespace std;
/* constants       */
float eps = 0.000001;
/* state variables */
float x, y, z;
/* functions    */
bool tri(float x, float y, float z);       // triangle
bool equal(float a, float b);              // equal, within eps
bool equi(float x, float y, float z);      // equilateral
bool iso(float x, float y, float z);       // isoceles
bool right(float x, float y, float z);     // right triangle
int main () {cout << "enter the triangle sides on one line"
<< endl;
   cin >> x >> y >> z;
   if (!tri(x,y,z)) {cout << "not a triangle" << endl;}
   if (tri(x,y,z) && equi(x,y,z)) {cout << "equilateral"
      << endl;}
   if (tri(x,y,z) && (!equi(x,y,z)) && iso(x,y,z) &&
      (!right(x,y,z)))
      {cout << "isoceles" << endl;}
  if (tri(x,y,z) && (!equi(x,y,z)) && (!iso(x,y,z)) &&
    right(x,y,z))
```

```
    {cout << "right" << endl;}
 if (tri(x,y,z) && (!equi(x,y,z)) && iso(x,y,z) && right(x,y,z))
    {cout << "isoceles right" << endl;}
 if (tri(x,y,z) && (!equi(x,y,z)) && (!iso(x,y,z)) &&
    (!right(x,y,z)))
    {cout << "scalene" << endl;}}
```

We can simplify this program by referring to the following identities:

- An equilateral triangle is isosceles; hence a non-isosceles triangle is not equilateral.
- A triplet (x, y, z) that satisfies $right(x, y, z)$ necessarily satisfies $tri(x, y, z)$.
- A triplet (x, y, z) that satisfies $equi(x, y, z)$ necessarily satisfies $tri(x, y, z)$.

We find:

```
int main () {cout << "enter the triangle sides on one line" << endl;
 cin >> x >> y >> z;
 if (!tri(x,y,z)) {cout << "not a triangle" << endl;}
 if (equi(x,y,z)) {cout << "equilateral" << endl;}
 if (tri(x,y,z) && (!equi(x,y,z)) && iso(x,y,z) &&
    (!right(x,y,z)))
    {cout << "isoceles" << endl;}
 if ((!iso(x,y,z)) && right(x,y,z)) {cout << "right" << endl;}
 if ((!equi(x,y,z)) && iso(x,y,z) && right(x,y,z))
    {cout << "isoceles right" << endl;}
 if (tri(x,y,z) && (!iso(x,y,z)) && (!right(x,y,z)))
    {cout << "scalene" << endl;}}
```

In this particular example, all the if-statements refer to the same values of variables x, y, and z. Indeed, though they are written sequentially, the if-statements are merely printing messages to the output stream and are not altering the program variables that are invoked in the conditions. A cursory inspection of the structure of the conditions reveals that the criterion of condition coverage is satisfied if we generated test data to ensure that each elementary function call returns both truth values, in turn. The following table shows sample test data that satisfies this criterion.

Condition	True	False
tri(x,y,z)	5 6 7	5 6 12
equi(x,y,z)	6 6 6	6 7 6
iso(x,y,z)	5 5 12	5 7 6
right(x,y,z)	3 4 5	3 4 6

Note that the data generated to make $iso(x, y, z)$ true does not define a triangle, nor does it have to—it only has to make $iso(x, y, z)$ true; such data will cause the program to declare that the data entered does not define a triangle.

10.2.4 Path Coverage

The criterion of path coverage provides that we generate test data to exercise every execution path of candidate programs. If the program has no loops, then the set of paths is finite, and can be easily catalogued; to get a sense of the work involved in this task, we consider the two versions of the triangle analysis program (the nested version and the sequential version). The flow chart of the nested version looks as follows (Fig. 10.2).

Paths in the program correspond to paths from the first node to the exit node in this graph; covering all the paths corresponds, in this case, to branch coverage. We

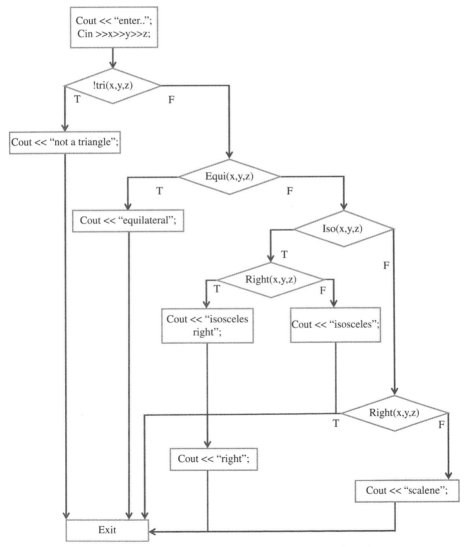

Figure 10.2 *Flowchart of a Triangle program: nested version.*

characterize each path by the sequence of conditions that it evaluates as it proceeds from the start to the exit node, and we find the following paths.

Path	Condition	Test Data		
		x	y	z
p1	`!tri()`	2	4	8
p2	`tri()&&equi()`	2	2	2
p3	`tri() && !equi() && iso() && right()`	1	1	$\sqrt{2}$
p4	`tri()&& !equi() && iso() && !right()`	4	4	3
p5	`tri() && !equi() && !iso() && right()`	3	4	5
p6	`tri() && !equi() && !iso() && !right()`	2	3	4

We consider now the sequential version of the triangle analysis program (Fig. 10.3). Topologically, this flowchart appears to have 2^6 paths, since it has six binary conditions in sequence; but in fact many of these paths are not executable (their path function is empty) due to the dependencies between the conditions. If we identify each path by the sequence of True/False (T/F) values of the conditions, we find the following paths:

Path	!tri	equi	tri && !equi && iso && !right	!iso && right	!equi && iso && right	tri && !iso && !right
p1	T	F	F	F	F	F
p2	F	T	F	F	F	F
p3	F	F	T	F	F	F
p4	F	F	F	T	F	F
p5	F	F	F	F	T	F
p6	F	F	F	F	F	T

Notice that in this table, each row is fully determined by the shaded area. For example, in the first row (path p1), consider that if condition (**!tri**) returns True, then all subsequent expressions necessarily return False: for example, the second column (condition: `equi`) returns False since a set of three identical numbers define a triangle; the third column (condition: **tri && !equi && iso && !right**) returns False since the first conjunct (**tri**) is already known to be False; etc. Hence the paths p1, p2, p3, p4, p5, p6 presented in this table are the only feasible paths (out of 2^6) of the program. The following table characterizes each one of these paths and proposes a data item that falls in their domain.

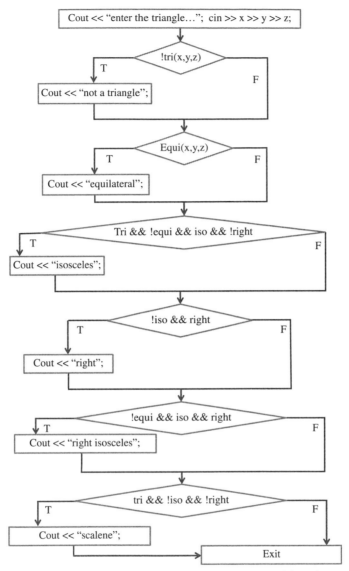

Figure 10.3 *Flowchart of a Triangle program: sequential version.*

Path	Path Condition	Test Data
p1	**!tri**	2 4 10
p2	`equi`	3 3 3
p3	**tri && !equi && iso && !right**	3 3 4

(continued)

(continued)

p4	!iso && right	3 4 5
p5	!equi && iso && right	$3\,3\,3\sqrt{2}$
p6	tri && !iso && !right	4 5 6

The sample examples we have studied so far have a finite number of paths, since they have no iterative statements; with while loops, we face the possibility of having an infinite number of paths; for such cases the criterion of path coverage cannot be fulfilled to the letter. We resort to approximations of this criterion, whereby we consider upper bounds on the number of iterations for each loop. Because we may have nested loops, even this approximate criterion may cause a combinatorial explosion, producing up to N^p paths, where N is the upper bound on the number of iterations and p is the depth of nesting of the loops.

As an example, we consider the gcd program discussed in Section 10.1:

```
{int x; int y; read(x); read(y);  // assuming x>0, y>0
while (x!=y) {if (x>y) {x=x-y;} else {y=y-x;}};
write(x);}
```

We resolve to apply the path coverage criterion to it, up to three iterations of the while loop. We find the following paths, classified according to the number of iterations:

- Path with Zero iterations:
  - p0: int x; int y; read(x); read(y);
    ((x!=y)? false); write(x);

- Paths with One iteration:
  - p11: int x; int y; read(x); read(y);
    ((x!=y)? true); ((x>y)? true); x=x-y;
    ((x!=y)? false); write(x);

  - p12: int x; int y; read(x); read(y);
    ((x!=y)? true); ((x>y)? false); y=y-x;
    ((x!=y)? false); write(x);

- Paths with Two iterations:
  - p21: int x; int y; read(x); read(y);
    ((x!=y)? true); ((x>y)? true); x=x-y;
    ((x!=y)? true); ((x>y)? true); x=x-y;
    ((x!=y)? false); write(x);

○ p22: `int x; int y; read(x); read(y);`
`((x!=y)? true); ((x>y)? false); y=y-x;`
`((x!=y)? true); ((x>y)? false); y=y-x;`
`((x!=y)? false); write(x);`

○ p23: `int x; int y; read(x); read(y);`
`((x!=y)? true); ((x>y)? true); x=x-y;`
`((x!=y)? true); ((x>y)? false); y=y-x;`
`((x!=y)? false); write(x);`

○ p24: `int x; int y; read(x); read(y);`
`((x!=y)? true); ((x>y)? false); y=y-x;`
`((x!=y)? true); ((x>y)? true); x=x-y;`
`((x!=y)? false); write(x);`

- Paths with Three iterations: In order to keep combinatorics under control, and because *x* and *y* play symmetric roles, we do not show all eight paths; but rather only four; the missing four can be retrieved by interchanging *x* and *y*.

○ p31: `int x; int y; read(x); read(y);`
`((x!=y)? true); ((x>y)? true); x=x-y;`
`((x!=y)? true); ((x>y)? true); x=x-y;`
`((x!=y)? true); ((x>y)? true); x=x-y;`
`((x!=y)? false); write(x);`

○ p32: `int x; int y; read(x); read(y);`
`((x!=y)? true); ((x>y)? true); x=x-y;`
`((x!=y)? true); ((x>y)? true); x=x-y;`
`((x!=y)? true); ((x>y)? false); y=y-x;`
`((x!=y)? false); write(x);`

○ p33: `int x; int y; read(x); read(y);`
`((x!=y)? true); ((x>y)? true); x=x-y;`
`((x!=y)? true); ((x>y)? false); y=y-x;`
`((x!=y)? true); ((x>y)? true); x=x-y;`
`((x!=y)? false); write(x);`

○ p34: `int x; int y; read(x); read(y);`
`((x!=y)? true); ((x>y)? true); x=x-y;`
`((x!=y)? true); ((x>y)? false); y=y-x; ;`
`((x!=y)? true); ((x>y)? false); y=y-x;`
`((x!=y)? false); write(x);`

We leave it as an exercise to the reader to compute the path functions and the path conditions of these paths; we show the results in the table below, along with test data that meets the path conditions.

Number of iterations	Path	Condition	Test data	
			x	y
0	p0	x=y	5	5
1	p11	x=2y	10	5
	p12	y=2x	5	10
2	p21	x=3y	15	5
	p22	y=3x	5	15
	p23	2x=3y	15	10
	p24	3x=2y	10	15
3	p31	x=4y	20	5
	p32	2x=5y	25	10
	p33	3x=5y	15	9
	p34	3x=4y	16	12

The test data for the four missing paths resulting from three iterations can be computed by merely interchanging x and y in the test data of the paths of length 3; we find,

Number of iterations	Path	Condition	Test data	
			x	y
3	p31	y=4x	5	20
	p32	2y=5x	10	25
	p33	3y=5x	9	15
	p34	3y=4x	12	16

10.3 DATA FLOW COVERAGE

Whereas in the previous section we explored how to generate test data by analyzing the control flow of candidate programs in execution, in this section we explore how we can use the data flow of the program as a guide to generate adequate test data.

10.3.1 Definitions and Uses

The life of a program variable during the execution of a program lasts from the time the variable becomes known as part of the program state to the time it is no longer accessible to the program as part of the state. Under static block-structured dynamic allocation, the name of a variable is known from the time of its declaration to the time when execution of the program exists the block where it is declared; under dynamic memory allocation, the name of a variable is known between the time the program creates the variable through an instantiation (by means of a _new_ statement), and the time when the program explicitly returns the name (implicitly relinquishing the memory space to which it refers) or terminates its execution. Several relevant events arise during the lifecycle of a variable, including:

- Assignment of a value to the variable, through an assignment statement, or through a read statement, or at instantiation time through invocation of the constructor method of a class, or at declaration time through compiler-generated initializations, or through parameter passing of the variable as a reference parameter to a routine. We refer to these events as _definitions_ of the variable.
- Use of the value of the variable, to compute an expression, or through a write statement, or in a branch condition, or as an index to an array, or through parameter passing of the variable as a value parameter to a routine. We refer to these events as _uses_ of the variable, and we distinguish between

  ○ _c-uses_, when the variable is used to compute an expression and

  ○ _p-uses_, when the variable is used to compute a Boolean condition that affects the program control.

  Notice that the same variable may be considered c-used and p-used if it intervenes in an expression to compute a Boolean condition; such is the case, for example, for variable x in the following Boolean condition:

  ```
  if ((x+2)>0) {…;}
  ```

  Notice also that in a statement such as

  ```
  a[i]=x+3;
  ```

  for example, we consider that a is defined, i is c-used (even though it is used to compute an address/a location rather than a value), and x is c-used; strictly speaking, this statement only defines the ith cell of array a, but since we cannot identify the exact cell that has been modified, we assume that all of a has been (re-) defined.

- Termination of the lifecycle of the variable, when the variable is no longer part of the state of the program, either because control has exited the block where it was declared (in block structured programs) or because it has been explicitly relinquished (as is the case with some dynamic allocation schemes) or the program terminates its execution.

As an illustration of definitions and uses, we consider the gcd program, which handles integer (natural) variables x and y:

```
{int x; int y;          //    1
read(x);                //    2
read(y);                //    3
while (x!=y)            //    4
```

```
{if (x>y)           //    5
   {x=x-y;}         //    6
else                //    7
   {y=y-x;}};       //    8
write(x);           //    9
}                   //   10
```

The following table shows for each variable the statements in which the variable is defined, c-used, p-used, and terminated.

Line	x				y			
	Defined	c-used	p-used	Terminated	Defined	c-used	p-used	Terminated
1								
2	√							
3					√			
4			√				√	
5			√				√	
6	√	√				√		
7								
8		√			√	√		
9		√						
10				√				√

We can write the lifecycle of each variable as follows, by indicating the sequence of events that arose in the lifecycle, along with the lines where they did:

- Variable x: defined(2); p-used(4); p-used(5); c-used(6); defined(6); c-used(8); terminated(10).
- Variable y: defined(3); p-used(4); p-used(5); c-used(6); c-used(8); defined(8); terminated(10).

If we observe a program in execution and focus on the sequence of events that take place during the lifecycle of any variable, we may find that some patterns are outright wrong, and some patterns, while they may be correct, look suspicious nevertheless, hence may deserve extra scrutiny. Among incorrect event sequences, we cite the following:

- A variable that is used (use, c-use, p-use) before being defined (without being assigned a value).
- A variable that is used after its termination.

As for suspicious patterns, we cite the following instances:

- A variable that is defined twice in sequence without being used in the intervening time.
- A variable that is defined and then killed without being reused.

These patterns do not necessarily indicate the presence of a fault, but they do warrant careful consideration. For strictly sequential programs, it is possible for the compiler to detect incorrect patterns and suspicious patterns; but with control structures such as if-then statements, if-then-else statements and loops, the compiler cannot predict execution sequences at compile time. The goal of data flow test generation criteria is to generate test data in such a way as to execute all the paths that may have incorrect or suspicious event sequences; we review a sample of these criteria in the following sections.

10.3.2 Test Generation Criteria

The purpose of dataflow-based test generation criteria is to force the execution of the program through combinations of definitions and uses in such a way as to detect all possible faults in the sequencing of these events. We discuss four such criteria:

- *All definition-use paths.* A path in the program is said to be a *definition-use path* (du-paths, for short) for some program variable x if and only if it starts with some statement that defines variable x and ends with a statement that uses variable x.
  - *All definition-clear paths.* A path in the program is said to be a *definition-clear path* for some program variable x if and only if it is a definition-use path for variable x and the definition statement with which it starts is the only definition statement for that variable in the path.

The criterion of *All definition-use paths* provides that one must generate test data to exercise all the definition-use paths for all the variables of the program. To apply this criterion, we proceed as follows:

- First, we list all the variables of the program.
- For each variable of the program, we list all the definition statements and all the use statements.
- For each definition/use pair, we check whether there exists a path from the definition statement to the use statement.
- For all the paths identified in the previous steps, we identify a pre-path, from the beginning of the execution to the first statement of the path, and a post-path, from the last statement of the path to the end of the execution.
- For each triplet made up of a pre-path, a definition-use path, and a post-path, we compute the function of the aggregate path.

○ For each aggregate path, we compute the path condition as the domain of the path function.

○ For each path that yields a non-False path condition, we generate test data that exercises this path.

The set of test data so obtained constitutes our test data.

- **All p-uses.** A *p-use path* for a program with respect to variable x is a definition-clear path from a definition of variable *x* to a p-use of *x*. The criterion of *All p-uses* provides that one must generate test data to exercise all the p-use paths for all the variables of the program. To apply this criterion, we proceed in the same way as we discuss above, but focusing exclusively on p-use paths.
- **All c-uses.** A *c-use path* for a program with respect to variable *x* is a definition-clear path from a definition of variable *x* to a c-use of *x*. The criterion of *All c-uses* provides that one must generate test data to exercise all the c-use paths for all the variables of the program. To apply this criterion, we proceed in the same way as we discuss above, but focusing exclusively on c-use paths.
- **All uses**. The criterion of *All uses* provides that one must generate test data to meet the All p-uses criterion and test data to meet the All c-uses criterion.
- **All definitions**. The criterion of *All definitions* provides that one must generate test data to ensure that all definitions are visited at least once.

For the sake of illustration, we briefly discuss the generation of test data according to the four criteria presented herein for the gcd program. We apply the criteria in turn, below:

- **All du-paths.** We consider in turn variable *x*, then variable *y*. For variable *x*, we find the following definition statements:
  ○ Statements 2 and 6.
  And the following use statements:
  ○ Statements 4, 5, 6, 8, and 9.

We choose the definition-use path that starts at the definition in statement 2 and ends at the use at statement 4. We write this path as follows:

```
read(x); read(y); ((x!=y)? XX);
```

The pre-path of this path is empty, since `read(x)` is the first executable statement of the program. There is an infinity of post-paths; for the sake of illustrations, we do not take the shortest/simplest post-path, but choose instead the following:

```
((x!=y)? true); ((x>y)? true); (x=x-y); ((x>y)? false);
    write(x);
```

We leave it to the reader to check that the function of this path is the following:

$$P = \{(s,s') | length(is) \geq 2 \wedge head(is) = 2 \times head(tail(is)) \wedge x' = head(tail(is))$$
$$\wedge y' = head(tail(is)) \wedge os' = os.head(tail(is))\}.$$

The domain of this function can be written as:

$$dom(P) = \{(s,s') | length(is) \geq 2 \wedge head(is) = 2 \times head(tail(is))\}.$$

Possible test data:

$$is = (24,12,...).$$

We leave it to the interested reader to continue reviewing other definition-use paths, including those obtained by the combinations of statements (2,5), (2,6), (2,8), (6,4), (6,5), and (6,8). Note that by the time we combine the selected path with a pre-path and a post-path, we may find an aggregate path that we have analyzed before; in that case, we can rely on the test data we have generated before.

We must do the same analysis for all the definition-use paths that pertain to variable y; to this effect, we list below the definition and use statements for variable y.

○ Definitions: statements 3 and 8.
○ Uses: statements 4, 5, 6, 8.

• **All p-uses.** This criterion provides for covering all the definition-clear paths that end with a p-use of some variable. The following table shows the list of definitions and p-uses of each variable of the program.

	x	y
Definitions	2, 6	3, 8
p-uses	4, 5	4, 5

This includes definition-clear paths (2,4), (2,5), (3,4), and (3,5).

• **All c-uses.** This criterion provides for covering all the definition-clear paths that end with a c-use of some variable. The following table shows the list of definitions and p-uses of each variable of the program.

	x	y
Definitions	2, 6	3, 8
c-uses	6, 8	6, 8

This includes definition-clear paths (2,6), (6,8), (3,8).

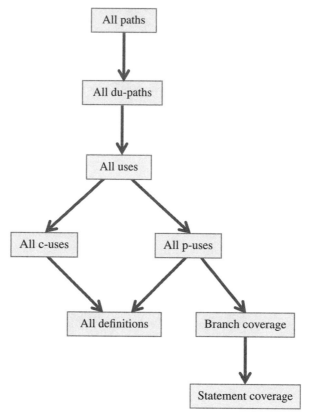

Figure 10.4 *Hierarchy of test generation criteria.*

- *All uses*. The test data generated for this criterion is the union of the test data generated by criterion All p-uses and criterion All c-uses.
- *All definitions*. The test data generated for this criterion must ensure that all the definition nodes are visited at least once; these are 2 and 6 for x, and 3 and 8 for y.

10.3.3   A Hierarchy of Criteria

A test data generation criterion C subsumes a test data generation criterion C' if and only if any test data set that satisfies C satisfies C'. The following subsumption relations hold between the criteria discussed in this section (Fig. 10.4).

10.4   FAULT-BASED TEST GENERATION

Whereas the previous sections focus on generating test data to cover the control flow and the data flow of the program, this section focuses on generating test data to expose specific types of faults, namely faults in Boolean conditions in the program.

We distinguish between the following types of faults in Boolean expressions and conditions:

- *Variable Reference Fault*, where a Boolean variable is replaced by another.
- *Variable Negation Fault*, where a Boolean variable is replaced by its negation.
- *Expression Negation Fault*, where a Boolean expression is replaced by its negation.
- *Associative Shift Fault*, where a Boolean expression is parenthesized incorrectly; for example, the expression $x \wedge y \vee z$ is written instead of $x \wedge (y \vee z)$.
- *Operator Reference Fault*, where the wrong Boolean operator is used in an expression; for example, the expression $x \wedge y$ is written instead of $x \vee y$.
- *Relational Operator Fault*, where the wrong relational operator is used in a Boolean valued expression; for example, the expression $x \geq y$ is used instead of $x > y$.

In this section, we discuss how we can generate test data to expose such faults, if they arise in Boolean conditions and Boolean expressions of a candidate program. To do so, we proceed in three steps:

1. First, for each type of fault, we want to characterize the local data that sensitizes the fault, and converts it into an error.
2. Second, we want to characterize the input data that generates the necessary local conditions for the fault to be sensitized.
3. Third, we want to further refine the data selection criterion to ensure that, in addition to generating an error, the data will also propagate the error to lead to an observable failure.

We review these three conditions in the following sections.

10.4.1 Sensitizing Faults

Let E be a Boolean expression in a program; we assume that E has one of the faults classified above, and we let E' be the Boolean expression obtained from E by correcting the fault in question. For example, let E be the Boolean expression $(x \wedge y) \vee (\neg x)$ and let there be a variable reference fault in E with respect to variable y (which should have been z, say), then E' is $(x \wedge z) \vee (\neg x)$. We are interested to determine under what condition (on program variables x, y, and z) can this fault be sensitized. In order for expression E to be different from expression E', the following condition has to hold:

$$E \oplus E',$$

where $\oplus$ represents the operator of exclusive or: $E \oplus E' = E \wedge \neg E' \vee \neg E \wedge E'$. This expression is true if and only if the Boolean values of expressions E and E' are distinct (one is True, the other is False). To understand the meaning of this condition, consider the following simple example:

- $E = (x \wedge y)$.
- $E' = (x \wedge z)$.

We find,

$E \oplus E'$

= {Substitution, expansion}

$(x \wedge y) \wedge \overline{(x \wedge z)} \vee \overline{(x \wedge y)} \wedge (x \wedge z)$

= {DeMorgan}

$(x \wedge y) \wedge (\bar{x} \vee \bar{z}) \vee (\bar{x} \vee \bar{y}) \wedge (x \wedge z)$

= {Distributivity, simplification}

$(x \wedge y \wedge \bar{z}) \vee (\bar{y} \wedge x \wedge z)$

= {Factoring, Definition of $\oplus$}

$x \wedge (y \oplus z)$.

Indeed, if expression E is faulty and expression E' is the correct expression, then the only way to sensitize this fault is to let x be true and let y be different from z. As long as y and z take the same values, we will never know that we are referring to the wrong variable (y rather than z); also, as long as x is false, the value of the expression is false regardless of whether the second term is y or z. Hence the condition $x \wedge (y \oplus z)$ is indeed the condition under which the fault can be sensitized and produce an error.

We review in turn all the classes of faults catalogued above and discuss what form the condition of fault sensitization has for them.

- *Variable Reference Fault.* If expression $E(x)$ depends on variable x and it should be referring to y instead of x, then the condition of sensitization is:

$$E(x) \oplus E(y).$$

An example of such a situation is given above.

- *Variable Negation Fault.* If expression $E(x)$ depends on variable x and it should be referring to $\bar{x}$ instead of x, then the condition of sensitization is:

$$E(x) \oplus E(\bar{x}).$$

As an illustrative example, we consider expression $E(x)$ defined as: $E(x) = (x \wedge y)$ and we assume that the reference to x should have been negated, hence $E'(x) = E(\bar{x}) = (\bar{x} \wedge y)$, then the condition of sensitization is:

$(x \wedge y) \oplus (\bar{x} \wedge y)$.

We analyze this expression, as follows:

$(x \wedge y) \oplus (\bar{x} \wedge y)$

$= \{\text{Expanding}\}$

$(x \wedge y) \wedge \overline{(\bar{x} \wedge y)} \vee \overline{(x \wedge y)} \wedge (\bar{x} \wedge y)$

$= \{\text{De Morgan}\}$

$(x \wedge y) \wedge (x \vee \bar{y}) \vee (\bar{x} \vee \bar{y}) \wedge (\bar{x} \wedge y)$

$= \{\text{Distribution, cancellation}\}$

$(x \wedge y) \vee (\bar{x} \wedge y)$

$= \{\text{Simplification}\}$

y.

Clearly, the only way to sensitize this fault is to let y be true, since if y were false then the expression would be false regardless of the value of x. Whereas with y at true, the expression would be equal to x and hence reflects whether we have the right value or its negation.

- *Expression Negation Fault.* If the faulty expression is the negation of the fault-free expression, then any evaluation of the expression sensitizes the fault. Indeed, we have, by definition

$$E \oplus \bar{E} = True$$

for all expression E.

- *Associative Shift Fault.* This fault arises when a Boolean expression is parenthesized wrong. As an illustrative example, we consider the following expression $E = x \wedge y \vee z$ and we assume that the fault free expression is $E' = x \wedge (y \vee z)$. We analyze the expression $E \oplus E'$ to determine under what condition this fault may be sensitized; rather than doing this algebraically (using logic identities), we use truth tables to compute the two expressions and then characterize the rows for which the two expressions are distinct:

x	y	z	x∧y	(y∨z)	E	E'	E⊕E'
F	F	F	F	F	F	F	F
F	F	T	F	T	T	F	T
F	T	F	F	T	F	F	F
F	T	T	F	T	T	F	T
T	F	F	F	F	F	F	F
T	F	T	F	T	T	T	F
T	T	F	T	T	T	T	F
T	T	T	T	T	T	T	F

Hence this condition can be simplified into $(z \wedge \bar{x})$. Indeed, if z is True and x is False, then $E = True$ regardless of the value of y and $E' = False$ regardless of the value of y.

- *Operator Reference Fault.* We let E be the original expression and E' be the corrected expression, and we compute/analyze the expression $E \oplus E'$. For example, if we let E be the expression $x \wedge y$ and E' be the expression $x \vee y$, then we find:

$E \oplus E'$

= {substitution, expansion}

$(x \wedge y) \wedge \overline{(x \vee y)} \vee \overline{(x \wedge y)} \wedge (x \vee y)$

= {De Morgan}

$(x \wedge y) \wedge (\bar{x} \wedge \bar{y}) \vee (\bar{x} \vee \bar{y}) \wedge (x \vee y)$

= {Distributing, simplifying}

$x \wedge \bar{y} \vee \bar{x} \wedge y$

= {Definition}

$x \oplus y$.

In other words, in order to sensitize this fault, we must submit distinct values for x and y ((true, false) or (false, true)); indeed, if x and y are identical, then their conjunction ($\wedge$) and their disjunction ($\vee$) are identical.

- *Relational Operator Fault.* If a relational operator is faulty, then we need to proceed in two steps: first, we choose data that yields different Boolean values for the relational expression; then we treat the relational expression as a variable reference fault. For example, let i and j be integer variables and let x be a Boolean variable (or another Boolean valued expression). We let expressions E and E' be defined as follows:

- $E = (x \wedge (i \leq j))$,
- $E' = (x \wedge (i < j))$.

Because $(i < j)$ logically implies $(i \leq j)$, the only way to make these conditions distinct is to let the first condition be false while the second is true. To this effect, we let i and j be equal. From then on, the question is how to make an expression $(x \wedge y)$ distinct from $(x \wedge z)$ given that y is different from z. We have seen in the study of the first class of fault that this requires the condition $x \wedge (y \oplus z)$. Since $(y \oplus z)$ is true by construction, the remaining condition for us is x.

All the sensitization conditions we have generated so far are local conditions, that is. conditions that refer to the value of program variables at the state where the Boolean expressions are evaluated; but generating test data requires that we compute conditions that input data must satisfy. In the following section, we consider how to generate test data that triggers sensitization conditions at chosen locations in the program, where the targeted Boolean conditions are evaluated.

10.4.2 Selecting Input Data for Fault Sensitization

For the sake of this discussion, we introduce a program label that indicates the first executable statement of the program, and we refer to it as the *begin* label. Also, we consider a Boolean expression E and designate the program label where this expression is evaluated by $\underline{L}$. We consider a possible fault in expression E (among the classes of faults catalogued in Section 10.4.1) and we let E' be the expression obtained from E when the fault is removed; also, we let C be the sensitization condition of the targeted fault at E, that is, $C = E \oplus E'$. We have the following criterion:

> We say that initial state s sensitizes the targeted fault in the Boolean expression E if and only if:
>
> - There exists a path p from label *begin* to label L; let P be the function of p (computed as shown in Section 10.1).
> - The post-restriction of P to sensitization condition C is not empty.
> - State s is in the domain of the post-restriction of P to sensitization condition C.

As an illustrative example, we consider an array a of size $2 \times N$ for some natural number N greater than 1 and an element x of the same data type as the contents of the array; we assume that we are interested in checking whether x is in the first half of the array. Hence we write the following program:

```
void main ()
   {itemtype a[2*N]; itemtype x; indextype i; bool found;
   i=0; L: while ((a[i]!=x) && (i<=N)) {i=i+1;}
   found = (a[i-1]==x);}
```

We have a relational operator fault in this program, as the loop condition should read `((a[i]!=x) && (i<N))` rather than `((a[i]!=x) && (i<=N))`. As we discuss in the previous section, this fault can be sensitized locally by ensuring that `(i<=N)` holds while `(i<N)` does not, and ensuring that `(a[i]!=x)` is true. To this effect, we let `i` be equal to `N` while ensuring that the condition `(a[N]!=x)` is true. We write the local sensitization condition as:

$$C \equiv ((i=N) \wedge (a[N] \neq x))$$

All these are local conditions; we must now determine what input data will create these local conditions at label L? To this effect, we compute a path from the start of the program to label L, take its post-restriction to the sensitization condition, check that it is nonempty, then compute its domain. We find:

Path: `i=0; ((((a[i]!=x) && (i<=N))? True) ; {i=i+1})*;`

where the * is used to refer to an arbitrary number of instances of a path. The function of this path is given by the following formula (where the star represents reflexive transitive closure):

P

= {Substitution}

$$\{(s,s')|i'=0 \wedge -(s)=-(s')\} \bullet \{(s,s')|a[i] \neq x \wedge i \leq N \wedge i'=i+1-(s)=-(s')\}^*$$

= {Transitive Closure}

$$\{(s,s')|i'=0 \wedge -(s)=-(s')\} \bullet \{(s,s')|\forall j:0 \leq j < i':a[j] \neq x \wedge j \leq N \wedge i' \geq i \wedge -(s)=-(s')\}$$

= {Relational Product}

$$\{(s,s')|\forall j:0 \leq j < i':a[j] \neq x \wedge j \leq N \wedge i' \geq 0 \wedge -(s)=-(s')\}$$

= {Simplification}

$$\{(s,s')|i' \geq 0 \wedge -(s)=-(s') \wedge i' \leq N+1 \wedge \forall j:0 \leq j < i':a[j] \neq x\}$$

Taking the post-restriction of this function to the sensitization condition, we find

$$P \bullet I(C)$$

$$= \{\text{Substitution}\}$$

$$\{(s,s') | i' \geq 0 \land -(s) = -(s') \land i' \leq N+1 \land (i'=N) \land (a[N] \neq x) \land \forall j : 0 \leq j < i' : a[j] \neq x\}$$

$$= \{\text{Simplification}\}$$

$$\{(s,s') | -(s) = -(s') \land (i'=N) \land \forall j : 0 \leq j \leq N : a[j] \neq x\}$$

The domain of this function is:

$$dom(P \bullet I(C)) = \{s | \forall j : 0 \leq j \leq N : a[j] \neq x\}.$$

Any initial state in this domain will sensitize the fault: Indeed, since the condition $(a[j] \neq x)$ holds for all indices between 0 and N inclusive, the second conjunct of the while condition determines the value of this condition: For i=N, the condition (**i<=N**) returns True, whereas the condition (**i<N**) returns False.

10.4.3   Selecting Input Data for Error Propagation

Whereas it is necessary to identify the conditions under which an initial state sensitizes a fault to create an error, it is not sufficient. We also need to make sure the error propagates to cause an observable failure. Whence the following criterion:

> We say that initial state s exposes the targeted fault in the Boolean expression E if and only if:
>
> - State s sensitizes the targeted fault in expression E.
> - Further, state s satisfies the following condition: $G(s) \neq G'(s)$, where G is the function of the original program g, and G' is the function of the modified program, in which expression E is replaced by expression E'.

The first condition ensures that the fault is sensitized and the second condition ensures that the resulting error is propagated to cause a failure, which can then be observed to infer the existence of the fault. As an illustration, consider again the search program we had introduced above:

```
void main ()
    {itemtype a[2*N]; itemtype x; indextype i; bool found;
    i=0; L: while ((a[i]!=x) && (i<=N)) {i=i+1;}
    found = (a[i-1]==x);}
```

If we let g' be the program obtained from g by changing the condition `(i<=N)` into the condition `(i<N)`, and we let s be an element of $dom(P \bullet I(C))$, then we find that application of functions G and G' to s yield the following results:

- For $G : x' = x \wedge a' = a \wedge i' = N + 1 \wedge found' = True$.
- For $G' : x' = x \wedge a' = a \wedge i' = N \wedge found' = True$.

Indeed, the images of s by G and G′ are distinct (distinct values of i′); hence the error caused by the identified fault is propagated to cause failure; had program G altered variable i in a non-injective manner, such as (for example):

```
void main ()
    {itemtype a[2*N]; itemtype x; indextype i; bool found;
     i=0; L: while ((a[i]!=x) && (i<=N)) {i=i+1;}
     found = (a[i-1]==x); i=0;}
```

then state s would no longer be an adequate choice to expose the selected fault, even though it does sensitize the fault and causes an error.

10.5 CHAPTER SUMMARY

Structural criteria for test data generation aim to generate test data not by analyzing the functional specification of the product but rather by analyzing the product itself; while the idea of using a product under test as a guide to test may be counter-intuitive, it does ensure some degree of coverage of the code that we are trying to test. Most criteria used in this chapter involve computing feasible execution paths through the code, then determining their path conditions, that is, for each path the condition under which that path will in effect be taken during an execution; hence the first topic we must address, and the most critical skill we must develop, is the ability to compute path conditions. We use this ability to study a number of test data generation criteria, including the following:

- Control flow criteria, which aim to ensure that we achieve a degree of coverage of control flow configurations.
- Dataflow criteria, which aim to ensure that we achieve a degree of coverage of various configurations of variable lifecycles.
- Fault-based criteria, which aim to ensure that we expose various configurations of specific faults in the code.

Whereas functional criteria focus on exposing possible software failures, structural criteria aim to expose various configurations of faults that may be causing observed failures.

10.6 EXERCISES

10.1. Consider the paths p0, p1, p2, and p3 derived on the gcd program of Section 10.1.

    a. Compute their *path function*.

    b. Compute their *path condition*.

    c. Derive test data to meet the path condition of each path.

10.2. Consider the paths p4, p5, p6, and p7 derived on the gcd program of Section 10.1.

    a. Compute their *path function*.

    b. Compute their *path condition*.

    c. Derive test data to meet the path condition of each path.

10.3. Generate four paths of the gcd program of Section 10.1 that proceed through the loop four times.

    a. Compute their *path function*.

    b. Compute their *path condition*.

    c. Derive test data to meet the path condition of each path.

    d. How many paths are there that iterate four times through the loop?

10.4. Consider the following program, whose goal is to check whether x is located in the second half of array a of size $2 \times N$, where $N > 1$:

```
void main ()
    {itemtype a[2*N]; itemtype x; indextype i; bool found;
    i=2*N-1; L: while ((a[i]!=x) && (i>N)) {i=i-1;}
    found = (a[i+1]==x);}
```

Find test data to sensitize the fault that the second conjunct of the loop condition should be `(i>=N)` rather than `(i>N)`.

10.5. Consider the following program, whose goal is to check whether x is located in the second half of array a of size $2 \times N$, where $N > 1$:

```
void main ()
    {itemtype a[2*N]; itemtype x; indextype i; bool found;
    i=2*N-1; L: while ((a[i]!=x) && (i>N)) {i=i-1;}
    found = (a[i+1]==x); i=N;}
```

Find test data to expose the fault that the second conjunct of the loop condition should be `(i>=N)` rather than `(i>N)`.

10.6. Consider the two paths proposed at the end of Section 10.2.1. Compute their path functions P1 and P2, then the domains of their path functions. Generate test data from them.

10.7. Consider the following program on space S defined by natural variables x, y, and z

```
{z=1; while (y!=0) {if (y%2==0) {y=y/2; x=x*x}
                    else {y=y-1; z=z+x;}}}.
```

    a. Generate the paths of this program that iterate no more than three times through the loop.

    b. Compute the function of each path and its path condition.

    c. Generate test data that satisfies the path condition of each path.

10.8. Complete test generation (started in Section 10.3.2) for the gcd program according to the criterion of *All du-paths*.

10.9. Complete test generation (started in Section 10.3.2) for the gcd program according to the criterion of *All c-uses*.

10.10. Complete test generation (started in Section 10.3.2) for the gcd program according to the criterion of *All p-uses*.

10.11. Complete test generation (started in Section 10.3.2) for the gcd program according to the criterion of *All definitions*.

10.12. Consider the following program on space S defined by natural variables x, y, and z

```
{z=0; while (y!=0) {if (y%2==0) {y=y/2; x=2*x}
                    else {y=y-1; z=z+x;}}}.
```

    Generate test data for this program using the criterion of All du-paths.

10.13. Consider the following program on space S defined by natural variables x, y, and z

```
{z=0; while (y!=0) {if (y%2==0) {y=y/2; x=2*x}
                    else {y=y-1; z=z+x;}}}.
```

    Generate test data for this program using the criterion of All u-uses.

10.14. Consider the following program on space S defined by natural variables x, y, and z

```
{z=0; while (y!=0) {if (y%2==0) {y=y/2; x=2*x}
                    else {y=y-1; z=z+x;}}}.
```

    Generate test data for this program using the criterion of All p-uses.

10.15. Consider the following program on space S defined by natural variables x, y, and z

```
{z=0; while (y!=0) {if (y%2==0) {y=y/2; x=2*x}
                    else {y=y-1; z=z+x;}}}.
```

Generate test data for this program using the criterion of All definitions.

10.16. Consider the following program on space S defined by natural variables x, y, and z

```
{z=1; while (y!=0) {if (y%2==0) {y=y/2; x=x*x}
                    else {y=y-1; z=z*x;}}}.
```

Generate test data for this program using the criterion of All du-paths.

10.17. Consider the following program on space S defined by natural variables x, y, and z

```
{z=1; while (y!=0) {if (y%2==0) {y=y/2; x=x*x}
                    else {y=y-1; z=z*x;}}}.
```

Generate test data for this program using the criterion of All u-uses.

10.18. Consider the following program on space S defined by natural variables x, y, and z

```
{z=1; while (y!=0) {if (y%2==0) {y=y/2; x=x*x}
                    else {y=y-1; z=z*x;}}}.
```

Generate test data for this program using the criterion of All p-uses.

10.19. Consider the following program on space S defined by natural variables x, y, and z

```
{z=1; while (y!=0) {if (y%2==0) {y=y/2; x=x*x}
                    else {y=y-1; z=z*x;}}}.
```

Generate test data for this program using the criterion of All definitions.

10.20. Consider the sequential form of the triangle analysis program discussed in Section 10.2.4. Review the table that characterizes paths p1–p6, and justify the way this table is filled.

10.21. Compute the path functions and the path conditions of the paths generated for the gcd program in Section 10.2.4.

10.22. Use fault-based test generation to produce test data for the sequential version of the triangle analysis program.

10.23. Use fault-based test generation to produce test data for the nested version of the triangle analysis program.

10.7 BIBLIOGRAPHIC NOTES

The discussion of fault-based test data generation uses results given by Kuhn (1999). The discussion of dataflow-based test data generation uses results from Rapps and Weyuker (1985) and Frankl and Weyuker (1988).

Part IV

Test Deployment
and Analysis

In Part III, we have explored ways to generate test data; the generation of test data is only a phase of the testing process. In this part, we discuss the remaining phases, which include the design of the test oracle, the design of the test driver, and the analysis of test outcomes; we devote one chapter to each one of these phases.

Software Testing: Concepts and Operations, First Edition. Ali Mili and Fairouz Tchier.
© 2015 John Wiley & Sons, Inc. Published 2015 by John Wiley & Sons, Inc.

11

Test Oracle Design

In this chapter, we discuss the design of the test oracle, that is, the agent whose task is to observe executions of the candidate program on sample test data and to rule on whether the program does or does not behave according to its specification. We review, in turn, the tradeoffs that arise in oracle design, how to design an oracle from a relational specification, and how to design an oracle for a state-based software product.

11.1 DILEMMAS OF ORACLE DESIGN

All the test data in the world do not help us unless we have an oracle, a correct oracle, to reliably check whether the candidate program behaves according to its specification. The choice of an oracle is both critical and difficult.

- It is critical to have a reliable oracle because otherwise we run the risk of over-looking faults (if failures are not detected) and the risk of acting on faulty diagnoses (if correct behavior is reported to be incorrect).
- It is difficult and error prone to monitor the behavior of a program by having a human operator watch its inputs and outputs; but developing automated oracles poses challenges of its own, which we discuss in this section.

The general framework in which an oracle is invoked can be written as follows (where g is the program under test and S is the space of the program):

```
main ()
      {s = testdata; s_init=s;
       g;  // modifies s, keeps s_init intact
       assert(oracle(s_init,s));}
```

Software Testing: Concepts and Operations, First Edition. Ali Mili and Fairouz Tchier.
© 2015 John Wiley & Sons, Inc. Published 2015 by John Wiley & Sons, Inc.

The design of the oracle is subject to the following criteria:

- *Simplicity.* The oracle must be simple enough that we can ensure its reliability with a great degree of confidence. In particular, it must be significantly simpler to write and analyze than candidate programs. If the oracle is as complex as the program being tested, then it is as likely to have faults as the candidate program; this, in turn, defeats the purpose of using the oracle to test the program.
- *Strength.* Ideally, we want the oracle to capture all the clauses of the requirements specification, so as to test all the relevant functional properties of the program. But this may prove too complex (hence violating the first criterion), too inefficient (in terms of resource usage), or too impractical (requiring a great deal of context, for example). Hence we may often have to settle for capturing a subset of the target requirements.

The criteria of strength and simplicity must be balanced against each other to reach a tradeoff where we derive an oracle that is sufficiently strong to be useful, yet sufficiently simple to be reliable. This tradeoff is very easy when it is easier to check that a final state is correct than to compute a correct final state. Consider for example a program that computes the roots of a quadratic equation: The space of this program is defined by real variables a, b, c that represent the coefficients of the quadratic equation, and real variables $x1$ and $x2$ that hold the roots. A specification of the quadratic equation may be written as follows:

$$R = \{(s, s') | positive(b^2\text{-}4ac) \wedge root(x1') \wedge root(x2') \wedge positive(x2'\text{-}x1')\}.$$

This specification provides that the quadratic equation is assumed to have two distinct roots, and that candidate programs are expected to produce the smaller root in $x1'$ and the larger root in $x2'$. To account for possible loss of precision in computer arithmetic, predicates *positive* and *root* are defined with respect to selected precision thresholds; for example,

- $positive(x) \equiv (x > \varepsilon)$,
- $root(x) \equiv (|ax^2 + bx + c| < \varepsilon)$,

for some small positive constant, ε. Whereas the program computes the roots of the quadratic equation constructively, the oracle merely checks that the computed values are indeed roots of the equation, and that they are distinct (hence the program is returning all the roots, rather than twice the same root). We can think of many other examples where computing a result is significantly more complex than checking that a computed result is correct:

- Consider the problem of computing the roots of a polynomial of higher degree, or the roots of a functional that has no polynomial form altogether, where no constructive solutions are known: candidate programs may compute the roots by some iterative method of successive approximations; yet all the oracle has to do is simply to check that the delivered values are indeed roots to the equation.

- Solving a large system of linear equations may be a complex affair (e.g., Gaussian elimination), where we have to worry not only about the correctness of the algorithm, but also about controlling round-off errors; yet checking that the solution is correct amounts to little more than multiplying a matrix by a vector.

- Computing the inverse of a $N \times N$ matrix involves complex calculations (e.g., N systems of linear equations), which are made all the more complex by the need to control round off errors; yet checking that the solution is correct amounts to little more than computing the product of two matrices.

- Computing the eigenvalues and eigenvectors of a $N \times N$ matrix involves solving polynomials of degree N, followed by solving systems of N linear equations, where again the control of runaway round-off errors is a major concern; yet checking that the solution is correct amounts to little more than multiplying a matrix by a vector.

In all these cases, it is possible to test a complex program using a simple, reliable oracle. There are ample cases, however, where checking that a final program state is correct is not much easier than generating a correct final state; in such cases, we may have to settle for generating an oracle that tests only some aspects of the target requirements specification, deferring the other aspects to other verification/quality assurance methods. As a simple illustrative example, consider the specification of a gcd program on natural variables x and y. The specification can be written as:

$$R = \{(s,s') \,|\, x>0 \wedge y>0 \wedge x' = \gcd(x,y)\}.$$

If we are given the initial values of variable x and y, and the final value x' of variable x, we have no easy way to tell whether x' is the gcd of x and y, except possibly to compute the gcd of x and y independently and compare it with x'. But doing so defeats the purpose of the oracle because it violates the requirement of simplicity: if the oracle is as complex as the program we are testing, we have no reason to trust the correctness of the oracle more than the correctness of the candidate program. As a substitute, we may want to settle for checking that x' is a common divisor of x and y, and renounce checking that it is the *greatest* common divisor. The specification that corresponds to such a scaled-down oracle can then be written as:

$$R' = \{(s,s') \,|\, x>0 \wedge y>0 \wedge x \bmod x' = 0 \wedge y \bmod x' = 0\}.$$

11.2 FROM SPECIFICATIONS TO ORACLES

Let g be a program on space S and let R be the specification against which we are testing g; as we discussed in the previous section, the general format for testing program g looks as follows:

```
main ()
      {s = testdata; s_init=s;
       g;  // modifies s, keeps s_init intact
       assert(oracle(s_init,s));}
```

The question we wish to address in this section is: How do we derive the oracle from specification R? A naïve solution would be to simply let `oracle(s_init,s)` be defined as: $(s_{init}, s) \in R$. As we will see in the following example, this is not a valid choice. We consider the following specification on space S defined by natural variables x and y (where we want to compute the greatest common divisor of integers greater than 10):

$$R = \{(s,s') | x > 10 \wedge y > 10 \wedge x' = \gcd(x,y)\},$$

and we consider the following program:

```
// gcd program
void gcd() {while (x!=y) {if (x>y) {x=x-y;} else {y=y-x;}};}
```

Because of the difficulties we have alluded to above, we resolve to test this program against a simpler specification than R, which checks that the final value of x is a common divisor of the original values of x and y, but not the greatest common divisor; this yields the following relation,

$$R' = \{(s,s') | x > 10 \wedge y > 10 \wedge x \bmod x' = 0 \wedge y \bmod x' = 0\},$$

Let us consider the following program, whose goal is to check the correctness of program gcd against specification R' for the input data $T = \{\langle 5,5 \rangle\}$.

```
#include <iostream>
using namespace std;
int x, y, x_init; y_init; void gcd();
int main () {x=0; y=0; x_init=x; y_init=y;
      gcd();  // modifies x and y, keeps x_init and y_init
      intact
      if (!(x_init>0 && y_init>0 &&
            x_init%x==0 && x_init%y==0))
          {cout << "test failure";}
      else {cout << "test success";}}
```

When we run this program on test data $T = \{\langle 5,5 \rangle\}$, it prints "test failure," which appears to suggest that the program is incorrect, when in fact this program is correct. The reason for this inconsistency is that the specification includes clauses on the initial state and clauses on the final state, which have different interpretations:

- Clauses on the initial state represent the conditions that candidate programs may assume to hold prior to their call, whereas
- Clauses on the final state represent the conditions that candidate programs are expected to ensure upon their execution.

An oracle ought to treat these two conditions separately:

1. If the condition on the initial state does not hold, then the program is off the hook: since its assumption does not hold, whatever it does must be considered correct.
2. The output condition of the specification is checked only if the input condition holds.

Hence the following proposition:

Proposition: Oracle Structure *In order to test a program g with respect to a specification R, we must use the following oracle:*

$$\text{oracle}(s_{\text{init}}, s) \equiv (s_{\text{init}} \notin \text{dom}(R)) \vee (s_{\text{init}}, s) \in R.$$

In Programming terms, we can write the generic form of the oracle as follows:

```
bool oracle (s_init, s)
  {return (!(domR(s_init)) || R(s_init,s));}
```

As an example, we consider again the gcd program, and we rewrite it as follows:

```
#include <iostream>                                    // 1
using namespace std;                                   // 2
int x, y, x_init, y_init; void gcd ();                 // 3
bool oracle (int x_init, int y_init, int x, int y);    // 4
bool domR(int x_init, int y_init);                     // 5
bool R(int x_init, int y_init, int x, int y);          // 6
int main () {x=355; y=215; x_init=x; y_init=y;         // 7
  gcd(); // changes x, y, keeps x_init and y_init      // 8
```

```
if (oracle(x_init,y_init,x,y))                         //  9
    {cout << "test success" << endl;}                  // 10
else {cout << "test failure" << endl;}  }              // 11
void gcd()
    {while (x!=y) {if (x>y) {x=x-y;} else {y=y-x;}};}   // 12
bool oracle(int x_init, int y_init, int x, int y)      // 13
  {return (!(domR(x_init,y_init)) ||
            R(x_init,y_init,x,y));}                     // 14
bool domR(int x_init, int y_init)
    {return (x_init>10 && y_init>10);}                 // 15
bool R(int x_init, int y_init, int x, int y)           // 16
  {return (x_init>10 && y_init>10 &&
          x_init%x==0);}                               // 17
```

The code of method '**bool oracle**' can be used as a general template for oracles (modulo differences in the state space): for any specification R, we must define Boolean functions **domR()** and **R()** with the appropriate parameters and let function oracle use them according to the formula of the proposition above.

As a second example, we consider the specification of the quadratic equation, which we define on space S represented by variables a, b, c (coefficients of the equation) and variables $x1$ and $x2$ (roots of the equation):

$$R = \{(s,s') | \text{positive}(b^2 - 4ac) \wedge \text{root}(x1') \wedge \text{root}(x2') \wedge \text{positive}(x2' - x1')\}.$$

From this definition, we infer the domain of this relation as:

$$\text{dom}(R) = \{(s,s') | \text{positive}(b^2 - 4ac)\}.$$

Hence the oracle can be written as:

```
bool oracle
(float a_init, float b_init, float c_init, float x1_init,
float x2_init, float a, float b, float c, float x1, float x2)
  {return (!(domR(a_init,b_init, c_init, x1_init,
    x2_init)) ||
  R(a_init, b_init, c_init, x1_init, x2_init, a, b, c,
    x1, x2));}
```

Where predicates **domR** and **R** are defined as follows:

```
bool domR
(float a_init, float b_init, float c_init, float x1_init,
  float x2_init)
  {return (positive(b_init*b_init-4*a_init*c_init));}
```

```
bool R(float a_init,float b_init, float c_init,
      float x1_init, float x2_init,
      float a, float b, float c, float x1, float x2)
 {return    (positive(b_init*b_init-4*a_init*c_init)&&
            root(x1)&&root(x2)&& positive(x2-x1));}
bool positive(float x) {return (x>epsilon);}
bool root(float x)
      {return (abs(a_init*x*x+b_init*x+c) <epsilon);}
```

The following segment shows how this code is called to run the quadratic equation program and test its operation:

```
int main ()
  {a=1; b=8; c=9; x1=0; x2=0;
   a_init=a; b_init=b; c_init=c; x1_init=x1; x2_init=x2;
   //saving init state
  quadratic(); // changes current state, keeps initial state
  if (oracle(a_init, b_init, c_init, x1_init, x2_init,
             a, b, c, x1, x2))
    {cout << "test success" << endl;}
  else {cout << "test failure" << endl;}}
```

where function quadratic is defined as follows:

```
void quadratic()
  {float delta; delta = b*b-4*a*c; delta=sqrt(delta);
  x1=(-b-delta)/2.*a; x2=(-b+delta)/2.*a;}
```

We have seen in Chapter 7 that the specification against which we test a software product depends to a great extent on the goal of the test; in particular, if our goal is to find (and remove) the maximum number of faults, then it is important to use the most refined (strongest) specification possible, namely one that capture every functional detail of the program as written. Hence, for the quadratic equation program, for example, the specification that captures all the functional detail would look like:

$$R = \{(s,s') | \text{positive}(b^2\text{-}4ac) \wedge \text{root}(x1') \wedge \text{root}(x2') \wedge \text{positive}(x2'\text{-}x1') \wedge$$

$$a' = a \wedge b' = b \wedge c' = c\}.$$

Also, for the *gcd* program, the specification that captures all the functional detail would look like:

$$R = \{(s,s') | x > 0 \wedge y > 0 \wedge x' = \gcd(x,y) \wedge y' = \gcd(x,y)\}.$$

As a tradeoff between simplicity and strength, we can use the following specification as a substitute for R:

$$R' = \{(s,s') \mid x > 0 \wedge y > 0 \wedge x \bmod x' = 0 \wedge y \bmod x' = 0 \wedge x' = y'\}.$$

This relation provides that x' is a common divisor of x and y, and that y' is equal to x'; but it does not provide that x' is the *greatest* common divisor of x and y; to ensure this latter property, we can write the following Boolean function:

```
bool greatest(int x_init, int y_init, int x)
  {// no number greater than x is a divisor of x_init and y_init;
   int min;
     if (x_init<y_init) {min=x_init;} else {min=y_init;};
   bool isgreatest; isgreatest=true;
   for (int i=x+1; i<=min; i++)
       {isgreatest = isgreatest &&
        !(x_init%i==0 && y_init%i==0);};
   return isgreatest;}
```

11.3 ORACLES FOR STATE-BASED PRODUCTS

In the previous section, we have discussed how to choose a specification against which we test a program and then how to derive a test oracle from a specification. In particular, we have focused our attention on two possible specifications:

- A specification that is appropriate for acceptance testing, which is the weakest specification that a user is willing to accept as a criterion for considering that the contract (between the software provider and the software user) is fulfilled.
- A specification that is appropriate for fault removal, which is the strongest possible specification that the candidate program must fulfill, reflecting the intent of the programmer and the minute details of the program.

In this section, we consider software products that are based on an internal state. As we have seen in Chapter 4, such products can be specified by means of relations from input histories to outputs. The main advantage of this specification model is that it absolves us from talking about system states, leaving this matter as a design decision rather than a specification decision.

We consider a specification of the form (X, Y, R), where R is a relation from $H = X^*$ to Y and we let g be a candidate implementation of the specification, in the form of a *class* (in the object oriented programming (OOP) sense). If we are interested in testing class g for the purpose of fault removal, then we can specify each of its methods in terms of how it affects the system state and how it generates outputs accordingly.

Each individual method can be viewed as a simple software component mapping an initial state into a final state; testing such components falls under the model we discussed in the previous section. Hence we focus our attention in this section on testing a state-based system against a specification of the form (X, Y, R), where R is a relation from $H = X^*$ to Y. We assume that such specifications are represented by means of axioms and rules, as we discuss in Chapter 4. The question then becomes: how do we test a candidate implementation against such a specification? More specifically, how do we map such an axiomatic specification into an oracle? In the following section we discuss, in turn, how we generate oracles from axioms and how we generate oracles from rules. In the discussions that follow, we assume that implementation g is a class that has a method for each symbol in X; for the sake of simplicity, we assume that each method has the same name as the corresponding symbol; we postfix method names with parentheses, even when they have no parameters.

11.3.1 From Axioms to Oracles

In the notation we introduced in Chapter 4, axioms have the form

- $R(h) = y$

where h is an (elementary) input history that ends with a *VX* symbol (representing a method that returns a value but does not change the state) and y is the corresponding output. History h can then be written as

- $h = h'.vop,$

where *vop* is a *VX* symbol. In order to test implementation g against this axiom, we write the following sequence of code:

```
vtype y; y=y0; // y0: output specified by the axiom
g.m1(); g.m2(); g.m3(); … g.mk(); // sequence h'
if (g.vop==y) {successfultest;} else {unsuccessfultest;}
```

where *vtype* is the data type returned by operation *vop*, and y is the output value provided by the axiom. As an illustration, we consider the following axioms from the stack specification discussed in Chapter 4 and generate an oracle for each.

- stack(init.top)=crror.

```
itemtype y; y=error; // data type returned by top
g.init(); // sequence h'
if (g.top==y) {successfultest;} else {unsuccessfultest;}
```

- stack(init.h.push(a).top)=a.

```
itemtype y; y=a;// data type returned by top
g.init();
g.xx(); g.yy(); ... g.zz(); // any sequence of AX methods
g.push(a);                   // arbitrary a
if (g.top==y) {successfultest;} else {unsuccessfultest;}
```

- stack(init.size)=0.

```
int y; y=0; // data type returned by size
g.init(); // sequence h'
if (g.size==y) {successfultest;} else {unsuccessfultest;}
```

- stack(init..empty)=true.

```
bool y; y=true; // data type returned by empty
g.init(); // sequence h'
if (g.empty==y) {successfultest;} else {unsuccessfultest;}
```

- stack(init.push(a).empty)=false.

```
bool y; y=false; // data type returned by empty
g.init(); g.push(a); // sequence h', arbitrary a
if (g.empty==y) {successfultest;} else {unsuccessfultest;}
```

11.3.2 From Rules to Oracles

The vast majority of rules in axiomatic specifications has the form of an equality between the images of two histories and expresses the property that two histories are equivalent for all subsequent input sequences. Typically the two histories are ordered (one is more complex than the other) and such rules can be used to infer the output of the complex history from the output of the simpler history. We focus on such rules first and then we consider other forms of rules.

Such rules can be written in generic form as:

$$\forall h: R(h'.h) = R(h''.h),$$

and can be interpreted as follows: for any input sequence h, the input sequence $h'. h$ yields the same outcome as the input sequence $h''. h$; in other words, the histories h' and h'' are equivalent now (if h is empty) and at any time in the future (if h is not empty). Examples of such rules, in the stack specification given in Chapter 4, include the following:

- stack(h′.init.h) = stack(init.h).
- stack(init.pop.h) = stack(init.h).
- stack(init.h.push(a).pop.h+) = stack(init.h.h+).
- stack(init.h.top.h+) = stack(init.h.h+).
- stack(init.h.size.h+) = stack(init.h.h+).
- stack(init.h.empty.h+) = stack(init.h.h+).

Some rules have h+ (nonempty sequences) instead of h (possibly empty), but they could be converted into rules with h by replacing h+ by xxx.h for each symbol xxx in X. Hence we make no distinction between rules that end with an arbitrary history h and rules that end with a nonempty history h^+. The same input sequence may lend itself to more than one rule, yielding a different oracle for each rule, as we discuss below. As an example, we consider the following input sequence:

- init.pop.push(a).size.push(b).pop.top.push(c).

We leave it to the reader to check that this input sequence lends itself to the following rules:

- The Init-Pop Rule that reduces the sequence to
  o init.push(a).size.push(b).pop.top.push(c).
- The VX Rule (for size and top) that reduces the sequence to
  o init.pop.push(a).push(b).pop.push(c).
- The Push-Pop Rule that reduces the sequence to
  o init.pop.push(a).size.top.push(c).

Each one of these rules provides that the original sequence places the stack in the same state as the simpler input sequence; since we want to write the oracle by inspecting the specification rather than candidate implementations (and we want the same oracle to work for all possible implementations), we abstain from referring to states. The question that arises then is: how can we say that two states are identical if we cannot refer to the states? The answer is that, as an approximation, we consider that two states are identical if all the VX operations return the same values at these two states. Hence if we have a rule of the form:

- R(init.h′.h) = R(init.h″.h),

where h″ is simpler than h′, then the general template for an oracle that is derived from the above rule is the following segment:

```
g.init(); g.m1(); g.m2(); … g.mk(); // sequence init.h'
if oracle() {successfultest();}
  else {unsuccessfultest();}
```

where `oracle()` is defined as follows:

```
bool oracle()
{vx1type vx1; vx2type vx2; vx3type vx3; // VX types
vx1 = g.vop1(); vx2 = g.vop2(); vx3 = g.vop3();
// storing the current state, following init.h'
g.init(); g.m1'(); g.m2'(); … g.mh'(); // sequence
init.h"
return ((vx1==g.vop1()) && (vx2==g.vop2()) &&
        (vx3==g.vop3())); }
```

As an illustration, we consider the following input sequence:

- init.pop.push(a).size.push(b).pop.top.push(c).

and we generate oracles to test it, according to various applicable rules.

- *The Init-Pop Rule.* In order to test this sequence against the Init-Pop rule, we apply the code pattern shown above, which we specialize to this rule.

```
itemtype a, b, c, v; int n;          // working variables
g.init(); g.pop(); g.push(a); n=g.size(); g.push(b);
g.pop(); v=g.top(); g.push(c);
if oracleinitpop(){successfultest();}
  else {unsuccessfultest();}
```

where we define `oracle()` as follows:

```
bool oracleinitpop()
{bool sempty; int ssize; itemtype stop;    // VX values
sempty=g.empty(); ssize=g.size(); stop=g.top();
g.init(); g.push(a); n=g.size(); g.push(b); g.pop();
v=g.top(); g.push(c);
return ((sempty == g.empty()) && (ssize==g.size) &&
        (stop==g.top())); }
```

- *The VX Rule (for size).* In order to test this sequence against the VX rule for size, we apply the code pattern shown above, which we specialize to this rule.

```
itemtype a, b, c, v; int n;          // working variables
g.init(); g.pop(); g.push(a); n=g.size(); g.push(b);
g.pop(); v=g.top(); g.push(c);
if oracleVXsize(){successfultest();}
  else {unsuccessfultest();}
```

where we define `oracle()` as follows:

```
bool oracleVXsize()
{bool sempty; int ssize; itemtype stop;    // VX values
sempty=g.empty(); ssize=g.size(); stop=g.top();
g.init(); g.pop(); g.push(a); g.push(b); g.pop();
v=g.top(); g.push(c);
return ((sempty == g.empty()) && (ssize==g.size) &&
        (stop==g.top())); }
```

- *The VX Rule (for top)*. In order to test this sequence against the VX rule for top, we apply the code pattern shown above, which we specialize to this rule.

```
itemtype a, b, c, v; int n;           // working variables
g.init(); g.pop(); g.push(a); n=g.size(); g.push(b);
g.pop(); v=g.top(); g.push(c);
if oracleVXtop(){successfultest();}
else {unsuccessfultest();}
```

where we define `oracle()` as follows:

```
bool oracleVXtop()
{bool sempty; int ssize; itemtype stop;    // VX values
sempty=g.empty(); ssize=g.size(); stop=g.top();
g.init(); g.pop(); g.push(a); n=g.size(); g.push(b);
g.pop(); g.push(c);
return ((sempty == g.empty()) && (ssize==g.size) &&
        (stop==g.top())); }
```

- *The Push-Pop Rule*. In order to test this sequence against the Push-Pop rule, we apply the code pattern shown above, which we specialize to this rule.

```
itemtype a, b, c, v; int n;           // working variables
g.init(); g.pop(); g.push(a); n=g.size(); g.push(b);
g.pop(); v=g.top(); g.push(c);
if oraclepushpop(){successfultest();}
  else {unsuccessfultest();}
```

where we define `oracle()` as follows:

```
bool oraclepushpop()
{bool sempty; int ssize; itemtype stop;    // VX values
sempty=g.empty(); ssize=g.size(); stop=g.top();
```

```
g.init(); g.pop(); g.push(a); n=g.size(); v=g.top();
g.push(c);
return ((sempty == g.empty()) && (ssize==g.size) &&
       (stop==g.top())); }
```

Whereas some rules provide that distinct input histories are equivalent, other rules describe how the value of a VX method depends on the structure of the input history. We write their general form as follows:

- C(R(init.h.vop), R(init.h′.vop)),

where C is a binary predicate between values returned by vop. As such, these rules are potentially applicable to any input sequence that ends with a *vop* symbol. The general format of their oracle can be written as follows, where we assume that sequence *h* is more complex than sequence *h'*:

```
g.init(); g.m1(); g.m2(); … g.mk();   // sequence init.h
if oraclevoprule() {successfultest();}
else {unsuccessfultest();}
```

where `oraclevoprule()` is defined as follows:

```
bool oraclevoprule()
{vxtype vx; vx = g.vop();            // store R(init.h.vop)
g.init(); g.m1'(); g.m2'(); … g.mh'(); // sequence init.h'
return (C(vx, g.vop); }
```

As an illustration, we consider the following input sequence

- init.pop.push(a).push(b).size.push(a).top.push(c).size

and we generate an oracle for it on the basis of the size rule. As we recall, the Size Rule of the stack specification provides:

- stack(init.h.push(a).size) = 1 + stack(init.h.size).

We find:

```
itemtype a, b, c, v; int n;            // working variables
g.init(); g.pop(); g.push(a); g.push(b); n=g.size();
g.push(a); v=g.top(); g.push(c);       // sequence init.h
if oraclesize() {successfultest();}
  else {unsuccessfultest();}
```

where **oraclesize()** is defined as follows:

```
bool oraclesize()
{int ssize; ssize = g.size();        // store R(init.h.vop)
g.init(); g.pop(); g.push(a); g.push(b); n=g.size();
g.push(a); v=g.top();               // sequence init.h'
return (ssize==g.size()+1);}
```

To illustrate the generation of oracles from the empty rules, we consider the following input sequence:

- init.pop.empty.push(a).push(b).size.pop.push(a).size.push(c).empty.

Using the two empty rules (copied from Chapter 4):

- stack(init.h.push(a).h'.empty) ⇒ stack(init.h.h'.empty)
- stack(init.h.h'.empty) ⇒ stack(init.h.pop.h'.empty)

From these rules, we generate the following oracles:

```
itemtype a, b, c, v; int n; bool e;        // working variables
g.init(); g.pop(); e=g.empty(); g.push(a); g.push(b);
n=g.size();
g.pop; g.push(a); n=g.size(); g.push(c); // sequence init.h
if oracleempty1() {successfultest();}
  else {unsuccessfultest();}
```

where **oracleempty1()** is defined as follows:

```
bool oracleempty1()
{bool sempty; sempty = g.empty();        // store R(init.h.vop)
g.init(); g.pop(); e=g.empty(); g.push(a); g.push(b);
n=g.size();
g.pop; n=g.size(); g.push(c); // sequence init.h'
return (!(sempty) || (g.empty()));}
// stack(init.h.push(a).h'.empty) →
// stack(init.h.h'.empty)
```

Whereas the first empty rule provides that removing a push operation makes the stack more empty (so to speak), the second empty rule provides that adding a pop operation also makes the stack more empty. Its oracle can be defined as follows, for the selected input sequence:

```
itemtype a, b, c, v; int n; bool e;   // working variables
g.init(); g.pop(); e=g.empty(); g.push(a); g.push(b); n=g.size();
g.push(a); n=g.size(); g.push(c); // sequence init.h
if oracleempty2() {successfultest();}
  else {unsuccessfultest();}
```

where **oracleempty2()** is defined as follows:

```
bool oracleempty2()
{bool sempty; sempty = g.empty();     // store R(init.h.vop)
g.init(); g.pop(); e=g.empty(); g.push(a); g.push(b); n=g.size();
g.pop(); g.push(a); n=g.size(); g.push(c); // sequence init.h'
return (!(sempty) || (g.empty())); }
            // stack(init.h.h'.empty) →
            // stack (init.h.pop.h'.empty)
```

So far we have used axioms and rules to generate test data and design oracles; but in fact, test data generation ought to be driven by coverage criteria. In Chapter 9, we had explored ways to generate test data for state-based software products, using the criteria that all states and all state transitions be visited at least once. In Chapter 12, we will see how the data generated in Chapter 9 can be combined with the oracles introduced herein to build test drivers.

11.4   CHAPTER SUMMARY

The subject of this chapter is the derivation of test oracles from relational specifications. This chapter covers two main themes, pertaining to the two main formats that specifications may take:

- For simple programs that operate by mapping an initial state to a final state, we find that if the specification of the program is a relation R, then the oracle has the form $Oracle(s,s') \equiv (s \in dom(R) \rightarrow (s,s') \in R)$.
- For state-based programs that maintain an internal state, we find that if the specification of such programs is represented by axioms and rules, then any sequence of method calls can be tested using an oracle derived from the axioms or from the rules (depending on the structure of the method call sequence).

We make it a point to separate the generation of test data from the generation of test oracles; in Chapter 12, we see how these two artifacts are put together to produce operational test drivers.

11.5 EXERCISES

11.1. We are interested in testing a program that searches an item x in an array a [1..N] of the same type as x. If x is in a, the array returns its index; if not, it returns 0.

    a. Write a specification that is appropriate for acceptance testing. Use it to derive a test oracle.

    b. Write a specification that is appropriate for fault removal, if you know that the candidate program operates by linear search starting from 1. Use it to derive a test oracle.

    c. Write a specification that is appropriate for fault removal, if you know that the candidate program operates by linear search starting from N. Use it to derive a test oracle.

    d. Write a specification that is appropriate for fault removal, if you know that the candidate program operates by binary search. Use it to derive a test oracle.

11.2. We are interested in testing a program that solves a system of linear equations of the form $AX = B$.

    a. Write a specification for this problem, to be used in acceptance testing, modulo some precision ε.

    b. Use it to write a test oracle, assuming that you have a built-in function that computes the determinant of a square matrix.

11.3. We are interested in testing a program that solves a cubic equation of the form $ax^3 + bx^2 + cx + d = 0$.

    a. Write a specification for this problem, which provides that the equation has three distinct roots, and that candidate programs must return these roots in variables $x1$, $x2$, and $x3$. Note: In order for a cubic equation to have three roots, its discriminant must be positive, where the discriminant is defined as $18abcd - 4b^3d + b^2c^2 - 4ac^3 - 27a^2d^2$.

    b. Use this specification to write a test oracle for acceptance testing.

    c. Write a program to solve this equation constructively (using analytical formulas for the roots) and derive a corresponding oracle for fault removal.

    d. Write a program to solve this equation iteratively (find the roots of the derivative and use these roots to apply the bisection method) and derive a corresponding oracle for fault removal.

11.4. Consider the specification of the queue in Chapter 4. Generate oracles for all the axioms of this specification and apply them to appropriate input sequences.

11.5. Consider the specification of the queue in Chapter 4. Generate an oracle for the Init Dequeue Rule of this specification and apply it to an appropriate input sequence.

11.6. Consider the specification of the queue in Chapter 4. Generate an oracle for the Enqueue Dequeue Rule of this specification and apply it to an appropriate input sequences.

11.7. Consider the specification of the queue in Chapter 4. Generate oracles for the Size Rule and the Empty Rules of this specification and apply them to appropriate input sequences.

11.8. Consider the specification of the queue in Chapter 4. Generate oracles for all the VX Rules of this specification and apply them to appropriate input sequences.

11.9. Consider the specification of the set in Chapter 4. Generate oracles for all the axioms of this specification and apply them to appropriate input sequences.

11.10. Consider the specification of the set in Chapter 4. Generate an oracle for the Null Delete Rule of this specification and apply it to an appropriate input sequence.

11.11. Consider the specification of the set in Chapter 4. Generate an oracle for the Insert Delete Rule of this specification and apply it to an appropriate input sequences.

11.12. Consider the specification of the set in Chapter 4. Generate an oracle for the Commutativity Rule of this specification and apply it to an appropriate input sequences.

11.13. Consider the specification of the set in Chapter 4. Generate oracles for the Size Rules of this specification and apply them to appropriate input sequences.

11.14. Consider the specification of the set in Chapter 4. Generate oracles for the Inductive Rules of this specification and apply them to appropriate input sequences.

11.15. Consider the specification of the set in Chapter 4. Generate oracles for all the VX Rules of this specification and apply them to appropriate input sequences.

11.16. Following the example of Section 11.3.2, generate applicable oracles for the following input sequence in the stack specification: *init.push(_).push(_). push(a).push(b).*

11.17. Following the example of Section 11.3.2, generate applicable oracles for the following input sequence in the stack specification: *init.push(_).push(_). push(a).push(b).size().*

11.18. Following the example of Section 11.3.2, generate applicable oracles for the following input sequence in the stack specification: *init.push(_).push(_). push(a).push(b).empty().*

$$12$$

Test Driver Design

In Part III, we have explored means to generate test data, and in Chapter 11, we have discussed ways to generate test oracles; in this chapter, we discuss how to compose test data and test oracles to develop a test driver.

12.1 SELECTING A SPECIFICATION

In Chapter 11, we have discussed how to map a specification against which we want to test a program into a test oracle; in this section, we discuss how to choose a specification. One may argue that the question of what specification to test a program against is moot, since we do not get to choose the specification. We argue that while we do not in general have the luxury of deciding what specification we must test a program against, we do have some latitude in choosing how to deploy different verification methods against different components of a complex, compound specification. Indeed, each family of verification methods (fault avoidance, fault removal, fault tolerance) works best for some type of specifications and works much less for others; the law of diminishing returns advocates that we use a wide range of methods, where each method is deployed against the specification components that are best adapted to it. We consider each broad family of methods and briefly characterize the properties of the specifications that are best adapted to it:

- *Fault Avoidance/Static Analysis of Program/Static Verification of Program Correctness*. We argue that specifications that are reflexive and transitive are very well adapted to static verification methods. Imagine that one has to prove the correctness of a complex program g with respect to a specification R that is represented by a reflexive transitive relation. If g is structured as a sequence of two subprograms, say $g = \{g_1; g_2\}$, then to prove that G refines R, it suffices to prove that G_1 and G_2 refine R (since R is transitive). Likewise, we find that if g is an

Software Testing: Concepts and Operations, First Edition. Ali Mili and Fairouz Tchier.
© 2015 John Wiley & Sons, Inc. Published 2015 by John Wiley & Sons, Inc.

if-then statement, then to prove that G refines R, it suffices to prove that the then-branch of g refines R; and that if g is an if-then-else statement, then to prove that G refines R, it suffices to prove that each branch of the statement refines R; and finally that if g is a while statement, then in order for G to refine R, it suffices that the loop body of g refines R. More generally, the reflexivity and transitivity of R greatly simplify the inductive arguments that are at the heart of many algorithms, whereby reflexivity supports the basis of induction and transitivity supports the inductive step.

As far as axiomatic program proofs are concerned (using Hoare's logic), it is well known that the most difficult aspects of such proofs (and the main obstacle to their automation) is the need to generate intermediate assertions and invariant assertions. When the specification at hand is reflexive and transitive, these assertions often take the simple form

$$(s_0, s) \in R,$$

where s_0 is the initial state and s is the current state. A small illustration of this situation is given in Chapter 6, where a reflexive transitive relation $(prm(s0,s))$ is uniformly used as an intermediate assertion and as an invariant assertion throughout the program, and all the verification conditions have the same assertion as precondition and postcondition.

- *Fault Removal/Software Testing*. The main criterion that a specification must satisfy to be an adequate choice for testing is the criterion of reliability: It must produce an oracle that can be implemented reliably, as a faulty oracle may throw the whole test off-balance and may insert faults into the software product, rather than remove existing faults.

- *Fault Tolerance*. In order to be an adequate specification for fault tolerance, a specification has to meet the following criteria: first, lend itself to a simple, reliable oracle (the same criterion as for testing, for the same rationale); second, it has to lend itself to an efficient run-time execution (since it may have to be checked at run-time to detect errors); third, and most importantly, it has to refer to current states rather than current and past states. In practice, this third requirement means that the specification is represented by an inverse vector, that is, a relation R such that $LR = R$. Such relations refer to the current state but not to any previous state; they offer the advantage that they can be checked by looking exclusively at the current state and spare us from the burden of storing previous states at designated checkpoints and from checking complex binary relations; hence they represent a savings in terms of memory space and processing time.

To illustrate the kind of rationale that governs the mapping of sub-specification to methods, we consider the following examples:

- We consider the example of the sorting routine discussed in Chapter 6, where we showed that such a program is difficult to prove using static methods, and difficult to test, but that that it is easy to prove its correctness with respect to some part of the specification and very easy and efficient to test it against the other part of the specification.

- We consider the specification of a program to perform a Gaussian elimination of a system of linear equations defined by a square matrix of size N and a column vector of size N. The specification that we consider for this program has the form:

$$Gauss = Eq \cap Tri,$$

where *Eq* means that the original system of equations has the same set of solutions as the final system of equations and *Tri* means that the final system of equations is triangular. It is difficult to prove the correctness of the program with respect to specification *Gauss* (since this requires that we deal with several nested loops, we check the start and end values of several index variables, we worry about the logic for finding optimal pivots, etc.); it is very complex, inefficient, and unreliable to test the program using an oracle derived from specification *Gauss* (due to the difficulty and inefficiency of ensuring that two systems of equations have the same set of solutions); it gives us a great return on investment (in terms of required effort vs. achieved impact) to verify the correctness of a candidate program with respect to specification *Eq* (since that can be done by merely checking that the system of equations is never modified except by replacing an equation by a linear combination of the equation with others) and to test it using an oracle derived from specification *Tri* (since this can be done by a simple scan of the lower half of the current matrix, without reference to any previously saved data). Note that as an equivalence relation, *Eq* is reflexive and transitive (hence satisfies the properties we have identified as making a specification adequate for proving correctness).

Hence when we say that the first step in designing a test driver is to decide what specification we want to test the program against, *we mean it*. The foregoing discussions illustrate in what sense and to what extent the software engineer does have some latitude in making this decision.

12.2 SELECTING A PROCESS

The structure of the test driver depends on the following (inter-dependent) parameters:

- *The Goal of the Test*. If the goal of the test is to certify the product or to rule on acceptance, then it is driven by the mandated test data; if the goal of the test is to find and remove faults, then it is driven by the observation of failures.
- *Whether the Test Data is Extracted from a Prepared Set or Generated by a Random Data Generator*. If the test data is extracted from a prepared test data set, then it runs until the set is exhausted; if the test data is generated at random

(according to some law of probability) by a test data generator, then some other criterion must be used to determine when the test terminates.

- *Whether the Test Must Stop at Each Failure or Merely Record the Failure and Continue*. Depending on the process of testing, we may have to stop the test whenever the program fails; this applies in particular if the test cycle includes a repair phase, which takes place off-line.
- *Whether Test Outcomes Are Recorded for Postmortem Analysis*. In some cases, such as certification testing or acceptance testing, the only relevant outcome of the test is whether the candidate program has passed the test successfully; in other cases, such as cases where the test results are used to identify and remove faults, each test execution (or perhaps each execution that leads to failure) must be documented for postmortem analysis.

As an example, a certification test based on a predefined test set may look like this:

```
bool certified ()
   {bool c=true; stateType s, init_s;
   while ! (testSet.empty())
   {testSet.remove(s); init_s=s;
   g; // program under test; manipulates s, preserves init_s;
   c = c && oracle(init_s, s);}
   return c;}
```

This function returns true if and only if the candidate program runs successfully on all the test data in **testSet**. If the same test data set is used for debugging purposes, then the test driver may look as follows:

```
void testReport()
   {stateType s, init_s;
   while ! (testSet.empty())
     {testSet.remove(s); init_s=s;
     g; // program under test; manipulates s, preserves init_s;
     if (oracle(init_s, s)) {successfulTest(init_s,s);}
     else {unsuccessfulTest(init_s,s);};}
   }
```

If we have a test data generator that can produce data indefinitely, and we are interested in running the test until the next failure (hopefully, the program will fail eventually, if not we have an infinite loop), then the test driver may look as follows:

```
void testUntilFailure()
   {stateType s, init_s;
```

```
repeat
  {generateTestData(s); init_s=s;
   g; // program under test; manipulates s, preserves init_s;
  }
until !oracle(init_s,s);
unsuccessfulTest(init_s, s);}
```

12.3 SELECTING A SPECIFICATION MODEL

For simple input/output programs, the test driver templates we have presented in the previous section can be used virtually verbatim; all we need to do is instantiate the functions that generate test data and execute the oracle. But for software products that have an internal state, such as abstract data types (ADT's), two complications arise:

- First, the oracle is not a closed form Boolean function, since the specification is represented by axioms and rules rather than by a closed form logic formula.
- Second, test data does not take the form of values assigned to variables but rather takes the form of method calls.

In this section, we discuss the design of test drivers for software products that carry an internal state; we cover, in turn, the case where test data is generated randomly, then the case where test data is pre-generated according to some criterion (such as those discussed in Chapter 9).

12.3.1 Random Test Generation

We consider the specification of a state-based software product in the form of axioms and rules, and we consider a candidate implementation in the form of a class (an encapsulated module that maintains an internal state and allows access to a number of externally accessible methods). In order to verify the correctness of the proposed implementation with respect to the specification, we resolve to proceed as follows:

- *Verify the Implementation Against the Axioms*. Each axiom of the specification can be mapped onto a Hoare formula, whose precondition is True and whose postcondition is a statement about the behavior specified by the axiom. We consider the following axiom in the specification of the stack ADT:

  stack(init.push(a).top)=a,

  and we let g be a candidate implementation that has a method of the same name as each input symbol of the specification. Then to verify the correctness of the implementation we generate the following formula:

v: {*true*} `g.init(); g.push(a); y=g.top(); {y = a}`

where *y* is a variable of type itemType and *a* is a constant of the same type. Such formulas typically deal with trivial cases (by definition) and hence involve none of the issues that usually make correctness proofs complicated; in particular, they typically give rise to simple intermediate assertions and do not involve complex invariant assertion generation.

- *Test the Implementation Against the Rules.* Rules are typically used to build an inductive argument linking the behavior of the specified product on simple input histories to its behavior on more complex input histories. The vast majority of rules fall into two broad classes: a class that provides that two input histories are equivalent and a class that provides an equation between the values of a VX operation at the end of a complex input history as a function of the value of the VX operation at the end of a simpler input history. Representative examples of these categories of rules for the stack specification include the following:

stack(init.h.push(a).pop.h+) = stack(init.h.h+).

stack(init.h.push(a).size) = 1+stack(init.h.size).

We resolve to test candidate implementations against specification rules by generating random sequences for h and h+ (the latter being necessarily nonempty) and checking these equalities for each random instance. For rules of the first category, which require that we check the equivalence of two states, we resolve to consider (as an approximation) that two states are equivalent if and only if they deliver identical values for all the XV operations.

In light of these decisions, we write the outermost structure of our test driver as follows:

```
#include <iostream>
#include "stack.cpp"
#include "rand.cpp"

using namespace std;

typedef int boolean;
typedef int itemtype;

const int testsize = 10000;
const int hlength = 9;
const int Xsize = 5;
const itemtype paramrange=7; // drawing parameter to push()

// random number generators
int randnat(int rangemax); int gt0randnat(int rangemax);
```

```
// rule testers
void initrule(); void initpoprule(); void pushpoprule();
void sizerule(); void emptyrulea(); void emptyruleb();
void vopruletop(); void voprulesize(); void vopruleempty();
// history generator
void historygenerator
  (int hl, int hop[hlength], itemtype hparam[hlength]);

/* State Variables   */
stack s; // test object
int nbf; // number of failures

int main ()
   {
   /* initialization */
   nbf=0;         // counting the number of failures
   SetSeed(825);   // random number generator

   for (int i=0; i<testsize; i++)
     {switch(i%9)
       {case 0: initrule(); break;
               case 1: initpoprule(); break;
         case 2: pushpoprule(); break;
               case 3: sizerule(); break;
         case 4: emptyrulea(); break;
               case 5: emptyruleb(); break;
         case 6: vopruletop(); break;
               case 7: voprulesize(); break;
         case 8: vopruleempty(); break;}
       }
 cout << "failure rate: " << nbf << " out of " << testsize << endl;
 }
```

This loop will cycle through the rules, testing them one by one successively. The factor **testsize** determines the overall size of the test data; because test data is generated automatically, this constant can be arbitrarily large, affording us an arbitrarily thorough test. The variable **nbf** represents the number of failing tests and is incremented by the routines that are invoked in the switch statement, whenever a test fails. For the sake of illustration, we consider the function pushpoprule(), which we detail below:

```
void pushpoprule()
   {
   // stack(init.h.push(a).pop.h+) = stack(init.h.h+)
```

```
int hl, hop[hlength]; itemtype hparam[hlength];
   // storing h
int hplusl, hplusop[hlength]; itemtype hplusparam
   [hlength]; // storing h+
int storesize;     // size in LHS
boolean storeempty; // empty in LHS
itemtype storetop;  // top in LHS
boolean successfultest; // successful test

// drawing h and h+ at random, storing them in hop, hplusop
hl = randnat(hlength);
for (int k=0; k<hl-1; k++)
   {hop[k]=gt0randnat(Xsize);
    if (hop[k]==1) {hparam[k]=randnat(paramrange);}}

hplusl = gt0randnat(hlength);
for (int k=0; k<hplusl-1; k++)
   {hplusop[k]=gt0randnat(Xsize);
    if (hplusop[k]==1) {hplusparam[k]=randnat
      (paramrange);}}

// left hand side of rule
s.sinit(); historygenerator(hl,hop,hparam);
itemtype a=randnat(paramrange); s.push(a); s.pop();
historygenerator(hplusl,hplusop,hplusparam);
// store resulting state
storesize = s.size(); storeempty=s.empty();
   storetop=s.top();

// right hand side of rule
s.sinit(); historygenerator(hl,hop,hparam);
historygenerator(hplusl,hplusop,hplusparam);
// compare current state with stored state
successfultest =
   (storesize==s.size()) && (storeempty==s.empty()) &&
   (storetop==s.top());
if (! successfultest) {nbf++;}
}
```

where function **historygenerator** (shown below) transforms an array of integers (which represent sequence h or h+) into a sequence of method calls, as shown below:

```
void historygenerator (int hl, int hop[hlength],
                       itemtype hparam[hlength])
```

```
{int dumsize; boolean dumempty; itemtype dumtop;
  for (int k=0; k<hl-1; k++)
    {switch (hop[k])
      {case 1: {itemtype a=hparam[k]; s.push(a);} break;
       case 2: s.pop(); break;
       case 3: dumsize=s.size(); break;
       case 4: dumempty=s.empty(); break;
       case 5: dumtop=s.top(); break;
      }
    }
}
```

and the random number generators are defined as follows:

```
int randnat(int rangemax)
  {// returns a random value between 0 and rangemax
  return (int) (rangemax+1)*NextRand();
  }
```

```
int gt0randnat(int rangemax)
  {// returns a random value between 1 and rangemax
  return 1 + randnat(rangemax-1);
  }
```

We have included comments in the code to explain it. Basically, this function proceeds as follows: First, it generates histories *h* and *h*+; then it executes the sequence *init.h.push(a).pop.h+*, for some arbitrary item *a*; then it takes a snapshot of the current state by calling all the VX operations and storing the values they return. Then it reinitializes the stack and calls the sequence *init.h.h+*; finally it verifies that the current state of the stack (as defined by the values returned by the VX operations) is identical to the state of the stack at the sequence given in the left hand side (which was previously stored). If the values are identical, then we declare a successful test; if not, we increment **nbf**.

As an example of the second class of rules, those that end with a VX operation, we consider the size rule, for which we write the following code:

```
void sizerule()
{// stack(init.h.push(a).size) = 1+stack(init.h.size)
  int hl, hop[hlength]; itemtype hparam[hlength];
    // storing h
  int storesize;    // size in LHS
  boolean successfultest; // successful test

  // drawing h and h+ at random,
  // storing them in hop, hplusop
```

```
hl = randnat(hlength);
for (int k=0; k<hl-1; k++)
  {hop[k]=gt0randnat(Xsize);
    if (hop[k]==1) {hparam[k]=randnat(paramrange);}}

// left hand side of rule
s.sinit(); historygenerator(hl,hop,hparam);
itemtype a=randnat(paramrange); s.push(a);
// store resulting state
storesize = s.size(); // size value on the left hand side

// right hand side of rule
s.sinit(); historygenerator(hl,hop,hparam);
// compare current state with stored state
successfultest = (storesize==1+s.size());
if (! successfultest) {nbf++;}
}
```

Once we generate a function for each of the nine rules, we can run the test driver with an arbitrary value of variable **testsize** (to make the test arbitrarily thorough), an arbitrary value of variable **hlength** (to make h sequences arbitrarily large), and an arbitrary value of variable **paramrange** (to let the items stored on the stack take their values from a wide range).

Execution of the test driver on our stack with the following parameter values

- **testsize** = 10000;
- **hlength** = 9;
- **paramrange** = 7;

yields the following outcome:

failure rate: 0 out of 10000

which means that all 10,000 executions of the stack were consistent with the rules of the stack specification. Of course, typically, when we are dealing with a large and complex module, a more likely outcome is to observe a number of failures. Notice that because test data generation and oracle design are both based on an analysis of the specification, we have written the test driver without looking at the candidate implementation; this means, in particular, that this test driver can be deployed on any implementation of the stack that purports to satisfy the specification we are using; we will uncover this implementation in Section 12.3.3.

12.3.2 Pre-Generated Test Data

In the previous section, we discussed how to develop a test driver using randomly generated test data. Because we had a way to generate data on demand, we focused the test driver on the rules of the specification; we let the rules determine what form the test data takes. In other words, for each rule, we generate test data that exercises the implementation of that rule. In this section, we take a different/complementary approach, which is driven by test data generation, in the following sense: we consider the test data that candidate implementations must be executed on, and for each test case, we design a test oracle by invoking all the rules that apply to the test case. This technique is best illustrated by an example, using the stack specification.

As we remember from Chapter 9, the criterion for visiting all the (virtual) states of the stack as well as making all the state transitions produced the following set of test data for stack implementations; so in order to meet this data selection criterion, we must run the candidate implementation on all these test sequences. As far as the test oracle is concerned, our discussions in Chapter 11 provide that for each sequence, we must invoke all the applicable rules and consider that candidate implementations are successful for a particular input sequence if and only if they satisfy all applicable rules.

		(X^*/E)			
		init	*init.push (_)*	*init.push(_). push(_)*	*init.push(_). push(_). push(_)*
VX	*top*	*init.top*	*init.push(a). top*	*init.push(_). push(a).top*	*init.push(_).push(_). push(a).top*
	size	*init.size*	*init.push(a). size*	*init.push(_). push(a).size*	*init.push(_).push(_). push(a).size*
	empty	*init.empty*	*init.push(a). empty*	*init.push(_). push(a).empty*	*init.push(_).push(_). push(a).empty*

AX	*VX*	(X^*/E)			
		init	*init.push (_)*	*init.push(_). push(_)*	*init.push(_). push(_). push(_)*
init	*top*	*init.init. top*	*init.push(a). init.top*	*init.push(_). push(a).init.top*	*init.push(_).push(_). push(a).init.top*
	size	*init.init. size*	*init.push(a). init.size*	*init.push(_). push(a).init.size*	*init.push(_).push(_). push(a).init.size*
	empty	*init.init. empty*	*init.push(a). init.empty*	*init.push(_). push(a).init. empty*	*init.push(_).push(_). push(a).init.empty*

(continued)

(continued)

push	top	init. push(b). top	init.push(a). push(b).top	init.push(_). push(a).push(b). top	init.push(_).push(_). push(a).push(b).top
	size	init. push(b). size	init.push(a). push(b).size	init.push(_). push(a).push(b). size	init.push(_).push(_). push(a).push(b).size
	empty	init. push(b). empty	init.push(a). push(b). empty	*init.push(_). push(a).push(b). empty*	init.push(_).push(_). push(a).push(b). empty
pop	top	init.pop. top	init.push(a). pop.top	init.push(_). push(a).pop.top	*init.push(_).push(_). push(a).pop.top*
	size	init.pop. size	init.push(a). pop.size	init.push(_). push(a).pop.size	init.push(_).push(_). push(a).pop.size
	empty	init.pop. empty	init.push(a). pop.empty	init.push(_). push(a).pop. empty	init.push(_).push(_). push(a).pop.empty

For the sake of illustration, we test a candidate implementation on a small sample of this test data set, specifically those test cases that are highlighted in the tables above. For each selected test case, we cite in the table below all the rules that apply to the case, as well as the input sequence that must be invoked in the process of applying the rule.

Test case	Applicable Rule	Resulting Oracle
init.push(a).init.top	*Init Rule*	*init.push(a).init.top = init.top*
init.push(_).push(_).push (a).size	*Size Rule*	*init.push(_).push(_).push(a).size = 1+init. push(_).push(_).size*
init.push(_).push(a).push (b).empty	*Empty Rule*	*init.push(_).push(a).empty ⇒ init.push(_). push(a).push(b).empty*
init.push(_).push(_).push (a).pop.top	*Push Pop Rule*	*init.push(_).push(_).push(a).pop.top = init. push(_).push(_).top*

To this effect, we develop the following program:

```cpp
#include <iostream>
#include <cassert>
#include "stack.cpp"
#include "rand.cpp"
```

```cpp
using namespace std;

typedef int boolean;
typedef int itemtype;

const int Xsize = 5;
const itemtype paramrange=8;  // drawing parameter to push()

// random number generators
int randnat(int rangemax);  int gt0randnat(int rangemax);
/* State Variables  */
stack s; // test object
int nbtest, nbf; // number of tests, failures
itemtype a, b, c; // push() parameters

bool storeempty;
itemtype storetop;
int storesize;

int main ()
  {
    /* initialization */
    nbf=0; nbtest=0;  // counting the number of tests and
                         failures
    SetSeed (825);    // random number generator
    a=randnat(paramrange); b=randnat(paramrange);
    c=randnat(paramrange);

    // first test case: init.push(a).init.top.
    // Init Rule
    nbtest++;
    s.sinit(); s.push(a); s.sinit(); storetop=s.top();
    s.sinit();
    if (!(s.top()==storetop)) {nbf++;}

    // second test case: init.push().push().push(a).size.
    // Size Rule
    nbtest++;
    s.sinit(); s.push(c); s.push(b); s.push(a);
    storesize = s.size();
    s.sinit(); s.push(c); s.push(b);
    if (!(storesize==1+s.size())) {nbf++;}

    // third test case: init.push().push(a).push(b).empty.
```

```
// Empty Rule
nbtest++;
s.sinit(); s.push(c); s.push(a); s.push(b);
storeempty=s.empty();
s.sinit(); s.push(c); s.push(a);
if (!(!(s.empty()) || storeempty)) {nbf++;}

// fourth test case: init.push().push().push(a).pop.top
// Push Pop Rule
nbtest++;
s.sinit(); s.push(c); s.push(b); s.push(a); s.pop();
storetop=s.top();
s.sinit(); s.push(c); s.push(b);
if (!(s.top()==storetop)) {nbf++;}

cout << "failure rate: " << nbf << " out of " << nbtest << endl;
}
```

Execution of this program produces the following output:

failure rate: 0 out of 4.

Hence the candidate program passed these tests successfully. Combining the test data generated in Chapter 9 with the oracle design techniques of Chapter 11 produces a complex test driver; fortunately, it is not difficult to automate the generation of the test driver from the test data and the rules.

12.3.3 Faults and Fault Detection

The test drivers we have generated in Sections 12.3.1 and 12.3.2 are both based on the ADT specification and hence can be developed and deployed on a candidate ADT without having to look at the ADT. The executions we have reported in Sections 12.3.1 and 12.3.2 refer in fact to two distinct implementations:

- A traditional implementation based on an array and an index
- An implementation based on a single integer that stores the elements of the stack as successive digits in a numeric representation. The base of the numeric representation is determined by the number of symbols that we wish to store in the stack.

The motivation of having two implementations is to highlight that the test driver does not depend on candidate implementations; the purpose of the second implementation, as counterintuitive as it is, is to highlight the fact that our specifications are behavioral, that is, they specify exclusively the externally observable behavior of software systems, and make no assumption/prescription on how this behavior ought to be implemented. Also note that the behavioral specifications that we use do not specify individually the behavior of each method; rather they specify collectively the inter-relationships between these methods, leaving all the necessary latitude to the designer to decide on the representation and the manipulation of the state data. The header files of the two implementations are virtually identical, except for different variable declarations (an array and an index in the first case, a single integer, and a constant base for the second). The .cpp files are shown below:

```
//*********************************************************
// Array based C++ implementation for the stack ADT.
// file stack.cpp, refers to header file stack.h.
//*********************************************************

#include "stack.h"

stack :: stack ()
  {
  };

void stack :: sinit ()
  {sindex =0;};

bool stack :: empty () const
  {return (sindex==0);}

void stack :: push (itemtype sitem)
  {sindex++;
   sarray[sindex]=sitem;}

void stack :: pop ()
  {if (sindex>0)
      { // stack is not empty
      sindex--;}
  }

itemtype stack :: top ()
  {int error = -9999;
   if (sindex>0)
      {return sarray[sindex];}
   else
      {return error;}
  }
```

```
int stack :: size ()
  {return sindex;}
```

As for the integer-based implementation, it is written as follows:

```
//*********************************************************
// Scalar based C++ implementation for the stack ADT.
// file stack.cpp, refers to header file stack.h.
//  base is declared as a constant in the header file, =8.
//*********************************************************

#include "stack.h"
#include <math.h>

stack :: stack ()
  {
  };

void stack :: sinit ()
  {n=1;};

bool stack :: empty () const
  {return (n==1);}

void stack :: push (itemtype sitem)
  {n = n*base + sitem;}

void stack :: pop ()
  {if (n>1) { // stack is not empty
      n = n / base;}
  }

itemtype stack :: top ()
  {int error = -9999;
   if (n>1)
      {return n % base;}
   else
      {return error;}
  }

int stack :: size ()
  {return (int) (log(n)/log(base));}
```

In order to assess the effectiveness of the test drivers we have developed, we have resolved to introduce faults into the array-based implementation and the scalar-based implementation, and to observe how the test drivers react in terms of detecting (or not detecting) failure.

Considering the array-based implementation, we present below some modifications we have made to the code, and document how this affects the performance of the test drivers (the test driver that generates random test data, presented in Section 12.3.1, and the test driver that uses pre-generated test data, presented in Section 12.3.2).

Locus	Modification	Random test data generation	Pre-generated test data
`pop();`	`sindex>0 → sindex>1`	failure rate: 561 out of 10000	failure rate: 0 out of 4
`push ();`	`sarray[sindex]=sitem; sindex++;`	failure rate: 19 out of 10000	failure rate: 0 out of 4
`push ();`	`sindex++; sarray[sindex]=sitem; sindex++;`	failure rate: 1964 out of 10000	failure rate: 1 out of 4

For the scalar-based implementation, we find the following results:

Locus	Modification	Random test data generation	Pre-generated test data
`pop();`	`n>1 → n>=1`	failure rate: 281 out of 10000	failure rate: 0 out of 4
`sinit();`	`n=1 → n=0`	failure rate: 822 out of 10000	failure rate: 0 out of 4
`push();`	`n=n*base+sitem → n=n+base*sitem`	failure rate: 1047 out of 10000	failure rate: 2 out of 4

12.4 TESTING BY SYMBOLIC EXECUTION

When we deploy a test driver on some test data and the oracle is satisfied, the only evidence of correct behavior that we have collected pertains to the precise test data on which the candidate program was tested; whether the test driver relies on randomly generated test data, or on targeted, pre-generated test data, the space covered by test data is typically a very small fraction of the domain of the specification. To overcome this limitation, it is possible to simulate the execution of a program without committing to a particular value of the input; to this effect, we represent the input values by symbolic names, rather than actual concrete values and analyze the effect of executing the program on these values, so as to compare them with the requirements imposed by the specification. For all intents and purposes, this is essentially a static verification method, but it is considered as part of the toolbox of the software tester; we refer to this technique as *symbolic testing* because it consists in effect in testing a program by executing it symbolically (rather than actually) on symbolic data (rather than actual concrete data). Whereas actual program execution produces an actual output for a specific actual input value, symbolic execution produces a symbolic expression of the output as a function of a symbolic representation of the input; this amounts, in effect, to computing the function of the program. In Chapter 5, we had talked about program functions without discussing how these are derived; in this section, we briefly discuss how this can be done in a bottom-up stepwise process, which proceeds inductively on the program structure.

We can think of a program function as mapping inputs (from an input stream, say) onto outputs (stored in an output stream); but very often, it is more interesting and more convenient to think of a program function as mapping initial states to final states. To accommodate these two perspectives without too much complexity overhead, we generally focus on state transformation, but we may sometimes (especially when we discuss I/O operations) assume that we have a default input stream (*is*) and a default output stream (*os*) as part of the state space. We consider a simple C-like programming language, and we consider, in turn, its elementary statements and then its compound statements.

Elementary statements include assignment statements and input/output statements (which we denote respectively by **read()** and **write()**). We denote by S the space of the program (whose function we are computing), and by s and s' arbitrary states of the program.

- *Assignment Statement.* Let x be a variable of some type T, let E be an expression on S that returns a value of type T, and let *def(E)* be the set of states on which expression E is defined (can be computed). Then

$$[x = E(s)] = \{(s, s') \mid s \in \mathrm{def}(E) \land x' = E(x) \land -(s') = -(s)\},$$

where $-(s)$ (respectively $-(s')$) designates all the variable names in s (respectively s') other than x.

- *Read Statement.* Let x be a variable of type T, and let *is* (the default input stream) be structured as a sequence of T-type values. Then,

$$[read(x)] = \{(s, s') \mid length(is) > 0 \land x' = head(is) \land is' = tail(is) \land -(s') = -(s)\},$$

where $-(s)$ (respectively $-(s')$) designates all the variable names in s (respectively s') other than x and *is*.

- *Write Statement.* Let x be a variable of type T, and let *os* be the default output stream of the program. Then,

$$[write(x)] = \{(s, s') | os' = os \oplus x \wedge -(s') = -(s)\},$$

where $-(s)$ (respectively $-(s')$) designates all the variable names in s (respectively s') other than *os* and $\oplus$ designates concatenation.

Compound statements include the structured control constructs of imperative programming languages, most notably:

- *The Sequence Statement,* whose rule is defined as follows:

$$[g_1; g_2] = [g_1] \bullet [g_2],$$

where $\cdot$ designates the relational product.

- *The Conditional Statement,* whose rule is defined as follows:

$$[if\ t\ \{g_1\}] = I(t) \bullet g_1 \cup I(\neg t),$$

where $I(t) = \{(s, s') | s' = s \wedge t(s)\}$.

- *The Alternative Statement,* whose rule is defined as follows:

$$[if\ t\{g_1\}\ else\{g_2\}] = I(t) \bullet g_1 \cup I(\neg t) \bullet g_2.$$

- *The Iterative Statement,* whose rule is defined as follows:

$$[while\ (t)\ \{b\}] = (I(t) \bullet [b])^* \bullet I(\neg t).$$

Because the formula of the while rule is difficult to apply in practice, we have a theorem that characterizes such functions.

Theorem: (due to H.D. Mills (1975)) *Let w:* while (t) {b} *be a while statement on space S and let W be a function on S. Then* **w** *computes function* W *if and only if the following conditions are satisfied*:

1. $dom(W)$ is the set of states on which the loop terminates normally.
2. $I(\neg t) \bullet W = I(\neg t)$.
3. $I(t) \bullet W = I(t) \bullet B \bullet W$.

In order to apply this theorem, we need to derive function W based on our understanding of what the loop does, then check that W verifies the conditions set forth above. We illustrate this theorem with two simple examples.

Let S be defined by variables x and y of type integer and let w be the following loop on S:

```
w: while (y!=0) {x=x+1; y=y-1;}.
```

We consider the following function W:

$$W = \{(s,s') | y \geq 0 \land x' = x+y \land y' = 0\}.$$

The first condition of the theorem is satisfied, since the domain of W is the set of states for which y is nonnegative, and that is exactly the set of states for which the loop terminates. As for the next two conditions, we check them briefly below:

$I(\neg t) \bullet W$

$= \{\text{substitution}\}$

$\{(s,s') | y = 0 \land s' = s\} \cdot \{(s,s') | y \leq 0 \land x' = x+y \land y' = 0\}$

$= \{\text{pre-restriction}\}$

$\{(s,s') | y = 0 \land y \geq 0 \land x' = x+y \land y' = 0\}$

$= \{\text{simplification}\}$

$\{(s,s') | y = 0 \land x' = x \land y' = y\}$

$= \{\text{substitution}\}$

$I(\neg t).$

As for the third condition, we write

$I(t) \bullet B \bullet W$

$= \{\text{substitution, pre-restriction}\}$

$\{(s,s') | y \neq 0 \land x' = x+1 \land y' = y-1\} \cdot \{(s,s') | y \geq 0 \land x' = x+y \land y' = 0\}$

$= \{\text{relational product}\}$

$\{(s,s') | y \neq 0 \land y-1 \geq 0 \land x' = (x+1)+(y-1) \land y' = 0\}$

= {simplification}

$\{(s,s')|y>0 \wedge x'=x+y \wedge y'=0\}$

= {pre-restriction}

$I(y \neq 0) \bullet \{(s,s')|y \geq 0 \wedge x'=x+y \wedge y'=0\}$

= {substitution}

$I(t) \bullet W$.

As a second example, we let S be defined by natural variables n, f, k, and we consider the following loop on space S:

```
w: while(k!=n+1) {f=f*k; k=k+1;}.
```

We let W be the function on S efined by:

$$W = \left\{(s,s')|k \leq n+1 \wedge n'=n \wedge f'=f \times \frac{n!}{(k-1)!} \wedge k'=n+1\right\}.$$

The domain of W is the set of states such that $k \leq n+1$, which is precisely the set of states on which the loop terminates. We check in turn the two remaining conditions of the theorem, as follows:

$I(\neg t) \bullet W$

= {substitution}

$$\{(s,s')|k=n+1 \wedge s'=s\} \bullet \left\{(s,s')|k \leq n+1 \wedge n'=n \wedge f'=f \times \frac{n!}{(k-1)!} \wedge k'=n+1\right\}$$

= {pre-restriction}

$$\left\{(s,s')|k=n+1 \wedge n'=n \wedge f'=f \times \frac{n!}{(k-1)!} \wedge k'=n+1\right\}$$

= {simplification}

$\{(s,s')|y=0 \wedge x'=x \wedge y'=y\}$

= {substitution}

$I(\neg t)$.

As for the third condition, we write

$I(t) \bullet B \bullet W$

= {substitution, pre-restriction}

$\{(s,s') \mid k \neq n+1 \wedge n' = n \wedge f' = f \times k \wedge k' = k+1\}$

$\bullet \left\{ (s,s) \mid k \leq n+1 \wedge n' = n \wedge f' = f \times \dfrac{n!}{(k-1)!} \wedge k' = n+1 \right\}$

= {relational product}

$\left\{ (s,s') \mid k \neq n+1 \wedge k \leq n+1 \wedge n' = n \wedge f' = f \times k \times \dfrac{n!}{(k+1-1)!} \wedge k' = n+1 \right\}$

= {simplification}

$\left\{ (s,s') \mid k < n+1 \wedge n' = n \wedge f' = f \times \dfrac{n!}{(k-1)!} \wedge k' = n+1 \right\}$

= {pre-restriction}

$I(k \neq n+1) \bullet \left\{ (s,s') \mid k \leq n+1 \wedge n' = n \wedge f' = f \times \dfrac{n!}{(k-1)!} \wedge k' = n+1 \right\}$

= {substitution}

$I(t) \bullet W.$

12.5 CHAPTER SUMMARY

In this chapter, we gather the artifacts we have collected in previous chapters to develop a test driver, which is responsible for running tests on a candidate software product and delivering a report from these tests. Specifically, we explore the following issues:

- In what sense and to what extent we have latitude in choosing the specification against which we can test a software product (whence the oracle that we derive for the test).
- How we can derive a test driver using a specific oracle (computed from a selected specification) and a specific test generation technique, for simple input/output programs and for software products that have an internal state.

- How we can overcome some of the limitations of software testing by means of symbolic execution, whereby we represent inputs by symbolic names (rather than concrete input values) and we represent outputs by symbolic expressions (rather than concrete output values).

12.6 EXERCISES

12.1. Consider the following C++ program:

```
void selectionSort () // given an array a of size N
  {indexType i, j, smallest;
   itemType t;
   for (i=N-1; i>0; i--)
     {smallest=0;
      for (j=1; j<=i; j++)
        {if (a[j]<a[smallest]) smallest=j;}
      t=a[smallest]; a[smallest]=a[i]; a[i]=t;}
  }
```

a. Prove the correctness of this program with respect to specification *Sort*.

b. Derive an oracle for this program from specification *Sort*.

c. Prove the correctness of this program with respect to specification *Prm*.

d. Derive an oracle for this program from specification *Ord*.

e. Conclude.

12.2. Same as Exercise 1, for a Gaussian elimination program, using the specification: *Gauss = Eq ∩ Tri*.

12.3. Consider the sort program of Exercise 1 and the specification *Ord*.

a. Derive a test oracle from specification *Ord*.

b. Consider the following test set (giving values for **N** and **a**), build a set datatype that has the relevant methods (empty, insert, remove), and load the test data therein:

N	a []
1	[6]
2	[6, 9]
2	[9, 6]
8	[32, 28, 24, 20, 16, 12, 8, 4]
8	[32, 8, 24, 16, 4, 12, 20, 28]

    c. Develop a test driver according to the pattern shown in Section 12.2 for certification testing.

12.4. Consider the sort program of Exercise 1 and the specification *Ord*.

    a. Derive a test oracle from specification *Ord*.

    b. Consider the following test set (giving values for **N** and **a**), build a set datatype that has the relevant methods (empty, insert, remove), and load the test data therein:

N	a []
1	[6]
2	[6, 9]
2	[9, 6]
8	[32, 28, 24, 20, 16, 12, 8, 4]
8	[32, 8, 24, 16, 4, 12, 20, 28]

    c. Develop a test driver according to the pattern shown in Section 12.2 for a test intended to record the outcome of each execution for subsequent analysis.

12.5. Consider the sort program of Exercise 1 and the specification *Ord*.

    a. Derive a test oracle from specification *Ord*.

    b. Alter the program in such a way as to make it incorrect.

    c. Develop a random test data generator that produces random values for **N** and **a**.

    d. Use the test data generator and the test oracle to develop a test driver that iterates until the first failure.

    e. How many executions did it take to cause the first failure?

12.6. In Section 12.3.1, we have shown the code for the push-pop rule. Taking inspiration from this code, write code for the init rule; run the resulting test driver on a candidate implementation of the stack.

12.7. In Section 12.3.1, we have shown the code for the push-pop rule. Taking inspiration from this code, write code for the init-pop rule; run the resulting test driver on a candidate implementation of the stack.

12.8. In Section 12.3.1, we have shown the code for the push-pop rule. Taking inspiration from this code, write code for the VX rules; run the resulting test driver on a candidate implementation of the stack.

12.9. In Section 12.3.1, we have shown the code for the size rule. Taking inspiration from this code, write code for the empty rule; run the resulting test driver on a candidate implementation of the stack.

12.10. In Section 12.3.1, we have shown the code for the size rule. Taking inspiration from this code, write code for the top rule; run the resulting test driver on a candidate implementation of the stack.

12.11. Consider the test data shown in the following table for the stack ADT. Select two test cases from each of the tables below and develop a test driver accordingly, following the pattern of Section 12.3.2 Deploy your test driver on the stack implementations given in Section 12.3.3.

		(X*/E)			
		init	*init.push(_)*	*init.push(_). push(_)*	*init.push(_). push(_). push(_)*
VX	top	*init.top*	*init.push(a). top*	*init.push(_). push(a).top*	*init.push(_).push(_). push(a).top*
	size	*init.size*	*init.push(a). size*	*init.push(_). push(a).size*	*init.push(_).push(_). push(a).size*
	empty	*init.empty*	*init.push(a). empty*	*init.push(_). push(a).empty*	*init.push(_).push(_). push(a).empty*

AX	VX	(X*/E)			
		init	*init.push(_)*	*init.push(_). push(_)*	*init.push(_). push (_). push(_)*
init	top	*init.init.top*	*init.push(a). init.top*	*init.push(_). push(a).init.top*	*init.push(_). push(_).push(a). init.top*
	size	*init.init.size*	*init.push(a). init.size*	*init.push(_). push(a).init.size*	*init.push(_). push(_).push(a). init.size*
	empty	*init.init. empty*	*init.push(a). init.empty*	*init.push(_). push(a).init. empty*	*init.push(_). push(_).push(a). init.empty*
push	top	*init.push(b). top*	*init.push(a). push(b).top*	*init.push(_). push(a). push(b).top*	*init.push(_). push(_).push(a). push(b).top*
	size	*init. push(b). size*	*init.push(a). push(b).size*	*init.push(_). push(a). push(b).size*	*init.push(_). push(_).push(a). push(b).size*
	empty	*init. push(b). empty*	*init.push(a). push(b). empty*	*init.push(_). push(a). push(b).empty*	*init.push(_). push(_).push(a). push(b).empty*

pop	top	init.pop.top	init.push(a). pop.top	init.push(_). push(a).pop.top	init.push(_). push(_).push(a). pop.top
	size	init.pop.size	init.push(a). pop.size	init.push(_). push(a).pop. size	init.push(_). push(_).push(a). pop.size
	empty	init.pop. empty	init.push(a). pop.empty	init.push(_). push(a).pop. empty	init.push(_). push(_).push(a). pop.empty

12.12. Use the technique discussed in Section 12.3.1 to write a test driver for a queue implementation of the queue ADT. Write an array-based queue implementation and a scalar based queue implementation and deploy the test driver to test them.

12.13. Use the technique discussed in Section 12.3.2 to write a test driver for a queue implementation of the queue ADT. Write an array-based queue implementation and a scalar-based queue implementation and deploy the test driver to test them.

12.14. Let x and y be integer variables and let MaxInt and MinInt be (respectively) the largest (smallest) integer that can be represented in a given programming language. Compute (by symbolic execution) the function of the following statements.

a. `x=x+1;`
b. `y=y-1;`
c. `x=x+1; x=x-1;`
d. `x=x-1; x=x+1;`
e. `x=x+1; y=y-1;`

12.15. Let S be the space defined by variables x, y, z of type integer, and let w be the following while loop:

`w: while (y!=0) {y=y-1; z=z+x;}`

And let W be the following function on S:

$$W = \{(s,s') | y \geq 0 \wedge x' = x \wedge y' = 0 \wedge z' = z + x \times y\}.$$

Prove that W is the function of **w**.

12.16. Let S be the space defined by integer variables x, y and z, and let w be the following while loop:

```
w: while (y!=0)
    {if (y%2==) {y=y/2; x=2*x;} else {y=y-1; z=z+x;}}
```

and let W be the following function on S:

$$W = \{(s,s') | y \geq 0 \wedge x' = x \wedge y' = 0 \wedge z' = z + x \times y\}.$$

Prove that W is the function of **w.**

12.17. Let S be the space defined by integer variables x, y and z, and let w be the following while loop:

```
w: while (y>0)
    {if (y%2==) {y=y/2; x=2*x;} else {y=y-1; z=z+x;}}
```

and let W be the following function on S:

$$W = I(y<0) \cup \{(s,s') | y \geq 0 \wedge x' = x \wedge y' = 0 \wedge z' = z + x \times y\}.$$

Prove that W is the function of **w.**

12.7 BIBLIOGRAPHIC NOTES

The theorem that captures the function of a program is due to H.D. Mills (1972). Because it requires a great deal of creativity (to derive a candidate function W), practitioners often replace it with an approximation of the loop function, whereby they do not compute the function of the loop for an arbitrary number of iterations (which is what this theorem does), but rather limit the number of iterations to a specific value and evaluate the function of the loop under these conditions; this produces an approximation of the program function, but still delivers much more information than a single execution of the program over a single input value.

13

Test Outcome Analysis

After we have gone through the trouble of generating test data, deriving a test oracle, designing a test driver, running/deploying the test, and collecting data about the test outcome, it is appropriate to ask the question: what claim can we now make about the program under test? This is the question we focus on in this chapter. The answer to this question depends, in fact, on the goal of the testing activity, which in turn affects the testing process as well as the conclusions that can be drawn therefrom.

We argue that if we test a software product without consideration of why are we doing it and what claims we can make about the product at the end of the test, then we are wasting our time. Testing a software product for the sole purpose of removing faults at random, in the absence of an overarching V&V plan, may be counterproductive for several reasons: First, because of the risks that we may be introducing faults as fast as we are removing other faults, or faster; second, because we have more faith in a software product in which we have not encountered the first fault than in a software product in which we have removed ten faults (hence our faith in the product may have dropped rather than risen as a result of the test); third, because faults have widely varying impacts on failure, hence are not equally worthy of our attention (we ought to budget our testing effort and maximize our return on investment by removing high impact faults before low impact faults).

We distinguish between two broad types of claims (of unequal value) that one can make from a testing activity:

1. Logical claims
2. Stochastic claims

We review these in turn, below.

Software Testing: Concepts and Operations, First Edition. Ali Mili and Fairouz Tchier.
© 2015 John Wiley & Sons, Inc. Published 2015 by John Wiley & Sons, Inc.

13.1 LOGICAL CLAIMS

13.1.1 Concrete Testing

We consider the scenario where we run a candidate program g on space S against an oracle derived from specification R, and we find that the program runs successfully on all elements of the test data set T; then we ask the question: what claims can be made about program g?

Before we answer this question, we need to specify precisely what we mean by *runs successfully* (in reference to a program under test). The first interpretation we adopt is that whenever the test oracle is executed, it returns *true*; we have no assurance that the oracle will ever be invoked (in particular, if the program under test does not terminate), but we know that if it is ever invoked, it returns *true*. Under this interpretation of a successful test, we observe that in order for the oracle to be invoked, the program g has to terminate its execution, that is, the initial state has to be an element of $dom(G)$. Hence we write:

$$\forall t \in T : t \in dom(G) \Rightarrow oracle(t, G(t)).$$

We rewrite this expression, replacing $oracle(t, G(t))$ by its expression as a function of the specification R (refer to the derivation of oracles from specifications, discussed in Chapter 9):

$$\forall t \in T : t \in dom(G) \Rightarrow (t \in dom(R) \Rightarrow (t, G(t)) \in R).$$

By logical simplification, we transform this as follows:

$$\forall t \in T : t \in dom(G) \wedge t \in dom(R) \Rightarrow (t, G(t)) \in R.$$

By changing the quantification, we rewrite this as follows:

$$\forall t \in S : t \in T \Rightarrow (t \in dom(G) \wedge t \in dom(R) \Rightarrow (t, G(t)) \in R).$$

By logical simplification, we rewrite this as follows:

$$\forall t \in S : t \in dom(G) \wedge t \in T \wedge t \in dom(R) \Rightarrow (t, G(t)) \in R.$$

By tautology, we rewrite this as follows:

$$\forall t \subset S : t \in dom(G) \wedge t \in T \wedge t \in dom(R) \Rightarrow t \in T \wedge (t, G(t)) \in R.$$

If we let R' be the pre-restriction of R to T, we can write this as:

$$\forall t \in S : t \in dom(G) \wedge t \in dom(R') \Rightarrow (t, G(t)) \in R'.$$

In other words, we have proven that program g is partially correct with respect to R', the pre-restriction of R to T. Whence the following proposition:

> *If we test program g on space S using an oracle derived from specification R on test data T and the program runs successfully for all the test data in T, we can conclude that program g is partially correct with respect to R', the pre-restriction of R to T.*

Because the domain of R' is typically a very small subset of the domain of R, this property is in effect very weak, in general. Yet, logically, this is all we can claim from the successful execution of the test; it is possible that the successful test gives us some confidence in the quality/reliability of the software product, but that is not a logical property.

13.1.2 Symbolic Testing

Symbolic testing is, in general very complex, for not only does it involve complex control structures such as loops, loops with complex loop bodies, nested loops, and so on, but it may also involve complex data structures. In order to model complex data structures, we need a rich vocabulary of relevant abstractions, as well as an adequate axiomatization pertaining to these abstractions.

Not only is symbolic testing complex and error prone, it is often wasteful and inefficient: Indeed, it is very common for programs to be much more refined than the specification they are intended to satisfy; hence by trying to compute the function of a program in all its minute detail, we may be dealing with functional detail that is ultimately irrelevant to the specification that the program is written to satisfy and even more irrelevant to the specification that the program is being tested against. Consider the example of a binary search, which searches an item x in an ordered array a by means of two indices l and h (for *low* and *high*), and imagine having to characterize the final values of l and h as a function of a and x; it is very difficult, as it depends on very minute details of the program (whether strict or loose inequalities are used) on whether x is in a or not, and on the position of x with respect to cells of a; and yet it is also of little relevance as the most important outcome of the search is to determine whether x is in a, and eventually at what location. Performing the symbolic execution of a binary search just to check whether it satisfies the specification of a search is like going through an 8000 feet pass to climb a 3000 feet peak.

If we do overcome the complexity, the error proneness, and the possibility of excessive (and irrelevant) detail that come with full blown symbolic execution of a program, then our reward is that we can prove any property we wish about the program in question, with respect to any specification we wish to consider. As a reminder, we present below a brief summary of the properties that we may want to prove about a candidate program g on space S once we have computed its function G.

> Given a program g on space S whose function is G, and given a specification R on S,
>
> - Program g is correct with respect to R if and only if:
>
> $$dom(R \cap G) = dom(R).$$
>
> - Program g is partially correct with respect to R if and only if:
>
> $$dom(R \cap G) = dom(R) \cap dom(G).$$
>
> - Program g is defined with respect to R if and only if:
>
> $$dom(R) \cap dom(G) = dom(R).$$

13.1.3 Concolic Testing

From a cursory analysis, it appears that

- Concrete testing, to the extent that it is carried out without fault removal, typically produces a very weak logical statement, pertaining to partial correctness with respect to a typically weak specification.
- Symbolic Execution, to the extent that it is deployed in full, enables us to prove any property we wish with respect to any specification, but it is very difficult to deploy, is very prone to errors, and forces us to deal with functional detail that may well be irrelevant to whatever property we wish to prove.

These two methods can be compared and contrasted in the following table.

Method	Process	Assumption	Scope	Assessment	
				Advantages	Drawbacks
Concrete testing	Dynamic execution and analysis	Faithful reflection of actual operating conditions	No limitation	Ease of deployment	Weak claims
Symbolic execution	Static analysis of the source code, impact of execution on symbolic data	Rules used for symbolic execution consistent with actual behavior of computer	Limited to aspects of programs that are easy to model	Arbitrarily strong claims with respect to arbitrary specifications	Difficulty/ complexity/ error proneness of deployment

Concolic testing is a technique that combines concrete testing and symbolic testing in an effort to achieve a greater return on investment than each method taken individually; the name *concolic* is in fact derived from combining the beginning of *concrete* with the ending of *symbolic*.

Concolic testing is essentially a form of concrete testing, where the program is executed on actual test data, but it uses symbolic execution techniques to compute the path conditions of various execution paths through the program, hence improves the coverage of the test. By focusing on execution paths rather than closed form control structures, and by targeting the derivation of path conditions rather than fully detailed path functions, concolic testing obviates the main difficulties of symbolic testing. On the other hand, by taking a systematic approach to the derivation of path conditions, it aims to achieve a degree of efficiency by ensuring that each new concrete test data exercises a new execution path, rather than a previously visited execution path.

13.2 STOCHASTIC CLAIMS: FAULT DENSITY

It appears from the previous section that testing does not yield much in terms of logical claims: Concrete testing yields very weak logical claims (in terms of partial correctness with respect to very partial specifications), while symbolic testing may yield stronger claims of correctness with respect to arbitrary specifications, provided we have extracted the function of candidate programs in all its minute detail (a tedious, complex, error-prone, and potentially wasteful task). In this and the following sections, we consider stochastic claims, which focus on likely properties rather than logically provable properties.

The first stochastic property we consider is fault density. A technique known as *fault seeding* consists in injecting faults into the source code of the candidate program and then submitting the program to a test data set T and counting:

- The number of seeded faults that have been uncovered and
- The number of unseeded faults that have been uncovered.

If we assume that the test data we have used detects the same proportion of seeded faults as unseeded faults, we can use this information to estimate the number of unseeded faults in the program. Specifically, if we let:

- D be the number of faults seeded into the program,
- D' be the number of seeded faults that were discovered through test data T,
- N' be the number of native faults that were discovered through test data T, and
- N be the total number of native faults in the program,

Then we can estimate the total number of native faults, say N, by means of the following formula:

$$\frac{N'}{N} = \frac{D'}{D},$$

Whence we can infer

$$N = \frac{N' \times D}{D'}.$$

This formula assumes that test T is as effective at finding seeded faults as it is at finding native faults (see Fig. 13.1) and the estimation is only as good as the assumption. Hence for example, if we seed 100 faults ($D = 100$) and we find that our test detects 70 faults of which 20 are seeded faults ($D' = 20$), we estimate the number of native faults as follows:

$$N = \frac{50 \times 100}{20} = 250.$$

This approach is based on the assumption that test T is as effective at exposing seeded faults as it is at exposing native faults. If we do not know enough about the type of native faults that the program has, or about the effectiveness of the test data set T to expose seeded and native faults, then we can use an alternative technique.

The alternative technique, which we call *cross testing*, consists in generating two test data sets of equivalent size, where the goal of each test is to expose as many faults as possible, then to analyze how many faults they expose in fact, and how many of these two sets of faults are common. We denote by:

- T1 and T2 the two test data sets.
- F1 and F2 the set of faults exposed by T1 and T2 (respectively); by abuse of notation, we may use F1 and F2 to designate the cardinality of the sets, in addition to the sets themselves.

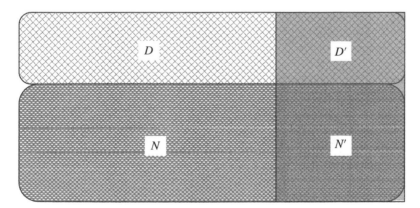

Figure 13.1 *Fault distribution (native vs. seeded).*

- Q the number of faults that are exposed by T1 and by T2.
- N the total number of faults that we estimate to be in the software product.

If we consider the set of faults exposed by T2, we can assume (in the absence of other sources of knowledge) that test data set T1 catches the same proportion of faults in T2 as it catches in the remainder of the input space (Fig. 13.2). Hence we write:

$$\frac{Q}{F2} = \frac{F1}{N},$$

From which we infer:

$$N = \frac{F1 \times F2}{Q}.$$

If test data $T1$ exposes 70 faults and test data $T2$ exposes 55 faults from which 30 are already exposed by $T1$ then we estimate the number of faults in the program to be:

$$N = \frac{70 \times 55}{30} \cong 128.$$

So far we have discussed fault density as though faults are independent attributes of the software product, which lend themselves to precise enumeration; in reality, faults are very dependent on each other so that removing one fault may

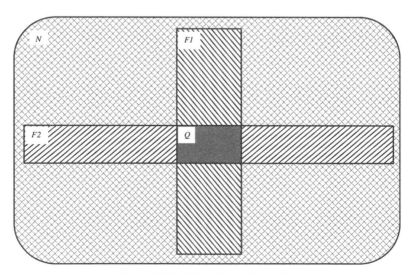

Figure 13.2 *Estimating native faults.*

well affect the existence, number, location, and nature of the other faults; this issue is addressed in the exercises at the end of the chapter. It is best to view fault density as an approximate measure of product quality rather than a precise census of precisely identified faults. Not only is the number of faults itself vaguely defined (see the discussions in Chapter 6), but their impact on failure rate varies widely in practice (from 1 to 50 according to some studies); hence a program with 50 low impact faults may be more reliable than a program with one high impact fault; this leads us to focus on failure probability as the next stochastic claim we study.

13.3 STOCHASTIC CLAIMS: FAILURE PROBABILITY

13.3.1 Faults Are Not Created Equal

In Section 13.1, we have discussed logic claims that can be made on the basis of testing a software product, and in Section 13.2 we have discussed probabilistic claims on the likely number of faults in a software product. In this section, we consider another probabilistic claim, namely failure probability (the probability of failure of any single execution) or the related concept of failure frequency (expected number of failures per unit of operation time); there are a number of conceptual and practical arguments to the effect that failure frequency is a more significant attribute of a software product than fault density.

- Not only is *fault* an evasive, hard to define, concept, as we have discussed in Chapter 6, but so is the concept of *fault density*. The reason is that faults are not independent attributes of the product but are rather highly interdependent. Saying that there are 30 black marbles in a bucket full of (otherwise) white marbles means that once we remove these 30 black marbles, we are left with a bucket of uniformly white marbles. But saying that we have 30 faults in a software product ought to be understood as an approximate indicator of product quality; whenever one of these faults is removed, this may affect the existence, number, location and/or nature of the other faults. Removing one black marble from a bucket that has 30 black marbles in the midst of white marbles leaves us with 29 black marbles, but removing a fault from a program that has 30 faults does not necessarily leave us with 29 faults (due to the interactions between faults).
- From the standpoint of a product's end-user, failure frequency is a much more meaningful measure of product quality/reliability than fault density. A typical end-user is not cognizant of the structure and properties of the software product, and hence cannot make any sense of an attribute such as fault density. But failure frequency is meaningful, for it pertains to an observable/actionable attribute of the software product: a passenger who boards an aircraft for a 3-hour flight may well know that aircrafts sometimes drop from the sky accidentally, but she/he does board anyway, because she/he estimates that the mean time to

failure of the aircraft is so large that the likelihood that a failure happens over the duration of the flight is negligible.

- Faults have widely varying impacts on product reliability. Some faults cause the software product to fail at virtually every execution, whereas others may cause it to fail under a very specific set of circumstances that arises very seldom (e.g., specific special cases of exception handling). Consequently, faults are not equally worthy of the tester's attention; in order to maximize the impact of the testing effort, testers ought to target high impact faults before lower impact faults. One can achieve that by pursuing a policy of reducing failure rates rather than a policy of reducing fault density. A key ingredient of this policy is to test the software product under the same circumstances as its expected usage profile; this ensures that the reliability growth that we observe through the testing phase will be borne out during the operational phase of the product.

Figure 13.3 shows the difference between testing a product according to its expected usage profile and testing it with a different profile; the horizontal axis represents time and the vertical axis represents the observed failure rate of the software product; the vertical line that runs across the charts represents the end of the testing phase and the migration of the software product from its test environment to its field usage environment. If we test the product according to its usage profile (by mimicking whatever circumstances it is expected to encounter in the field) then the observation of reliability growth during test (as a result of fault removal) will be borne out once the product has migrated to field usage, because most of the faults that the user is likely to expose (sensitize) have already

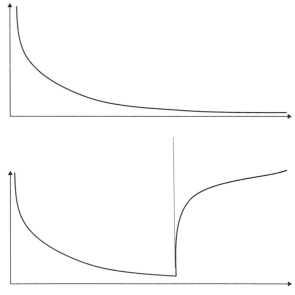

Figure 13.3 *Impact of usage patterns.*

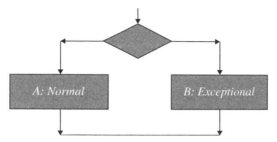

Figure 13.4 *Targeted test coverage.*

been exposed and removed; this is illustrated in the upper chart. If the product has been tested under different circumstances from its usage profile, then the tester likely removed many faults that have little or no impact on the user, while failing to remove faults that end users are likely to expose/sensitize; hence when the product is delivered, its failure rate may jump due to residual high impact faults.

- If a fault is very hard to expose, it may well be because it is not worth exposing. Consider, as a simple example, a software product that is structured as an alternative between two processing components: one (say, A) for normal circumstances and one (say, B) for highly exceptional circumstances. Imagine that in routine field usage, component B is called once for every ten thousand (10000) times more often than A is called. Then we ought to focus our attention on removing faults from A until the most frequent fault of B becomes more likely to cause failure than any remaining fault in A (Fig. 13.4).

  So that if faults in B prove to be very difficult to expose because executing B requires a set of very precise circumstances that are difficult to achieve, the proper response may be to focus on testing A until B becomes the bottleneck of reliability, rather than to invest resources in removing faults in B at the cost of neglecting faults in A that are more likely to cause failure.

For all these reasons, estimating the number of faults in a software product is generally of limited value; in the remainder of this section, we focus our attention on estimating failure frequency rather than fault density.

13.3.2 Defining/Quantifying Reliability

The reliability of a software product reflects, broadly speaking, the product's likelihood of operating free of failure for long periods of time. Whereas correctness is a logical property (a program is or is not correct), reliability is a probabilistic property (quantifying the likelihood that the program operates failure free for some unit of time). The first matter that we need to address in trying to define reliability is to decide what concept of time we are talking about. To this effect we consider three broad classes of software products, which refer to three different scales of time:

1. A process control system, such as a system controlling a nuclear reactor, a chemical plant, an electric grid, a telephone switch, a flight control system, an autonomous vehicle, and so on. Such systems iterate constantly through a control loop, whereby they probe sensors, analyze their input along with possible state data, compute control parameters and feed them to actuators. For such systems, time can be measured by clock time or possibly by the number of iterations that the system goes through; these two measures are related by a linear formula, since the sampling time for such system is usually fixed (e.g., take a sample of sensor data every 0.1 second).

2. A transaction processing system, such as an e-commerce system, an airline reservation system, or an online query system. Such system operates on a stimulus–response cycle, whereby they await user transactions, and whenever a transaction arises, they process it, respond to it, and get ready for the next transaction. Because such systems are driven by user demands, there is no direct relation between actual time and the number of transaction cycles they go through; for such systems, the passage of time can be measured by the number of transactions they process.

3. Simple input/output programs, which carry no internal state, and merely compute an output from an input provided by a user, whenever they are invoked. For such software product, time is equated with number of invocations/executions.

Hence when we talk about time in the remainder of this chapter, we may be referring to different measures for different types of programs.

Another matter that we must pin down prior to discussing reliability is the matter of input to a program; referring back to the distinction made earlier about three families of software products, we observe that only the third family of software products operates exclusively on simple inputs; software products in the other two families operate on state information in addition to the current input data. When we talk about the input to a program, we refer generally to input data provided by the user as well as relevant state data or context/environment data.

As a measure of failure avoidance over time, reliability can be quantified in a number of ways, which we explore briefly:

- Probability that the execution of the product on a random input completes without failure.
- Mean time to the next failure.
- Mean time between failures.
- Mean number of failures for a given period of time.
- Probability of failure free-operation for a given period of time.

It is important to note that reliability is always defined with respect to an implicit (or sometimes, explicit) *user profile* (or *usage pattern*). A user profile is defined by a probability distribution over the input space; if the input space is a discrete set, then the probability distribution is defined by means of a function from the set to the interval [0.0 .. 1.0]; if the set is a continuous domain, then the probability distribution is defined by a function whose integral over the input space gives 1.0 (the integral over any subset of the input space represents the probability that the input falls in that subset). User profile (or usage pattern) is important in the study of reliability because the same system may have different reliabilities for different user profiles.

It is common, in the study of reliability, to classify failures into several categories, depending on the impact of the failure, ranging from minor inconvenience to a catastrophic impact involving loss of life, mission failure, national security threats, and so on. We postpone this aspect of the discussion to Section 13.4, where we explore an economic measure of reliability, which refines the concept of failure classification.

13.3.3 Modeling Software Reliability

A software reliability model is a statistical model that represents the reliability of a software product as a function of relevant parameters; each model can be characterized by the assumptions it makes about relevant parameters, their properties, and their impact on the likelihood of product failure. It is customary to classify reliability models according to the following criteria:

- *Time Domain*. Some models are based on wall clock time whereas others measure time in terms of the number of executions.
- *Type*. The type of a model is defined by the probability distribution function of the number of failures experienced by the software product as a function of time.
- *Category*. Models are divided into two categories depending on the number of failures they can experience over an infinite amount of operation time: models for which this number is finite and models for which it is infinite.
  - *For Finite Failures Category*. Functional form of the failure intensity in terms of time.
  - *For Infinite Failures Category*. Functional form of the failure intensity in terms of the number of observed failures.

We consider the reliability of a system under the assumption that the number of failures it can experience is finite, and we let $M(t)$ be the random variable that represents the number of failures experienced by a software product from its first execution (or from the start of its test phase) to time t. We denote by $\mu(t)$ the expected value of $M(t)$ at time t and we assume that $\mu(t)$ is a non-decreasing, continuous, and differentiable function of t and we let $\lambda(t)$ be the derivative of $\mu(t)$ with respect to time:

$$\lambda(t) = \frac{d\mu(t)}{dt}.$$

This function represents the rate of increase of function $\mu(t)$ with time; we refer to it the *failure intensity* (or the *failure rate*) of the software product. If this failure rate is constant (independent of time), which is a reasonable assumption so long as the software product is not modified (no fault removal) and its operating conditions (usage pattern) are maintained, then we find:

$$\mu(t) = \lambda t + c,$$

for some constant c; given that time $t = 0$ corresponds to the first execution of the product under observation, no failures are observed at $t = 0$, hence we find $\mu(t) = \lambda t$.

A common model of software reliability for constant failure intensity provides the following equation between failure, intensity, time, and the probability of failure free operation:

$$R(t) = e^{-\lambda t}$$

The probability $F(t)$ that the system has failed at least once by time t is the complement of $R(t)$, that is,

$$F(t) = 1 - R(t) = 1 - e^{-\lambda t}.$$

The probability density function f(t) of probability F(t) is the derivative of F(t) with respect to time, which is:

$$f(t) = \lambda e^{-\lambda t}.$$

The probability that a failure occurs between time t_0 and time t_1 is given by the following integral:

$$\int_{t_0}^{t_1} f(t) dt = \int_{t_0}^{t_1} \lambda e^{-\lambda t} dt = -e^{-\lambda t}\big]_{t_0}^{t_1} = e^{-\lambda t^0} - e^{-\lambda t_1}.$$

The probability that a failure occurs before time t is a special case of this formula, for $t_0 = 0$ and $t_1 = t$, which yields:

$$F(t) = 1 - e^{-\lambda t},$$

which is what we had found earlier using the definition of R(t). The mean time to failure of the system can be estimated by integrating, for t from 0 to infinity, the function that represents the product of t by the probability that the failure occurs at time t. We write this as:

$$MTTF = \int_0^\infty t\lambda e^{-\lambda t} dt.$$

We compute this integral using integration by parts:

$$\int_0^\infty t\lambda e^{-\lambda t} dt$$

$= \{\text{integration by parts}\}$

$$\int_0^\infty e^{-\lambda t} dt - te^{-\lambda t}]_0^\infty$$

$= \{\text{evaluating the second term, which is zero at both ends}\}$

$$\int_0^\infty e^{-\lambda t} dt$$

$= \{\text{simple integral}\}$

$$-\frac{1}{\lambda} e^{-\lambda t}]_0^\infty$$

$= \{\text{value at zero}\}$

$$\frac{1}{\lambda}.$$

We highlight this result:

> Under the exponential reliability model, the mean time to failure is the inverse of the failure intensity.

This equation enables us to correlate the mean time to failure with all the relevant probabilities of system failure. For example, the following table shows the probability that the system operates failure-free for a length of time t, for various values of t, assuming that the system's mean time to failure is 10,000 hours:

Operation time, t (in hours)	Probability of failure free operation
0	1.0
1	0.9999
10	0.999
100	0.99005
1,000	0.904837
10,000	0.367879
100,000	4.53999×10^{-5}
Probabilities of failure free operation for MTTF = 10,000 hours	

From this table, we can estimate the probability that a failure occurs in each of the intervals indicated in the table below, by virtue of the formula

$$P(t_0 \leq t \leq t_1) = e^{-\lambda t^0} - e^{-\lambda t_1}$$

where $P(t_0 \leq t \leq t_1)$ designates the probability that the failure occurs between time t_0 and time t_1.

Operation time, t (in hours)	Probability of failure free operation
Within the first hour	0.0001
After the first hour, within 10 hours	0.0009
After the first 10 hours, within 100 hours	0.00895
After the first 100 hours, within 1,000 hours	0.085213
After the first 1,000 hours, within 10,000 hours	0.536958
After the first 10,000 hours, within 10,0000 hours	0.367834
After the first 100, 000 hours	0.0000454
Total	1.0
Probabilities of failure per interval of operation time, for MTTF = 10, 000 hours	

13.3.4 Certification Testing

Imagine that we must test a software product to certify that its reliability meets or exceeds a given value; this situation may arise at acceptance testing if a reliability standard is part of the product requirements. If the candidate program passes a long enough test without any failure, we ought to certify it; the question that arises, of course, is how long does the program have to run failure-free to be certified. The length of the certification test depends on the following parameters:

- The *target reliability standard*, which we quantify by the *MTTF* (or its inverse, the failure intensity).
- The *discrimination ratio* (γ), which is the tolerance of error we are willing to accept around the estimate of the target reliability; for example, if the target reliability is 10,000 hours and we are willing to certify a product whose actual reliability is 8,000, or to reject a product whose actual reliability is 12,500, then $\gamma = 1.25$.
- The *producer risk* (α), which is the probability that the producer tolerates of having his product rejected as unreliable even though it does meet the reliability criterion.

- The *consumer risk* (β), which is the probability that the consumer tolerates of accepting a product that has been certified even though it does not meet the reliability criterion.

The length of the certification test is given by the following formula:

$$t = MTTF \times \frac{\log\left(\frac{1-\alpha}{\beta}\right)}{\lambda - 1}.$$

As an illustrative example, assume that the target reliability MTTF has been fixed at 10,000 hours and the discrimination ratio γ has been fixed at 1.25. Further, assume that:

- The producer tolerates no more than a probability of 0.1 that his product be unfairly/inadvertently declined (due to estimation errors) even though its reliability actually exceeds 12,500 hours; this means α is given value 0.1.
- Due to the criticality of the application, the consumer tolerates no more than a probability of 0.06 that his product be inadvertently accepted (due to estimation errors) even though its actual reliability falls below 8,000; this means β is given value 0.06.

Using this data, we find that the size of the certification test set:

$$t = 10,000 \times \frac{\log(15)}{0.25} = 108,322 \text{ hours.}$$

If we were to run this test in real-time, this would take about 12 years; but of course we do not have to, provided we have an estimate of the number of times that the product is invoked per hour, say N, then we convert hours into number of executions/invocations, and we obtain the number of tests we must run the program on, say n:

$$n = 108322 \times N,$$

a much more realistic target.

13.3.5 Reliability Estimation and Reliability Improvement

The purpose of this section is to discuss how we can use testing to estimate the reliability of a software product and how to use testing and fault removal to improve the reliability of a product up to a predefined standard.

If we are given

- a software product,
- a specification that describes its requirements,

- an oracle that is derived from the specification, and
- a usage profile of the product in the form of a probability distribution over the domain of the specification,

then the simplest way to estimate its reliability is to run the product on randomly generated test data according to the given usage profile, to record all the failures of the product, and to compute the average time (number of tests/executions) that elapses between successive failures. One may argue that what we are measuring herein is actually the MTBF rather than the MTTF; while we agree that strictly speaking this experiment is measuring the MTBF, we argue that it provides an adequate indication of the mean time to failure.

The simple procedure outlined herein applies when the software product is unchanged throughout the testing process and our purpose is to estimate its mean time to failure as is. We now consider the case of a software product which is due to undergo a system-level test for the purpose of removing faults therein until the system's reliability reaches or exceeds a target reliability requirement. This process applies to the aggregate made up of the following artifacts:

- the software product under test,
- the specification against which the product is being tested, and the oracle that is derived from this specification,
- a usage profile of the product in the form of a probability distribution over the domain of the specification,
- a target reliability requirement that the product must reach or exceed upon delivery, in the form of a MTTF,

and iterates through the following cycle until the estimated product reliability reaches or exceeds the target MTTF requirement:

- Run the software product on randomly generated test data according to the product's anticipated usage pattern and deploy the oracle derived from the selected specification, until a failure is disclosed by the oracle.
- Analyze (off-line) the failure, identify the fault that caused it, and remove it.
- Compute a new estimate of the product reliability, in light of the latest removed fault.

The first step of this iterative process can be automated by means of the following test driver:

```
void testRun (int runLength)
     {stateType initS, s; bool moreTests;
      runLength=0; moreTests=true;
      while moreTests
          {generateRandom(s); initS=s; runLength++;
```

```
    g();      // modifies s, preserves initS
  moreTests = oracle(initS,s);}
runLength--;}
```

The second step is carried out off-line; each execution of the test driver and removal of the corresponding fault is referred to as a *test run*. As for the third step, a question of how we estimate/update the reliability of the software product after each test run is raised. The obvious (and useless) answer to this question is: it depends on what fault we have removed; indeed, we know that the impact of faults on reliability varies a great deal from one fault to another; some faults cause more frequent failures than others, hence their removal produces a greater increase in reliability.

Cleanroom reliability testing assumes that each fault removal increases the mean time to failure by a constant amount starting from a base value and uses the testing phase to estimate the initial mean time to failure as well as the ratio by which the mean time to failure increases after each fault removal. This model is based on the following assumptions:

- Unit testing is replaced by static analysis of the source code, using verification techniques similar to those we discuss in Chapter 5.
- Reliability testing replaces integration testing and applies to the whole system, in which no part has been previously tested.
- Reliability testing records all executions of the system starting from its first execution.

It we let $MTTF_0$ be the mean time to failure of the system upon its integration and we denote by $MTTF_N$ the mean time to failure of the system after the removal of the N first faults (resulting from the N first failures), then we can write (according to our modeling assumption):

$$MTTF_N = MTTF_0 \times R^N,$$

where R is the reliability growth factor, which reflects by what multiplicative factor the MTTF grows, on average, after each fault is removed. At the end of N runs, we know what N is, of course; we need to determine the remaining constants, namely $MTTF_0$ and R. To determine these two constants, we use the historic data we have collected on the N first runs, and we take a linear regression on the logarithmic version of the equation above:

$$\log(MTTF_N) = \log(MTTF_0) + N \times log(R).$$

We perform a linear regression where $log(MTTF_N)$ is the dependent variable and N is the independent variable. For the sake of argument, we show in the following table a sample record of a reliability test, where the first column shows the ordinal of the runs and the second column shows the length of each run (measured in terms of the number of executions before failure).

N	Inter-failure run	Log
0	24	1.33
1	20	1.30
2	36	1.56
3	400	2.60
4	510	2.71
5	10000	4.0

In the third column, we record the logarithm of the length of the test runs. When we perform a regression using the third column as dependent variable and the first column as independent variable, we find the following result:

$$\text{Log MTTF} = 0.95 + 0.52 * N.$$

Figure 13.5 gives a graphic representation of the regression, on a logarithmic scale. The least squares linear regression gives the Y intercept and the slope of the regression as follows:

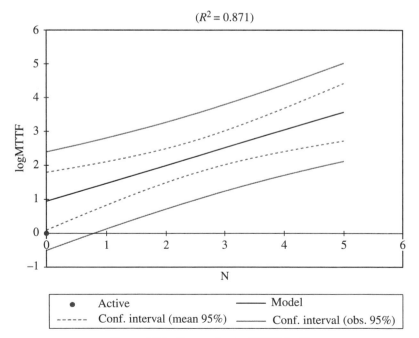

Figure 13.5 *Regression log(MTTF) by N.*

$$MTTF_0 = 10^{0.95} = 8.83.$$

$$R = 10^{0.52} = 3.35.$$

From this, we infer the mean time to failure at the conclusion of the testing phase as follows:

$$MTTF = 8.83 \times 3.35^5 = 3725.$$

In other words, if this software product is delivered in its current form, it is expected to execute 3725 times before its next failure. If this reliability attains or exceeds the required standard, then the testing phase ends; else, we proceed with the next test run.

13.3.6 Reliability Standards

So far in this chapter, we have discussed how to certify a product to a given reliability standard or how to improve a product to meet a particular reliability standard, but we have not discussed how to set such reliability standards according to the application domain or to the stakes that are involved in the operation of the software product; this matter is the focus of this section. Broadly speaking, industry standards provide for $1 per hour for tolerable financial losses; the following table shows the required reliability of a software product as a function of the financial loss that a system failure causes.

Stakes/cost of failure ($)	Required reliability, MTTF
$1	1 hour
$10	10 hours
$100	4 days
$1,000	6 weeks
$1,000,000	114 years

When human lives are at stake, the default industry standard is that the MTTF must exceed typical life expectancy; if more than one life is at stake, this value must be adjusted accordingly. The following table, due to Musa (1999), shows the link between mean time to failure values and the probability of failure free operation for 1 hour:

Mean time to failure	Probability of failure free operation for 1 hour
1 hour	0.368
1 day	0.959
100 hours	0.990
1 week	0.994
1 month	0.9986
A month and a half	0.999
A year	0.99989

13.3.7 Reliability as an Economic Function

So far we have made several simplifying assumptions as we analyze the reliability of a software product; in this section, we tentatively challenge these assumptions and offer a more refined definition of reliability that lifts these restrictive assumptions:

- We have assumed that the stakeholders in the operation of a software product are a monolithic community, with a common stake in the reliable behavior of the system. In reality, a system may have several different stakeholders, having widely varying stakes in its reliable operation. Hence reliability is best viewed, not as a property of the product, but rather as an attribute of a product and a stakeholder. We represent it, not by a scalar (the MTTF), but rather as a vector, which has one entry per relevant stakeholder.
- We have assumed that the specification is a monolith, which carries a unique stake for each stakeholder, when in fact typical specifications are aggregates of several sub-specifications, representing distinct requirements whose stakes for any given stakeholder may vary widely. Hence whereas in the previous section we talked about the cost of a system failure as an attribute of the system, in this section we consider the structure of a specification, and we associate different costs to different sub-specification, for each stakeholder.
- We have assumed that failure is a Boolean condition, whereby an execution either fails or succeeds, when in fact failure is rather a composite event, where the same system may succeed with respect to some requirements but fail with respect to others. Hence in estimating probabilities of failure, we do not consider failure as a single event, but rather as different events, having possibly different probabilities of occurrence and carrying different stakes even for the same stakeholder (let alone for different stakeholders).

To take into account all these dimensions of heterogeneity, we consider the random variable $FC(H)$, which represents, for stakeholder H, the cost per unit of time that she/

he stands to incur as a result of possible system failures (FC stands for failure cost), and we let $MFC(H)$ be the mean of variable $FC(H)$ over various instances of system operation. To fix our ideas, we quantify $MFC(H)$ in terms of dollars per hour of operation, which we abbreviate by $/h. With this measure, it is no longer necessary to distinguish between reliability (freedom from failure with respect to common requirements) and safety (freedom from failure with respect to high stakes requirements), since the mean failure cost takes into account the costs associated with all relevant requirements, ranging from low stakes requirements to high stakes requirements.

We consider a system whose community of stakeholders includes n members $H_1, H_2, H_3, \ldots H_n$, and whose specification R is structured as the aggregate of several requirements, say

$$R = R_1 \oplus R_2 \oplus R_3 \oplus \ldots R_m,$$

and we let $P = (P_1, P_2, P_3, \ldots P_m)$ be the probabilities that the system fails to satisfy requirements $R_1, R_2, R_3, \ldots R_m$ during a unitary operation time (say, 1 hour of operation time). If we let $ST(H_i, R_j)$ be the stakes that stakeholder H_i has in meeting requirement R_j, then the mean failure cost of stakeholder H_i can be approximated by the following formula:

$$MFC(H_i) = \sum_{j=1}^{m} ST\left(H_i, R_j\right) \times P_j.$$

This formula is not an exact estimate of the mean failure cost but is an approximation thereof; this stems from two reasons, both of which result from the fact that specifications $R_1, R_2, R_3, \ldots R_m$ are not orthogonal, but rather overlap:

- Costs are not additive: when we consider the costs associated with failure to satisfy two distinct requirements R_i and R_j, the same loss may be counted twice because the two specifications are not totally orthogonal, hence their failures represent related events.
- Probabilities are not multiplicative: If we consider two distinct specification components R_i and R_j that are part of the system specification, failure with respect to R_i and failure with respect to R_j are not statistically independent because the same error may cause both events.

Hence strictly speaking, the formula above is best understood as an upper bound of the mean failure cost, rather than an exact estimate; nevertheless, we use it as a convenient (easy to compute) approximation. We recast the formula of MFC given above in matrix form, by means of the following notations:

- We let MFC be the column vector that has one entry per stakeholder, such that $MFC(H_i)$ represents the mean failure cost of stakeholder H_i.

- We let P be the column vector that has one more entry than there are specification components, such that $P(R_j)$ represents the probability that the system fails to satisfy requirement R_j during a unitary execution time (e.g., 1 hour) and the extra entry represents the probability that no requirement is violated during a unitary execution time.
- We let ST be the matrix that has as many rows as there are stakeholders and as many columns as there are specification components and such that $ST(H_i, R_j)$ represents the loss that stakeholder H_i incurs if requirement R_j is violated; we consider an additional column that represents the event that no requirement is violated.

Then the formula of mean failure cost can be written in relational form as follows (where • represents matrix product):

$$MFC = ST \bullet P.$$

As a simple (and simple-minded) illustrative example, we consider the flight control system of a commercial aircraft, and we list in turn, a sample of its stakeholders, a sample of its requirements, then we try to fill the stakes matrix (ST) and the failure probability vector (P). For a sample of stakeholders, we cite the following:

- PL: The aircraft pilot
- PS: A passenger
- LIF: The passenger's life insurance company
- AC: The airline company that operates the aircraft
- AM: The aircraft manufacturer
- INS: The insurance company insuring the aircraft
- FAA: The Civil Aviation Authority (e.g., FAA),
- NGO: An environmental NGO
- RES: A resident in the neighborhood of the origin or destination airport

Among the (massively overlapping and very partial/anecdotal) requirements, we consider the following:

- AP: Adherence to the autopilot settings within acceptable tolerance thresholds
- SM: Smoothness of the transition between different autopilot settings
- ECO: Maximizing fuel economy
- NOI: Minimizing noise pollution
- CO2: Minimizing CO_2 pollution
- SAF: Safety critical requirements

We review the stakeholders in turn and discuss for each, the stakes they have in each requirement, as well as a tentative quantification of these stakes in dollar terms; specifically, the quantitative figure represents the amount of money that a stakeholder stands to lose if the cited requirement is violated. In the column labeled XS, we write X if the quantification is deemed exact and S if it is deemed a mere estimate.

The Pilot:

Requirement	Stake	XS	Value ($)
AP	Professional obligation	S	100.00
SM	Professional satisfaction, personal comfort	S	60.00
ECO	Professional satisfaction, loyalty to employer	S	40.00
NOI	Professional satisfaction, good citizenship	S	30.00
CO2	Environmental consciousness, good citizenship	S	70.00
SAF	Professional duty, own safety	S	1.0 M

The Passenger:

Requirement	Stake	XS	Value ($)
AP	No direct stake, so long as safety is not at stake	S	0.00
SM	Personal comfort	S	60.00
ECO	No direct stake	X	0.00
NOI	No direct stake	X	0.00
CO2	Reducing carbon footprint	S	40.00
SAF	Personal safety	S	1.0 M

The Passenger's Life Insurance Company:

Requirement	Stake	XS	Value ($)
AP	Indirect impact, through increased risk	S	80.00
SM	No direct stake	X	0.00
ECO	No direct stake	X	0.00
NOI	No direct stake	X	0.00
CO2	No direct stake	X	0.00
SAF	Life Insurance Payout	X	1.0 M

The Airline Company that operates the aircraft:

Requirement	Stake	XS	Value ($)
AP	Indicator of Fleet Quality	S	1000.00
SM	Positive Passenger Experience	S	800.00
ECO	Direct Pocketbook impact	X	700.00
NOI	Good corporate citizenship, PR value	S	400.00
CO2	Good corporate citizenship, promotional value	S	600.00
SAF	Loss of aircraft, civil liability, corporate reputation, etc	X	15.0 M

The Aircraft Manufacturer:

Requirement	Stake	XS	Value ($)
AP	Pilot confidence in aircraft quality	S	1000.00
SM	Positive Passenger Experience, impact on corporate reputation	S	800.00
ECO	Lower Operating Costs as a Sales Pitch	S	800.00
NOI	Good corporate citizenship, adherence to civil regulations	S	900.00
CO2	Good corporate citizenship, corporate image	S	800.00
SAF	Corporate reputation, viability of aircraft, civil liability	X	120.0 M

The Insurance Company Insuring the Aircraft:

Requirement	Stake	XS	Value ($)
AP	Indirect impact on safety	S	1000.00
SM	No direct stake	X	0.00
ECO	No direct stake	X	0.00
NOI	No direct stake	X	0.00
CO2	No direct stake	X	0.00
SAF	Insurance Payout (price of aircraft + $1 M/passenger)	X	350.0 M

The Civil Aviation Authority:

Requirement	Stake	XS	Value ($)
AP	Core agency mission	S	1000.00
SM	No direct stake	X	0.00
ECO	No direct stake	X	0.00
NOI	Secondary agency mission	S	200.00
CO2	Secondary agency mission	S	200.00
SAF	Core agency mission	X	1000.00

An Environmental NGO:

Requirement	Stake	XS	Value ($)
AP	No direct stake	X	0.00
SM	No direct stake	X	0.00
ECO	No direct stake	X	0.00
NOI	Secondary organizational mission	S	100.00
CO2	Core organizational mission	S	600.00
SAF	No direct stake	X	0.00

A Resident in the Proximity of the Relevant Airports:

Requirement	Stake	XS	Value ($)
AP	Indirect stake, due to safety implications	S	200.00
SM	No direct stake	X	0.00
ECO	No direct stake	X	0.00
NOI	Viability of home, home value	S	2000.00
CO2	Secondary homeowner/health concern	S	20.00
SAF	Indirect stake, due to safety implications	S	200.00

In light of this discussion, we find the following Stakes matrix, where the column labeled NOF refers to the event that no failure has occurred during a unitary operation time.

	AP	SM	ECO	NOI	CO2	SAF	NOF
PL	100	60	40	30	70	1,000,000	0
PS	0	60	0	0	40	1,000,000	0
LIF	80	0	0	0	0	1,000,000	0
AC	1000	800	700	400	600	15,000,000	0
AM	1000	800	800	900	800	120,000,000	0
INS	1000	0	0	0	0	350,000,000	0
FAA	1000	0	0	200	200	1,000	0
NGO	0	0	0	100	600	0	0
RES	200	0	0	200	20	200	0

As for computing the vector of probabilities, we advocate to proceed as follows:

- Design oracles for each of the requirements introduced above.
- Run reliability tests of the software product to estimate the reliability of the product with respect to each relevant requirement.
- Use the estimates of reliability to determine the probability that the product fails during a unitary operation time (e.g., 1 hour of operation).

For the sake of illustration, we consider the following vector of probabilities:

Requirement	Probability of failure per hour
AP	0.01
SM	0.01
ECO	0.005
NOI	0.005
CO2	0.008
SAF	0.0000001
NOF	0.9619999

Computing the product of the stakes matrix with the probability vector, we find the following vector of mean failure costs, which has one entry per stakeholder and is quantified in dollars per hour.

Stakeholder	Mean failure cost ($/hour)
PL	2.61
PS	1.02
LIF	0.90
AC	29.80
AM	44.90
INS	45.00
FAA	12.60
NGO	5.30
RES	3.16

This table represents, for each stakeholder, the mean of their loss, per hour of operation, as a result of possible system failure; this quantity is measured in dollars per hour and can be used to make economically justified decisions.

13.4 CHAPTER SUMMARY

Testing is useless unless it can help us reach relevant, verifiable conclusions about the product under test. The purpose of this chapter is to survey the various uses of a software test, in terms of the claims that can be made about the product. We consider in turn a number of claims:

- *Logical Claims*: The successful execution of a program under test on a given test data set can be used as the basis of a claim of correctness of the product with respect to the specification that gives rise to the test oracle. The trouble with such claims is that they pertain to specifications that are very weak, hence are of little value.
- *Probabilistic Claims: Fault Density.* Testing can be used in conjunction with some assumptions on fault patterns in the program to estimate the density of faults in candidate products. The trouble with this approach is that fault density, even when estimated with great precision, is only tenuously correlated with failure frequency; and from the standpoint of a user, failure frequency is the only meaningful measure of product quality.
- *Probabilistic Claims: Failure Frequency.* Carefully designed testing experiments can be used to estimate the failure frequency of a product and can also

be used to enhance (lower) failure frequency beyond (below) a target value. Once we know the failure frequency of a software product, we can compute a number of relevant reliability attributes, such as the probability of failure within a given time interval, or the mean time to failure.

Once we know the failure frequency of a software product with respect to a given product requirement, and the stakes that a stakeholder has in meeting that requirement, we can estimate the mean of the random variable that represents the loss that the stakeholder stands to incur as a result of possible system failure with respect to that requirement. If we integrate with respect to all the requirements, we obtain the system's mean failure cost for each stakeholder, measured in dollars per unit of time.

13.5 EXERCISES

13.1. Consider the discussion of Section 13.1.1 and revisit its conclusion under the assumption that a successful execution of the test means that for all test cases (elements of T), the candidate program does terminate and the oracle, when invoked, returns true.

13.2. If you seed 65 faults into your software product and test it using test data T, which exposes 70 faults of which 30 are seeded, how many faults do you estimate to exist in your product prior to removing all the exposed faults? How many do you estimate to exist after removal of all exposed faults?

13.3. If you run your program on two test data sets, say T1 and T2, and you find that T1 exposes 65 faults, and T2 exposes 58 faults of which 28 are also exposed by T1, how many faults do you estimate to exist in your product prior to removing all the exposed faults? How many do you estimate to exist after removal of all exposed faults?

13.4. A flight control system has a mean time to failure with respect to safety critical requirements of 20,000 hours.

    a. If you take a 5 hour flight from Newark to Los Angeles, what is the likelihood that the system will experience a safety critical failure during your flight?

    b. If the aircraft operates 8 hours a day of actual flying time, what is the likelihood that it will experience a safety critical violation on a given day?

    c. If the aircraft operates 8 hours a day of actual flight and is grounded for maintenance one day a month, what is the likelihood that it will experience a safety critical failure in its first ten years of operation?

    d. Under the conditions cited above, what is the likelihood that its first safety critical failure occurs during its 11th year of operation?

13.5. We want to certify the reliability of a software product to the MTTF standard of 25,000 executions.

    a. Given a discrimination ratio of 1.5, a producer risk of 0.25 and a consumer risk of 0.15, how long does the certification test have to be?

    b. This software product is used to control an industrial process in which data is sampled every minute, analyzed, and actuators are adjusted accordingly. What is the probability that this product will operate failure-free during its first year of operation?

13.6. Consider a software product undergoing a process of reliability testing, whereby it is repeatedly tested on randomly generated test data until it fails, the failure is analyzed to identify and remove the presumed fault causing the failure. Assume that the successive test runs that this experiment gives rise to are as follows:

Number of faults removed	Number of executions between failures
0	14
1	48
2	36
3	260
4	1,020
5	8,060
6	10,435

    Estimate the failure intensity of this product with respect to the selected oracle, in terms of number of executions. If this product is invoked every ten minutes around the clock, what is the mean time to failure of this product in days and in months (assuming 30 days per month)?

13.7. Consider a software product that has a mean time to failure of 10 months.

    a. What is the probability that this product will fail within its first hour of operation?

    b. What is the probability that this product will fail within its first day of operation?

    c. What is the probability that this product will fail within its first month of operation?

    d. What is the probability that this product will fail within its first year of operation?

    e. What is the probability that this product will fail within its 6th month of operation?

13.8. Consider a cloud computing infrastructure of a cloud services provider.

    a. Identify classes of typical stakeholders.

    b. Identify typical system requirements.

    c. Estimate the corresponding stakes matrix.

    d. Consider a realistic probability distribution of system failures, assuming the system may not fail with respect to more than one requirement per unit of time (e.g., an hour).

    e. Estimate the mean failure cost of the system with respect to all the stakeholders.

13.6 PROBLEMS

13.1. Consider that the fault seeding technique of fault density estimation assumes that faults are independent of each other and that one can identify a number of faults and then remove them. But the remedy to each fault may very well depend on previously removed faults. Explore the consequences of this premise on the technique of fault seeding.

13.2. Consider that the cross testing technique of fault density estimation assumes that faults are independent of each other and that one can identify a number of faults and then remove them. But the remedy to each fault may very well depend on previously removed faults. Explore the consequences of this premise on the technique of cross testing.

13.7 BIBLIOGRAPHIC NOTES

For more information on software reliability engineering, consult Musa (1999) and O'Connor (2002). A recent snapshot of the state of the art in symbolic testing is given by Cadar and Sen (2013); note that in this reference, as well as in many references on symbolic execution, the focus is on individual execution paths rather than a comprehensive view of the program; as a result, loops are usually unfurled and converted into an arbitrary number of iterations and treated as sequence (rather than captured by means of Mills' Theorem, as we do in this chapter). Concolic testing was introduced by Larson and Austin (2003); for an example of a concolic testing paradigm, refer Sen et al. (2005). The technique of Fault Seeding introduced in Section 13.1.1 is due to Harlan D. Mills (1972); as for the technique of fault density estimation by cross-testing, it is due to Shari Laurence Pfleeger and Joanne M. Atlee (2009).

Part V

Management of Software Testing

In Parts I–IV, we have focused primarily on technical aspects of software testing, including test data generation, oracle design, test driver design, and test outcome analysis. In this part, we consider some managerial aspects of software testing, including software metrics, software tools, and software product line testing.

- In Chapter 14, we review some software metrics that are relevant from the standpoint of software testing. These include metrics that quantify such aspects of software testing as fault density, error proneness, failure probability, fault tolerance, the ease of identifying faults from static analysis, and the ease of detecting errors at run time.

- In Chapter 15, we review some representative software testing tools, which we classify into six broad, slightly overlapping families of tools: scripting tools that help engineers write test drivers; record and replay tools that help engineers record complex user interactions for the purpose of test replay; performance testing tools that enable the engineer to test a software product under specified operating conditions; oracle design tools that help the engineer to design and record a test oracle; exception discovery tools that help the engineer check a software product for possible run-time exceptions; and finally collaborative tools that are primarily intended to support collaborative multiparty communication in the context of software testing.

- In Chapter 16, we briefly review the emerging paradigm of software product line engineering and discuss the unique issues that this paradigm raises with respect to software testing; we explore some general principles that pertain to the management of testing resources within this paradigm and illustrate them by a sample example.

Software Testing: Concepts and Operations, First Edition. Ali Mili and Fairouz Tchier.
© 2015 John Wiley & Sons, Inc. Published 2015 by John Wiley & Sons, Inc.

14

Metrics for Software Testing

The discipline of software metrics is concerned with defining quality attributes of software products and sizing them up with quantitative functions; such quantitative functions can then be used to assess the quality attributes of interest and thereby provide a basis for quantitative analysis and decision-making. Metrics have been used to capture such quality attributes as reliability, maintainability, modularity, verifiability, complexity, and so on. In this chapter, we focus our attention on software metrics that are relevant to testing and test-related attributes. We classify the proposed metrics into six categories that espouse the lifecycle of a system failure, namely:

- Fault proneness—the density of faults within the source code.
- Fault detectability—the ease of detecting faults in the source code.
- Error detectability—the ease of detecting errors in the state of a program in execution.
- Error maskability—the likelihood that an error that arises during the execution of a program gets masked before it causes a program failure.
- Failure avoidance—the ease of detecting and avoiding program failure with respect to its intended function.
- Failure tolerance—the likelihood that a program satisfies its specification despite failing to compute its intended function.

We review these metrics in turn, below. But first, we briefly introduce some elements of information theory, which we use in subsequent sections of this chapter. Given a random variable X on a finite set X (by abuse of notation we use the same name for the random variable and the set from which it takes its values), we let the entropy of X be the function denoted by $H(X)$ and defined by:

$$H(X) = -\sum_{x \in X} p(x) \log(p(x)),$$

Software Testing: Concepts and Operations, First Edition. Ali Mili and Fairouz Tchier.
© 2015 John Wiley & Sons, Inc. Published 2015 by John Wiley & Sons, Inc.

where $p(x)$ is the probability of occurrence of the event $X=x$ and log is (by default) the base 2 logarithm. We take the convention that $0 \log(0) = 0$, and we find that $H(X)$ is nonnegative for all probability distributions. $H(X)$ is expressed in bits and represents the amount of uncertainty we have about the outcome of random variable X; for a set of given size n, this function takes its maximal value for the uniform distribution on X, where $p(x) = 1/n$ for all x; the maximal value in question is then equal to $\log(n)$.

Given a random variable X on set X and a random variable Y on set Y, we consider the joint random variable $(X; Y)$ on the set $(X \times Y)$ with the probability distribution $p2$ (x, y) on $(X \times Y)$ defined as the probability that variable X takes value x while variable Y takes value y. Then we define the *joint entropy* of X and Y as the entropy of the random variable $(X; Y)$ on the set $(X \times Y)$ with respect to the probability distribution $p2(x, y)$. Using joint entropy, we let the *conditional entropy* of X with respect to Y be the function denoted by H(X|Y) and defined by:

$$H(X|Y) = H(X;Y) - H(Y).$$

The conditional entropy of X with respect to Y represents the uncertainty we have about the outcome of random variable X once we know what is the outcome of random variable Y.

If we let X be a random variable on set X and Y be a random variable on set Y, and if we let G be a function from X to Y then we have

$$H(X) \geq H(Y),$$

where the probability distribution of Y is derived from that of X by the following formula:

$$p(Y=y) = \sum_{x \in G^{-1}(y)} p(x).$$

Entropies and conditional entropies will be used to define some of the metrics that we discuss in the remainder of this chapter.

14.1 FAULT PRONENESS

What makes a software product prone to faults is its complexity; hence complexity metrics are adequate measures of fault proneness. Empirical studies routinely show a significant correlation between complexity metrics and fault density in software products. In this section, we present two widely known, routinely used metrics of structural complexity of control structures.

14.1.1 Cyclomatic Complexity

In its simplest expression, the *cyclomatic complexity* of a program reflects the complexity of its control structure and is computed by drawing the flowchart (say, F) of the program, then deriving the value of the expression as:

$$v(F) = e - n + 2,$$

where

- e is the number of edges in F and
- n is the number of nodes in F.

We know from graph theory that if the flowchart is a planar graph (i.e., a graph that can be drawn on a planar surface without any two edges crossing each other) then $v(F)$ represents the number of regions in F. Also, note that if the flowchart is merely a linear sequence of nodes, then its cyclomatic complexity is 1, regardless of the number of nodes; hence a single statement (corresponding to $e = 0$ and $n = 1$) has the same cyclomatic complexity as a sequence of 100 statements ($e = 99$ and $n = 100$). This is consistent with our intuitive understanding of complexity as an orthogonal attribute to size: a sequence of 100 statements is longer than a single statement but is not more complex. As an illustration of this metric, we consider the following sample example:

```
int product (int a, int b)
  {
    int c; c=0;
    while (b!=0)
      {if (b%2==0) {b=b/2; a=2*a;}
       else         {b=b-1; c=c+a;}}
    return c;
  }
```

The flowchart of this program is given in Figure 14.1. From this flowchart, we compute the number of nodes and edges, and we find:

- $e=7$,
- $n=6$

whence

$$v(F) = 3.$$

Exercises 1 and 2 in Section 14.8 explore how this figure is affected after we make the program more complex by additional tests.

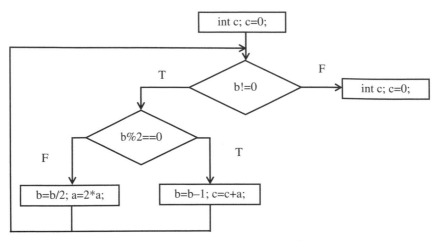

Figure 14.1 *Counting nodes and edges.*

14.1.2 Volume

Whereas cyclomatic complexity measures the complexity of a program by considering the density of its control structure, the metric of program volume measures complexity by the amount of intellectual effort that it took to develop the program. We can argue that unlike the cyclomatic complexity, which measures structure independently of size, program volume captures size along with structural complexity. Specifically, program volume is computed as follows:

- If N is the number of lexemes (operators, operands, symbols, constants, etc.) in a program and
- n is the number of distinct lexemes (operators, operands, symbols, constants, etc.) in the program,

then the volume of the program is given by the following formula:

$$V = N \times \log_2(n).$$

Interpretation: n is the size of the vocabulary in which the program is written; $\log_2(n)$ measures the number of binary decisions one has to make to select one symbol in a vocabulary of size n; $N \times \log_2(n)$ measures the total development effort of the program, viewed as the selection of N symbols in a vocabulary of size n, and quantified in terms of binary decisions. Alternatively, $\log_2(n)$ can be interpreted as the entropy of the random variable that represents each symbol of the program and $N \times \log_2(n)$ is then the entropy of the whole program (quantity of information contained within its source text).

If we consider again the **product** program given above, we find the following quantities:

- Number of lexemes, N: 66.
- Vocabulary: {int, product, (, a, ',', b,), {, c, :, =, 0, while, !=, if, %, 2, ==, /, *, }, else, $-$, 1, +, return}. Hence $n=26$.

The volume of this program is:

$$V = 66 \times \log_2(26) = 310.23 \text{ bits.}$$

Generating this program requires the equivalent of 310 binary (yes/no) decisions.

14.2 FAULT DETECTABILITY

Whereas complexity is a reliable indicator of fault proneness/fault density, the metrics we explore in this section reflect the ease of detecting the presence of faults (in a testing environment) or, conversely, the likelihood of fault sensitization (in an operating environment).

We consider a program g on space S and a specification R on S, and we let T be a test data set which is a subset of $dom(R)$. Assuming that program g is faulty, we define the following metrics that reflect the level of effectiveness of T in exposing faults in g:

- *The P-Measure*, which is the probability that at least one failure is detected through the execution of the program on test data T.
- *The E-Measure*, which is the expected number of failures detected through the execution of the program on test data T.
- *The F-Measure*, which is the number of elements of test data T that we expect to execute on average before we experience the first failure of program g.

These metrics can be seen as indicators of the effectiveness of test set T in exposing program faults, but if we let T be a random test data set, then these metrics can be seen as characterizing the ease of exposing faults in program g.

These three metrics can be estimated in terms of the failure rate of the program (say, θ), which is the probability that the execution of the program on a random element s of the domain of R produces an image $G(s)$ such that $(s, G(s)) \notin R$. Under the assumption of random test generation (where the same initial state may be generated more than once), we find the following expressions:

- *The P-Measure*. The probability that n tests generated at random do not cause the program to fail is $(1-\theta)^n$. Hence the P-measure of the program is:

$$P = 1 - (1-\theta)^n.$$

- *The E-Measure.* The expected number of failures experienced through the execution of the program on n randomly generated test data is:

$$E = n^*\theta.$$

- *The F-Measure.* Under the assumption of random test generation, the probability that the first test failure occurs at the ith test is $(1-\theta)^{i-1}\theta$. Statistical analysis shows that for this probability distribution, the mean $(\bar{F})$ and the median (F_{med}) of the number of tests before the first failure are respectively:

$$\bar{F} = \frac{1}{\theta}.$$

$$F_{med} = \left\lceil \frac{-\log(2)}{\log(1-\theta)} \right\rceil,$$

where $\lceil \ \rceil$ is the ceiling operator in the set of natural numbers.

All these calculations depend on an estimation of θ, the probability of failure of the execution of the program on a randomly chosen initial state. This probability depends on the following two parameters:

- The set of initial states on which the candidate program g fails to satisfy specification R; as we have seen in Chapter 6, this set is defined (in relational form) as $\overline{dom(R \cap G)}$.
- The probability distribution of initial states.

If the space of the program is finite and if the probability distribution is finite then the probability of failure can be written as:

$$\theta = \frac{\left| dom(R) \cap \overline{dom(R \cap G)} \right|}{|dom(R)|}$$

where $|\ |$ represents set cardinality.

As an illustrative example, we consider the space S defined by natural variables x, y, and z, and the following specification R on S.

$$R = \{(s,s') \mid y' = x + y \wedge z' < 99\}.$$

We let g be the following program on space S:

```
g: {y = x+y; z = y%100;}
```

whose function is:

$$G = \{(s,s') \mid x' = x \wedge y' = x + y \wedge z' = (x+y) \bmod 100\}.$$

To estimate the probability of failure () of this program, we compute $dom(R \cap G)$.

$dom(R \cap G)$

={substitution}

$dom(\{(s,s')|\, y' = x + y \wedge z' < 99 \wedge x' = x \wedge y' = x + y \wedge z' = (x+y) \, mod \, 100\})$

={simplification}

$dom(\{(s,s')|\, (x+y) \, mod \, 100 < 99 \wedge x' = x \, \wedge y' = x + y \wedge z' = (x+y) \, mod \, 100\})$

={taking the domain}

$(\{s|\, \exists s' :\, (x+y) \, mod \, 100 < 99 \wedge x' = x \wedge y' = x + y \wedge z' = (x+y) \, mod \, 100\})$

={logical simplification}

$(\{s|\, (x+y) \, mod \, 100 < 99 \wedge (\exists s' :\, x' = x \wedge y' = x + y \wedge z' = (x+y) \, mod \, 100)\})$

={logical simplification}

$(\{s|\, (x+y) \, mod \, 100 < 99\})$

Taking the complement of this relation, we find:

$\overline{dom(R \cap G)}$

={logic}

$\{s|\, (x+y) \, mod \, 100 \geq 99\}$

={since a mod 100 function returns values between 0 and 99}

$\{s|\, (x+y) \, mod \, 100 = 99\}$

Hence $\theta = 0.01$, since 99 is one value out of 100 that the mod function may take. With this value of probability failure, we can now compute the various measures of interest for a random test sample of size, say, 400:

- *P-Measure.*

$$P = 1 - (1-\theta)^n = 1 - 0.99^{400} = 0.98205$$

- *E-Measure.*

$$E = n^*\theta = 400^*0.01 = 4.$$

- *F-Measure.*
  - *Mean*:

$$\bar{F} = \frac{1}{\theta} = 100.$$

  - *Median*:

$$F_{\text{med}} = \left\lceil \frac{-\log(2)}{\log(1-\theta)} \right\rceil = \left\lceil \frac{-\log(2)}{\log(0.99)} \right\rceil = \lceil 68.9676 \rceil = 69.$$

In other words, there is a 0.98205 probability that a random test of size 400 will expose at least one failure, the expected number of failures exposed by a random test of size 400 is four, the mean number of random tests before we observe the first failure is 100, and the median number of tests before we observe the first failure is 69.

Of course, in practice, these metrics are not computed analytically in the way we have just shown; rather they are estimated or derived empirically by extrapolating from field observations. Also regardless of how accurately we can (or cannot) estimate them, these metrics are useful in the sense that they enable us to reason about how easy it is to expose faults in a program and what test generation strategies enable us to optimize test removal effectiveness.

14.3 ERROR DETECTABILITY

What makes it possible to detect errors in a program? We argue that redundancy does; more specifically, what makes it possible to detect errors is the redundancy in the way program states are represented. When we declare variables in a program to represent data, we have in mind a relation between the data we want to manipulate and the representation of this data by means of the program variables. We refer to this relation as the representation relation; ideally, we may want a representation relation to have the following properties:

- *Totality*: each datum has at least one representation.
- *Determinacy*: each datum has at most one representation.
- *Injectivity*: different data have different representations.
- *Surjectivity*: all representations represent valid data.

It is very common for representation relations to fall short of these properties: in fact it is common to have none of them.

- When a representation relation is not total, we observe an *incomplete representation*: for example, not all integers can be represented in computer arithmetic.

- When a representation is not deterministic, we observe *ambivalence*: for example, in a sign-magnitude representation of integers, zero has two distinct representations, −0 and +0.

- When a representation is not injective, we observe a *loss of precision*: for example, real numbers in the neighborhood of a representable floating point value are all mapped to that value.

- When a representation is not surjective, we observe redundancy: for example, in a parity-bit representation scheme of bytes, not all 8-bit patterns represent legitimate bytes.

More generally, redundancy in the representation of data in a program stems from the non-surjectivity of the representation relation of program data, which maps a small data set to a vast state space of the program. If the representation relation were surjective, then all representations would be legitimate; hence if by mistake one representation were altered to produce another representation, we would have no way to detect the error; by contrast, if the representation relation were not surjective, and one representation were altered to produce another representation that is outside the range of the representation relation, then we would know for sure that we have an error. Hence the essence of state redundancy is the non-surjectivity of the representation relation. Whence the definition:

Definition: State Redundancy *Let g be a program on space S, and let σ be the random variable that represents actual values that the program state may take at a particular stage in its execution. The state redundancy of program g at a stage in its computation is defined as the difference between the entropy of its state space S and the entropy of σ at that stage; the state redundancy of program g is defined as the interval formed by its state redundancy at its initial state and its state redundancy at its final state.*

As an illustration, let us consider three program variables that we use to represent: the year of birth of a person, the age of the person, and the current year. The variable declarations of the program would look like:

```
int yob, age, thisyear;
```

If we assume that integer variables are coded in 32 bits, then the entropy of the program state is 3×32 bits $= 96$ bits. As for the entropy of the actual set of values that we want to represent, we assume that ages range between 0 and 150, years of birth range between 1990 and 2090 (101 different values), and current year ranges between 2014 and 2140 (127 different values). Because we have the equation *yob* +*age* = *thisyear*, the condition that age is between 0 and 150 is redundant and age can be inferred from the other two variables. Hence the entropy of the set of actual values is $\log(101) + \log(127) = 27.62$ bits. Hence the redundancy (excess bits) is $96 - 27.62 = 62.38$ bits.

> The redundancy of a state reflects the strength of an assertion that we can check about the state. For example, a redundancy of 32 bits means that we can check an assertion in the form of an equality between two 32-bit integer expressions.

Now that we know how to compute the redundancy of a state, we use it to define the redundancy of a program: to this effect, we observe that while the set of program variables remains unchanged through the execution of the program, the range of values that program states may take shrinks, as the program establishes new relations between program variables; for example, a sorting routine starts with an array whose cells are in random order and rearrange them in increasing order. Given that the entropy of a random variable decreases as we apply functions to it, we can infer that the entropy of the final state of a program is smaller than the entropy of the initial state (prior to applying the function of the program) and the redundancy of the final state is greater than the redundancy of the initial state (assuming the set of program variables remains unchanged, that is, no variables have been declared or returned through the execution of the program). We can define the redundancy of a program by

- The state redundancy of its initial state, or
- The (larger) state redundancy of its final state, or
- The pair of values representing the initial and final state redundancies.

As an illustration, we consider the following program that reads two integers between 1 and 1024 and computes their greatest common divisor.

```
{int x, y; cin << x << y ;
     // initial state
     While (x!=y) {if (x>y) {x=x-y;} else {y=y-x;}}
     // final state
}
```

The set defined by the declared variables which are two integers; which we assume to be 32 bits wide; hence the entropy of the declared state is 2×32 bits $= 64$ bits. Because the variables range from 1 to 1024, the entropy of the set of values that these variables take is actually $2 \times \log(1024) = 20$ bits. Hence the redundancy of the initial state is 44 bits. In the final state the two variables are identical and hence the entropy of the final state is merely $\log(1024)$, which is 10 bits. Hence the redundancy of the final state is 54 bits. The state redundancy of this program can be represented by the pair (44 bits, 54 bits).

14.4 ERROR MASKABILITY

Maskability is the ability of a program to mask an error that arises during its execution. In the testing phase, maskability may be seen as an obstacle to fault diagnosis, since (by definition) it masks errors and hence prevents the observer from exposing the impact of faults, while in the operating phase, maskability may be seen as a blessing, since it helps the program avoid failure. Either way, this metric is relevant from the standpoint of testing.

If we consider deterministic programs, tha is, programs that map initial states into uniquely determined final states, then each program defines an equivalence class on its domain that places in the same class all the initial states that map to the same final state. See Figure 14.2.

A program is all the more non-injective that the equivalence class of each final state is larger. To quantify this attribute, we let X be the random variable that represents the initial states of the program and we let Y be the random variable that represents the final states of the program. Then one way to quantify the size of a (typical) equivalence class is to compute the conditional entropy of X with respect to Y; in other words, we quantify the non-injectivity of a program by the uncertainty we have about the initial state of the program if we know its final state; the more initial states map to the same final state (the essence of non-injectivity), the larger this conditional entropy. Whence the definition:

Definition: Non-injectivity *Let g be a program on space S, let X be a random variable that takes its values in the domain of G and Y a random variable that takes its values in the range of G. The non-injectivity of g is defined as the following conditional entropy:*

$$\mu(g) = H(X|Y).$$

Because Y is a function of X, this conditional entropy can simply be written as:

$$\mu(g) = H(X) - H(Y).$$

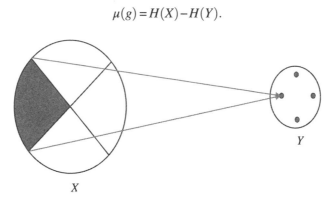

Figure 14.2 *Measuring non-injectivity.*

As illustrative examples, we consider the following:

- Let g be the following program on space S defined by a single integer variable i: $g = \{i=i+1;\}$. Then $\mu(g) = 0$, since $H(X) = w$, and $H(Y) = w$, where w is the width of an integer variable. Ignoring the possibility of overflow, this program is injective; if variable i has an erroneous value prior to this statement, then it has an erroneous value after this statement.
- Let g be the following program on space S defined by three integer variables i, j, and k: $g = \{i=j+k;\}$ Then $\mu(g) = w$, since $H(X) = 3w$, and $H(Y) = 2w$, where w is the width of an integer variable. Indeed, this program has the potential to mask an error of size w: if variable i had a wrong value prior to this statement, then that error will be masked by this statement since the wrong value is overridden.
- Let g be the following program on space S defined by three integer variables i, j, and k: $g = \{i=0; j=1; k=2;\}$. Then $\mu(g) = 3w$, since $H(X) = 3w$, and $H(Y) = 0$, where w is the width of an integer variable. Indeed, this program has the potential to mask an error of size $3 \times w$: if variables i, j, and k had wrong values prior to this statement, then that error will be masked by this statement since all the wrong values are overridden.

We submit the following interpretation:

> The non-injectivity of a program measures the size of damage to its state (error) that the program can mask by its execution.

The more non-injective a program, the more damage it can mask; in fact non-injectivity aims to measure in bits the amount of erroneous information that can be masked by the program.

14.5 FAILURE AVOIDANCE

Whereas state redundancy reflects excess information in representing a state, functional redundancy represents excess information in representing the result of a function. For example, if a function is duplicated (for the sake of error detection) or triplicated (for the sake of error recovery) then in principle we are getting one or (respectively) two extra copies, that is, two instances of excess information. But functional redundancy need not proceed in discrete quantities; as we define in this section, functional redundancy quantifies the (continuous) duplication of functional information. In the same way that state redundancy stems from the non-surjectivity of representation functions, functional redundancy stems from the non-surjectivity of program functions. Figure 14.3 illustrates graphically in what sense a duplicated function is more redundant than a single function, by virtue of being less-surjective: while the range of function F is isomorphic to the range of the duplicated function $\langle F, F \rangle$, the output space of $\langle F, F \rangle$ is much larger than the output space of F, making for a smaller ratio of range over output space, which is the essence of non-surjectivity.

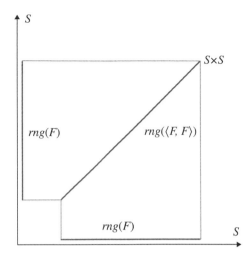

Figure 14.3 *Enlarging the output space, preserving the range.*

Definition: Functional Redundancy *We consider a program g that computes a function G from input space X to output space Y, and we let ρ be a random variable that takes its values in the range of G. Then the functional redundancy of g is denoted by φ(g) and defined by:* $\varphi(g) = \frac{H(Y)}{H(\rho)} - 1$.

Whereas we are accustomed to talking about a program space as a structure that holds input data and output data, in this definition we refer separately to the input space and the output space of the program. There is no contradiction between these two views: X may encompass some program variables along with input media (keyboard, sensors, input files, communication devices, etc.) and Y may encompass some program variables along with some media (screen, actuator, output file, communication devices, etc.).

As an illustration, we consider the following functions and show for each function: its input space (X), its output space (Y), its expression, its range (ρ), its functional redundancy (φ), and possibly some explanation of the result. We let B5 be the set of natural numbers that can be represented in a word of five bits.

Name	Exp	X	Y	ρ	φ	Comments
F1	X	B5	B5	B5	0	All 5 bits are used
F2	$2X$	B5	B5	{0, 2, ..30}	0.25	Rightmost bit always 0
F3	$X \% 4$	B5	B5	{0,1,2,3}	1.5	2 bits of information, 3 bits at 0
F4	$X \% 16$	B5	B5	{0,1,.. 15}	0.25	4 bits of information, 1 bit at 0
F5	$X / 2$	B5	B5	{0,1,.. 15}	0.25	Leftmost bit always 0

G1	$\langle F1, F1 \rangle$	B5	B5×B5	B5×B5	1.0	1+2×ϕ(F1)
G2	$\langle F2, F2 \rangle$	B5	B5×B5	$\{0, 2, ..30\}^2$	1.5	1+2×ϕ(F2)
G3	$\langle F3, F3 \rangle$	B5	B5×B5	$\{0, 1, 2, 3\}^2$	4.0	1+2×ϕ(F3)
G4	$\langle F4, F4 \rangle$	B5	B5×B5	$\{0, 1,.. 15\}^2$	1.5	1+2×ϕ(F4)
G5	$\langle F5, F5 \rangle$	B5	B5×B5	$\{0, 1,.. 15\}^2$	1.5	1+2×ϕ(F5)

14.6 FAILURE TOLERANCE

The quality attributes of software products such as reliability, safety, security, and availability depend not only on the products themselves but also on their specifications. Hence, if we want to define metrics that reflect software quality attributes, our metrics need to take into account specifications as well as software product per se. In this section, we consider a metric that captures relevant attributes of specifications.

Functional redundancy, which we have discussed in the previous section, reflects the ability of a software product to avoid failure and compute the intended behavior despite the presence and sensitization of faults and the emergence of errors. But if a specification is sufficiently non-deterministic, a program may fail to compute its exact intended function and still satisfy the specification. The question that we raise in this regard is: How do we measure the extent to which a program may deviate from its intended behavior without violating its specification. The measure of specification non-determinacy is an attempt to answer this question.

> We consider a relation R on space S and we let X and Y be random variables that take their values in the domain (respectively) and range of R. The non-determinacy of R is the conditional entropy $v(R) = H(Y|X)$.

The conditional entropy of Y with respect to X represents the uncertainty we have about the value of Y if we know the value of X. The bigger the non-determinacy of R, the bigger this conditional entropy. As an illustrative example, we consider the following relation on space S defined by three variables $i, j,$ and k.

$$R = \left\{ (s, s') \mid k = 2i + j \wedge i' = i + j \wedge j' = i - j \right\}.$$

The non-determinacy of this relation is $v(R) = H(Y|X) = H(X; Y) - H(X)$. The reader may notice that (in this particular case) the inverse of relation R is a function; in other words, X is a function of Y, hence the join entropy H(X,Y) is the same as the entropy of Y. Hence the non-determinacy of this specification can be written as:

$$v(R) = H(Y) - H(X).$$

In order to derive the entropies of X and Y, we must first compute the domain and range of relation R. We find:

$$X = dom(R)$$
$$= \{(s,s') \mid \exists s' : k = 2i + j \wedge i' = i + j \wedge j' = i - j\}$$
$$= \{(s,s') \mid k = 2i + j \wedge \exists s' : i' = i + j \wedge j' = i - j\}$$
$$= \{(s,s') \mid k = 2i + j\}.$$

$$Y = rng(R)$$
$$= \{(s,s') \mid \exists s' : k' = 2i' + j' \wedge i = i' + j' \wedge j = i' - j'\}$$
$$= S.$$

Hence, under the assumption of uniform probability distribution, we find $H(X) = 2w$, since we have only two independent variables (i and j), and $H(Y) = 3w$, since we have three independent variables. We find:

$$v(R) = H(Y) - H(X) = w,$$

which we interpret as follows: A program may lose as much as w bits of information (i.e., the width of an integer value) and still not violate specification R. Indeed, specification R mandates final values for i and j, but no final value for k, which means that a candidate program may lose track of k and still be correct; this is the meaning of non-determinacy.

14.7 AN ILLUSTRATIVE EXAMPLE

As further illustration, we consider the following sorting program and briefly compute its metrics as well as the non-determinacy of three possible sorting specifications that the program may be tested against.

```
int N=100;
void sort ()
   {int c, d, p, swap; c=0;
   while (c<N-1)
        {p=c; d=c+1;
        while (d<N) {if (a[p]>a[d]) {p=d;} d++;}
        if (p!=c) {swap=a[c]; a[c]=a[p];
                   a[p]=swap;} c++;}}
```

14.7.1 Cyclomatic Complexity

If we draw the flowchart of this program, we find that it has 14 edges and 11 nodes. Hence its cyclomatic complexity is $14 - 11 + 2 = 5$.

14.7.2 Volume

If we analyze the source code of this program, we find that it has 108 lexemes taken from a vocabulary of 27 distinct lexemes. The volume of this program is:

$$108 \times \log(27) = 513.53.$$

14.7.3 State Redundancy

If we assume that integer variables are represented by 32 bits, then the entropy of the state of this program is 104×32 bits = 3328 bits. Now, if we assume that the cells of the array (as well as variable swap) range between 1 and 400 and that index variables (c, d, p) range between 0 and 100, then the entropy of the random variable that represents the initial data of the program is $101 \times \log(400) + 3 \times \log(100) = 893$ bits. Hence the state redundancy of the initial state is $3328 - 893$ bits = 2435 bits.

In order to compute the state redundancy of the final state of this program, we refer to a result to the effect that when an array of size N is sorted, its entropy drops by $N \times \log(N)$. Hence the entropy of the final sorted array is $N \times \log(400) - N \times \log(N)$. For $N = 100$, this expression evaluates to 200 bits. Because the final values of variables c and d are determined by the program, they are not counted in the entropy of the final state; we only count the entropy of the array and that of variables p and *swap*. We find that $200 + \log(101) + \log(400) = 213$ bits. Hence the redundancy of the final state is $3328 - 213$ bits = 3115 bits. Therefore, the state redundancy of this program can be represented by the interval: [2435 bits ... 3115 bits]; the state redundancy of the program evolves from 2435 initially to 3115 in the final state. State redundancy measures the bandwidth of assertions that can be checked between variables of the state; in the final state it is almost 10 integers' worth of assertions (i.e., nearly 10 assertions that equate 2 integer expressions to each other).

14.7.4 Functional Redundancy

According to the definition of functional redundancy, the functional redundancy of the sort program is obtained by the following formula,

$$\frac{H(Y)}{H(\rho)} - 1,$$

where Y is the output space of the program and ρ is the (random variable representing the) range of the program. For the output space, we let Y be the space of the S program, whose entropy we have found to be 3328 bits. For the range of the program, we have computed its entropy in the previous section and found it to be 213 bits. Hence the functional redundancy of this program is:

$$\frac{3328}{213} - 1 = 14.62.$$

Much of this redundancy stems from the fact that we are using 32-bit words (100 of them) to represent integers between 1 and 400 only (when 9 bits would have been sufficient). Another factor that further reduces the entropy of the output (hence increases its redundancy) is that the output array is sorted; as a result, each cell of the array limits the range of possible values for the remainder of the array (e.g., if the first cell is 200, then the remainder of the array is restricted to the range [201...400] rather than [1...400]).

14.7.5 Non-injectivity

The non-injectivity of a program is the conditional entropy of its input (or initial state) given its output (or final state). Because this program sorts arrays, we know that each sorted array of size N stems from N! distinct initial arrays (assuming, as we do, that all array cells are distinct). If we take the hypothesis of uniform probability distribution, and if we focus on the array (rather than auxiliary index variables), we find that this conditional entropy is $\log(N!)$. According to Stirling's approximation, this quantity can be approximated by

$$N \times \log(N) - N = 564 \text{ bits,}$$

for $N = 100$.

14.7.6 Non-determinacy

While all the previous metrics reflect properties of the program, non-determinacy reflects properties of the specification that the program is intended to satisfy and against which it is judged and tested. We consider three possible specifications for the sort program and compute the non-determinacy of each:

- *Ord*, which specifies that the output is ordered.
- *Prm*, which specifies that the final array is a permutation of the initial array.
- *Sort* = *Ord* ∩ *Prm*.

According to the definition of non-determinacy, we must compute the conditional entropy $H(Y|X)$, where X is the random variable that takes its values over the domain of the specification and Y is the random variable that ranges over the image set of X by R (i.e., such that $(X, Y) \in R$). We find the following:

- *Ord*: This specification provides that the output array is sorted but bears no relation to the input array. In this case, $H(Y|X) = H(Y)$. The entropy of a sorted array of size N whose values may take V values (in our case $V = 400$) is given by the formula $N \times W - N \times \log(N)$. For $N = 100$ and $V = 400$, we find $H(Y) = 2536$ *bits*. This is the extent to which a candidate program can deviate from the function of sorting and still not violate the specification *Ord*.

- *Prm*: This specification provides that the final array is a permutation of the initial array but it does not stipulate that it must be ordered. For an array of size N (whose cells we assume to be distinct), there exist N! distinct arrays that satisfy this specification. Under the assumption of uniform probability, this entropy is $H(Y|X) = \log(N!)$, which we estimate by means of the Sterling approximation as $N \times \log(N) - N = 564$ bits. This is the extent to which a candidate program can deviate from the function of sorting and still not violate the specification *Prm*.

- *Sort*: Because this specification is deterministic, $H(Y|X) = 0$. Any deviation of a candidate program from the mission of sorting the array will violate this specification.

14.7.7 SUMMARY

The following table summarizes the discussion of the sorting routine's metrics.

Metric		Value	Unit	Interpretation/meaning/relation to testing
Cyclomatic complexity		5		Fault proneness
Volume		513.53		Fault proneness
State Redundancy		2435 3115	Bits	Bandwidth of assertions that can check for errors, in initial state and final state
Functional Redundancy		14.62		Factor by which state space is larger than the result of the computation
Non-injectivity		564	Bits	Bandwidth of data that the program may lose and still recover spontaneously
Non Determinacy	Ord	2536	Bits	Amount of data a program can lose and still manage to satisfy the specification
	Prm	564		
	Sort	0		

14.8 CHAPTER SUMMARY

In this chapter, we have presented syntactic and semantic metrics that have relevance from the standpoint of software testing and fault analysis:

- Fault proneness—the density of faults within the source code.
- Fault detectability—the ease of detecting faults in the source code.
- Error detectability—the ease of detecting errors in the state of a program in execution.

- Error maskability—the likelihood that an error that arises during the execution of a program gets masked before it causes a program failure.
- Failure avoidance—the ease of detecting and avoiding program failure with respect to its intended function.
- Failure tolerance—the extent to which a program may satisfy its specification despite failing to compute its intended function.

14.9 EXERCISES

14.1. Consider the **product** routine given in Section 14.1.1. Imagine that for the sake of speeding up the calculation of the product, we add a test for **(b% 4==0)**, and if the test is positive we divide b by 4 and multiply a by 4. Change the program accordingly and compute the new cyclomatic complexity.

14.2. Consider the **product** routine given in Section 14.1.1. Imagine that for the sake of robustness (to avoid divergence) we check whether b is nonnegative before we engage in the loop. Change the program accordingly and compute the new cyclomatic complexity.

14.3. Consider the **product** routine given in Section 14.1.1. Imagine that for the sake of speeding up the calculation of the product, we add a test for **(b% 4==0)**, and if the test is positive we divide b by 4 and multiply a by 4. Change the program accordingly and compute the volume of the new program.

14.4. Consider the **product** routine given in Section 14.1.1. Imagine that for the sake of robustness (to avoid divergence) we check whether b is nonnegative before we engage in the loop. Change the program accordingly and compute the volume of the new program.

14.5. Redo the calculations of the P-measure, E-measure, and F-measures on the program given in Section 14.2, with respect to the following specification:

$$R = \{(s,s') | y' = x + y \wedge z' < 90\}.$$

14.6. Redo the calculations of the P-measure, E-measure, and F-measures on the program given in Section 14.2, with respect to the following specification:

$$R = \{(s,s') | y' = x + y \wedge z' > 4\}.$$

14.7. Draw the flowchart of the sort program shown in Section 14.7, and compute its cyclomatic complexity.

14.8. Continuing the discussion of Section 14.7.6, compute the non-determinacy of the following specification:

a. $EqSum = \{(s,s')| \sum_{i=1}^{N} a[i] = \sum_{i=1}^{N} a'[i]\}.$

b. $EqSum \cap Sort.$

c. $EqSum \cap prm.$

14.10 BIBLIOGRAPHIC NOTES

The definition of cyclomatic complexity is due to Thomas McCabe (1976). The volume metric is due to Maurice Halstead (1977). The semantic metrics presented in this chapter are due to Mili et al. (2014). Other semantic metrics may be found in Bansyia et al. (1999), Etzkorn and Gholston (2002), Gall et al. (2008), Morell and Murill (1993), Morell and Voas (1993), and Voas and Miller (1993). For more information on Software Metrics, consult Abran (2012), Ebert and Dumke (2007), and Fenton and Pfleeger (1997). For more information on entropy functions and information theory, consult Csiszar and Koerner (2011).

15

Software Testing Tools

Like all software engineering activities, software testing is a labor-intensive task that is difficult to automate because it depends on a great deal of creativity and because it is difficult to cast in a systematic process. Still, there is much scope for automated support, to help with clerical or repetitive aspects of software testing. The subject of this chapter is to review some of the tools that are available in the market and to classify them by means of some orthogonal attributes.

15.1 A CLASSIFICATION SCHEME

When we look at all the software products that purport to be testing tools, it is difficult to imagine that they bear the same name, given how different they look. To help characterize each tool, we propose a classification scheme, which is defined by a number of attributes and a set of values for each attribute. The classification scheme includes the following attributes:

- Life cycle phase: unit testing, integration testing, system testing, acceptance testing.
- Test data generation method: specification-based, code-based, scenario-based.
- Testing phase/activity: test data generation, test driver design, test execution, test outcome analysis.
- Target language, if applicable: some tools are restricted to specific languages or are geared toward programs written in a specific language.
- Target development environment, if applicable: some tools are compatible with a limited set of development environments.

In addition to information pertaining to these attributes, we may present, for each tool, information such as the following: URL where the tool is described, whether the

Software Testing: Concepts and Operations, First Edition. Ali Mili and Fairouz Tchier.
© 2015 John Wiley & Sons, Inc. Published 2015 by John Wiley & Sons, Inc.

tool is available for purchase or it is free, whether it is open source, whether it has a trial version, and so on.

Of course, our purpose is not to promote nor to unduly criticize any tool we review but merely to give the reader some sense of the kind of functionality that existing testing tools may provide; we do our best to represent our experience with each tool as faithfully and as objectively as possible. Note that the information reported in this chapter is based on a survey conducted in the summer of 2013, hence reflects the attributes of the tools as of that date.

We have reviewed a total of 14 tools; rather than presenting a monolithic sequence of tools, we have resolved to enhance readability by grouping them into six broad categories, which are as follows:

1. *Scripting Tools*, which enable us to codify and store test data and test execution traces for repeated use; these tools are useful to test an application after each fault removal (in corrective maintenance, for example); they are not directly useful in adaptive maintenance because they cannot be reused if the specification changes.

2. *Record-and-Replay Tools*, which can be used in applications with a complex interface (such as web applications) to record the scenario of interactions of the tester with the application. This scenario can be replayed whenever we want to reexecute the test (e.g., after each corrective maintenance operation to retest the application).

3. *Performance-Testing Tools*, which simulate workload conditions for applications under test to check how their performance evolves according to their workload or how they behave under specific workload conditions.

4. *Oracle Design Tools*, which enable the tester to write code to codify the oracle of a test for the sake of automation.

5. *Exception Discovery Tools*, which alert the tester to the possibility that the program may run into an exceptional condition, such as an infinite loop, an overflow/underflow, an array reference out of bounds, an illegal pointer reference, or a division by zero.

6. *Collaborative Tools*, which are tools whose main function is to serve as communication media between the stakeholders of a test, including end users, developers, and testers.

In the remainder of this chapter, we devote one section to each family of tools.

15.2 SCRIPTING TOOLS

15.2.1 CppTest

CppUnit is a unit-testing framework for the C++ programming language, described as a C++ port for JUnit. The library can be compiled for a variety of portable operating systems interface (POSIX) platforms, allowing unit testing of "C" sources as well as C++ with minimal source modifications.

CppTest	
Source	Freeware
Web page	http://sourceforge.net/apps/mediawiki/cppunit/index.php?title=Main_Page
Access	Open source
Target language(s)	C++
Life cycle phase	Unit testing
Test phase	Test driver design and execution

Test scripts are written in the syntax of a C++ class and include specialized **test_add()** statements, where each **test_add()** statement refers to separately defined routines that invoke tests in the form of logical assertions. Each such a routine is declared as a **void** C++ method that includes assertions of the form **TEST_ASSERT()**, which takes logical assertions as parameters. Using these statements and structures, the tester can define arbitrarily complex test scripts.

In order to run a test script, the user has to define an output handler, which records and organizes the output produced by the **TEST_ASSERT()** statements; a number of formats are available, including a text format, that may be shipped to the **stdout** stream and an html format, among others.

Among the strengths of CppTest, we cite that it puts the power of C++ at the disposal of the tester, to define arbitrarily sophisticated test scripts; in particular, the tester may use the exception-handling mechanisms of C++ in conjunction with the assert statements of CppUnit to handle any exceptions that may arise during the test in a controlled manner.

15.2.2 SilkTest

SilkTest is a suite of related test tools that offer a range of interrelated functionalities, including the following:

- SilkTest Classic, which uses a domain-specific scripting language inspired from C to support the development of test scripts.
- Silk4J, which uses Java as a scripting language to support the derivation of test scripts in Eclipse.
- Silk4Net, which uses Visual Basic or C# as a scripting language to support the derivation of test scripts in Visual Studio.
- SilkTest Workbench, which uses VB.NET as a scripting language to support test automation.

SilkTest	
Source	Borland Software
Web page	http://www.borland.com/products/silktest/
Access	Commercial
Target language(s)	Java, visual basic (VB), C#
Life cycle phase	System-level
Test phase	Test management

In order to operate SilkTest, we open a new project, give it a name, associate the project name to the application we want to test (possibly a web-based application), configure SilkTest to a particular browser, then record the sequence of tests we want to run. This sequence of tests defines the test script; once this script is saved, it can be run by merely calling the project name and invoking its execution, possibly unattended.

Among the strengths of this tool, we cite its ability to support integrated testing of graphical user interface (GUI) applications, its ease of use (notably that it does not require any programming knowledge, hence can be operated by the end user of the application), and the availability of test templates that provide standard test frameworks. Silk has two drawbacks: first, it can only support two browsers, namely, Internet Explorer (© Microsoft) and Firefox (© Mozilla). Also, it does not support migration between the two browsers, that is, a script composed on one browser cannot be run on the other.

SilkTest can be seen as a scripting tool but can also be seen as a save-and-replay tool, to the extent that it stores tests by recording an interactive session on the web-based application. The tools of the next section fall exclusively in the latter category.

15.3 RECORD-AND-REPLAY TOOLS

15.3.1 TestComplete

TestComplete is an automated testing tool that aims to enable testers to create, record, edit, and save complex test scripts; it also saves failure logs that correspond to test scripts.

TestComplete	
Source	SmartBear
Web page	http://smartbear.com/products/qa-tools/automated-testing-tools/
Access	Commercial
Target language(s)	No restriction
Life cycle phase	Performance testing, reliability testing
Test phase	Test data generation, test outcome analysis

Sample example of use: We use this tool to edit, save, then replay a test sequence.

- First, we click on the button labeled "record a new test" on the TestComplete start page.
- This brings up the window to create a new test project and allows us to give it a name and to decide where to save it; also, it allows us to associate the project to an application that we want to test.
- Upon this, the TestComplete window minimizes down to a small recording toolbar; from now on and until we click on the stop button, everything we do with the selected application is recorded in the test script.
- Once the test script is saved, it can be reexecuted by clicking on the button labeled "run the test" in the window that corresponds to the TestComplete project.

Among its strengths, TestComplete offers the ability to record arbitrary interactions between the tester and the application, can run unattended, and does not require any programming or scripting skills. Nevertheless, for users who have adequate programming skills, TestComplete offers the ability to integrate sophisticated testing scenarios written in a wide variety of scripting languages, such as VBScript, JScript, C++Script, C#Script, or DelphiScript.

15.3.2 Selenium IDE

Selenium interactive development environment (IDE) is a Mozilla Firefox add-on that provides an interface for running test cases or complete test suites via a simple mechanism of record and playback of browser transactions. It can be applied to any application whose user interface is supported by a browser; this includes virtually all web applications.

Selenium IDE	
Source	Freeware
Web page	http://docs.seleniumhq.org/
Access	Open source
Target language(s)	SQL, http, Java
Life cycle phase	System-level
Test phase	Test data generation, test data recording, test execution

Sample example of use: We can start an experiment by opening a tab of Firefox and running the Selenium IDE through its Tools tab; once Selenium IDE is on, we push the record button to start the recording process. From then on, Selenium IDE records any operation we do on the browser, such as visiting URLs, navigating through Web pages, and searching keywords on Web pages. When we initiate the replay, Selenium runs all the interactions that were recorded and displays the reactions of the web application under test.

Among the strengths of Selenium IDE, we cite that it requires no programming experience, hence can be run by an end user; that it provides for extensions and customizations; and that its scripts can be converted to a variety of programming languages, such as Java, Ruby, C#, and Python. The main weakness of Selenium IDE is, of course, that it can only run on Mozilla Firefox.

15.4 PERFORMANCE-TESTING TOOLS

15.4.1 LoadRunner

LoadRunner is a testing tool for performance and load testing of software applications; it proceeds by simulating arbitrary levels of workload (in the form of concurrent users) on an application under test and observing its behavior.

LoadRunner	
Source	Hewlett Packard
Web page	http://www8.hp.com/us/en/software-solutions/loadrunner-load-testing/index.html?#.Udr82zs9-td
Access	Commercial
Target language(s)	Web apps, mail, databases, and so on
Life cycle phase	Performance testing
Test phase	Test management

Sample example of use: The main artifact that LoadRunner deals with is that of a load scenario; a load scenario is defined by a set of virtual users, along with characteristics of their demands on the system under test. LoadRunner enables the tester to create, edit, save, and invoke load scenarios. When a load scenario is invoked on an application, it enables the tester to observe and analyze the behavior of the system under the workload imposed by the load scenario. Once the scenario has completed its execution, Load Runner delivers a table of statistics, which may include such details as the following:

- Tables showing the number of active virtual users, the number of processed transactions, and the number of failed transactions.
- Graphs plotting a variety of parameters as a function of time, including number of virtual users, response time, number of hits per second, and system resources.

- Statistics (such as Max, Min, Average, and Standard deviation) of relevant parameters, such as rate of occupancy of processor time, file data operations per second, processor queue length, and page faults per second.

The main strength of LoadRunner is clearly its ability to simulate arbitrary levels of workload, along with its ability to capture detailed statistical information on the behavior of the program under test; this information is a great resource to a tester who wants to analyze the operational properties of a software application.

15.4.2 Grinder

Grinder is a desktop application that enables the tester to test a software application under controlled workload conditions; to this effect, Grinder uses a specialized scripting language called Jython, which is derived from Python.

Grinder	
Source	Freeware
Web page	http://grinder.sourceforge.net/
Access	Open source
Target language(s)	Web applications
Life cycle phase	Performance testing, load testing
Test phase	Test management

Sample example of use: When Grinder is called, a window opens with four tabs, labeled Graphs, Results, Processes, and Scripts. Under the Processes tab, we configure the agent processes that act upon the application under test. Under the Script tab, we are given the opportunity to edit test scripts or to invoke test scripts that are already written in Jython. We start the test codified in the selected script by pressing the button labeled "start process." Upon completion of the test, we obtain statistics about the performance of the target application. For a transaction processing application, these may include such details as the following:

- Number of tests, divided into number of successful tests and number of failures.
- Mean number of transactions per second and peak number of transactions per second.
- Mean response time, divided into mean time to resolve host, mean time to establish connection, and mean time to access the first byte.
- Mean response length and number of response bytes per second.

Among the strengths of the Grinder, we can cite its ability to load test any application that has a Java API, its ability to support detailed test scripts written in Jython, and its ability to deploy a wide range of distributed load injectors (i.e., processes that simulate the workload on the system).

15.4.3 QF-Test

QF-Test is a tool for the creation, execution, and management of automated system and load tests for Java and Web applications with a GUI. It is compatible with a wide range of development technologies and development environments, including Swing, JavaFX, and SWT and supports cross-browser testing of web GUI. It can test static html web pages as well as dynamic web applications developed in Ajax technologies.

QF-Test	
Source	Quality first software
Web page	http://www.qfs.de/
Access	Commercial
Target language(s)	Java, web applications
Life cycle phase	Performance testing, reliability testing
Test phase	Test management

Sample example of use: QF-Test has a capture-and-replay function that enables it to run individual tests or complete test suites by merely starting the recording function then manually executing whatever test script the tester wants. Whenever the test script is invoked, it executes the test on the application and produces a configurable report of the execution including statistics about possible errors. Because of its scalability, this tool can be used for system-level testing.

15.4.4 Appvance PerformanceCloud

Appvance PerformanceCloud is a tool that specializes in testing the performance and load capabilities of web applications. It is compatible with Ajax development environments, supports end-to-end testing to a great level of detail through all the steps of the application, can simulate millions of simultaneous users using a wide variety of web browsers, down to fine detail such as every keystroke and every message transfer, and supports pervasive agile integration. In addition, it requires little or no coding and supports customizable report generation, thereby providing faster test development.

Appvance performanceCloud	
Source	Appvance
Web page	http://appvance.com/products/#sthash.ihZqzsRq.dpbs
Access	Commercial, free demo, free trial
Target language(s)	Web applications
Life cycle phase	Performance testing, load testing
Test phase	Test scripts, test execution

For a simulated user load, the tool provides a detailed analysis of system performance, including information about the performance of individual transactions, their rate of success, their resource usage, their execution path, and so on. It also offers a large menu of measures one can collect on the application under test, such as its overall resource usage, its failure history, its performance scalability, or its throughput.

15.4.5 JMeter

Apache JMeter enables the tester to analyze the performance of an application under controllable workload conditions; it can be used to evaluate system performance on static and dynamic resources and to simulate a transaction load on a server, a group of servers, or a network. It provides performance data under a wide variety of textual and graphic formats, under arbitrarily controllable heavy workloads.

Apache JMeter	
Source	Apache software foundation
Web page	http://jmeter.apache.org/
Access	Open source
Target language(s)	SQL, http, Java
Life cycle phase	System-level
Test phase	Test driver design and execution, test outcome analysis, performance analysis

Sample example of use: The basic artifact in JMeter testing is the test plan, which is a sequence of steps that JMeter executes whenever it is invoked. JMeter supports the tester in editing a test plan, which may contain any combination of the following elements:

- One or more thread groups, where each thread group is a collection of concurrent processes submitting simultaneous queries to the system under test.

- Logic controllers, which coordinate the deployment of the thread groups by means of control constructs (similar to programming language constructs).
- Sample-generating controllers, which generate requests (e.g., http requests) that each thread group will produce when they are activated.
- Listeners, which are JMeter functions that collect performance data and store it as part of the application performance analysis.
- Assertions, which are test scripts that enable the tester to check whether the application under test is returning the expected results.

The output of JMeter depends on the format the tester has specified in the Listener and may include detailed information about the execution of the system under test (functions invoked in the system, number of http queries, number of database queries, number of ftp requests, number of active and sleeping tasks, etc.) as well as the resource usage of the system (CPU usage, memory usage, buffer usage, communication infrastructure bandwidth, etc.).

Among the strengths of JMeter, we may mention the following:

- Because JMeter is an open-source tool, a user may adapt to her/his needs and customize it as needed.
- One may build a relatively sophisticated test plan without prior knowledge of test scripts or scripting languages; also, the process of constructing test plans is fairly simple, thanks to a user-friendly GUI.

15.5 ORACLE DESIGN TOOLS

15.5.1 JUnit

JUnit is an open-source framework for writing test oracles in Java to perform unit testing on Java code. It comes with a .jar executable file that must be added as an external jar file to libraries in the user's project. It enables the user to deploy predefined functions to perform unit testing. Oracles are modeled as Java classes that compute Boolean assertions.

JUnit	
Source	Freeware
Web page	http://www.junit.org/
Access	Open source
Target language(s)	Java
Life cycle phase	Unit testing
Test phase	Oracle design

Sample example of use: JUnit oracles can be composed by means of Java classes of type @Test and can be arbitrarily hierarchical (higher-level oracles calling more elementary oracles). Once a JUnit class is written, it can be compiled in Java; its execution yields a report in the form of a tree structure showing each assertion of the hierarchy, and whether it returned true or not.

The main strength of JUnit is that it enables the user to write arbitrarily complex test oracles in a structured, hierarchical manner; also, it supports a neat separation between production code and test code and makes it possible for developers and testers to work independently.

15.5.2 TestNG

TestNG is a testing framework for the Java programming language; it is designed to cover a wide range of testing categories, including unit testing, integration testing, system testing, and so on. TestNG is an annotation-based testing framework that aims to make up for some of the shortcomings of JUnit by offering a higher level of flexibility; whereas JUnit tests are structured by means of the class hierarchy of Java, TestNG tests are composed from elementary test classes by means of an XML file structure.

TestNG	
Source	Freeware
Web page	http://www.testng.org/
Access	Open source
Target language(s)	Java
Life cycle phase	Unit testing, integration, system-level
Test phase	Oracle design, test execution

Sample example of use: In order to build a test suite in TestNG, the tester must write elementary tests in Java classes; then he must compose these elementary tests into suites by means of an XML file structure. Execution of the test suite returns a report on which elements of the suite were successful and which elements were not; whereas in JUnit a test that fails causes its dependent tests to fail, in TestNG, when a test fails, its dependent tests are skipped, and the remainder of the test suite is allowed to proceed.

15.6 EXCEPTION DISCOVERY

15.6.1 Rational Purify

Rational Purify is a testing tool that checks for run-time memory-related exceptions, such as out-of-bounds array references, pointer references, uninitialized memory references, buffer overflow, inappropriate deallocation of memory, unauthorized write operations, and so on. It supports a diverse set of languages (Java, C++, and .NET) and a wide range of development environments (Visual Studio, .NET, and Eclipse).

Rational purify	
Source	Rational IBM
Web page	http://www-03.ibm.com/software/products/en/rational-purify-family/
Access	Commercial
Target language(s)	Java, C++, .Net
Life cycle phase	Unit testing, integration testing
Test phase	Test driver design and execution

Sample example of use: Rational Purify requires no setup in the way that other tools do; all we need is to run the tool on the source code of the program under test; the tool returns its diagnosis in the way a compiler does, that is, by pointing to the offending statement and posting an appropriate error message. This tool operates on intact source code; no modifications are needed, provided it is written in one of the supported programming notations.

15.6.2 Astree

Astree takes its name from the French translation of Real-Time Embedded Software Static Analyzer. It is a static analyzer of C code whose purpose is to check C programs for a range of run-time errors. The operation of this tool is based on the theory of abstract interpretation, which reasons about program semantics by means of abstractions. The abstractions must be selected in such a way as to be sufficiently high to be computationally tractable yet sufficiently detailed to enable effective reasoning.

Astree	
Source	Ecole Normale Superieure, Paris, France
Web page	http://astree.ens.fr/, http://www.absint.de/astree/
Access	Commercial
Target language(s)	C
Life cycle phase	Unit testing, integration testing, system testing
Test phase	Test deployment, outcome analysis

Astree is deployed on source code and produces a report in the form of possible warnings or error messages pertaining to run-time errors such as arithmetic overflow or underflow, array references out of bounds, division by zero, as well as any user-defined assert statements. Astree is guaranteed to signal all possible errors, though it can also signal errors that cannot happen (i.e., false alarms).

15.7 COLLABORATIVE TOOLS

15.7.1 FitNesse

FitNesse is a collaborative tool whose purpose is to serve as a medium for communication between the various stakeholders of testing, namely, programmers, testers, customers, verification and validation (V&V) team members, and so on. It is essentially a wiki that enables stakeholders to share information and artifacts pertaining to the testing activities of an ongoing software development and evolution process.

FitNesse	
Source	Freeware
Web page	http://www.fitnesse.org/
Access	Open source
Target language(s)	Primarily Java but also C++, Python, Ruby, Delphi, C#
Life cycle phase	Integration, acceptance
Test phase	Records generated data, posts expected output versus actual output

Sample example of use: Imagine that we want to test a division function. FitNesse offers the means to develop a routine to check the operation of this function by providing a set of test data and a test oracle. Regardless of which stakeholder provides which information, the fact that this information is shared in FitNesse ensures that it is double checked and vetted by all relevant stakeholders.

15.8 CHAPTER SUMMARY

In this chapter, we have presented a set of 14 software testing tools, which we have tentatively divided into 6 (non-disjoint) classes, which are as follows:

1. *Scripting Tools*
2. *Record-and-Replay Tools*
3. *Performance-Testing Tools*

4. *Oracle Design Tools*
5. *Exception Discovery Tools*
6. *Collaborative Tools*

It is clear, from a casual reading of this chapter, that most software tools presented herein do not support any of the creative (and difficult) aspects of software testing; rather, they support many of the tedious, clerical, bookkeeping aspects of testing. This does not make them any less useful but does mean that the tester remains in charge in terms of generating test data, deciding on and codifying the test oracle, and analyzing and interpreting the outcome of the test.

16

Testing Product Lines

Like all engineering disciplines, software engineering relies on a reuse discipline to achieve economies of scale, improved product quality, shorter production cycles, and reduced process risk. But contrary to all other engineering disciplines, reuse is very difficult in software engineering and has been found to be effective only within the confines of product line engineering (PLE). The purpose of this chapter is to briefly introduce the reader to the reuse discipline of PLE and to focus specifically on testing software products produced and evolved within this discipline.

16.1 PLE: A STREAMLINED REUSE MODEL

Given that software is very labor-intensive (hence hard to automate), that software labor is very expensive (as it requires a great deal of specialized expertise), and that software products are very hard to produce (due to their size and complexity), one would expect software reuse to be an indispensable component of software engineering. Indeed, for an industry that is under as much stress as the software industry, reuse offers a number of significant advantages, including the following:

- *Enhanced productivity*, which stems from using the same product in a wide variety of applications at little or no extra cost.
- *Enhanced quality*, which stems from investing an adequate amount of effort in the quality assurance of the product, with the knowledge that this effort will be amortized through the multiple uses of the product.
- *Shorter time to market*, which can be achieved by saving, not only the development effort but also the development schedule required for a custom product development.

Software Testing: Concepts and Operations, First Edition. Ali Mili and Fairouz Tchier.
© 2015 John Wiley & Sons, Inc. Published 2015 by John Wiley & Sons, Inc.

• *Reduced risk*, which stems from trading the risk inherent in any software project development for the safety and predictability of using an existing component that has survived extensive field testing and field usage.

Despite all these advantages, software reuse has not caught on as a general routine practice in software engineering, for a number of reasons, chief among them is the absence of a reference architecture in software products. Indeed, in order for reuse to happen, the party that produces reusable assets and the party that consumes them need to have a shared product architecture in mind. In the automobile industry, for example, component reuse has been a routine practice for over a century because the basic architecture of automobiles has not changed since the late nineteenth century: All cars are made up of a chassis, four wheels, a cab, an engine, a transmission, a steering mechanism, a braking mechanism, a battery, an electric circuitry, a fuel tank, an exhaust pipe, an air-conditioning system, and so on. As a result of this standard architecture, many industries emerge around the production of specific parts of this architecture, such as tire manufacturers, battery manufacturers, transmission manufacturers, exhaust manufacturers, and air-conditioning manufacturers, as well as other more specialized (and less visible to the average user) auto parts manufacturers. This standard architecture supports reuse on a large scale: when they design a new automobile, car manufacturers do not reinvent what is a car every time; rather, they may make some design decision pertaining to look, styling, engine performance characteristics, standard features, and optional features, then pick up their phone and order all the auto parts that they envision for their new car. Unfortunately, such an efficient/ flexible process is not possible for software products, for lack of a standard architecture for such products.

But while software products have no common architecture across the broad range of applications where software is prevalent, they may have a common architecture within specific application domains—whence PLE. PLE is a software development and evolution process that represents a streamlined form of software reuse. It is geared toward the production of a family of related software products within a particular application domain and includes two major phases, which are as follows:

• *Domain Engineering*, which consists in developing the necessary infrastructure to build and evolve applications within the selected application domain. This phase includes the following steps/activities:
  ○ *Domain Analysis*, which is the PLE equivalent of the requirements engineering phase in traditional waterfall lifecycles and consists of analyzing the application domain to understand its domain-specific knowledge (abstractions, assumptions, axioms, rules, etc.).
  ○ *Domain Scoping*, which consists of determining the boundaries of the domain by specifying which applications fall within and which fall outside the selected domain.
  ○ *Economic Rationale*, which consists of making a case for the product line based on an estimation of the return on investment achieved by this product

line; the calculation of the return on investment depends on the domain engineering costs, the application engineering costs, the number of applications we envision to sell every year, and the number of years we envision the product line to be active.

○ *Variability/Commonality Analysis*, which consists of deciding what features domain applications have in common (to maximize reuse potential) and how they differ from each other (to broaden the market that can be served by the domain). Variabilities are defined by specifying what features vary from one application to another and what values each feature may take. For example, if we are talking about database applications, then one variability could be the back-end database, and the values on offer could include Oracle, SQL, and Access.

○ *Reference Architecture*, which consists in deriving a common architecture for all the applications in the domain.

○ *Asset Development*, which consists in developing adaptable components that fit in the proposed architecture and support the variabilities that have been selected in the aforementioned analysis.

○ *Application Modeling Language (AML)*: For well-designed, well-modeled product lines, it is possible to define a language in which one can specify or uniquely characterize individual products within the application domain. In some simple cases, it is possible to design translators that map a specification written in this AML onto a finished application.

○ *Application Engineering Process*: In addition to producing the necessary assets that the application engineer needs to compose an application, the domain engineering team must deliver a systematic application engineering process that explains how applications are produced from domain engineering assets according to application requirements.

• *Application Engineering*, which consists in using the assets produced in the domain engineering phase to build an application according to the steps detailed in the application engineering process.

As a simple illustration, consider a product line developed to cater to the IT needs of banks in some jurisdiction (e.g., the state of New Jersey in the United States).

• *Domain analysis* consists of getting acquainted with the banking domain and with the relevant requirements of an IT application in the selected jurisdiction. This may require that we read relevant documentation and legislation in the jurisdiction of the bank and that we talk to bank managers, bank employees, bank tellers, bank customers, fiscal authorities, state and federal regulators of the banking sector, and so on. At the end of this phase, we ought to become fluent in the banking domain; we also need to record our expertise and domain knowledge in the form of domain models, including relevant abstractions, rules, terminology, and so on.

• *Domain scoping* consists of deciding what applications are or are not part of our domain. For example, we consider all the types of banks, such as retail banks, investment banks, credit unions, online banks, savings and loans banks, local banks, statewide banks, nationwide banks, offshore banks, and international banks.

- To build an *economic rationale* for our product line, we must consider the scope that we have defined earlier and evaluate the cost of developing a product line to cater for banks within our scope, then balance this cost against the benefits reaped from selling applications to banks; this, in turn, requires that we estimate the length of our investment cycle, the discount rate that we want to apply from one year to the next, the number of applications that we envision to sell to banks, the price at which we envision to sell the applications, and so on.

- *Variability/Commonality Analysis*: Once we have defined the scope of our domain, we can analyze the common attributes that the applications of our domain have: for example, if we decide to cater to nationwide retail banks, commonalities include that they are all subject to federal banking laws, federal tax laws, and federal employment laws; other commonalities include that they all maintain bank accounts, customer databases, loan departments, and so on. As for variabilities,

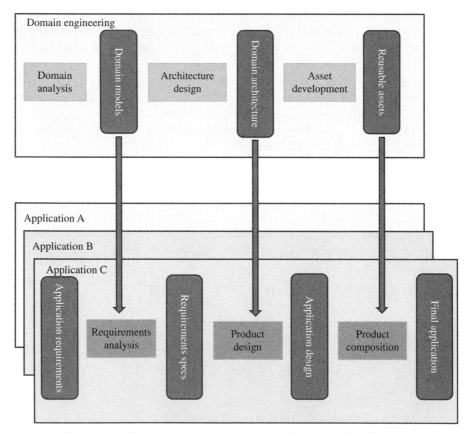

Figure 16.1 *Domain engineering and application engineering lifecycles.*

banks may be subject to different state laws depending on where they are headquartered, they may have significantly distinct banking policies, they may differ by the range of services that they offer their clients, and so on.

- *Reference Architecture*: Once we know what kinds of banks we are catering to and what kinds of commonalities and variabilities exist among the needs of these banks, we can draw an *architecture* that may be shared by all applications of the domain. Such an architecture may include a database of accounts, a database of customers, and a database of loans, along with a customer interface (for online customer transactions), a teller interface (for teller in-branch operations), an automatic teller interface (for ATMs), and so on.

- Once the common architecture is drawn, we can proceed with developing *adaptable software components*, which can be adjusted to fulfill specific customer needs within the scope of the product line and integrated into the architectural framework to produce a complete application.

Figure 16.1 illustrates the lifecycles of domain engineering and application engineering and how they relate to each other.

16.2 TESTING ISSUES

To get a sense of the issues that arise in testing product lines, we review the traditional lifecycle of software testing then we explore how this lifecycle can be combined with the PLE process discussed earlier (and illustrated in Fig. 16.1). Given a software product P and a specification R, and given that we want to test whether P is correct with respect to R, we proceed through the following phases:

- *Test Data Generation*, whereby we inspect program P or specification R or both to generate test data T on which we envision to test P.
- *Test Oracle Design*, whereby we derive a test oracle Ω from specification R, which for any element s of T tells whether the pair $(s, P(s))$ represents a correct execution of program P on initial state s.
- *Test Driver Design*, whereby we combine the test data generation criterion with the oracle design to derive a test driver that runs program P on test data T and stores the outcome.
- *Test Outcome Analysis*, whereby we analyze the outcome of the test and take action according to the goal of the test (fault density estimation, fault removal, reliability estimation, product certification, etc.).

Of course, we can carry out these steps for each application that we develop at the application engineering phase, but this raises the following issues:

- *This is extremely inefficient*: Indeed, each application is made up of common parts (that stem from commonality analysis) and application-specific parts (that stem from the specific variabilities of the application). The common parts have been tested each time an application is tested; and the variable parts have been tested each time an application with the same variability has been tested. Ideally, we would like to focus the testing effort on those aspects of the application that have not received adequate coverage.

- *This is incompatible with the spirit of PLE*: The whole paradigm of PLE revolves around streamlined reuse of reuse artifacts and processes; it is only fitting that reuse should extend to testing artifacts (such as test data) and processes (such as testing common features only once, rather than repeatedly for each application).

- *This alters the Economics of PLE*: The economics of PLE is based on the assumption that a great deal of effort is invested in domain engineering in order to support the rapid, efficient, cost-effective production of applications at application engineering time. If we burden the application engineering phase with the task of testing each application, this may undermine the economic rationale of the product line.

- *The application specification is not self-contained*: The specification of an application for the purposes of application engineering (written in the AML, for example) is cast in the context of domain engineering and merely specifies the attributes that characterize the application within the scope of the domain; as such, it is not self-contained. To write the specification of the application in a self-contained manner (for the purpose of oracle design), one needs to refer to all the implicit domain requirements that arise in domain engineering.

In light of these issues, it is legitimate to consider shifting the bulk of testing to the domain engineering phase, rather than the application engineering phase. Unfortunately, this option raises a host of issues as well, such as the following:

- *Absence of Executable Assets*: At the end of domain engineering, we do not have any self-contained executable assets to speak of. What we typically have are adaptable software components that are intended to be used as part of complete applications.

- *Absence of Verifiable Specifications*: Not only do we not have completely defined operational software products we also do not have precise requirements specifications to test applications against. Instead, we have domain models and feature models that capture domain knowledge and represent domain variabilities.

- *Combinatorics of Variabilities*: Testing a single software product is already hard enough due to the massive size of typical input spaces. PLE compounds that complexity by adding the extra dimensions of variability: If a product line has five dimensions of variability, and each variability may take four possible values (considered a toy-size example), we have in effect $4^5 = 1024$ possible configurations to test. If we assume that (some or all of) the variabilities are optional (i.e., a user may opt out of a variability), then the number of application configurations can reach $5^5 = 3125$.

- *Feature Interactions*: One way to deal with the combinatorial explosion alluded to earlier is to consider the variabilities one at a time, falling back on default options. The trouble with that option is that it fails to uncover problems that arise when variabilities are combined; in particular, it fails to detect feature interactions that may arise.

- *Failure to Certify the Composition Step*: Testing that takes place at the domain engineering phase precedes, by definition, the application engineering phase, hence it fails to detect issues that may arise at the latter phase. In particular, it fails to ensure that variabilities are bound appropriately according to the specification.

16.3 TESTING APPROACHES

There is no simple, integrated, widely accepted, solution to the problems raised earlier. Rather, there are general guidelines that one ought to pursue in designing a testing policy for any particular product line; we review these guidelines in this section and illustrate them on a simple example in the next section. These guidelines are driven by the following principles:

- All commonalities must be tested at domain engineering time. This principle is intended to save testing effort: commonalities are thoroughly tested at domain engineering time so that we do not need to retest them at application engineering time for each application. We envision two broad methods to optimize commonality testing at domain engineering time:
  - Either through the creation of a reference application that may take default variability values or, alternatively, frequently used variability values.
  - Or, if we are confident about the validity of the reference architecture and the soundness of component specifications, through individual testing of the various components of the reference architecture.

- Variability-specific test artifacts must be generated at domain engineering time and deployed at application engineering time. This principle is intended to save test data generation effort: For each variability option, the application engineering has a set of test data that she/he must use to test the variability within the application.

- Variability bindings must be tested at application engineering time. Because variability bindings are application-specific, it is fitting that they should be carried out by the application engineer.

- Applications must undergo some degree of integration testing, to make sure the composition of the application was carried out properly and that the components of the application work together as intended.

These principles are illustrated in the next section, through a sample product line, its implementation, and its test.

16.4 ILLUSTRATION

16.4.1 Domain Analysis

We wish to develop a product line of applications that simulate the behavior of waiting queues at service stations. These may represent customers standing in line at checkout counters at a store, travelers standing at airline check-in counters at an airport, arriving passengers standing at immigration stations in an international arrivals terminal, postal customers standing in line for service at a post office, or processes being queued at a shared resource allocation post. The purpose of the applications in this product line is to enable managers to simulate various queuing and servicing policies and analyze their performance in terms of waiting time, fairness, throughput, and so on.

Among the commonalities that we envision between all the applications of this product line, we cite the following:

- *The Input Data to the Simulation*: The user must enter the following information:
  - The duration of the simulation, as a function of a virtual unit of time (e.g., the minute for simulations of customers and the millisecond for simulations of processor allocation).
  - The arrival rate, that is, the average length of time between two successive arrivals, expressed in the unit time selected earlier. If there are more than one category of customers, then a rate for each category.
  - The service rate, that is, the average length of service time required by each customer. If there are more than one category of customers, then a rate for each category.
- *The Format of the Output Data*: The user may be interested to collect a variety of statistics pertaining to the simulation. The set of possible functions she/he may be interested in varies from one application to another and is determined at application engineering time, as we discuss later.
- *A Standard Record Structure for Customers*: We could make the customer record structure a variability, but for the sake of simplicity we choose to adopt a generic structure that will represent most of the relevant data, such as some identification of the customer, his time of arrival, his category (if there are more than one), his requested service time, his priority (if queuing is based on priority), and his time of departure.
- *An Illustration of the Simulation*: The simulation may be illustrated at run time by showing the evolution of the waiting queues and the service stations throughout the simulation process.

Among the variabilities between applications in this product line, we cite the following:

- *Topology of Service Stations*: An application may have a single service station or several service stations; if there are several service stations, they may be interchangeable (offering the same service) or not (offering different services, e.g., first-class passengers vs. business-class passengers vs. coach passengers at an airline check-in area; or self check-out counters vs. attended check-out counters vs. check-out counters for small orders at a store's cash registers; or citizens vs. permanent residents vs. visitors at immigration posts at an international arrivals hall of an airport). Another dimension of variability is whether a service station, if it is available, may serve customers from a different class, if such customers are not being served by their corresponding service station (e.g., if a first-class check-in station is available and there are coach passengers in the coach waiting queue, we may want to have them served at the first-class station).

- *Service Time*: The service time of a customer may be fixed (the same for all customers) or it may be variable (most typical, in practice). If it is variable, its length may depend solely on the customer (some customers need more service than others) or it may depend on the customer and on the service station (combining the customer needs with the productivity/efficiency of the service station attendant). If the service time is variable, it may be subject to a maximum allocation (as is the case in round-robin allocation of CPU cycles to competing processes in an operating system).

- *Topology of Queues*: Given a configuration of service stations (one or many, interchangeable or distinct, with or without cross-servicing), we may have one queue per service station or one queue per category of service stations.

- *Arrival Distribution*: We can imagine a number of probability laws that govern the arrival of new customers. Possible options may include the following:
  - A uniform probability distribution
  - A Markovian probability distribution
  - A Poisson probability distribution

- *Queuing Policy*: This policy deals with two questions: given an arriving customer, what queue do we put him in, and where in the queue do we place him. In terms of the first question, options include the following:
  - Each category of customers is assigned to a particular type of queue, if there is one queue per category.
  - Each category of customers is assigned to the shortest queue that corresponds to his category, if there are more than one queue per category.
  - Customers are randomly assigned to a queue that corresponds to their category.

  As for how to place each customer in the selected queue, we consider two options: an FIFO policy or a priority-based policy.

- *Dispatching Policy*: Whereas queuing policy deals with where to place an incoming customer in the queue system, the dispatching policy deals with which customers to pick for service whenever a service station becomes available. The simplest situation is to have a queue associated to each service station and not to allow cross-queue transfers. Other options include the situation where several interchangeable service stations take their customers from a shared queue and the situation where an idle service station can take customers from the queue of another service station.

- *Measurements*: Measurements include any combination of the following:
  - ○ Average, median, minimum, or maximum waiting time, that is, time spent in waiting queues.
  - ○ Average, median, minimum, or maximum sojourn time, that is, time spent in the system overall.
  - ○ Fairness, that is, the extent to which waiting time is proportional to requested service time.
  - ○ Occupancy rate of the service stations, that is, the extent to which service stations were busy.
  - ○ Throughput of the service stations, that is, the number of customers serviced per unit of time.
  - ○ Total duration of the simulation (if the simulation is allowed to proceed until all customers are serviced).
  - ○ Total number of customers serviced.
- *Wrap Up Policy*: When the user of an application determines the length of the experiment, a number of decisions must be made as to how the simulation winds down:
  - ○ The simulation is stopped abruptly when the selected time elapses; then all remaining customers are flushed out, possibly taking their statistics.
  - ○ When the time of the simulation is exhausted, no new customers are generated but the simulation continues until all the current customers have been serviced and have exited the system.

In the next section, we consider a possible reference architecture for applications in this domain, then we implement some reusable/adaptable components of this architecture and outline how such components are composed to produce an application.

16.4.2 Domain Modeling

We have to make provisions for all possible configurations of the service stations and corresponding queues, namely, variable number of service stations, variable number of queues, variable number of service station types, various mappings from queues to service stations, and so on. In order to cater for all possible configurations, we resolve to introduce a basic building block, which we call the queue-station block; each such a block is made up of a number of interchangeable service stations and a single queue feeding customers to these stations. We represent such a block by the symbol $QS(n)$, where n is the number of service stations and QS stands for queue-service station. We leave it to the reader to check that all possible queue/station configurations can be implemented by a set of such blocks, with varying values of n. For example, if we want to simulate the situation of an airline check in counter that has two stations for first class, three stations for business class, and five stations for coach, we write (in the style of a type-variable declaration) as follows:

QS(2) firstclass; QS(3) businessclass; QS(5) coach.

In addition to specifying the number of service stations in a QS component, we may want to also specify the queuing policy; if we want the first-class and business-class queues to adopt an FIFO policy but want to adopt a priority-based policy for coach queues (e.g., award some privileges to frequent flyers who still fly coach), we may write the following:

QS(FIFO, 2) firstclass; QS(FIFO, 3) businessclass; QS(PRIORITY, 5) coach.

If, for example, we want to simulate the situation of waiting queues at a gas station, where each pump has its own queue of cars and cars are served by order of arrival, then we write the following:

QS(FIFO, 1) pump1, pump2, pump3, pump4, pump5;

In addition to specifying the configuration of queue/station sets, we may also want to specify policies pertaining to how some service station may serve the queues of other service stations; for example, in an airline check-in counter, it is common for first-class stations to serve coach passengers if the station is free and the coach queue is not empty. To this effect, we use the feature *CrossStation*, and we consider the following options to this feature:

- CrossStation(NONE): no such a possibility is available.
- CrossStation(S,Q): specifies the station that offers the service and the queue to which the service is offered.

For example, in the case of an airline check-in counter, we may write the following:

- CrossStation(firstclass, businessclass);
- CrossStation(firstclass, coach);
- CrossStation(businessclass, coach).

To feed customers to the simulation, we create a component called *Arrivals*, which generates customers according to the arrival rate provided by the user at run time. This component implements the arrivals distribution of the application and is responsible for the implementation of the queuing policy, at least as far as dispatching arriving customers to QSs, according to their category or to some other criterion. We assume that the Arrivals component takes two parameters, which are as follows:

1. The law of probability that determines the arrival of new customers at each unit of clock time: UNI (for uniform), MARKOV (for Markov), or POISSON (for Poisson).
2. The rule that determines where each new arriving customer is queued: We assume that we have three options, as discussed earlier, namely, CAT

(by category), SHORT (to shortest queue), and ANY (random assignment to queues).

In addition to specifying where incoming customers are placed, we may also want to specify whether the assignment of customers to queues is permanent (until the customer is served) or whether a customer may jump from one queue to another. We use the feature *CrossQueue* to this effect, and we consider the following options to this feature:

- CrossQueue(NONE): The assignment of customers to queues is permanent.
- CrossQueue(FRONT, n), where n is a natural number: If a queue is of length *n* or greater and another queue is empty, the front of the first queue is sent to the empty queue.
- CrossQueue(BACK, n), where n is a natural number: if a queue Q1 is longer than a queue Q2 by *n* elements or more, then the back of queue Q1 is moved to the back of queue Q2.

We assume that CrossQueue transfers take place only within QS sets of the same category.

Also, to collect statistics pertaining to the simulation, we create a component called *Statistics*, that is called by the QSs whenever a customer is about to leave the system after being serviced; it may also be called by the QSs at each iteration if the user is interested in measuring the rate of occupancy of service stations. This component collects data about individual customers, then computes simulation-wide statistics at the end of the simulation and posts it to the user. We assume that this component lists as parameters all the statistics that are selected at application engineering time, including the following:

- Waiting Time (parameter: WT), including minimum, maximum, average, median
- System Response Time (parameter: SRT), that is, time spent by customers in the system, including minimum, maximum, average, median
- Occupancy rate for each station (parameter: OR)
- Maximum queue length for each queue (parameter: MQL)
- Throughput of the system, that is, number of customers served per unit of time (parameter: TP)
- System Fairness (parameter: FAIR)

It is possible to envision an AML that we use to characterize each application of this domain. In addition to all the details specified earlier, the language may include an indication of whether the simulation ends abruptly when the simulation time runs out or whether it winds down smoothly until all residual customers have been serviced and leave the system. This can be written as follows:

- WrapUp (ABRUPT) or
- WrapUp (SMOOTH)

Hence, for example, if we wanted to specify the simulation of waiting queues in a gas station, we would write the following:

Simulation gasStation
{
QS(FIFO, 1) pump1, pump2, pump3, pump4; // four gas pumps
CrossStation(NONE); // each pump services its own queue
Arrivals (MARKOV, ANY); // arrival law, random assignment to queues
CrossQueue(NONE); // each car stays in its queue
Statistics (WT, OR, MQL); // wait time, occupancy rate, maximum queue length
WrapUp (SMOOTH); // at closing, serve remaining cars
}

Ideally, one may want to define a formal AML, and build a compiler for it, in such a way that an application description such as this could be compiled into a finished application.

16.4.3 A Reference Architecture

The foregoing discussion yields a natural reference architecture for the proposed product line, whose main components include instances of the queue/station structure (QS), an Arrivals component, a Statistics component, and a main program to coordinate all these; this is illustrated in Figure 16.2. This figure describes the dataflow between these components; as for the control flow, it is basically limited to the main component invoking all the others in a sequential manner.

We review the variabilities that we have listed in Section 16.4.1 and see how these map onto this architecture; in other words, once we decide on the value of a variability, we must determine which components must be modified and how. We consider the variabilities, in turn:

- *Topology of Service Stations*: This variability affects the main program, as well as the queue/station instances. This variability determines the number of QS instances we create and the number of service stations we declare for each.
- *Service Time*: This variability affects the Arrivals component as it determines how service requests are computed for incoming customers.
- *Topology of Queues*: This variability affects the main program, as well as the queue/station instances. This variability determines the number of QS instances we create and how queues are associated with service stations.
- *Arrival Distribution*: This variability affects the Arrivals component.
- *Queuing Policy*: This variability affects the declared instances of the QS components, as well as the relationships between them.
- *Dispatching Policy*: This variability affects the declared instances of the QS components, in the sense that it determines how idle stations determine where

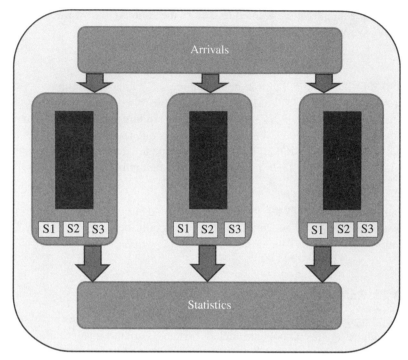

Figure 16.2 *Reference architecture of the queue simulation product line.*

their next customer comes from; it also affects whether an idle station may take a customer from another QS component.

- *Measurements*: This variability affects the Statistics component, by determining what functions to collect data for during the simulation and to summarize at the end of the simulation.
- *Wrap Up Policy*: This variability affects the main program, in the sense that it determines the main simulation loop of the main program, by dictating the exit condition of the loop: To exit when the end of the simulation is up (abrupt) or when all the customers have cleared the system (smooth).

16.4.4 Domain Implementation

We choose to implement this product line in C++. In this section, we outline the broad structure of the main program, then we implement the main building blocks that are used in this product line. The main program reads as follows:

```
#include <iostream>                          line 1
#include "qs.cpp"                                  2
#include "arrivals.cpp"                            3
#include "statistics.cpp"                          4
```

```
using namespace std;                                      5
typedef int clocktimetype;                                6
typedef int durationtype;                                 7
    /* State Objects */                                   8
    qsclass qs1, qs2;                                      9
    arclass arrivals;                                     10
    stclass stats;                                        11
    /* State Variables */                                 12
    durationtype expduration;                             13
    int arrivalrate1, servicerate1;  // for class 1       14
    int arrivalrate2, servicerate2;  // for class 2       15
    int nbcustomers;                                      16
    /* Working Variables */                               17
    clocktimetype clocktime;                              18
    customertype customer;                                19
    bool newarrival;                                      20
    int locsum, locmin, locmax;                           21
/* functions */                                           22
bool ongoingSimulation();                                 23
void elicitParameters();                                  24
int main ()                                               25
    {                                                     26
    elicitParameters();                                   27
    while (ongoingSimulation())                           28
        {                                                 29
        arrivals.drawcustomer(clocktime, expduration,     30
        arrivalrate1, servicerate1, customer, newarrival);  31
        if (newarrival) {nbcustomers++; qs1.enqueue
            (customer);}                                  32
        arrivals.drawcustomer(clocktime, expduration,     33
        arrivalrate2, servicerate2, customer,
            newarrival);                                  34
        if (newarrival) {nbcustomers++; qs2.enqueue
            (customer);}                                  35
        qs1.update(clocktime, locsum, locmin, locmax);    36
        stats.record(locsum,locmin,locmax);              37
        qs2.update(clocktime, locsum, locmin, locmax);    38
        stats.record(locsum,locmin,locmax);              39
        clocktime++;                                      40
        };                                                41
    cout << "concluded at time: " << clocktime << endl;   42
    stats.summary(nbcustomers);                           43
    }                                                     44
bool ongoingSimulation()                                  45
```

```
{                                                            46
    return ((clocktime<=expduration) ||                      47
           (!qs1.done()) || (!qs2.done()));                  48
};                                                           49
void elicitParameters()                                      50
{                                                            51
    nbcustomers=0;                                           52
    cout << "Length of Simulation" << endl;                  53
    cin >> expduration;                                      54
    cout << "Arrival rate, Service Rate, Station 1" << endl; 55
    cin >> arrivalrate1 >> servicerate1;                     56
    cout << "Arrival rate, Service Rate, Station 2" << endl; 57
    cin >> arrivalrate2 >> servicerate2;                     58
};                                                           59
```

As written, this main program refers to two identical QS components; but in general, it may refer to more than one type of QS components (as we recall, QS components may differ by their number of stations and their queuing policy). Also, this main program refers to an arrivals component, that determines the rate of customer arrivals, and a statistics component, that collects statistics. For the sake of simplicity, we have opted for a straightforward (tree-like) #include hierarchy between the various components of this program; the price of this choice is that most data has to transfer through the main program rather than directly between the subordinate components. Hence the decision of whether there is a new arrival and the selection of the new customer parameters transits through the main program (lines 30 31 and 32–34) on its way to the QS component that stores incoming customers (lines 32 and 35); likewise, statistical data is sent from the QS components (lines 36 and 38) to the statistics components (lines 37 and 39) via the main program. Note that while the topology and configuration of the queues and service stations is decided at application engineering time, the actual simulation parameters (experiment duration, arrival rate of each class of customers, service rate of each class of customers) are decided at run-time (line 27).

The QS component is defined by the following header file:

```
//*********************************************************
// Header file qs.h
//
//*********************************************************
const int maxq = 1000;     // max size of queue        line 1
const int nbs  = 3;        // number of stations for
                           // single queue                 2
const int largewait=2000;  // used for min wait            3
typedef int clocktimetype;                                 4
typedef int servicetimetype;                               5
typedef int durationtype;                                  6
typedef int customeridtype;                                7
```

```
typedef int indextype;                                        8
typedef struct                                                9
   {customeridtype cid;                                      10
   clocktimetype at;                                         11
   servicetimetype st;                                       12
   int ccat;                                                 13
   } customertype;                                           14
typedef struct                                               15
   {customertype guest;                                      16
   durationtype busytime;                                    17
   int busyrate;                                             18
   } stationtype;                                            19
class qsclass                                                20
   {public:                                                  21
       qsclass ();  // default constructor                  22
       bool done ();                                         23
       void update (clocktimetype clocktime,                24
                 int& locsum, int& locmin, int& locmax);    25
       bool emptyq () const; // tells whether q is empty    26
       void enqueue (customertype qitem);                   27
       void dequeue ();                                      28
       void checkfront (customertype& qitem) const;         29
       int queuelength ();                                  30
                                                            31
   private:                                                 32
       customertype qarray [maxq];                          33
       stationtype sarray [nbs];                            34
       indextype front;                                     35
       indextype back;                                      36
       int qsize;                                           37
   };                                                       38
```

The *nbs* parameter in this header file (line 2) indicates the number of service stations in the QS component; ideally, we would like to define a single QS component for each queuing policy (e.g., FIFO), and let *nbs* be a parameter (hence, e.g., writing QS(3) or QS(5) depending on the number of stations we want to have for each queue) but we do not believe C++ allows that; hence in practice we write a separate QS class for each different value of nbs and each different value of the queuing policy; in the case of this product line, if we adopt FIFO as the only queuing policy and *nbs* = 3 as the only viable number of stations per queue, then only one QS class is needed. The state variables of this class include the queue infrastructure (qarray, front, back, qsize) as well as an array of service stations, of size *nbs*. In addition to the queue methods (emptyq, queuelength, checkfront, enqueue, dequeue), this class has two QS-specific methods, which are (Boolean-valued) done() and (void) update(clocktime, locsum, locmin, locmax). The former indicates that the QS component has no residual customers in its queue or its service stations; the latter updates the queue and service stations on the grounds that a new unit of time (minute, second, millisecond, etc.) has elapsed:

- If a service station is still busy, it updates the remaining busy time thereof.
- If a service station has just completed serving a customer, it frees the customer and collects statistical data on it.
- If a service station is free and the queue is not empty, then it dequeues the customer at the front of the queue and loads it on the service station.

The arrivals component reads as follows:

```
***************************************************** line 1
//                                                          2
// arrivals component;                                      3
// file arrivals.cpp, refers to header file arrivals.h.     4
//                                                          5
//***************************************************        6
#include "arrivals.h"                                        7
#include "rand.cpp"                                          8
arclass :: arclass ()                                        9
   {SetSeed(673); customerid=1001;                          10
   };                                                       11
void arclass :: drawcustomer (clocktimetype clocktime,
                              int expduration,              12
                              int arrivalrate,
                              int servicerate,              13
                              customertype& customer,
                              bool& newarrival)             14
   {float draw = NextRand();                                15
   newarrival = ((clocktime<=expduration) &&                16
           (draw<(1.0/float(arrivalrate))));                17
   if (newarrival)                                          18
      {customer.cid = customerid; customerid =
      customerid+3;                                         19
      customer.at = clocktime;                              20
      customer.st = 1+int(NextRand()*servicerate);          21
      }                                                     22
   }                                                        23
```

This component calls a random number generator using the parameters of arrival time to determine whether or not there is an arrival at time clocktime, and if there is an arrival, it uses the parameter of service time to draw the length of service needed by the new arriving customer, assigns it a customer ID, and timestamps its arrival time. This information is used subsequently for reporting purposes and/ or to compute statistics.

The header of the statistics component reads as follows:

```
//**********************************************    line 1
// Header file statistics.h                              2
//                                                        3
//**********************************************          4
class stclass                                             5
   {public:                                               6
       stclass (); // default constructor                 7
       void summary (int nbcustomers);                    8
       void record (int locsum, int locmin, int locmax);  9
   private:                                              10
       int totalwait, minwait, maxwait;                  11
       int totalstay, minstay, maxstay;                  12
   };                                                    13
```

As written, this component maintains some information about wait times and stay times of customers in the system; it is adequate if all we are interested in are statistics about these two quantities; but it needs to be expanded if we are to support all the variabilities listed in Section 16.4.1. As written, this component has two main functions, which are as follows:

1. Collecting data pertaining to wait times and stay times, which transits through the main program (rather than directly from the QS components)
2. Summarizing the collected data and printing it to the output at the end of the simulation

16.4.5 Testing at Domain Engineering

In order to test the product line commonalities at domain engineering, we can proceed in one of the following two ways:

1. Either we consider the components of the architecture, derive their specification as it emerges from the design of the reference architecture, and test them as self-standing components.
2. Or we derive a reference application, that takes default values for the domain variabilities, or adopts frequently used variabilities.

Focusing on the first approach, we propose to consider individual components, pin down their specification as precisely as possible to derive their test oracle, build dedicated test drivers for them, and test them to an arbitrary level of thoroughness, as a way to gain confidence in the correctness and soundness of the product line assets.

As an illustration, we consider, for example, the arrivals components, and write a test driver for it, in such a way that its behavior can be checked easily. For example, if we invoke the arrivals component 10,000 times with an arrival rate of 4 and a service rate of 20, then we expect to generate about 2,500 new customers whose average service rate is about 10 units of time. Note that to write this test driver, we need not see the file arrivals.cpp (in fact it is better not to, for the sake of redundancy); we only need to see the (specification) file arrivals.h. We propose the following test driver:

```
#include <iostream>                                          line 1
#include "qs.cpp"                                                 2
#include "arrivals.cpp"                                           3
using namespace std;                                             4
typedef int clocktimetype;                                       5
typedef int durationtype;                                        6
    /* State Objects */                                          7
    arclass arrivals;                                            8
    /* Working Variables */                                      9
    customertype customer; bool newarrival;                     10
    int nbcustomers; durationtype totalst;                      11
int main ()                                                     12
   {for (int clocktime=1; clocktime<=10000;
   clocktime++)                                                 13
      {arrivals.drawcustomer(clocktime,10000,4,20,
       customer,newarrival);                                    14
       if (newarrival) {nbcustomers++;
       totalst=totalst+customer.st;}                            15
      };                                                        16
   cout << "nb customers: " << nbcustomers << endl;            17
   cout << "average service time: " << float(totalst)/
      nbcustomers << endl;18
   }                                                            19
```

Execution of this test driver yields the following output:

```
nb customers: 2506
average service time: 10.7027
```

which corresponds to our expectation and enhances our faith in the arrivals component.

We could, likewise, test the QS component by generating and storing a number of customers in its queue, then monitoring how it handles the load. For example, we can generate 300 customers that each requires 20 units of service time, and see to it that it schedules them in 2000 minutes. We consider the following test driver:

```
#include <iostream>                                          line 1
#include "qs.cpp"                                                 2
#include "statistics.cpp"                                         3
using namespace std;                                             4
```

```
typedef int clocktimetype;                               5
typedef int durationtype;                                6
                                                         7
/* State Objects */                                      8
qsclass qs;                                              9
stclass stats;                                          10
/* Working Variables */                                 11
clocktimetype clocktime;                                12
customertype customer;                                  13
durationtype expduration; int nbcustomers;              14
int locsum, locmin, locmax;                             15
/* functions */                                         16
bool ongoingSimulation();                               17
                                                        18
                                                        19
int main ()                                             20
   {clocktime=0;                                        21
    expduration = 0; // terminate whenever qs is empty  22
    customer.cid=1001; customer.at=0; customer.st=20;   23
    for (int i=1; i<=300; i++) {qs.enqueue(customer);}; 24
    nbcustomers=300;                                    25
    while (ongoingSimulation())                         26
        {qs.update(clocktime, locsum, locmin, locmax);  27
         stats.record(locsum,locmin,locmax);            28
         clocktime++;                                   29
        };                                              30
    cout << "concluded at time: " << clocktime << endl; 31
    stats.summary(nbcustomers);                         32
   }                                                    33
bool ongoingSimulation()                                34
   {return ((clocktime<=expduration) ||(!qs.done()));   35
   };                                                   36
```

The outcome of the execution of this test driver is the following output, which corresponds to our expectation: The 300 customers kept the 3 stations busy nonstop for a total of 100×20 minutes, that is, 2000 minutes. The sum of waiting times is an arithmetic series, of the form

$$(1+2+3+\cdots+99)20.$$

Dividing this sum by the number of customers on each station (100) and replacing the arithmetic series by its closed form expression, we find

$$\frac{9,910,020}{2,100} = 990.$$

The minimum waiting time is 0, of course since the stations were available at the start of the experiment. The maximum waiting time is the waiting time of the last customer in each queue, which had to wait for the 99 customers before it, hence the maximum waiting time is $99 \times 20 = 1980$. All this is confirmed in the following output, delivered by the test driver (except for the minor detail that the test driver shows the closing time at 2001 rather than 2000, but that is because the main loop increments the clocktime at the bottom of the loop body).

```
concluded at time: 2001
nb customers 300
statistics, wait time (total, avg, min, max):
297000 990 0 1980
```

Interestingly, running this test driver enabled us to uncover and remove a fault in the code of the QS component, which was measuring stay time rather than wait time. As far as domain engineering is concerned, we can perform testing under the following conditions:

- We test individual components rather than whole applications. Individual components lend themselves more easily to simple, compact specifications, which can be used as oracles.
- We test preferably components that have the least variability, or whose variabilities are trivial. Ideally, we want any confidence we gain about the correctness of a component to survive as the component is adapted to other applications.

In our case study, we have tested component qs with $nbs = 3$; we can be reasonably confident that changing the value of nbs for the purposes of another application does not alter significantly the confidence we have in its correctness. But changing the queuing policy, however, (e.g., from FIFO to priority) will require a new testing effort. We are able to single out individual components, write test drivers for them, and design targeted test data that will exercise specific functionalities, and for which we know exactly what outcome to expect.

All the testing effort that we carry out at the domain engineering phase is expended once, but will benefit every application that is produced from this product line. While the test we have conducted so far, and other tests focused on system components one at a time, give us confidence in the correctness of the individual components, they give us no confidence in the soundness of the architecture, nor in the integration of the components to form an application.

One way to test the architecture is to run experiments that exercise the interactions between different components of the architecture. Consider, for example, the interaction between two queue-station components in the context of a CrossStation() relation. We assume that the queue-station components are declared by the following AML statements:

```
QS(3) coach; QS(2) firstclass;
CrossStation(firstclass, coach);
Wrap-Up(Abrupt);
```

Then one way to test the interaction between the two queue-station components is to run the simulation with far more coach passengers than the coach service station can serve, and virtually no first passengers at all, and observe that the simulation proceeds as though we had a single coach queue for five coach stations. A sample of data that makes it possible is as follows:

1. Coach arrival rate: one every 2 minutes, on average
2. Coach service rate: 20 minutes, on average
3. First Class arrival rate: 4000 minutes
4. First Class service rate: 1 minute
5. Duration of the Simulation: 2000 minutes

Then upon termination of the simulation, we may find that all five workstations were busy virtually 100% of the time.

16.4.6 Testing at Application Engineering

In the application engineering phase, we take the domain engineering assets and use them to build an application on the basis of specific requirement specifications. In application engineering, we avail ourselves of an executable product for which we have a product specification; hence we have everything we need to run a test; the issue here is to maximize return on investment by targeting test data to those aspects of the application that have not been adequately tested at domain engineering or have not been adequately covered by the test of other applications within the same domain. Also, we must test that the variabilities are bound correctly with respect to the AML specification.

We consider a sample application in our queue simulation domain, specified by the following AML statements:

```
Simulation airlineCheckin
{
    QS(FIFO, 4)  coach;
    QS(FIFO, 2)  firstClass;
    CrossStation(NONE);          // each class services its own queue
    Arrivals (UNIFORM, CAT);     // arrival law, assignment by category
    CrossQueue(NONE);            // each passenger stays in his/her queue
    Statistics (WT);             // wait time
    WrapUp (SMOOTH);             // when check-in ends, take no new
                                 // passengers, but clear lines
}
```

In light of this specification, we propose to define two QS classes, one with four service stations, and one with two service stations. Also, we envision that the user specifies the arrival rate and service rate of each class of service (coach, first class), and to deliver statistics about wait times. This yields the following simulation program.

```cpp
#include <iostream>
#include "qs2.cpp"
#include "qs4.cpp"
#include "arrivals.cpp"
#include "statistics.cpp"
using namespace std;

typedef int clocktimetype;
typedef int durationtype;
/* State Objects */
qsclass2 qs2;
qsclass4 qs4;
arclass arrivals;
stclass stats;
/* State Variables */
durationtype expduration;
int arrivalrate2, servicerate2; // for class 2
int arrivalrate4, servicerate4; // for class 4
int nbcustomers;
/* Working Variables */
clocktimetype clocktime;
customertype customer;
bool newarrival, newdeparture;
int locsum, locmin, locmax;
/* functions */
bool ongoingSimulation();
void elicitParameters();
int main ()
   {elicitParameters();
    while (ongoingSimulation())
       {arrivals.drawcustomer(clocktime, expduration,
          arrivalrate2, servicerate2, customer, newarrival);
        if (newarrival) {nbcustomers++; qs2.enqueue
          (customer);}
        arrivals.drawcustomer(clocktime, expduration,
          arrivalrate4, servicerate4, customer,
          newarrival);
        if (newarrival) {nbcustomers++; qs4.enqueue
          (customer);}
        qs2.update(clocktime, locsum, locmin, locmax);
```

```
    stats.record(locsum,locmin,locmax);
    qs4.update(clocktime, locsum, locmin, locmax);
    stats.record(locsum,locmin,locmax);
    clocktime++;
    };
  cout << "concluded at time: " << clocktime << endl;
  stats.summary(nbcustomers);
}
bool ongoingSimulation()
  {return ((clocktime<=expduration) || (!qs2.done())
  || (!qs4.done()));
  };

void elicitParameters()
  {nbcustomers=0;
  cout << "Length of Simulation" << endl;
  cin >> expduration;
  cout << "Arrival rate, Service Rate, First Class" << endl;
  cin >> arrivalrate2 >> servicerate2;
  cout << "Arrival rate, Service Rate, Coach" << endl;
  cin >> arrivalrate4 >> servicerate4;
  };
```

Successive executions of this program with different arrival rates and service rates give the following results:

Duration	First class		Coach		Time ended	Customers served	Average wait	Maximum wait
	Arrival rate	Service rate	Arrival rate	Service Rate				
900	4	24	3	19	1573	542	152	665
900	4	20	3	15	1321	542	95	415
900	4	16	3	12	1076	542	41	173
900	4	14	2	7	987	688	13	92
900	4	10	2	5	906	688	0.89	13
1000	5	20	4	14	1086	465	21	82

This table shows the test data used for the experiment, as well as the output produced by the simulation. For completeness, we need an oracle that tells us whether the output produced by the simulation is correct; because of the random nature of the simulation, the oracle is not a deterministic function but rather the mean of a random variable. Hence, in terms of an oracle, we need to build an analytical model that shows the expected results of the simulation according to the parameters of the application (decided at application engineering time) and according to the parameters of the simulation (decided at run time). This model would be developed at domain engineering and applied for each application to serve as a test oracle.

16.5 CHAPTER SUMMARY

This chapter highlights the difficulty of testing software product lines, due to unbound specifications and to the combinatorial explosion that stems from multiple variabilities, and proposes some general principles to guide the testing process, which are as follows:

- All commonalities must be tested at domain engineering time.
- Variability-specific test artifacts must be generated at domain engineering time and deployed at application engineering time.
- Variability bindings must be tested at application engineering time.
- Applications must undergo some degree of integration testing, to make sure the composition of the application was carried out properly and that the components of the application work together as intended.

16.6 EXERCISES

16.1. Consider the following application specification in the domain of queue simulation, which represents a gas station that has four pumps:
Simulation gasStation
{
   QS(FIFO, 1) pump1, pump2, pump3, pump4;
   CrossStation(NONE);   // each pump services its own queue
   Arrivals (UNIFORM);   // arrival law
   CrossQueue(NONE);   // each car stays in its queue
   Statistics (WT);   // wait time
   WrapUp (ABRUPT);   // when the station closes, the pumps stop
}
Develop a reference application according to the AML specification and use it to test the commonalities of the product line.

16.2. Insert five faults in the code of the queue simulation presented in Section 16.4. Deploy domain engineering tests and application engineering tests and identify which tests uncover the faults and which faults have been uncovered.

16.7 PROBLEMS

16.1. Build an analytical statistical model of the queue simulation that can predict, for each configuration and each set of input parameters, what are the expected values of the various statistical functions cited in the queue simulation.

16.2. Develop a product line that simulates the behavior of a prey–predator model, develop it, and design a testing policy for the product line. Consider that the model may involve an arbitrary number of species, with an arbitrary network of prey–predator relationships, and an arbitrary array of external factors (drought, disease, floods, etc.) that may affect some or all of the species.

16.8 BIBLIOGRAPHIC REFERENCES

The field of software product line testing is still in its infancy; while many researchers agree on the broad challenges facing the discipline, there is no consensus on a general solution. John McGregor (2001) was the first to draw attention to the unique nature and unique challenges of product line testing. Recent surveys of the field include Machado et al. (2014) and Engstrom and Runeson (2011). The sample example of the queue simulation product line is due to Mili et al. (2002). The domain engineering methodology adopted in this chapter is FAST, which is due to Weiss and Lai (1999). For more on software product lines, consult Weiss and lai (1999), Pohl et al. (2005), or Linden et al. (2007). Another source is the annual Software Product Line Conference(s) (SPLC) conferences at http://www.splc.net/.

Bibliography

Abran A. *Software Metrics and Software Metrology*. Hoboken (NJ): Wiley; 2012.

Abrial JR. *The B Book: Assigning Programs to Meanings*. Cambridge: Cambridge University Press; 1996.

Avizienis A, Laprie JC, Randell B, Landwehr C. Basic concepts and taxonomy of dependable and secure computing. IEEE Trans Dependable Secure Comput 2004;**1** (1):11–33.

Bansyia J, Davis C, Etzkorn L. An entropy based complexity measure for object oriented designs. Theory Pract Object Syst 1999;**5** (2):1–9.

Black R. *Pragmatic Software Testing: Becoming an Effective and Efficient Test Professional*. Indianapolis (IN): Wiley; 2007.

Bochm BW. *Software Engineering Economics*. Englewood Cliffs (NJ): Prentice-Hall; 1981.

Boehm BW, Abts C, Brown AW, Chulani S, Clark BK, Horowitz E, Madachy R, Reifer DJ, Steece B. *Software Cost Estimation with COCOMO II*. Upper Saddle River (NJ): Prentice Hall; 2000.

Cadar C, Sen K. Symbolic execution for software testing. Commun ACM 2013;**56** (2):82–90.

Csiszar I, Koerner J. *Information Theory: Coding Theorems for Discrete Memoryless Systems*. Cambridge: Cambridge University Press; 2011.

Culbertson R, Brown C, Cobb G. *Rapid Testing*. Upper Saddle River (NJ): Prentice Hall; 2002.

DeMillo RA, Lipton RJ, Sayward FG. Hints on test data selection: Help for the practicing programmer. IEEE Comput 1978;**11** (4):34–41.

Ebert C, Dumke R. *Software Measurement: Establish, Extract, Evaluate, Execute*. Berlin: Springer Verlag; 2007.

Engstrom E, Runeson P. Software product line testing: a systematic mapping study. Inf Softw Technol 2011;**52** (1):2–13.

Etzkorn L, Gholston S. A semantic entropy metric. J Softw Maint Evol Res Pract 2002;**14**:293–310.

Fenton NE, Pfleeger SL. *Software Metrics: A Rigorous and Practical Approach*. London: PWS Publishing Co.; 1997.

Software Testing: Concepts and Operations, First Edition. Ali Mili and Fairouz Tchier.
© 2015 John Wiley & Sons, Inc. Published 2015 by John Wiley & Sons, Inc.

Frankl PG, Weyuker EJ. An applicable family of dataflow testing criteria. IEEE Trans Softw Eng 1988;**14** (10):1483–1498.

Gall CS, Lukin S, Etzkorn L, Gholston S, Farrington P, Utley D, Fortune J, Virani S. Semantic software metrics computed from natural language design specifications. IET Softw 2008;**2** (1):17–26.

Goodenough JB, Gerhart SL. Towards a theory of test data selection. IEEE Trans Softw Eng 1975;**SE-1**:26–37.

Habrias H, Frappier M. *Software Specification Methods*. Hoboken (NJ): John Wiley & Sons; 2013. ISTE series.

Halstead MH. *Elements of Software Science*. Amsterdam: North-Holland; 1977.

Hoare CAR. An axiomatic basis for computer programming. Commun ACM 1969;**12** (10):576–585.

Jackson D. *Software Abstractions: Logic, Language and Analysis*. Cambridge (MA): MIT Press; 2011.

Janicki R, Khedhri R. On a formal semantics of tabular expressions. Sci Comput Program 2001;**39** (2, 3):189–213.

Janicki R, Parnas DL, Zucker JI. Tabular representations in relational documents. In: Brink C, Kahl W, Schmidt G, editors. *Relational Methods in Computer Science*. New York: Springer Verlag; 1997. p 184–196.

Jet Propulsion Laboratory. *NASA Study on Flight Software Complexity*. 2009. Available at http://www.nasa.gov/pdf/418878main_FSWC_Final_Report.pdf. Accessed November 26, 2014.

Kaner C, Falk J, Nguyen HQ. *Testing Computer Software*. 2nd ed. New York: John Wiley & Sons; 1999.

Kit E. *Software Testing in the Real World: Improving the Process*. Reading (MA): Addison-Wesley; 1995.

Kuhn DR. Fault classification and error detection capability of specification based testing. ACM Trans Softw Eng Methodol 1999;**8** (4):411–424.

Laprie J-C. Dependability: a unifying concept for reliable, safe, secure computing. IFIP Congress 1992;**1**:585–593.

Laprie J-C. Dependability: its attributes, impairments, and means. In: Randell B, Laprie J-C, Kopetz H, Littlewood B, editors. *Predictably Dependable Computing Systems*. New York: Springer; 1995. p 3–24.

Larson E, Austin T. High coverage detection of input-related security faults. Proceedings of the 12th USENIX Security Symposium; August 4–8, 2003, Washington, DC.

Linden FJ, Schmidt K, Rommes E. *Software Product Lines in Action: The Best Industrial Practice in Product Line Engineering*. Berlin: Springer Verlag; 2007.

Linger RC, Mills HD, Witt BI. *Structured Programming: Theory and Practice*. Reading (MA): Addison-Wesley; 1979.

Machado I d C, McGregor JD, Cavalcanti YC, de Almeida ES. On strategies for testing software product lines: a systematic literature review. Inf Softw Technol 2014;**56**:1183–1199.

Mathur AP. *Foundations of Software Testing: Fundamental Algorithms and Techniques*. Upper Saddle River (NJ): Pearson Education; 2002.

McCabe TJ. A complexity measure. IEEE Trans Softw Eng 1976;**2** (4):308–320.

McGregor JD. Testing a software product line. Technical report, CMU/SEI-2001-TR-022. Pittsburgh (PA): Carnegie Mellon University; 2001.

Mili A, Desharnais J, Mili F. *Computer Program Construction*. New York: Oxford University Press; 1994.

Mili H, Mili A, Yacoub S, Addy E. *Reuse Based Software Engineering: Techniques, Organization and Controls*. New York: John Wiley & Sons; 2002.

Mili A, Frias MF, Jaoua A. On faults and faulty programs. Proceedings, RAMICS 2014; April 28–May 1, 2014; Marienstatt, Germany. p 191–207.

Mills HD. *Mathematical Foundations for Structured Programming*. Gaithersburg, MD: IBM Federal Systems Division; 1972.

Mills HD. The new math of computer programming. Commun ACM 1975;**18** (1):43–48.

Mills HD, Basili VR, Gannon JD, Hamlet RG. *Principles of Computer Programming: A Mathematical Approach*. New York: McGraw Hill; 1986.

Morell L, Murill B. Semantic metrics through error flow analysis. J Syst Softw 1993;**20** (3):207–216.

Morell L, Voas JM. A framework for defining semantic metrics. J Syst Softw 1993;**20** (3):245–251.

Musa J. *Software Reliability Engineering: More Reliable Software, Faster Development and Testing*. New York: McGraw Hill; 1999.

Naik K, Tripathy P. *Software Testing and Quality Assurance: Theory and Practice*. Hoboken (NJ): John Wiley & Sons; 2008.

Nicol DM, Sanders WH, Trivedi K. Model based evaluation: from dependability to security. IEEE Trans Dependable Secure Comput 2004;**1** (1):48–65.

O'Connor PDT. *Practical Reliability Engineering*. 4th ed. New York: Wiley; 2002.

Offutt AJ, Hayes JH. A semantic model of program faults. Proceedings of 1996 International Symposium on Software Testing and Analysis; January 1996; San Diego, CA. ACM Press. p 195–200.

Perry WE. *Effective Methods for Software Testing*. Indianapolis (IN): Wiley; 2002.

Pfleeger SL, Atlee JM. *Software Engineering: Theory and Practice*. Prentice Hall: Upper Saddle River (NJ); 2009.

Pohl K, Boeckle G, Linden FJ. *Software Product Line Engineering: Foundations, Principles and Techniques*. New York: Springer Verlag; 2005.

Rapps S, Weyuker EJ. Selecting test data using dataflow information. IEEE Trans Softw Eng 1985;**11** (4):367–375.

Sen K, Marinov D, Agha G. CUTE: a concolic unit testing engine for C. Proceeding, Fifth Joint Meeting of the European Software Engineering Conference and ACM SIGSOFT Symposium on the Foundations of Software Engineering; 2005; Lisbon, Portugal. p 263–272.

Somerville I. *Software Engineering*. 7th ed. Harlow: Pearson Education; 2004.

Spivey JM. *The Z Notation: A Reference Manual*. Englewood Cliffs (NJ): Prentice Hall; 1998.

Voas J, Miller K. Semantic metrics for software testability. J Syst Softw 1993;**20** (3):207–216.

Weiss DM, Lai CTR. *Software Product Line Engineering: A Family Based Software Development Process*. Reading (MA): Addison-Wesley; 1999.

Whittaker JA. *Exploratory Software Testing: Tips, Tricks, Tours and Techniques to guide Test Design*. Upper Saddle River (NJ): Addison-Wesley/Pearson Education; 2010.

Index

Software Testing: Concepts and Operations, First Edition. Ali Mili and Fairouz Tchier.
© 2015 John Wiley & Sons, Inc. Published 2015 by John Wiley & Sons, Inc.